Understanding
19th-Century
Slave Narratives

Understanding 19th-Century Slave Narratives

Sterling Lecater Bland Jr., Editor

BLOOMSBURY ACADEMIC
NEW YORK • LONDON • OXFORD • NEW DELHI • SYDNEY

BLOOMSBURY ACADEMIC
Bloomsbury Publishing Inc
1385 Broadway, New York, NY 10018, USA
50 Bedford Square, London, WC1B 3DP, UK
29 Earlsfort Terrace, Dublin 2, Ireland

BLOOMSBURY, BLOOMSBURY ACADEMIC and the Diana logo
are trademarks of Bloomsbury Publishing Plc

First published in the United States of America by ABC-CLIO 2016
Paperback edition published by Bloomsbury Academic 2024

Copyright © Bloomsbury Publishing Inc, 2024

Cover design by Silverander Communications
Cover photo: *Effects of the Fugitive Slave Law*. Anti-Fugitive Slave Act cartoon, 1850.
(Sarin Images/Granger, NYC)

All rights reserved. No part of this publication may be reproduced or
transmitted in any form or by any means, electronic or mechanical,
including photocopying, recording, or any information storage or retrieval
system, without prior permission in writing from the publishers.

Bloomsbury Publishing Inc does not have any control over, or responsibility for,
any third-party websites referred to or in this book. All internet addresses given
in this book were correct at the time of going to press. The author and publisher
regret any inconvenience caused if addresses have changed or sites have
ceased to exist, but can accept no responsibility for any such changes.

Library of Congress Cataloging-in-Publication Data
Names: Bland, Sterling Lecater, 1961- editor.
Title: Understanding 19th-century slave narratives / Sterling Lecater Bland Jr., editor.
Description: Santa Barbara, California: Greenwood, 2016. |
Includes bibliographical references and index.
Identifiers: LCCN 2015048663 | ISBN 9781440844638 (print: alk. paper) |
ISBN 9781440844645
Subjects: LCSH: Slaves' writings, American. | Slaves—United States—Biography. |
Fugitive slaves—United States—Biography. | Freedmen—United States—Biography. |
Slaves—United States—Social conditions—19th century. | Slavery—United States—
History—19th century—Sources.
Classification: LCC E444.U54 2016 | DDC 306.3/62092—dc23
LC record available at http://lccn.loc.gov/2015048663

ISBN: HB: 978-1-4408-4463-8
PB: 979-8-7651-2085-9
ePDF: 978-1-4408-4464-5
eBook: 979-8-2161-5902-5

To find out more about our authors and books visit www.bloomsbury.com
and sign up for our newsletters.

For Freddie Belk, one who believed
19 January 1904–20 February 2000

Behold, God is my salvation; I will trust, and not be afraid:
for the Lord Jehovah is my strength and my song;
he also is become my salvation.
—Isaiah 12:2

[The fugitive slaves] encounter a whole Iliad of woes, not in plundering and enslaving others, but in recovering for themselves those rights which they have been deprived from birth. Or if the Iliad should be thought not to present a parallel case, we know not where one who wished to write a modern Odyssey could find a better subject than in the adventures of a fugitive slave. What a combination of qualities and deeds and sufferings most fitted to attract human sympathy in each particular case!
        —Ephraim Peabody, "Narrative of Fugitive Slaves"
        (*Christian Examiner*, July 1949)

Thou shalt not deliver unto his master the servant which is escaped from his master unto thee: He shall dwell with thee, even among you, in that place which he shall choose in one of thy gates, where it liketh him best: thou shalt not oppress him.
        —Deuteronomy 23:15–16

Contents

Preface	xi
Introduction	1
Bearing Witness: The Fugitive Slave Narrative and Its Traditions	
Chapter 1. Nat Turner (1800–1831)	19
The Confessions of Nat Turner, The Leader of the Late Insurrection in Southampton, Va. (1831)	
Chapter 2. Lunsford Lane (1803–?)	43
The Narrative of Lunsford Lane, Formerly of Raleigh, N.C. (1842)	
Chapter 3. William Wells Brown (1814–1884)	73
Narrative of William W. Brown, a Fugitive Slave, Written by Himself (1847)	
Chapter 4. Henry "Box" Brown (1816–?)	121
Narrative of Henry Box Brown, Who Escaped from Slavery Enclosed in a Box 3 Feet Long and 2 Wide. Written from a Statement of Facts Made by Himself. With Remarks Upon the Remedy for Slavery by Charles Stearns (1849)	
Chapter 5. James W. C. Pennington (1807–1870)	179
The Fugitive Blacksmith; or, Events in the History of James W. C. Pennington, Pastor of a Presbyterian Church, New York, Formerly a Slave in the State of Maryland, United States (1849)	
Chapter 6. William (1826?–1900) and Ellen Craft (1826–1891)	237
Running a Thousand Miles for Freedom; or, the Escape of William and Ellen Craft from Slavery (1860)	
Bibliography	293
Index	301

Preface

> [W]hen we get a little farther from the conflict, some brave and truth-loving man, with all the facts before him . . . will gather from here and there the scattered fragments . . . and give those who shall come after us an impartial history of this the grandest moral conflict of the century. [For] Truth is patient and time is just.
> —Frederick Douglass, 1891

Like many others, I was first introduced to the power of African American slave narrative writing by reading the *Narrative of the Life of Frederick Douglass* (1845). When I began research on fugitive slave narratives, the influential subgenre of African American slave narrative writing, it became increasingly clear that there are many other voices besides Douglass's that contribute to the tradition of which Douglass's *Narrative* is such an exemplary part. This anthology represents my attempt to offer some of those lesser-known voices in the context of the social and political circumstances that contributed to their composition and widespread influence. This volume is not conceived as an encyclopedic recitation of the approximately seventy fugitive slave narratives produced as books in the three decades preceding the Civil War. Instead, this is an attempt to use a selection of these narrative works as a starting point for discussing the ways African American writing and American culture influenced and ultimately grew out of each other. I have chosen the writings I have because they, in and of themselves, provide a certain level of nuance and because they provide an avenue for encountering a variety of literary and cultural subjects.

My greatest objective in gathering these narratives together is to bring students and their instructors to voices that are not often heard in anthologies. The works contained in this anthology merit preservation and deserve classroom attention. Students will find in this selection of narratives the opportunity to explore and engage with an important, relevant area of African American literary expression. These narratives give students—those new to this area of African American intellectual history as well as those with more experience in the subject—a broadly nuanced understanding of an important literary tradition. Instructors and the students they teach will find a volume that presents a collection of unabridged, annotated, primary documents in conversation with scholarship that contextualizes its literary and historical significance. In doing so, these documents become part of a larger discussion that makes this collection of nineteenth century narratives relevant to the contemporary ways African American literature is taught and understood.

These narratives each convey a genuine sense of the ways these writers used language, structured their writing, and chose which aspects of their lives to present and extrapolate into deeper significance regarding themselves as individuals and the relationship of that individual self to the collective. Taken together, these narratives articulate thoughts and feelings that have an aesthetic beauty as well as a practical relevance to the lives of their writers and their audience.

This literature is also representative of the interconnectedness that exists among cultures. African American antebellum writing mainly focuses on the issue of slavery. It primarily addresses this issue in terms of actual experiences of physical bondage. It also expresses this issue from a spiritual perspective that emphasizes a spiritual journey from sin to redemption. It is the experience of slavery and the literature that experience produced that contribute to the feelings of double consciousness that W.E.B. Du Bois describes in *The Souls of Black Folk* (1903). Slavery undoubtedly altered Western culture and the ways that culture perceived and expressed itself. These narratives document and expand the discussion surrounding these writings and their relation to a variety of cultural, political, social, and class-based conditions. Slave narrative writing incorporates, directly and indirectly, its African origins while also addressing the ways it simultaneously influenced and was influenced by the cultures with which it interacted.

My greatest acknowledgments for this anthology are to those who contributed to its initial conception and subsequent compilation. I am grateful to Kenneth Silverman, who first encouraged me to undertake this project as my interest in slave narrative writing was developing. I am especially thankful to the general and humanities reference librarians at Firestone Library (Princeton University) and at Alexander Library, Mabel Smith Douglass Library, and Dana Library (Rutgers University) who made it possible for me to identify and locate the wide variety of materials I required to complete this project. I am particularly grateful to Mary George and Emily Belcher at Firestone Library for patiently offering assistance, guidance, and direction. I owe a special debt of gratitude to Marian Perales at ABC-CLIO for suggesting the idea of publishing a single-volume collection of narratives and for bringing the project to fruition with steadiness and close attention to detail.

The community I have experienced while teaching and writing at Rutgers University in Newark, New Jersey, has made my work both enjoyable and intellectually stimulating. I am particularly grateful to Fran Bartkowski, Barbara Foley,

Gabriel Miller, and Clement Price for being welcoming, encouraging about my work, and generous with their help. I would especially like to acknowledge the students who participated in the undergraduate classes and seminars I have taught on African American literature and the students in the graduate seminars I have taught on the African American novel and twentieth-century American literature. Their interest in African American literature and their sense of intellectual curiosity continues to make my own explorations into ways to examine slave narrative writing fun, challenging, and exciting.

During the years in which the ideas for this book were formulated, given shape, and revised, I benefited from the stimulus, inspiration, and vision of teachers, fellow students, colleagues, friends, family, and acquaintances far too numerous to name. Several, however, deserve specific mention: David Carroll, Isabelle Kaminski, Marilyn Campbell, Jane Low, Alessandra Bocco, Jennifer Manlowe, Eileen Reilly, Julie Armstrong, Jacqueline Ivens, Laurie Altman, Carolyn Fox, Edward Murray, Scott Murray, and Janice Bland. I am particularly grateful to Steven Chang and David Yule.

My wife, Wendy Donat, has been an unwavering source of love and support. My deepest thanks and acknowledgment continue to go to the memory of my parents, Ula and Sterling Bland Sr., for their unceasing love and constant encouragement. This book is lovingly dedicated to the memory of my grandmother, Freddie Belk.

In bringing these narratives together for this volume, I have attempted, as much as possible, to avoid modernizing or trying to make consistent various styles of capitalization, grammar, spelling, and punctuation. Unless there are obvious areas of confusion for contemporary readers, I have retained these elements as they were used in the original texts. I have, however, silently corrected obvious errors. The texts of the narratives included here are presented in their entirety and are not abridged or condensed in any way.

■ INTRODUCTION
Bearing Witness: The Fugitive Slave Narrative and Its Traditions

> This fugitive slave literature is destined to be a powerful lever. We have the most profound conviction of its potency. We see in it the easy and infallible means of abolitionizing the free States. Argument provokes argument, reason is met by sophistry. But narratives of slaves go right to the hearts of men.
> —Boston *Chronotype*, quoted in *Anti Slavery Bugle*, November 3, 1849

This anthology presents a selection of the narratives produced by African American ex-slaves between roughly 1830 and 1865. With the notable exception of Nat Turner, who was tried and hanged for organizing a slave rebellion in Southampton, Virginia, these narrators had all escaped southern bondage.[1] They were writing, often with the encouragement of abolitionist sponsorship, firsthand accounts of their lives as slaves, their personal (and often spiritual) development, their desire for freedom, and their subsequent escape. Like the experiences they contain, African American fugitive slave narratives represent the kinds of tensions involved in trying to bring together disparate thoughts and experiences within the borders of what is fundamentally a generic literary form. The narratives these writers produced are illuminating in terms of what they say, what they refrain from saying, and the varying techniques used to achieve their intended results.

The popularity of the nineteenth-century fugitive slave narrative as a genre was based on a number of circumstances. These included the complex interrelationship between the increasing influence of abolitionist activity, the increasing political debate about slavery, the public desire to read about the experiences of slaves, and an increasing interest in the first-person accounts of the effects of slavery on individuals.

Slave narratives are both historical documents and important literary documents. They explain the experiences of their narrators and document the inequality that existed between the ideals contained in the nation's founding documents and the lived experiences of the nation's African American citizens. Slave narratives also occupy an important relationship to the presentation of race and inequality in canonical literature like *Uncle Tom's Cabin* by Harriet Beecher Stowe and Mark Twain's *Adventures of Huckleberry Finn* (1884). Their influence can also be felt both in contemporary autobiographical literature like Richard Wright's *Black Boy* (1945) and Malcolm X's *Autobiography of Malcolm X* (1965) and fictional literature like William Styron's *Confessions of Nat Turner* (1967), Toni Morrison's *Beloved* (1987), *The Known World* (2003) by Edward P. Jones, and Manu Herbstein's *Brave Music of a Distant Drum* (2011). Slave narrators like William Wells Brown or James W. C. Pennington and the fictional characters inspired by their experience provide important commentary on the nation's ongoing conversation about race, inequality, and identity.

STYLISTIC DEVELOPMENTS

While the lives of southern blacks were sharply defined by the hardships of chattel slavery, the lives of blacks throughout the nation were also defined by economic hardship, legal constraint, the inability to vote, and other forms of racial discrimination. The conditions of blacks throughout the country and in the Caribbean created an environment in which black insurrection was a constant possibility. Among many others, organized uprisings were led by Toussaint L'Ouverture in the French colony of Saint-Domingue, which led to the establishment of the Republic of Haiti (1793–1801), Gabriel Prosser in Richmond, Virginia (1800), Denmark Vesey in Charleston, South Carolina (1822), and Nat Turner in Southampton, Virginia (1831). With the exception of the Saint-Domingue revolution, most of the other insurrections resulted in the capture and eventual execution of their organizers.[2] Though the uprisings themselves were often contained relatively quickly, their effects were often substantial. Repressive measures were taken with the objective of making it difficult for blacks to communicate and organize. Especially in the South, increasingly restrictive legislation ("slave codes") made education and peaceful congregation illegal for blacks. Travel for slaves and free blacks throughout the South was closely monitored. Contact between blacks was sharply limited and bearing arms or engaging in certain kinds of occupations without white consent was prohibited.

The slave narrative as it developed out of this repressive climate represents the ways former-slave writers were willing to adapt prevailing narrative forms to their needs. Simultaneously, however, they undercut the very notion of a "traditional" form by co-opting these forms for distinctly non-traditional uses. The eighteenth-century slave narrative form was strongly shaped by the literary conventions from which it drew. These stylistic techniques, while certainly popular throughout the eighteenth and early third of the nineteenth centuries, were endowed with a certain amount of urgency as political differences began to escalate and the role of the slave narrator became co-opted by the growth of the New England abolitionist movement. These changes initiated shifts in the ways slave narrators were encouraged to present their work as well as the ways their audiences received their work. With the publication of popular slave narratives that went through multiple printings and were translated into several languages, the slave narrative became fairly well established as a genre of narrative writing that had the potential to attract a large audience. But as political pressures in the North intensified to persuade the South to bring about the end of slavery, the objectives of the slave narratives sought more directly to address the antislavery impulse.

The renewed interest of white Americans in the abolitionist cause during the late 1820s and early 1830s sparked an abolitionist need for first-person accounts of slavery and its effects. The abolitionists saw slave narratives as an instrument that could be used to sway public opinion in their favor. Slaves were eagerly approached by abolitionists and encouraged to write their narratives. Public demand for more narratives greatly increased. The triangularity of this relationship helped fuse antebellum black writing with prevailing socio-political conditions. One of the fundamental shifts specific to blacks was that direct connections to Africa began to disappear. Eighteenth-century writers provided first-person accounts of the narrator's African experiences.[3] The experiences recounted in their narratives were very much a function of their recollections of their lives in Africa. But the African-born freeman who expressed his independence by attempting to gain control over his financial, spiritual, and social affairs was gradually replaced by the fugitive slave narrator who coupled explicit examples of physical violence and psychological abuse with candid objections to the morality of self-professed Christians who allowed the system to continue. Fugitive slave narrators no longer relied on extended philosophical examinations of slavery and were instead encouraged, by abolitionists and their reading public, to highlight the most lurid and sensational accounts of their lives. The abolition of slavery, rather than simply the eradication of the slave trade, became the primary focus. In order to achieve that goal, the slave narrative adjusted to accommodate.[4]

THE ERASURE OF ORIGINS

Eighteenth-century slave narratives were an indirect product of enlightened thinking, emphasizing fundamental, individual freedoms—whether religious, intellectual, political, or social. These influences became considerably more focused and concentrated on the institution of slavery in the 1830s. For blacks, the shift from African origins to farm- and plantation-based origins brought with it a subtle but important shift in the kinds of stock episodes that comprised the narratives. Though both eighteenth- and nineteenth-century narratives often began with details concerning the birth of the narrator, the nineteenth-century narrative moved on to specific descriptions of slavery. Eighteenth-century narrators routinely presented the idealized African experiences of its narrators and then contrasted the order and humanity of Africa with the inhumane brutality of European culture. Nautical adventures involving danger, excitement, and a certain amount of autonomy for the eighteenth-century narrator were replaced with nineteenth-century accounts of farms and plantations in which the names of savage slaveholders were given and individual personalities were described. Slavery was no longer presented as a large, impersonal issue, but rather as a situation in which one group of individuals unjustly enslaved another group of individuals.

Even as slave narratives shifted their perspective away from shipboard adventures and Native American captivities, they still possessed many elements that endeared them to a large reading audience. They described sympathetic characters who were mistreated by cruel, heartless male and female slaveholders. The slaves were distinctly exotic and wondrously strange to their readership. Plots were moved forward by the excitement of slaves' plans for escape and their eventual arrival in a free state.

While slave narratives benefited from the attention given them by abolitionists, they also owed a portion of their increasing popularity to larger cultural changes within the United States, like national literacy, an expanding reading public, and improvements in printing procedures. The number of magazines, for instance, rapidly grew from the five magazines published in the United States in 1794 to about 100 in 1825, and eventually reached more than 500 by 1865. Improvements in the postal system allowed for the timely dispersal of periodic reading material to ever-increasing areas. The expansion of the penny press, through such newspapers as the *New York Herald* and the *New York Sun*, offered mass circulation.[5]

POLITICAL ENTRENCHMENT AND INCREASING IDEOLOGICAL DISCORD

Nineteenth-century slave experiences were shaped by the close interaction of slaves with masters and overseers on farms and plantations. Slaves were forced to participate in a system in desperate need of inexpensive labor, but a system nonetheless seriously threatened by abolitionist pressures from without and the fear of slave revolt from within. By the 1820s, the abolitionist movement was slowly beginning to gather momentum. In 1820, John Quincy Adams wrote in his diary his belief that slavery was "the great and foul stain upon the North American Union" and that slavery would undoubtedly be the question upon which the future existence of the Union would be decided.[6]

Though Adams chose only to express these sentiments privately, others, like Benjamin Lundy, who edited a Baltimore newspaper called *The Genius of Universal Emancipation*, publicly called for the federal government to involve itself in influencing the South to abolish slavery. Lundy's assistant, William Lloyd Garrison, was more confrontational in his stance against slavery and rejected the use of political methods to achieve his ends. Instead, he frequently burned the Constitution at public lectures as a gesture indicating the institutionalized bias of the government against willingly enacting legislation that would bring about the end of slavery. Garrison's incendiary speeches were not always well received by others, who felt threatened by their implied violence.[7]

Though relatively small in number, Garrison's followers had a strong effect on the abolitionist debate. His ideas about the need to bring about full equality for blacks rather than simply the need for abolitionists to "free" blacks was also important in shaping the abolitionist agenda. As the South galvanized itself to the growing Northern objection to slavery, it also became more sensitive and reactive to slave insurrection and the threat of slave insurrection. Southerners reacted quickly and violently to any hint of slave revolt. The threat of slave revolt, for instance, was quickly extinguished when rumors revealed the insurrection planned by Denmark Vesey in 1822. In retaliation, Southerners killed thirty-seven slaves and deported another thirty. Although there was no actual uprising, even the *threat* of rebellion was enough to bring about this kind of reaction.

Actual rebellions were treated with equal severity.[8] After a slave revolt in Louisiana, sixteen blacks were captured and killed. Their heads were placed on poles along the Mississippi River in an attempt to intimidate others who may have considered formulating similar plans. The famous Nat Turner rebellion in Southampton, Virginia, in 1831 became seen as one of the more dramatic examples of the dangers for Southerners of slave revolts. At least fifty-five white people were killed before control was eventually regained. The effects of the rebellion were felt throughout the South. Runaway slaves were relentlessly tracked, and Southern states made it increasingly difficult for slave owners to free their slaves.[9]

From this perspective, the patterns leading to the development of an organized abolitionist movement are fairly clear. The very institution of slavery itself formed the basis for slave unrest and raised the potential for slave revolt. Slave revolt became a fundamental way of expressing a desire for freedom and a willingness to fight and die for it. White abolitionism was built upon what was essentially black abolitionism or, more precisely, a sustained revolutionary conflict. The abolitionist movement was initiated by blacks and appropriated by nonblacks who were troubled, on moral and religious grounds, by the thought of Southern denial of human rights. This nonblack abolitionist movement was as troubling to proslavery advocates as actual slave uprisings.[10] Abolitionists were perceived as being outside troublemakers who did not fully understand the facts of the matter. The assertion that abolitionism was very much a function of slave discontent did not appear in most literature of the white abolitionist movement. But the fact that slaves did indeed revolt indicates that slaves did not readily accept their subordinate position.

The increased scrutiny and draconian restrictions placed upon slaves as a result of pressures by abolitionists and the possibility of slave revolts caused many slaves to view escape as their only hope for survival.[11] The internalization of the escape motif became the primary structuring device of most slave narratives.[12] Nineteenth-century slave narratives were placed in a position in which they had to present a slave as a sympathetic character who may have been forced to lie, steal, and use other deceptions to gain his or her freedom. Slave narrative writers were deeply aware of their positions as Americans who contributed, under the harshest conditions, to the development of the country. But because of the conditions in which they lived, blacks were also acutely conscious of their alienation from a complete involvement with the country they were helping to create. Virtually all slave narratives seek, at some level, to explore the disparity between blackness and cultural, political, social, spiritual, and economic assimilation.

ABOLITIONIST EXPANSION AND ITS APPROPRIATION OF THE EX-SLAVE'S VOICE

Ex-slaves were increasingly encouraged to tell their stories both as public orations and as written narratives. The oral, performative component of the narrative is especially significant. It is probable that by initially presenting their experiences as an oral presentation, slave narrators were able to gauge and revise the effectiveness of various combinations of experience before composing the written version of the narrative.

The abolitionist movement can be seen as one of the many reform movements that existed in the United States during the pre–Civil War era, including the temperance movement, the creation of utopian communities, and the women's rights movement.[13] The atmosphere that was created by the antislavery movement also permeated other movements seeking civil rights. It was a political movement that, among other things, enabled black writers to find avenues to literary expression that they otherwise would not have found.

But as instrumental as the antislavery movement was to the literary expression of black experiences, it should also be underscored that the directions of the antislavery movement were very much influenced by the involvement of blacks as well as whites. The movement came to be identified with the cause of white, New England liberals, but that cause grew directly out of the enslavement of blacks and their individual and collective reactions to that enslavement. In an individual response to their captivity, slaves ran away and sought to find ways in which they could buy their freedom. In a collective response, slaves planned insurrections, arranged networks through which other slaves could escape to the North, organized antislavery groups, and published antislavery pamphlets. All of this activity preceded the white abolitionist groups that developed during the 1820s and 1830s. Though overshadowed by white activists, blacks, as the people most directly affected by the successes and failures of the antislavery movement, remained involved and were acutely instrumental in its success.

In 1830, there were about fifty black abolitionist societies in existence and actively working to bring an end to slavery.[14] After 1830, these groups grew in size and influence by associating themselves with white abolitionist groups. White abolitionist groups found it very beneficial to the advancement of their cause to be able to present black speakers who were willing to speak at their meetings and provide firsthand examples of the experiences of being enslaved.[15] These oratorical accounts were rendered in a way that was intended to arouse a certain amount of sympathy and support from the audience.

These speeches did not require a great deal of artistry. What was important was the heartfelt expression of experiences. Given the nature of these lectures, there was less of an emphasis on a full and complete oral history and more interest given to the incidents that were most vivid and moving for the audience. Indeed, if the speaker were too polished in his or her delivery, the audience would begin to doubt that the speaker had ever been a slave. The written narratives often grew out of these lectures and primarily adhered to similar rules. The narratives were episodic in structure and contained vivid descriptions of beatings. Narrators noted when they felt the beginnings of a desire to escape and discussed the plotting of the escape (and possibly false starts at making that escape), the eventual escape itself, the creation of a new life in free territory, and reflections on slavery and its effects on both blacks and whites. The most successful narratives went through multiple printings and were widely read in the United States and Great Britain.

RELIGION

Black writing was as deeply shaped by the intersection of abolition and religion as it was by various social, cultural, and individual imperatives. The religious influences on the black experience in America have their basis in Africa and in the transferal of those influences to the status of blacks in America.[16] In a literary sense, these religious influences recur throughout the structures and themes of the narratives. But religion was also a fundamental component of abolitionism. Religion was used both to defend slavery and to argue for its elimination. Slaveholders and slaves each professed a deep sense of religiosity, though clearly the outward manifestation of the lessons they absorbed were fundamentally different.

In attempting to renovate the fundamental ways in which the country viewed and responded to issues concerning race, black and white abolitionists also created a climate that questioned the traditional ways in which religion was practiced. Abolitionists believed that their campaign against slavery demanded that they create a humanized picture of the slave while simultaneously depicting a starkly inhuman system that encouraged the unfair subjugation of one human by another. Abolitionists sought to sway public opinion by gathering the most persuasive accounts of slavery they could muster.

Clearly, slavery was not abolished solely on the basis of slave narratives. But for abolitionist sponsors, these narratives achieved the goal they sought to attain: slave narratives created a climate in which the victims of slavery were humanized and presented as sympathetic figures simply seeking the freedom they deserved. This placed an undue stress on the narrators. They were simultaneously forced to present themselves as individual characters, as representatives of their race, and as embodiments of the injustices visited upon the race. If whites could have earlier claimed a certain amount of ignorance regarding the kinds of exploitation African slaves faced, fugitive slaves graphically presented examples of the nature of the exploitation as well as the physical and mental abuses that accompanied that exploitation. Southerners, however, were under no illusions regarding their need for slaves and the inevitability of a system that demanded a large, unskilled labor pool to run it.

> Nay, supposing that we were all convinced, and thought of slavery precisely as you do, at what ear of "Moral suasion" do you imagine you could prevail on us to give up a thousand millions of dollars in the value of our slaves, and a thousand millions of dollars more in the depreciation of our lands, in consequence of the want of laborers to cultivate them?[17]

"WHAT IF I AM A WOMAN?": WOMEN, RELIGION, AND THE ANTISLAVERY MOVEMENT

The questioning of American religious practice through abolitionist activity was especially evident in the thoughts of organized antislavery women and the reactions to their work. For many women who involved themselves in the antislavery movement during the 1830s and 1840s, the stand against slavery and racism indicated a more central evangelically based belief that social change could be used to bring moral redemption to American culture.[18] Though they needed to present their ideas in a public platform, women faced the constrictions of the private, domestic sphere within which they were supposed to operate. Maria W. Stewart, a black antislavery activist living in Boston, argued in 1831 that blacks should enjoy the same rights as whites, and that blacks themselves needed to stand up and assert those rights: "All the nations of the earth are crying out for Liberty and Equality. Away, away with tyranny and oppression! And shall Afric's [sic] sons be silent any longer?"[19] Though she acknowledged societal difference in attitudes toward women working in the public arena, it was the responsibility of women as much as men to respond: "What if I am a woman? . . . God at this eventful period" has "raise[d] up . . . females to strive, by their example both in public and private to assist" in the social and political progress of African Americans.[20]

Stewart was the first American woman, black or white, in recorded American history to speak publicly about black civil rights and women's rights. Her message, both in lectures and political writings, challenged her listeners, who were most often black, to organize against slavery in the South and racism in the North. Her language and many of the themes she used relied heavily on the language and allusion of the Old Testament, especially Jeremiah and Lamentations, as well as the prophets Isaiah and Ezekiel. She frequently turned to the book of Revelation, possibly because of its emphasis on written language and on the final, catastrophic war of good and evil and because of its didactically prophetic nature. But her position as a woman speaking before audiences of men and women (or "promiscuous" audiences, as they were called) is especially striking. She relied on biblical precedent to support her work: "The spirit of God came before me and I spake before many . . . reflecting on what I had said, I felt ashamed. . . . And something said within my breast 'press forward, I will be with thee.' And my heart made this reply, 'Lord, if thou wilt be with me, then I will speak for thee as long as I live.'"[21]

Comments arguing for a public presence for women in the antislavery movement and employing a deep awareness of evangelical doctrine caused hostile reactions outside antislavery organizations as well as division within. Though women saw an evangelical foundation for their actions, religious leaders often found their thoughts and activities threatening.

In an article published in *The Liberator* on September 1, 1837, titled "Appeal of Clerical Abolitionists on Anti-Slavery Measures," several notable Boston ministers wrote to express their belief that women were actually using the overthrow of "slavery to overthrow government, civil and domestic, the Sabbath and the church and ministry." This was the beginning of a major division in the antislavery agenda. One of the primary issues of conflict was the question of how women could best be involved. Garrison urged his followers to accept women as full members, which they did. But in reaction to the decision by the Massachusetts Anti-Slavery Society and the New England Anti-Slavery Society to accept women members, religious-based groups decided to establish the Massachusetts Abolition Society, which would exclude women members. This intersection of religion and the abolitionist movement defined the direction of the abolitionist agenda and certainly delineated the ways in which the abolitionist movement influenced the development of slave narrative writing and the forms (male centered and adventure oriented) that writing was encouraged to take.

In terms of these elements and the production of women's slave narratives, it is also important to note that women were sought out proportionately less than men to tell their stories on abolitionist platforms. This is partially a function of the bias against women speaking in public and partially because of the nineteenth-century emphasis on women being domestic and submissive. It should come as no surprise that the loudest criticism of women serving as public speakers initially came from those who were made most uncomfortable by what they saw as threats to their authority.[22]

THE SAMENESS OF THE NARRATIVES

Structurally and thematically, there is an overwhelming sameness throughout slave narrative writing. This sameness became increasingly rigid over the course of the eighteenth-century, until the involvement of the abolitionist movement securely codified this style of black writing through the Civil War. Among other conventions, the basic outlines of the narratives usually include on the title page the assertion that the narrative was either written by the slave or dictated to some friend who did the actual writing. Before the beginning of the actual narrative, there are usually a series of introductions or prefaces that serve as testimonials to the character of the narrator and the accuracy of the narrative. This introductory material is customarily written by white abolitionist supporters or white editors and authors who served as literary benefactors to the slave writer. The functions of these prefaces are to emphasize the fundamental truth of the narrative to follow, the connections between the preface writer and the narrative writer, and the fact that the narrative understates rather than overstates the effects of the slave system.

The narratives themselves tend to open at the beginning of the narrator's life, with a short discussion of what facts the narrator actually knows about his or her birth. These customarily do not include precise information about the date of birth, but are usually very specific in designating the geographic location of the birth. Parentage is frequently an issue with the slave narrator. As often as not, there is a question of parentage that suggests the possibility of a white ancestor. Having established basic facts concerning the narrator, the narrative tends to shift to external conditions. Central to these conditions are the heartless slave owner and the precarious nature of the slave's existence. Descriptions of the slave auction served to show the uncertain nature of the slaves' lives. Christianity, or at least the Christianity professed by most slaveholders, was routinely shown to be of little help to the slave. Indeed, the slaveholders claiming Christian faith were characteristically described as being especially malicious.

There are a number of other recurrent elements in the fugitive slave narrative genre. They include accounts of the restrictions and obstacles that slaves faced in obtaining an education and learning to read and write; descriptions and summaries of the efforts of others to escape to freedom; successful and unsuccessful attempts on the part of the narrator to escape; final thoughts on slavery and the toll it takes on both the slaveholder and the enslaved; and supplementary material following the conclusion of the narrative (such as more letters from supporters or other endorsements) that serves as a kind of framing counterpoint to the material preceding the narrative.[23]

What becomes clear from even a cursory look at several narratives is that all of this structural apparatus leaves very little room for the voice of the narrator to come through. The narratives virtually all look outward to the reality of slavery in hopes of addressing the reading audience and encouraging it to express its political strength in expectation of bringing an end to slavery. The lives of the narrators became secondary to the political issues at hand. Though central to the narrative, their lives more than anything illustrate what slavery was and what slavery was about. The detail the reader gets is formulaic and not overly revealing of the personal thoughts and desires of the narrator. The only interior life discussed by the narrator is the life directly related to slavery and its abolition. At heart, this was the single, guiding principle behind virtually all fugitive slave narrative writing. Their literary sponsors sought to use a well-defined genre to serve a particular, well-defined political agenda. Everyone involved with the narratives—including the narrators themselves, their sponsors, and their intended audience—understood the objectives the narratives sought to accomplish. It is inevitable that most of the narratives bear striking similarities to each other.[24]

THE RECONSTRUCTIVE VOICE

Having argued for the deeply formulaic nature of the slave narrative as a genre, it is also worth noting that the kind of reconstructive voice that appears at the beginning of the narrative is also a fairly stock ingredient in the American autobiographical form of the early- to mid-nineteenth century. Narrators created a place for themselves in the minds of their readers by associating themselves with any number of geographic and familial coordinates. The primary difference, of course, between the narratives of former slaves and the autobiographies of white writers is that white writers were likely to spend more time remarking on why they chose to write their autobiographies and considerably less time commenting on the nature and circumstances surrounding their birth. For the ex-slave writer, the purpose of the narrative was fairly clear, as writers wanted to write about the slave system and bring about its collapse. Though the *why* of the autobiography was fairly unchanging, the *who* of the autobiography differed. The reader is paradoxically denied access to any particularities because these are the details that are most often shadowy and indistinct.

Black narratives play off the expectations initiated by white autobiographies because black narratives are not able to present the kinds of details the white autobiographer was able to draw upon to identify himself or herself. Black autobiography became distinct from white autobiography in the fundamental inability of the ex-slave to write his or her autobiography using the features common to white autobiography. Parentage is unclear or sketchy. At best, it goes back only as far as a grandparent. Brothers and sisters often do not share a common father, so the idea of a family name is useless. Perhaps this is one of the reasons why a recurring component of the slave narrative involves taking a new last name once the slave achieves relative freedom. As the last name did not signify an intrinsic connection to any kind of conventional familial structure, former slaves felt free to change their last name to correspond with their newly won freedom. In losing this customary method of gaining the reader's attention, black narrators were forced to find other ways to engage the reader's interest.[25] So, while the black narrator adopted the narrative form, he or she relinquished any claim on the conventions intrinsic to that form.

Former slaves were very aware that their audience was largely white. They were acutely alert to the fact that their readers might not find their portrayals of their captivity or their captors particularly barbarous or horrific. This seems to be one of the primary reasons for the kinds of authenticating documents supplied by whites at the beginning and the end of the narrative. Because of the source of the narrative, slave narratives required white corroboration to achieve any kind of resonance with readers. This layer of validation was particular to black autobiographies written for a white audience, as white narratives of Native American captivities or explorations of inhospitable places around the world seldom used these same kinds of framing devices to add a patina of legitimacy.[26]

The ways in which the narratives may be read are very much a function of the relationship that was constructed between the author, the author's experiences, and the intended audience. Black writers interpreted for whites, by way of various levels of mediation, the experiences of blacks. One way they did this was to focus the readers' attention outside of the usual parameters of their existence. At the most literal level, this was done by directing the audience's attention to a specific geographic region. At a more figurative level, the successive experiences of the narrator, eventually leading to a decision to seek freedom followed by episodic accounts of the escape, serve to displace the reader from a comfortable, isolated emotional space.[27]

Slave narrators used various strategies to approach their audience, but this approach was always a function of the writer's conception of the audience and the kind of response the writer sought to rouse. Such writers as Lunsford Lane and

James W. C. Pennington try to show their audience that slaves are essentially hardworking, honest, and spiritual people who were driven to lie, cheat, and steal by the extremity of the conditions in which they lived. Slave narrators were engaged in a fierce struggle for the right to create themselves rhetorically, but first they had to revise some of their audience's negative perceptions about black life.

In framing my discussion of the slave narrative in the way I have, my intention is to argue for a view that sees them, from their very beginning, as triangular narratives whose meanings are a function of the relationship that was rhetorically developed between the writer of the narrative, the mediators who facilitated the production of the narrative and served as its gatekeepers, and the intended audience. Implicit within this configuration are elements of religion. These aspects are reflected in explicit Christian references and influences as well as in the implicit structuring of the narrative. The life of the fugitive slave is depicted as being a literal journey to freedom that involves the same kind of escape from physical oppression that the soul experiences in its attempts to free itself from the spiritual tyranny of sin. The narrative depicts a similar movement from bondage to freedom.

But the influences that bound the slave writer as closely to form and structure as slaveholders bound the slave to the plantation were abolitionists and their political agenda. The development of the abolitionist political agenda offered slaves a literal and figurative platform for widespread expression of their experiences within the framework of a literature offering clearly defined didactic patterns. But these patterns of self-expression were ultimately as limiting as they were freeing. As with the physical movement from slavery to freedom or the movement from South to North—where slaves often realized that they had traded one kind of oppression for another—so, too, did the literary articulation of their experiences ultimately become limiting.

Though the slave's narrative was closely controlled, it is important to note that it was one of several forms, including the novel, the essay, and poetry, that black writers actively chose to use. Such writers as James W. C. Pennington and William Wells Brown, who went on to explore other literary outlets, were well aware of the limitations as well as the possibilities of the slave narrative genre. Virtually all writings by fugitive slaves seek to establish a didactic purpose. Their writings move with a sense of direction and political purpose that is reflected in works by succeeding black writers. This cultural and political commitment eventually reached a similar pinnacle of political involvement in the black writings of the 1960s.[28]

THE LITERARY LEGACY OF THE NARRATIVES

The legacy of the narratives is as much a function of social and political conditions as the narratives themselves. As the narratives of former slaves suggest, racial awareness was inexorably fused with the desire for freedom and autonomy.

For the slave writer, these elements were rendered in physical and, to a somewhat lesser extent, spiritual terms. Subsequent African American writers rendered these desires in broader cultural and political terms. In the generation or so following the end of the Civil War, such African American writers as Elizabeth Keckley in *Behind the Scenes: Thirty Years a Slave and Four Years in the White House* (1868) and, probably most famously, Booker T. Washington in *Up from Slavery* (1901) continued to overtly use the slave narrative form. The realities of slavery and its effects were acknowledged, but now the emphasis shifted away from descriptions of past oppression and toward an awareness of the possibilities for the future.

The New Negro Renaissance that occurred during the 1920s opened a creative dialogue between black poets, novelists, playwrights, musicians, visual artists, and intellectuals and their African American and African pasts. Such anthologies as the *Book of American Negro Poetry* (1922), which was compiled by James Weldon Johnson, and *The New Negro* (1925), compiled by Alain Locke, sought to clarify and describe the vast web of cultural and literary traditions that linked a large and increasingly disparate body of African American writing. One of the difficulties inherent in an examination of the slave narrative is that the relationship of the individual to the genre is particularly diffuse. The technique that used individual identity in the service of a collective presence ultimately produced stories and narrative voices that mistakenly gave the impression of a single, unique, and homogeneous identity. Twentieth- and twenty-first-century writing based on the foundation of fugitive slave narrative writing refutes this essentialized view of African American culture and experience. The past in general (and slavery in particular) was seen as a pastiche of many stories, each equally valid. Out of the increased awareness of the explicit relationship between the past and the present, mid-twentieth-century works used the first-person narrative voice as a way of examining racial interaction.

Contemporary African American writers recognize—in a variety of imaginative frameworks—the relevance of slavery and the body of narratives the experience produced. While not trying to replicate the narrative descriptions of oppression and its influence on the interior lives of those who experienced and witnessed that oppression, contemporary writers have drawn on the form and what it expressed as starting points for creative reimaginings of those experiences. The legacy of experiences the narratives describe are as varied and complicated as its narratives. Broadly speaking, contemporary writers recognized and incorporated into their imaginations the ways in which slavery was an intrinsic component in the development of modernity and in modernity's assumptions about race, power, economics, and national power. By extension and influence, fugitive slave writers became members of a transnational community that actively recognized and embraced the contributions and unique experiences of all people of African descent. But the influence of fugitive slave narrative writers should not be entirely relegated to imaginative remappings of the past and its influences on the present. They also contribute to the areas of African American literature that imagine the future.

By situating slavery within modernity's increasingly globalized, transnational, and futurist contexts, contemporary artists and thinkers are seeing the slave experience as something much larger than a "peculiar institution" simply inflicted upon Africans and their descendants. In this enlarged context of examination, slavery is an integral thread running throughout the fabric of Western culture. The global framework of contemporary evaluations of slavery returns slavery to the fundamental points that early slave narrative writers articulated several centuries earlier: Slavery was a blight on all of Western culture. It ultimately infected everyone it touched and continues to have individual and collective literary and cultural legacies.

NOTES

1. Daniel S. Fabricant, "Thomas R. Gray and William Styron: Finally, a Critical Look at the 1831 *Confessions of Nat Turner*," *American Journal of Legal History* 37 (July 1993): 332–61; Stephen B. Oates, *The Fires of Jubilee: Nat Turner's Fierce Rebellion* (New York: Harper and Row, 1975); Eric J. Sundquist, *To Wake the Nations: Race in the Making of American Literature* (Cambridge, MA: Belknap Press of Harvard University Press, 1993); Kenneth S. Greenberg, ed., *The Confessions of Nat Turner and Related Documents* (Boston: Bedford Books of St. Martin's Press, 1996).

2. Douglas R. Egerton, "The Scenes Which Are Acted in St. Domingo: The Legacy of Revolutionary Violence in Early National Virginia," in *Antislavery Violence: Sectional, Racial, and Cultural Conflict in Antebellum America*, edited by John R. McKivigan and Stanley Harrold (Knoxville: University of Tennessee Press, 1999), 41–64.

3. Marion Wilson Starling, *The Slave Narrative: Its Place in American History*, 2nd ed. (Washington, D.C.: Howard University Press, 1988), 59; Frances Smith Foster, *Witnessing Slavery: The Development of Antebellum Slave Narratives* (Westport, CT: Greenwood Press, 1979), 52–53; Angelo Costanzo, *Surprising Narrative: Olaudah Equiano and the Beginnings of Black Autobiography* (Westport, CT: Greenwood Press, 1987), 41–90, 109–13.

4. Foster, *Witnessing Slavery*, 148; Jean Fagan Yellin, *The Intricate Knot: Black Figures in American Literature, 1776–1863* (New York: New York University Press, 1972), 166; William L. Andrews, *To Tell a Free Story: The First Century of Afro-American Autobiography, 1760–1865* (Urbana: University of Illinois Press, 1986), 61–96.

5. George McMichael, ed., *Anthology of American Literature*, vol. 1, *Colonial through Romantic* (New York: Macmillan, 1974), 550.

6. John A. Garraty, *A Short History of the American Nation* (New York: Harper Collins, 1993), 1:184–86. See also Charles Joyner, "A Single Southern Culture: Cultural Interaction in the Old South," in *Black and White Cultural Interaction in the Antebellum South*, edited by Ted Ownby (Jackson: University Press of Mississippi, 1993), 3–22; Eugene D. Genovese, *Roll, Jordan, Roll: The World the Slaves Made* (New York: Pantheon Books, 1974), 3–158.

7. Garraty, *A Short History of the American Nation*, vol. 1, 184–85; Henry Mayer, *All on Fire: William Lloyd Garrison and the Abolition of Slavery* (New York: St. Martin's Press, 1998), 3–70, 213–99, 333–481; Mason Lowance, *Against Slavery: An Abolitionist Reader* (New York: Penguin Books, 2000), 92–130.

8. Joseph Cephas Carroll, *Slave Insurrections in the United States, 1800–1865* (New York: Negro Universities Press, 1968), 47–82, 83–117, 129–44.

9. Garraty, *A Short History of the American Nation*, 1:221–22.

10. Drew Gilpin Faust, ed., *The Ideology of Slavery: Proslavery Thought in the Antebellum South, 1830–1860* (Baton Rouge: Louisiana State University Press, 1981), 1–20.

11. John Hope Franklin and Loren Schweninger, *Runaway Slaves: Rebels on the Plantation* (New York: Oxford University Press, 1999), 209–33. See also Charles L. Blockson, *The Underground Railroad* (New York: Prentice-Hall, 1987), esp. 23–155, 163–209.

12. Robert Hedin, "The American Slave Narrative: The Justification of the Picaro," *American Literature* 53 (January 1982): 635–36; Starling, *The Slave Narrative*, 29–33.

13. Louis Filler, *The Crusade against Slavery, 1830–1860* (New York: Harper, 1960), 28–47.

14. Edward Magdol, *The Antislavery Rank and File: A Social Profile of the Abolitionists' Constituency* (Westport, CT: Greenwood Press, 1986), 3–14, 43–51, 61–99; Lewis Perry, *Radical Abolitionism: Anarchy and the Government of God in Antislavery Thought* (Ithaca, NY: Cornell University Press, 1973), 92–128; Filler, *The Crusade against Slavery, 1830–1860*, 10–27; Rice, *The Rise and Fall of Black Slavery* (London: Macmillan, 1975), 305–52.

15. Garraty, *A Short History of the American Nation*, 1:184–85; Stanley Harrold, *The Abolitionists and the South, 1831–1861* (Lexington: University of Kentucky Press, 1995), 26–63.

16. Albert J. Raboteau, *Slave Religion: The "Invisible Institution" in the Antebellum South* (New York: Oxford University Press, 1978), 211–88, 290–318.

17. Charles H. Nichols, *Many Thousand Gone: The Ex-Slaves' Account of Their Bondage and Freedom* (Leiden, Netherlands: E. J. Brill, 1963), 180; also quoted in Herbert Aptheker, *Essays in the History of the American Negro* (New York: International Publishers, 1983), 137.

18. Patricia Morton, ed., *Discovering the Women in Slavery: Emancipating Perspectives on the American Past* (Athens: University of Georgia Press, 1996), 1–26. See also Jennifer Fleischner, *Mastering Slavery: Memory, Family, and Identity in Women's Slave Narratives* (New York: New York University Press, 1996), 11–32.

19. Loewenberg and Bogin, eds., *Black Women in Nineteenth-Century Life: Their Words, Their Thoughts, Their Feelings* (University Park: Pennsylvania State University Press, 1976), 186. Also quoted in Yellin and Van Horne, eds., *The Abolitionist Sisterhood*, 4.

20. Bert James Loewenberg and Ruth Bogin, eds., *Black Women in Nineteenth-Century Life*, 198, 199. Also quoted in Jean Fagan Yellin and John C. Van Horne, eds., *The Abolitionist Sisterhood: Women's Political Culture in Antebellum America* (Ithaca, NY: Cornell University Press, 1994), 4.

21. Quoted in Marilyn Richardson, ed., *Maria Stewart: America's First Black Woman Political Writer* (Bloomington: Indiana University Press, 1987), 19.

22. Foster, *Witnessing Slavery*, 58–59; Erlene Stetson, "Studying Slavery: Some Literary and Pedagogical Considerations on the Black Female Slave," in *All the Women Are White, All the Blacks Are Men, but Some of Us Are Brave: Black Women's Studies*, edited by Gloria T. Hull, Patricia Bell Scott, and Barbara Smith (Old Westbury, NY: Feminist Press, 1982), 83; Joanne M. Braxton, *Black Women Writing Autobiography: A Tradition within a Tradition* (Philadelphia: Temple University Press, 1989), 39–79; Deborah Gray White, *Ar'n't I a Woman? Female Slaves in the Plantation South* (New York: Norton, 1985), 62–90.

23. James Olney, "'I Was Born': Slave Narratives, Their Status as Autobiography and as Literature," in *The Slave's Narrative*, edited by Charles T. Davis and Henry Louis Gates Jr., 148–75 (New York: Oxford University Press, 1985), 152–54.

24. Olney, "'I Was Born,'" 152–54.

25. Olney, "'I Was Born,'" 153–56; Andrews, *To Tell a Free Story*, 27–29.

26. Andrews, *To Tell a Free Story*, 26; Henry Louis Gates Jr., *Figures in Black: Words, Signs, and the "Racial" Self* (New York: Oxford University Press, 1987), 89.

27. Elizabeth W. Bruss, *Autobiographical Acts: The Changing Situation of a Literary Genre* (Baltimore: Johns Hopkins University Press, 1976), 23; Julia Swindells, *The Uses of Autobiography* (London: Taylor and Francis, 1995), 1–30, 89–97.

28. Stephen Butterfield, *Black Autobiography in America* (Amherst: University of Massachusetts Press, 1974), 23–31; Robert B. Stepto, *From behind the Veil: A Study of Afro-American Narrative* (Urbana: University of Illinois Press, 1979), 3–31; Nathan Irvin Huggins, *Black Odyssey: The Afro-American Ordeal in Slavery* (New York: Pantheon Books, 1977), 114–53, 203–42.

■ CHAPTER 1
Nat Turner (1800–1831)

THE CONFESSIONS OF NAT TURNER

In 1831, Southampton, Virginia, was a small county that was inhabited by approximately 16,000 people, including whites, a relatively high proportion of free blacks, and slaves.[1] Southampton County is in the southeastern portion of Virginia, near the North Carolina border. Though slavery had been a fixture in the South since the seventeenth century, there had never been a sustained slave insurrection. In 1790, there was a large-scale uprising on the island of Santo Domingo. The rebellion overthrew French control and established Haiti, the first independent black republic in the New World.[2]

In 1800, the year Nat Turner was born, Gabriel Prosser formed plans in Richmond, Virginia, for blacks to revolt on the belief that the ideals of life, liberty, and the pursuit of happiness contained in the Declaration of Independence should apply to blacks as well as whites. Though Prosser's plans were entirely confined to Richmond, Virginia, authorities promptly responded by activating the state militia and arresting Gabriel Prosser and about thirty-four of his followers. All were eventually tried and sentenced to death by hanging. Though no whites were killed and Prosser's plans were stopped before they began, the question remained about whether or not large-scale black revolution, similar to what had occurred on Santo Domingo, where some 60,000 people died, could ever occur in the American South.

That question was emphatically answered during August 21 through August 23, 1831, when Nat Turner and a small group of collaborators (initially a group of six that expanded to possibly as many as fifty or sixty) carried on an insurrection in Southampton that resulted in the deaths of at least fifty-five white people. Most of Turner's group was captured by August 23, though Turner himself remained at large before being captured around noon on October 30, 1831.

While *The Confessions of Nat Turner* is only one of several accounts of the insurrection that were published at the time, it emerged, almost from its initial publication, as the most influential. In the days following his capture, Nat Turner was asked by Thomas R. Gray, a white southern lawyer and slaveholder, to provide a firsthand account of his actions and the motives propelling those actions. Though Gray entitled the resulting document a "confession," it is not an actual transcript of Turner's trial. It was dictated to Gray, who then wrote, edited, and commented upon it in his introduction, in his conclusion, and at various places throughout the narrative. While Turner's control of the narrative is clearly compromised by Gray's close involvement with it and by some disparity between the narrative and official court documents, its details are largely corroborated by unrelated, contemporaneous documentation.

The full extent of Gray's editorial involvement with Turner's story is unclear. What is abundantly clear, however, is that neither voice can fully exist as a freestanding, authorized voice on its own. Each voice needs the limiting and defining qualities of the other for its own existence and significance. Gray furthermore needed the hysteria created by Turner's insurrection in order to sell the booklet itself. The compressed time frame of composition (Gray interviewed Turner on November 1–3, 1831, he acquired a copyright on November 10, Turner was hanged on November 11, and the booklet was published in Baltimore less than two weeks later) closely coincides with the fact that Gray's financial fortunes were quickly diminishing from the relative prosperity he enjoyed in 1829, when he had twenty-one slaves and eight hundred acres of land, to the single horse he reported as property just three years later.[3]

Turner's vision of revolution both encompassed and transcended physical enslavement. For Turner, slavery in the South served as the basis for his holy war. He saw himself as a prophet in the lineage of Christ. His narrative suggests that he saw his childhood intelligence and prophetic visions as evidence of that fact. Several events in Turner's life contribute to his outlook: the agreement by both blacks and whites that from childhood Turner was intelligent and would be dissatisfied as a slave; his father's escape to the North; and his literacy, religious visions, status as a lay preacher, and intense sense of mission. Most emphatically, Turner's narrative indicates the ways in which the religious rhetoric used by slaveholders as a means of control and justification of the slave system could be inverted and used as a justification for violent revolution and social change. Turner's story has served as the inspiration for a number of fictional accounts, including *The Old Dominion; or, The Southampton Massacre* (1856) by G[eorge] P[ayne] R[ainsford] James; *Dred: A Tale of the Great Dismal Swamp Together with Anti-Slavery Tales and Papers, and Life in Florida after the War* (1856) by Harriet Beecher Stowe; *Homoselle* (1881) by Mary Spear Tiernan; *Their Shadows Before: A Story of the Southampton Insurrection* (1899) by Pauline Carrington [Rust] Bouve; *Ol' Prophet Nat* (1967) by Daniel Panger; *The Confessions of Nat Turner* (1967) by William Styron; *Dessa Rose* (1986) by Sherley Anne Williams; the graphic novel *Nat Turner* (2008) by Kyle Baker; and the film *The Birth of a Nation* (2016) written, produced, and directed by Nate Parker.

The Confessions of Nat Turner reprinted here is from the original edition of the booklet published by Thomas R. Gray in 1831.

Further Reading

Andrews, William L. "Inter(racial)textuality in Nineteenth-Century Southern Narrative." In *Influence and Intertextuality in Literary History*, edited by Jay Clayton and Eric Rothstein. Madison: University of Wisconsin Press, 1991, 298–317; Andrews, William L. *To Tell a Free Story: The First Century of Afro-American Autobiography, 1760–1865*. Urbana: University of Illinois Press, 1986; Aptheker, Herbert. *American Negro Slave Revolts*. New York: International Publishers, 1983; Aptheker, Herbert. *Nat Turner's Slave Rebellion. Together with the Full Text of the So-Called "Confessions" of Nat Turner Made in Prison in 1831*. New York: Humanities Press, 1966; Bland, Sterling Lecater Jr. *Voices of the Fugitives: Runaway Slave Stories and Their Fictions of Self-Creation*. Westport, CT: Greenwood Press, 2000; Browne, Stephen Howard. "'This Unparalleled and Inhuman Massacre': The Gothic, the Sacred, and the Meaning of Nat Turner." *Rhetoric and Public Affairs* 3 (Fall 2000): 309–32; Clarke, John Henrik, ed. *William Styron's Nat Turner: Ten Black Writers Respond*. Boston: Beacon Press, 1968; Egerton, Douglas R. *Gabriel's Revolution: The Virginia Slave Conspiracies of 1800 and 1802*. Chapel Hill: University of North Carolina Press, 1993; Egerton, Douglas R. "The Scenes Which Are Acted in St. Domingo: The Legacy of Revolutionary Violence in Early National Virginia." In *Antislavery Violence: Sectional, Racial, and Cultural Conflict in Antebellum America*, edited by John R. McKivigan and Stanley Harrold, Knoxville: University of Tennessee Press, 1999, 41–64; Fabricant, Daniel S. "Thomas R. Gray and William Styron: Finally, a Critical Look at the 1831 *Confessions of Nat Turner*." *American Journal of Legal History* 37 (July 1993): 332–61; Foner, Eric, ed. *Nat Turner*. Englewood Cliffs, NJ: Prentice-Hall, 1971; Freehling, Alison Goodyear. *Drift toward Dissolution: The Virginia Slavery Debate of 1831–1832*. Baton Rouge: Louisiana State University Press, 1982; Genovese, Eugene D. *From Rebellion to Revolution: Afro-American Slave Revolts in the Making of the Modern World*. Baton Rouge: Louisiana State University Press, 1979; Genovese, Eugene D. *Roll, Jordan, Roll: The World the Slaves Made*. New York: Pantheon Books, 1974; Greenberg, Kenneth, S., ed. *The Confessions of Nat Turner and Related Documents*. Boston: Bedford Books of St. Martin's Press, 1996; Gross, Seymour L., and Eileen Bender, "History, Politics, and Literature: The Myth of Nat Turner." *American Quarterly* 23 (1971): 487–518; Harding, Vincent. *There Is a River: The Black Struggle for Freedom in America*. New York: Harcourt Brace Jovanovich, 1981; Harding, Vincent. "You've Taken My Nat and Gone." In *The Critical Response to William Styron*, edited by Daniel W. Ross. Westport, CT: Greenwood Press, 1995, 133–39; Kolchin, Peter. *Unfree Labor: American Slavery and Russian Serfdom*. Cambridge, MA: Belknap Press of Harvard University Press, 1987; Levine, Lawrence W. *Black Culture and Black Consciousness: Afro-American Folk Thought from Slavery to Freedom*. New York: Oxford University Press, 1977; Oates, Stephen B. *The Fires of Jubilee: Nat Turner's Fierce Rebellion*. New York: Harper and Row, 1975; Parramore, Thomas C. *Southampton County, Virginia*. Charlottesville: University Press of Virginia, 1978; Raboteau, Albert J. *Slave Religion: The "Invisible Institution" in the Antebellum South*. New York: Oxford University Press, 1978; Sobel, Mechal. *Trabelin' On: The Slave Journey to an Afro-Baptist Faith*.

Princeton, NJ: Princeton University Press, 1988; Starling, Marion Wilson. *The Slave Narrative: Its Place in American History*. 2nd ed. Washington, D.C.: Howard University Press, 1988; Stone, Albert E. *The Return of Nat Turner: History, Literature, and Cultural Politics in Sixties America*. Athens: University of Georgia Press, 1992; Styron, William. *The Confessions of Nat Turner*. New York: Modern Library, 1994. Originally published New York: Random House, 1967.; Sundquist, Eric J. *To Wake the Nations: Race in the Making of American Literature*. Cambridge, MA: Belknap Press of Harvard University Press, 1993; Swift, David E. *Black Prophets of Justice: Activist Clergy before the Civil War*. Baton Rouge: Louisiana State University Press, 1989; Tragle, Henry Irving. *The Southampton Slave Revolt of 1831: A Compilation of Source Material*. Amherst: University of Massachusetts Press, 1971; West, James L. W., III, ed. *Conversations with William Styron*. Jackson: University Press of Mississippi, 1985; White, Deborah Gray. *Ar'n't I a Woman? Female Slaves in the Plantation South*. New York: Norton, 1985; Wood, Peter H. "Nat Turner: The Unknown Slave as Visionary Leader." In *Black Leaders of the Nineteenth Century*, edited by Leon Litwack and August Meier. Urbana: University of Illinois Press, 1988, 21–40.

THE CONFESSIONS of NAT TURNER,
The Leader of the Late INSURRECTION IN SOUTHAMPTON, VA.

As fully and voluntarily made to
THOMAS R. GRAY,

In the prison where he was confined, and acknowledged by him to be such when read before the Court of Southampton; with the certificate, under seal of the Court, convened at Jerusalem,[4] Nov. 5, 1831, for his trial.

Also, An Authentic ACCOUNT OF THE WHOLE INSURRECTION.
With Lists Of The Whites Who Were Murdered.
And Of The Negroes Brought Before The Court Of Southampton, And There Sentenced, &.

Baltimore:
PUBLISHED BY THOMAS R. GRAY.
Lucas & Deaver, print.
1831.

DISTRICT OF COLUMBIA, TO WIT

Be it remembered, That on this tenth day of November, Anno Domini, eighteen hundred and thirty-one, Thomas R. Gray[5] of the said District, deposited in this office the title of a book, which is in the words as following:

"The Confessions of Nat Turner, the leader of the late insurrection in Southampton, Virginia, as fully and voluntarily made to Thomas R. Gray, in the prison where he was confined, and acknowledged by him to be such when read before the Court of Southampton; with the certificate, under seal, of the Court convened at Jerusalem, November 5, 1831, for his trial. Also, an authentic account of the whole insurrection, with lists of the whites who were murdered, and of the negroes brought before the Court of Southampton, and there sentenced, &. the right whereof he claims as proprietor, in conformity with an Act of Congress, entitled "An act to amend the several acts respecting Copy Rights."

(Seal.)

EDMUND J. LEE, Clerk of the District.

In testimony that the above is a true copy, from the record of the District Court for the District of Columbia, I, Edmund J. Lee, the Clerk thereof, have hereunto set my hand and affixed the seal of my office, this 10th day of November, 1831.

EDMUND J. LEE, C.D.C.

TO THE PUBLIC

The late insurrection in Southampton has greatly excited the public mind, and led to a thousand idle, exaggerated and mischievous reports.[6] It is the first instance in our history of an open rebellion of the slaves, and attended with such atrocious circumstances of cruelty and destruction, as could not fail to leave a deep impression, not only upon the minds of the community where this fearful tragedy was wrought, but throughout every portion of our country, in which this population is to be found. Public curiosity has been on the stretch to understand the origin and progress of this dreadful conspiracy, and the motives which influence its diabolical actors. The insurgent slaves had all been destroyed, or apprehended, tried and executed, (with the exception of the leader,) without revealing any thing at all satisfactory, as to the motives which governed them, or the means by which they expected to accomplish their object. Every thing connected with the sad affair was wrapt in mystery, until Nat Turner, the leader of this ferocious band, whose name has resounded throughout our widely extended empire, was captured. This "great Bandit" was taken by a single individual, in a cave near the residence of his late owner, on Sunday, the thirtieth of October, without attempting to make the slightest resistance, and on the following day safely lodged in the jail of the County. His captor was Benjamin

Phipps, armed with a shot gun well charged. Nat's only weapon was a small light sword which he immediately surrendered, and begged that his life might be spared. Since his confinement, by permission of the Jailor, I have had ready access to him, and finding that he was willing to make a full and free confession of the origin, progress and consummation of the insurrectory movements of the slaves of which he was the contriver and head; I determined for the gratification of public curiosity to commit his statements to writing, and publish them, with little or no variation, from his own words. That this is a faithful record of his confessions, the annexed certificate of the County Court of Southampton, will attest. They certainly bear one stamp of truth and sincerity. He makes no attempt (as all the other insurgents who were examined did,) to exculpate himself, but frankly acknowledges his full participation in all the guilt of the transaction. He was not only the contriver of the conspiracy, but gave the first blow towards its execution.

It will thus appear, that whilst every thing upon the surface of society wore a calm and peaceful aspect; whilst not one note of preparation was heard to warn the devoted inhabitants of woe and death, a gloomy fanatic was revolving in the recesses of his own dark, bewildered, and overwrought mind, schemes of indiscriminate massacre to the whites. Schemes too fearfully executed as far as his fiendish band proceeded in their desolating march. No cry for mercy penetrated their flinty bosoms. No acts of remembered kindness made the least impression upon these remorseless murderers. Men, women and children, from hoary age to helpless infancy were involved in the same cruel fate. Never did a band of savages do their work of death more unsparingly. Apprehension for their own personal safety seems to have been the only principle of restraint in the whole course of their bloody proceedings. And it is not the least remarkable feature in this horrid transaction, that a band actuated by such hellish purposes, should have resisted so feebly, when met by the whites in arms. Desperation alone, one would think, might have led to greater efforts. More than twenty of them attacked Dr. Blunt's house on Tuesday morning, a little before day-break, defended by two men and three boys. They fled precipitately at the first fire; and their future plans of mischief, were entirely disconcerted and broken up. Escaping thence, each individual sought his own safety either in concealment, or by returning home, with the hope that his participation might escape detection, and all were shot down in the course of a few days, or captured and brought to trial and punishment. Nat has survived all his followers, and the gallows will speedily close his career. His own account of the conspiracy is submitted to the public, without comment. It reads an awful, and it is hoped, a useful lesson, as to the operations of a mind like his, endeavoring to grapple with things beyond its reach. How it first became bewildered and confounded, and finally corrupted and led to the conception and perpetration of the most atrocious and heart-rending deeds. It is calculated also to demonstrate the policy of our laws in restraint of this class of our population, and to induce all those entrusted with their execution, as well as our citizens generally, to see that they are strictly and rigidly enforced. Each particular community should look to its own safety, whilst the general guardians of the laws, keep a watchful eye over all. If Nat's statements can be relied on, the insurrection in this county was entirely local, and his designs confided but to a few, and these in his immediate vicinity. It was not instigated by motives of revenge or sudden anger, but the results of long deliberation, and a settled purpose of mind. The offspring of gloomy fanaticism, acting upon materials but too well prepared for such impressions. It will be long remembered in the annals of our country, and many a mother as she presses her infant darling to her bosom, will shudder at the recollection of Nat Turner, and his band of ferocious miscreants.

Believing the following narrative, by removing doubts and conjectures from the public mind which otherwise must have remained, would give general satisfaction, it is respectfully submitted to the public by their ob't serv't,

T. R. GRAY.

Jerusalem, Southampton, Va. Nov. 5, 1831.

We the undersigned, members of the Court convened at Jerusalem, on Saturday, the 5th day of Nov. 1831, for the trial of Nat, *alias* Nat Turner, a negro slave, late the property of Putnam Moore,[7] deceased, do hereby certify, that the confessions of Nat, to Thomas R. Gray, was read to him in our presence, and that Nat acknowledged the same to be full, free, and voluntary; and that furthermore, when called upon by the presiding Magistrate of the Court, to state if he had any thing to say, why sentence of death should not be passed upon him, replied he had nothing further than he had communicated to Mr. Gray. Given under our hands and seals at Jerusalem, this 5th day of November, 1831.

JEREMIAH COBB, [Seal.]
THOMAS PRETLOW, [Seal.]
JAMES W. PARKER [Seal.]
CARR BOWERS, [Seal.]
SAMUEL B. HINES, [Seal.]
ORRIS A. BROWNE, [Seal.]

State of Virginia, Southampton County, to wit:

I, James Rochelle, Clerk of the County Court of Southampton in the State of Virginia, do hereby certify, that Jeremiah Cobb, Thomas Pretlow, James W. Parker, Carr Bowers, Samuel B. Hines, and Orris A. Browne, esqr's are acting Justices of the Peace, in and for the County aforesaid, and were members of the Court which convened at Jerusalem, on Saturday the 5th day of November, 1831, for the trial of Nat *alias* Nat Turner, a negro slave, late the property of Putnam Moore, deceased, who was tried and convicted, as an insurgent in the late insurrection in the county of Southampton aforesaid, and that full faith and credit are due, and ought to be given to their acts as Justices of the peace aforesaid.

[Seal.]

In testimony whereof, I have hereunto set my hand and caused the seal of the Court aforesaid, to be affixed this 5th day of November, 1831

JAMES ROCHELLE, C.S.C.C.

CONFESSION

Agreeable to his own appointment, on the evening he was committed to prison, with permission of the jailer, I visited NAT on Tuesday the 1st November, when, without being questioned at all, he commenced his narrative in the following words:—

SIR,—You have asked me to give a history of the motives which induced me to undertake the late insurrection,[8] as you call it—To do so I must go back to the days of my infancy, and even before I was born. I was thirty-one years of age the 2nd of October last, and born the property of Benj. Turner, of this county. In my childhood a circumstance occurred which made an indelible impression on my mind, and laid the ground work of that enthusiasm, which has terminated so fatally to many, both white and black, and for which I am about to atone at the gallows. It is here necessary to relate this circumstance—trifling as it may seem, it was the commencement of that belief which has grown with time, and even now, sir, in this dungeon, helpless and forsaken as I am, I cannot divest myself of. Being at play with other children, when three or four years old, I was telling them something, which my mother overhearing, said it had happened before I was born—I stuck to my story, however, and related somethings which went, in her opinion, to confirm it—others being called on were greatly astonished, knowing that these things had happened, and caused them to say in my hearing, I surely would be a prophet, as the Lord had shewn me things that had happened before my birth. And my father and mother strengthened me in this my first impression, saying in my presence, I was intended for some great purpose, which they had always thought from certain marks on my head and breast—[a parcel of excrescences which I believe are not at all uncommon, particularly among negroes, as I have seen several with the same. In this case he has either cut them off or they have nearly disappeared]—My grandmother, who was very religious, and to whom I was much attached—my master, who belonged to the church, and other religious persons who visited the house, and whom I often saw at prayers, noticing the singularity of my manners, I suppose, and my uncommon intelligence for a child, remarked I had too much sense to be raised, and if I was, I would never be of any service to any one as a slave—To a mind like mine, restless, inquisitive and observant of every thing that was passing, it is easy to suppose that religion was the subject to which it would be directed, and although this subject principally occupied my thoughts—there was nothing that I saw or heard of to which my attention was not directed—The manner in which I learned to read and write, not only had great influence on my own mind, as I acquired it with the most perfect ease, so much so, that I have no recollection whatever of learning the alphabet—but to the astonishment of the family, one day, when a book was shewn to me to keep me from crying, I began spelling the names of different objects—this was a source of wonder to all in the neighborhood, particularly the blacks—and this learning was constantly improved at all opportunities—when I got large enough to go to work, while employed, I was reflecting on many things that would present themselves to my imagination, and whenever an opportunity occurred of looking at a book, when the school children were getting their lessons, I would find many things that the fertility of my own imagination had depicted to me before; all my time, not devoted to my master's service, was spent either in prayer, or in making experiments in casting different things in moulds made of earth, in attempting to make paper, gun-powder, and many other experiments, that although I could not perfect, yet convinced me of its practicablity if I had the means.* I was not addicted to stealing in my youth, nor have ever been—Yet such was the confidence of the negroes in the neighborhood, even at this early period of my life, in my superior judgment, that they would often carry me with them when they were going on any roguery, to plan for them. Growing up among them, with this confidence in my superior judgment, and when this, in their opinions, was perfected by Divine inspiration, from the circumstances already alluded to in my infancy, and which belief was ever afterwards zealously inculcated by the austerity of my life and manners, which became the subject of remark by white and black.—Having soon discovered to be great, I must appear so, and therefore studiously avoided mixing in society, and wrapped myself in mystery, devoting my time to fasting and prayer—By this time, having arrived to man's estate,[9] and hearing the scriptures commented on at meetings, I was struck with that particular passage which says: "Seek ye the kingdom of Heaven and all things shall be added unto you."[10] I reflected much on this passage, and prayed daily for light on this subject—As I was praying one day at my plough, the spirit spoke to me, saying "Seek ye the kingdom of Heaven and all things shall be added unto you." *Question*—what do you mean by the Spirit. *Ans.* The Spirit that spoke to the prophets in former days—and I was greatly astonished, and for two years prayed continually, whenever my duty would permit—and then again I had the same revelation, which fully confirmed me in the impression that I was ordained for some great purpose in the hands of the Almighty. Several years rolled round, in which many events

---

*When questioned as to the manner of manufacturing those different articles, he was found well informed on the subject.

occurred to strengthen me in this my belief. At this time I reverted in my mind to the remarks made of me in my childhood, and the things that had been shewn me—and as it had been said of me in my childhood by those by whom I had been taught to pray, both white and black, and in whom I had the greatest confidence, that I had too much sense to be raised, and if I was, I would never be of any use to any one as a slave. Now finding I had arrived to man's estate, and was a slave, and these revelations being made known to me, I began to direct my attention to this great object, to fulfil the purpose for which, by this time, I felt assured I was intended. Knowing the influence I had obtained over the minds of my fellow servants, (not by the means of conjuring and such like tricks—for to them I always spoke of such things with contempt) but by the communion of the Spirit whose revelations I often communicated to them, and they believed and said my wisdom came from God. I now began to prepare them for my purpose, by telling them something was about to happen that would terminate in fulfilling the great promise that had been made to me—About this time I was placed under an overseer, from whom I ranaway—and after remaining in the woods thirty days, I returned, to the astonishment of the negroes on the plantation, who thought I had made my escape to some other part of the country, as my father had done before. But the reason of my return was, that the Spirit appeared to me and said I had my wishes directed to the things of this world, and not to the kingdom of Heaven, and that I should return to the service of my earthly master—"For he who knoweth his Master's will, and doeth it not, shall be beaten with many stripes, and thus have I chastened you."[11] And the negroes found fault, and murmured against me, saying that if they had my sense they would not serve any master in the world. And about this time I had a vision—and I saw white spirits and black spirits engaged in battle, and the sun was darkened—the thunder rolled in the Heavens, and blood flowed in streams—and I heard a voice saying, "Such is your luck, such you are called to see, and let it come rough or smooth, you must surely bare it. I now withdrew myself as much as my situation would permit, from the intercourse of my fellow servants, for the avowed purpose of serving the Spirit more fully—and it appeared to me, and reminded me of the things it had already shown me, and that it would then reveal to me the knowledge of the elements, the revolution of the planets, the operation of tides, and changes of the seasons. After this revelation in the year of 1825, and the knowledge of the elements being made known to me, I sought more than ever to obtain true holiness before the great day of judgment should appear, and then I began to receive the true knowledge of faith. And from the first steps of righteousness until the last, was I made perfect; and the Holy Ghost was with me, and said, "Behold me as I stand in the Heavens"—and I looked and saw the forms of men in different attitudes—and there were lights in the sky to which the children of darkness gave other names than what they really were—for they were the lights of the Savior's hands, stretched forth from east to west, even as they were extended on the cross on Calvary for the redemption of sinners. And I wondered greatly at these miracles, and prayed to be informed of a certainty of the meaning thereof—and shortly afterwards, while laboring in the field, I discovered drops of blood on the corn as though it were dew from heaven—and I communicated it to many, both white and black, in the neighborhood—and I then found on the leaves in the woods hieroglyphic characters, and numbers, with the forms of men in different attitudes, portrayed in blood, and representing the figures I had seen before in the heavens. And now the Holy Ghost had revealed itself to me, and made plain the miracles it had shown me—For as the blood of Christ had been shed on this earth, and had ascended to heaven for the salvation of sinners, and was now returning to earth again in the form of dew—and as the leaves on the trees bore the impression of the figures I had seen in the heavens, it was plain to me that the Savior was about to lay down the yoke he had borne for the sins of men, and the great day of judgment was at hand. About this time I told these things to a white man, (Etheldred T. Brantley) on whom it had a wonderful effect—and he ceased from his wickedness, and was attacked immediately with a cutaneous eruption, and blood oozed from the pores of his skin, and after praying and fasting nine days, he was healed, and the Spirit appeared to me again, and said, as the Savior had been baptised so should we be also—and when the white people would not let us be baptised by the church, we went down into the water together, in the sight of many who reviled us, and were baptised by the Spirit—After this I rejoiced greatly, and gave thanks to God. And on the 12th of May, 1828, I heard a loud noise in the heavens, and the Spirit instantly appeared to me and said the Serpent was loosened, and Christ had laid down the yoke he had borne for the sins of men, and that I should take it on and fight against the Serpent, for the time was fast approaching when the first should be last and the last should be first.[12] *Ques.* Do you not find yourself mistaken now? *Ans.* Was not Christ crucified? And by signs in the heavens that it would make known to me when I should commence the great work—and until the first sign appeared, I should conceal it from the knowledge of men—And on the appearance of the sign, (the eclipse of the sun last February) I should arise and prepare myself, and slay my enemies with their own weapons. And immediately on the sign appearing in the heavens, the seal was removed from my lips, and I communicated the great work laid out for me to do, to four in whom I had the greatest confidence, (Henry, Hark, Nelson, and Sam)—It was intended by us to have begun the work of death on the 4th July last—Many were the plans formed and rejected by us, and it affected my mind to such a degree, that I fell sick, and the time passed without our coming to any determination how to commence—Still forming new schemes and rejecting them, when the sign appeared again, which determined me not to wait longer.

Since the commencement of 1830, I had been living with Mr. Joseph Travis, who was to me a kind master, and placed the greatest confidence in me; in fact, I had no cause to complain of his treatment to me. On Saturday evening, the 20th of August, it was agreed between Henry, Hark and myself, to prepare a dinner the next day for the men we expected, and then to concert a plan, as we had not yet determined on any. Hark, on the following morning, brought a pig, and Henry brandy, and being joined by Sam, Nelson, Will and Jack, they prepared in the woods a dinner, where, about three o'clock, I joined them.

Q. Why were you so backward in joining them.

A. The same reason that had caused me not to mix with them for years before.

I saluted them on coming up, and asked Will how came he there, he answered, his life was worth no more than others, and his liberty as dear to him. I asked him if he thought to obtain it? He said he would, or lose his life. This was enough to put him in full confidence. Jack, I knew, was only a tool in the hands of Hark, it was quickly agreed we should commence at home (Mr. J. Travis') on that night, and until we had armed and equipped ourselves, and gathered sufficient force, neither age nor sex was to be spared,[13] (which was invariably adhered to). We remained at the feast, until about two hours in the night, when we went to the house and found Austin; they all went to the cider press and drank, except myself. On returning to the house, Hark went to the door with an axe, for the purpose of breaking it open, as we knew we were strong enough to murder the family, if they were awaked by the noise; but reflecting that it might create an alarm in the neighborhood, we determined to enter the house secretly, and murder them whilst sleeping. Hark got a ladder and set it against the chimney, on which I ascended, and hoisting a window, entered and came down stairs, unbarred the door, and removed the guns from their places. It was then observed that I must spill the first blood. On which, armed with a hatchet, and accompanied by Will, I entered my master's chamber, it being dark, I could not give a death blow, the hatchet glanced from his head, he sprang from the bed and called his wife, it was his last word, Will laid him dead, with a blow of his axe, and Mrs. Travis shared the same fate, as she lay in bed. The murder of this family, five in number, was the work of a moment, not one of them awoke; there was a little infant sleeping in a cradle, that was forgotten, until we had left the house and gone some distance, when Henry and Will returned and killed it; we got here, four guns that would shoot, and several old muskets, with a pound or two of powder. We remained some time at the barn, where we paraded; I formed them in a line as soldiers, and after carrying them through all the manoeuvres I was master of marched them off to Mr. Salathul Francis', about six hundred yards distant. Sam and Will went to the door and knocked. Mr. Francis asked who was there, Sam replied it was him, and he had a letter for him, on which he got up and came to the door; they immediately seized him, and dragging him out a little from the door, he was dispatched by repeated blows on the head; there was no other white person in the family. We started from there for Mrs. Reese's, maintaining the most perfect silence on our march, where finding the door unlocked, we entered, and murdered Mrs. Reese in her bed, while sleeping; her son awoke, but it was only to sleep the sleep of death, he had only time to say who is that, and he was no more. From Mrs. Reese's we went to Mrs. Turner's, a mile distant, which we reached about sunrise, on Monday morning. Henry, Austin, and Sam, went to the still, where, finding Mr. Peebles, Austin shot him, and the rest of us went to the house; as we approached, the family discovered us, and shut the door. Vain hope! Will, with one stroke of his axe, opened it, and we entered and found Mrs. Turner and Mrs. Newsome in the middle of a room, almost frightened to death. Will immediately killed Mrs. Turner, with one blow of his axe. I took Mrs. Newsome by the hand, and with the sword I had when I was apprehended, I struck her several blows over the head, but not being able to kill her, as the sword was dull. Will turning around and discovering it, despatched her also. A general destruction of property and search for money and ammunition, always succeeded the murders. By this time my company amounted to fifteen, and nine men mounted, who started for Mrs. Whitehead's, (the other six were to go through a by way to Mr. Bryant's, and rejoin us at Mrs. Whitehead's,) as we approached the house we discovered Mr. Richard Whitehead standing in the cotton patch, near the lane fence; we called him over into the lane, and Will, the executioner, was near at hand, with his fatal axe, to send him to an untimely grave. As we pushed on to the house, I discovered some one run round the garden, and thinking it was some of the white family, I pursued them, but finding it was a servant girl belonging to the house, I returned to commence the work of death, but they whom I left, had not been idle; all the family were already murdered, but Mrs. Whitehead and her daughter Margaret. As I came round to the door I saw Will pulling Mrs. Whitehead out of the house, and at the step he nearly severed her head from her body, with his broad axe. Miss Margaret, when I discovered her, had concealed herself in the corner, formed by the projection of cellar cap from the house; on my approach she fled, but was soon overtaken, and after repeated blows with a sword, I killed her by a blow on the head, with a fence rail. By this time, the six who had gone by Mr. Bryant's, rejoined us, and informed me they had done the work of death assigned them. We again divided, part going to Mr. Richard Porter's, and from thence to Nathaniel Francis', the others to Mr. Howell Harris', and Mr. T. Doyles. On my reaching Mr. Porter's, he had escaped with his family. I understood there, that the alarm had already spread, and I immediately returned to bring up those sent to Mr. Doyles, and Mr. Howell Harris'; the party I left going on to Mr. Francis', having told them I would join them in that neighborhood. I met these sent to Mr. Doyles' and Mr. Harris' returning, having met Mr. Doyle on the road and killed him; and learning from some who joined them, that Mr. Harris was from home, I immediately pursued the course taken by the party gone on before; but knowing they would complete the work of death and pillage, at Mr. Francis' before I could get there, I went to Mr. Peter Edwards', expecting to find them there, but they had been here also. I then went to Mr. John T. Barrow's, they had been here and murdered him. I pursued on their track to Capt. Newit Harris', where I found the greater part mounted, and ready to start; the men now amounting to about forty, shouted and hurraed as I rode up, some were in the yard, loading their guns, others drinking. They said Captain Harris and his family had escaped, the property in the house they destroyed, robbing him of money and other valuables. I ordered them to mount and march instantly, this was about nine or ten o'clock, Monday morning. I proceeded to Mr. Levi Waller's, two or three miles distant. I took my station in the rear, and as it was my object to carry terror and devastation wherever we went, I placed fifteen or twenty of the best armed and most relied on, in front, who generally approached the houses as fast as their horses could run; this was for two purposes, to prevent escape and strike terror to the inhabitants—on this account I never got to the houses, after leaving Mrs. Whitehead's, until the murders were committed, except in one case. I sometimes got in sight in time to see the work of death completed, viewed the mangled bodies as they lay, in silent satisfaction, and immediately started in quest of other victims—Having murdered Mrs. Waller and ten children, we started for Mr. William Williams'—having killed him and two little boys that were there; while engaged in this, Mrs. Williams fled and got some distance from the house, but she was pursued, overtaken, and compelled to get up behind one of the company, who brought her back, and after showing her the mangled body of her lifeless husband, she was told to get down and lay by his side, where she was shot dead. I then started for Mr. Jacob Williams, where the family were murdered—Here he found a young man named Drury, who had come on business with Mr. Williams—he was pursued, overtaken and shot. Mrs. Vaughan was the next place we visited—and after murdering the family here, I determined on starting for Jerusalem—Our number amounted now to fifty or sixty, all mounted and armed with guns, axes, swords and clubs—On reaching Mr. James W. Parker's gate, immediately on the road leading to Jerusalem, and about three miles distant, it was proposed to me to call there, but I objected, as I knew he was gone to Jerusalem, and my object was to reach there as soon as possible; but some of the men having relations at Mr. Parker's it was agreed that they might call and get his people. I remained at the gate on the road, with seven or eight; the others going across the field to the house, about half a mile off. After waiting some time for them, I became impatient, and started to the house for them, and on our return we were met by a party of white men, who had pursued our blood-stained track, and who had fired on those at the gate, and dispersed them, which I knew nothing of, not having been at that time rejoined by any of them—Immediately on discovering the whites, I ordered my men to halt and form, as they appeared to be alarmed—The white men, eighteen in number, approached us in about one hundred yards, when one of them fired, (this was against the positive orders of Captain Alexander P. Peete, who commanded, and who had directed the men to reserve their fire until within thirty paces)—And I discovered about half of them retreating, I then ordered my men to fire and rush on them; the few remaining stood their ground until we approached within fifty yards, when they fired and retreated. We pursued and overtook some of them who we thought we left dead; (they were not killed) after pursuing them about two hundred yards, and rising a little hill, I discovered they were met by another party, and had halted, and were re-loading their guns, (this was a small party from Jerusalem who knew the negroes were in the field, and had just tied their horses to await their return to the road, knowing that Mr. Parker and family were in Jerusalem, but knew nothing of the party that had gone in with Captain Peete; on hearing the firing they immediately rushed to the spot and arrived just in time to arrest the progress of these barbarous villians, and save the lives of their friends and fellow citizens). Thinking that those who retreated first, and the party who fired on us at fifty or sixty yards distant, had all fallen back to meet others with ammunition. As I saw them reloading their guns, and more coming up than I saw at first, and several of my bravest men being wounded, the others became panick struck and squandered over the field; the white men pursued and fired on us several times. Hark had his horse shot under him, and I caught another for him as it was running by me; five or six of my men were wounded, but none left on the field; finding myself defeated here I instantly determined to go through a private way, and cross the Nottoway river at the Cypress Bridge, three miles below Jerusalem, and attack that place in the rear, as I expected they would look for me on the other road, and I had a great desire to get there to procure arms and ammunition. After going a short distance in this private way, accompanied by about twenty men, I overtook two or three who told me the others were dispersed in every direction. After trying in vain to collect a sufficient force to proceed to Jerusalem, I determined to return, as I was sure they would make back to their old neighborhood, where they would rejoin me, make new recruits, and come down again. On my way back, I called at Mrs. Thomas's, Mrs. Spencer's, and several other places, the white families having fled, we found no more victims to gratify our thirst for blood, we stopped at Majr. Ridley's quarter for the night, and being joined by four of his men, with the recruits made since my defeat, we mustered now about forty strong. After placing out sentinels, I laid down to sleep, but was quickly roused by a great racket; starting up, I found some mounted, and others in great confusion; one of the sentinels having given the alarm that we were about to be attacked, I ordered some to ride round and reconnoitre, and on their return the others being more alarmed, not knowing who they were, fled in different ways, so that I was reduced to about twenty again; with this I determined to attempt to recruit, and proceed on to rally in the neighborhood, I had left. Dr. Blunt's was the nearest house, which we reached just before day; on riding up the yard, Hark fired a gun. We expected Dr. Blunt and his family were at Maj. Ridley's, as I knew there was a company of men there; the gun was fired to ascertain if any of the family were at home; we were immediately fired upon and retreated, leaving several of my men. I do not know what became of them, as I never saw them afterwards. Pursuing our course back and coming in sight of Captain Harris', where we had been the day before, we discovered a party of white men at the house, on which all deserted me but two, (Jacob and Nat), we concealed ourselves in the woods until near night, when I sent them in search of Henry, Sam, Nelson, and Hark, and directed them to rally all they could, at the place we had had our dinner the Sunday before, where they would find me, and I accordingly returned there as soon as it was dark and remained until Wednesday evening, when discovering white men riding around the place as though they were looking for some one, and none of my men joining me, I concluded Jacob and Nat had been taken, and compelled to betray me. On this I gave up all hope for the present; and on Thursday night after having supplied myself with provisions from Mr. Travis's, I scratched a hole under a pile of fence rails in a field, where I concealed myself for six weeks, never leaving my hiding place but for a few minutes in the dead of night to get water which was very near; thinking by this time I could venture out, I began to go about in the night and eaves drop the houses in the neighborhood; pursuing this course for about a fortnight and gathering little or no intelligence, afraid of speaking to any human being, and returning every morning to my cave before the dawn of day. I know not how long I might have led this life, if accident had not betrayed me, a dog in the neighborhood passing by my hiding place one night while I was out, was attracted by some meat I had in my cave, and crawled in and stole it, and was coming out just as I returned. A few nights after, two negroes having started to go hunting with the same dog, and passed that way, the dog came again to the place, and having just gone out to walk about, discovered me and barked, on which thinking myself discovered, I spoke to them to beg concealment. On making myself known they fled from me. Knowing then they would betray me, I immediately left my hiding place, and was pursued almost incessantly until I was taken a fortnight afterwards by Mr. Benjamin Phipps, in a little hole I had dugout with my sword, for the purpose of concealment, under the top of a fallen tree. On Mr. Phipps' discovering the place of my concealment, he cocked his gun and aimed at me. I requested him not to shoot and I would give up, upon which he demanded my sword. I delivered it to him, and he brought me to prison. During the time I was pursued, I had many hair breadth escapes, which your time will not permit you to relate. I am here loaded with chains, and willing to suffer the fate that awaits me.

I here proceeded to make some inquiries of him, after assuring him of the certain death that awaited him, and that concealment would only bring destruction on the innocent as well as guilty, of his own color, if he knew of any extensive or concerted plan. His answer was, I do not. When I questioned him as to the insurrection in North Carolina happening about the same time, he denied any knowledge of it; and when I looked him in the face as though I would search his inmost thoughts, he replied, "I see sir, you doubt my word; but can you not think the same ideas, and strange appearances about this time in the heaven's might prompt others, as well as myself, to this undertaking." I now had much conversation with and asked him many questions, having forborne to do so previously, except in the cases noted in parenthesis; but during his statement, I had, unnoticed by him, taken notes as to some particular circumstances, and having the advantage of his statement before me in writing, on the evening of the third day that I had been with him, I began a cross examination, and found his statement corroborated by every circumstance coming within my own knowledge or the confessions of others who had been either killed or executed, and whom he had not seen nor had any knowledge since 22d of August last, he expressed himself fully satisfied as to the impracticability of his attempt. It has been said he was ignorant and cowardly, and that his object was to murder and rob for the purpose of obtaining money to make his escape. It is notorious, that he was never known to have a dollar in his life; to swear an oath, or drink a drop of spirits. As to his ignorance, he certainly never had the advantages of education, but he can read and write, (it was taught him by his parents,) and for natural intelligence and quickness of apprehension, is surpassed by few men I have ever seen. As to his being a coward, his reason as given for not resisting Mr. Phipps, shews the decision of his character. When he saw Mr. Phipps present his gun, he said he knew it was impossible for him to escape as the woods were full of men; he therefore thought it was better to surrender, and trust to fortune for his escape. He is a complete fanatic, or plays his part most admirably. On other subjects he possesses an uncommon share of intelligence, with a mind capable of attaining any thing; but warped and perverted by the influence of early impressions. He is below the ordinary stature, though strong and active, having the true negro face, every feature of which is strongly marked. I shall not attempt to describe the effect of his narrative, as told and commented on by himself, in the condemned hole of the prison. The calm, deliberate composure with which he spoke of his late deeds and intentions, the expression of his fiend-like face when excited by enthusiasm, still bearing the stains of the blood of helpless innocence about him; clothed with rags and covered with chains; yet daring to raise his manacled hands to heaven, with a spirit soaring above the attributes of man; I looked on him and my blood curdled in my veins.

I will not shock the feelings of humanity, nor wound afresh the bosoms of the disconsolate sufferers in this unparalleled and inhuman massacre, by detailing the deeds of their fiend-like barbarity. There were two or three who were in the power of these wretches, had they known it, and who escaped in the most providential manner. There were two whom they thought they left dead on the field at Mr. Parker's, but who were only stunned by the blows of their guns, as they did not take time to re-load when they charged on them. The escape of a little girl who went to school at Mr. Waller's, and where the children were collecting for that purpose, excited general sympathy. As their teacher had not arrived, they were at play in the yard, and seeing the negroes approach, she ran up on a dirt chimney, (such as are common to log houses,) and remained there unnoticed during the massacre of the eleven that were killed at this place. She remained on her hiding place till just before the arrival of a party, who were in pursuit of the murderers, when she came down and fled to a swamp, where, a mere child as she was, with the horrors of the late scene before her, she lay concealed until the next day, when seeing a party go up to the house, she came up, and on being asked how she escaped, replied with the utmost simplicity, "The Lord helped her." She was taken up behind a gentleman of the party, and returned to the arms of her weeping mother. Miss Whitehead concealed herself between the bed and the mat that supported it, while they murdered her sister in the same room, without discovering her. She was afterwards carried off, and concealed for protection by a slave of the family, who gave evidence against several of them on their trial. Mrs. Nathaniel Francis, while concealed in a closet heard their blows, and the shrieks of the victims of these ruthless savages; they then entered the closet, where she was concealed, and went out without discovering her. While in this hiding place, she heard two of her women in a quarrel about the division of her clothes. Mr. John T. Baron, discovering them approaching his house, told his wife to make her escape, and scorning to fly, fell fighting on his own threshold. After firing his rifle, he discharged his gun at them, and then broke it over the villain who first approached him, but he was overpowered, and slain. His bravery, however, saved from the hands of these monsters, his lovely and amiable wife, who will long lament a husband so deserving of her love. As directed by him, she attempted to escape through the garden, when she was caught and held by one of her servant girls, but another coming to her rescue, she fled to the woods, and concealed herself. Few indeed, were those who escaped their work of death. But fortunate for society, the hand of retributive justice has overtaken them; and not one that was known to be concerned has escaped.

The Commonwealth, vs. Nat Turner

Charged with making insurrection, and plotting to take away the lives of divers free white persons, &c. on the 22d of August, 1831.

The court composed of———, having met for the trial of Nat Turner, the prisoner was brought in and arraigned, and upon his arraignment pleaded *Not guilty*; saying to his counsel, that he did not feel so.

On the part of the Commonwealth, Levi Waller was introduced, who being sworn, deposed as follows: (*agreeably to Nat's own Confession.*) Col. Trezvant[*] was then introduced, who being sworn, narrated Nat's Confession to him, as follows: (*his Confession as given to Mr. Gray.*) The prisoner introduced no evidence, and the case was submitted without argument to the court, who having found him guilty, Jeremiah Cobb, Esq. Chairman, pronounced the sentence of the court, in the

---

[*] The committing Magistrate.

following words: Nat Turner! Stand up. Have you any thing to say why sentence of death should not be pronounced against you?

Ans. I have not. I have made a full confession to Mr. Gray, and I have nothing more to say.

Attend then to the sentence of the Court. You have been arraigned and tried before this court, and convicted of one of the highest crimes in our criminal code. You have been convicted of plotting in cold blood, the indiscriminate destruction of men, of helpless women, and of infant children. The evidence before us leaves not a shadow of doubt, but that your hands were often imbrued in the blood of the innocent; and your own confession tells us that they were stained with the blood of a master; in your own language, "too indulgent." Could I stop here, your crime would be sufficiently aggravated. But the original contriver of a plan, deep and deadly, one that never can be effected, you managed so far to put it into execution, as to deprive us of many of our most valuable citizens; and this was done when they were asleep, and defenseless; under circumstances shocking to humanity. And while upon this part of the subject, I cannot but call your attention to the poor misguided wretches who have gone before you. They are not few in number—they were your bosom associates; and the blood of all cries aloud, and calls upon you, as the author of their misfortune. Yes! You forced them unprepared, from Time to Eternity. Borne down by this load of guilt, your only justification is, that you were led away by fanaticism. If this be true, from my soul I pity you; and while you have my sympathies, I am, nevertheless called upon to pass the sentence of the court. The time between this and your execution, will necessarily be very short; and your only hope must be in another world. The judgment of the court is, that you be taken hence to the jail from whence you came, thence to the place of execution, and on Friday next, between the hours of 10 A.M. and 2 P.M. be hung by the neck until you are dead! dead! dead! and may the Lord have mercy upon your soul.

A list of persons murdered in the Insurrection, on the 21st and 22nd of August, 1831

Joseph Travers and wife and three children, Mrs. Elizabeth Turner, Hartwell Prebles, Sarah Newsome, Mrs. P. Reese and son William, Trajan Doyle, Henry Bryant and wife and child, and wife's mother, Mrs. Catharine Whitehead, son Richard and four daughters and grand-child, Salathiel Francis, Nathaniel Francis' overseer and two children, John T. Barrow, George Vaughan, Mrs. Levi Waller and ten children, William Williams, wife and two boys, Mrs. Caswell Worrell and child, Mrs. Rebecca Vaughan, Ann Eliza Vaughan, and son Arthur, Mrs. John K. Williams and child, Mrs. Jacob Williams and three children, and Edwin Drury—amounting to fifty-five.[14]

A List of Negroes Brought before the Court of Southampton, with Their Owners' Names, and Sentence.

Daniel,	Richard Porter,	Convicted.
Moses	J. T. Barrow,	Do.
Tom,	Caty Whitehead,	Discharged.
Jack and Andrew,	Caty Whitehead	Con. and transported.
Jacob,	Geo. H. Charlton,	Disch'd without trial.
Isaac,	Ditto,	Convi. and transported.
Jack,	Everett Bryant,	Discharged.
Nathan,	Benj. Blunt's estate,	Convicted.
Nathan, Tom, and Davy, (boys,)	Nathaniel Francis,	Convicted and transported.
Davy	Elizabeth Turner,	Convicted.
Curtis,	Thomas Ridley,	Do.
Stephen,	Do.	Do.
Hardy and Isham,	Benjamin Edwards,	Convicted and transp'd.
Sam,	Nathaniel Francis,	Convicted.
Hark,	Joseph Travis' estate.	Do.
Moses, (a boy,)	Do.	Do. and transported.
Davy,	Levi Waller,	Convicted.
Nelson,	Jacob Williams,	Do.
Nat,	Edm'd Turner's estate,	Do.
Jack,	Wm. Reese's estate	Do.
Dred,	Nathaniel Francis,	Do.
Arnold, Artist, (free)		Discharged.
Sam,	J. W. Parker,	Acquitted.
Ferry and Archer,	J. W. Parker,	Disch'd. without trial.
Jim,	William Vaughan,	Acquitted.
Bob,	Temperance Parker,	Do.
Davy,	Joseph Parker,	
Daniel,	Solomon D. Parker	Disch'd without trial.
Thomas Haithcock, (free,)		Sent on for further trial.
Joe,	John C. Turner,	Convicted.
Lucy,	John T. Barrow,	Do.
Matt,	Thomas Ridley,	Acquitted.
Jim,	Richard Porter,	Do.
Exum Artes, (free,)		Sent on for further trial.
Joe,	Richard P. Briggs,	Disch'd without trial.
Bury Newsome, (free,)		Sent on for further trial.
Stephen,	James Bell,	Acquitted.
Jim and Isaac,	Samuel Champion,	Convicted and trans'd.
Preston,	Hannah Williamson	Acquitted.
Frank,	Solomon D. Parker	Convi'd and transp'd.
Jack and Shadrach,	Nathaniel Simmons	Acquitted.[15]

Nelson,	Benj. Blunt's estate,	Do.
Sam,	Peter Edwards,	Convicted.
Archer,	Arthur G. Reese,	Acquitted.
Isham Turner, (free,)		Sent on for further trial.
Nat Turner,	Putnam Moore, dec'd.	Convicted.

NOTES

1. According to the 1830 census, the total population of Southampton was 16,074, consisting of 6,573 free whites, 1,745 free blacks, and 7,756 slaves. See Henry Irving Tragle, *The Southampton Slave Revolt of 1831: A Compilation of Source Material* (Amherst: University of Massachusetts Press, 1971), 15.

2. Douglas R. Egerton, "The Scenes Which Are Acted in St. Domingo: The Legacy of Revolutionary Violence in Early National Virginia," in *Antislavery Violence: Sectional, Racial, and Cultural Conflict in Antebellum America*, edited by John R. McKivigan and Stanley Harrold (Knoxville: University of Tennessee Press, 1999), 41–64.

3. Daniel S. Fabricant, "Thomas R. Gray and William Styron: Finally, a Critical Look at the 1831 *Confessions of Nat Turner*," *American Journal of Legal History* 37 (July 1993): 339–40; Eric J. Sundquist, *To Wake the Nations: Race in the Making of American Literature* (Cambridge, MA: Belknap Press of Harvard University Press, 1993), 46–47; Tragle, *The Southampton Slave Revolt of 1831*, 402–9.

4. In 1634, Virginia was divided into eight districts, or shires. One was called Warrasqyoyocke or Smith's Hundred. Its boundaries included the James River on the north and the North Carolina border to the south. In 1637, the name was changed to Isle of Wight Plantation. In 1749, the tract was separated into two parts, with the Blackwater River as the dividing line. While the upper portion remained Isle of Wight Plantation, the southern portion became known as Southampton County. A courthouse was built a few years later on the banks of the Nottoway River. The village that grew up in the vicinity became known as Jerusalem. It was incorporated by the state legislature as a town in 1888, and the name was changed to Courtland. See Tragle, *The Southampton Slave Revolt of 1831*, 13–14, 15.

5. Thomas Ruffin Gray, a lawyer and slaveholder, served as legal council for several of Turner's coconspirators, though not for Turner himself. His decision to gain access to Turner and elicit his story is most likely some combination of his desire to perform the public service of explaining Turner's motives and to profit from public interest in the insurrection by publishing the firsthand account of its leader.

6. Newspapers like the *Richmond Enquirer*, the *Richmond Constitutional Whig*, and the *Norfolk American Beacon* sought to allay fears of widespread revolt but also insisted on the possibility of far-reaching insurrection and the need for vigilance. There was no indication in the adjacent counties in North Carolina that similar slave activity was planned. The newspapers incited hysteria, however, and many blacks, slave and free, were lynched, jailed, and otherwise harassed. See Tragle, *The Southampton Slave Revolt of 1831*, 4–5; Elliot, "The Nat Turner Insurrection as Reported in the North Carolina Press," 1–18.

7. Nat Turner was initially owned by Benjamin Turner. Upon the death of his owner sometime around 1822, Nat Turner was purchased by Thomas Moore for his infant son, Putnam, who became Nat Turner's legal owner. At the time of the insurrection, Nat Turner was working for Moore's widow, who had remarried Joseph Travis.

8. Turner refutes Gray's use of the word "insurrection," as have subsequent authorities. "Insurrection" refers to an actual uprising against the government in open resistance. "Revolt" is generally seen as an uprising against a civil government (though it may also be directed toward a military government). A "rebellion" goes beyond an "insurrection" by actively seeking to overthrow the government. See Aptheker, *Nat Turner's Slave Rebellion*, 2 n.2; Tragle, *The Southampton Slave Revolt of 1831*, 21–22.

9. Referring to the attainment of a particular mental, physical, or material condition of life.

10. Luke 12:31, "But rather seek ye the kingdom of God; and all these things shall be added unto you."

11. Luke 12:47, "And that servant, which knew his lord's will, and prepared not himself, neither did according to his will, shall be beaten with many stripes."

12. Matthew 19:30, "But many that are first shall be last; and the last shall be first"; Matthew 20:16, "So the last shall be first, and the first last: for many be called, but few chosen"; Mark 10:31, "But many that are first shall be last; and the last first"; Luke 13:30, "And, behold, there are last which shall be first, and there are first which shall be last."

13. The conspirators planned indiscriminately to attack all white men, women, and children.

14. Fifty-five may be inaccurate. Fifty-seven is more commonly given, and there are references to as many as sixty-four. This disparity may be caused by a number of children killed whose names are not included here. See Tragle, *The Southampton Slave Revolt of 1831*, 4.

15. Jack and Shadrach had their charges of "treason against the Commonwealth" dismissed by the Southampton County court on October 17, 1831. The court ruled that slaves could not be tried for treason. See Tragle, *The Southampton Slave Revolt of 1831*, 22.

■ CHAPTER 2
Lunsford Lane (1803–?)

THE NARRATIVE OF LUNSFORD LANE

What is known about Lunsford Lane is primarily contained in the information he presents in his *Narrative*. Lane was born near Raleigh, North Carolina, on May 30, 1803. The *Narrative* is a Franklinesque story illustrating the importance of hard work and economic independence as necessary steps toward freedom and self-determination. Lane's *Narrative* places the potential his entrepreneurial skills provide him in direct relationship to the confining, limiting nature of the slave system. Even his earliest awareness of slavery is juxtaposed against his mindfulness that the slave system, above all things, functions around the buying and selling of human bodies as much as it operates on the concept of subjugation based on race. Lane writes that "To know, also, that I was never to consult my own will, but was, while I lived, to be entirely under the control of another, was another state of mind hard for me to bear. Indeed all things now made me *feel*, what I had before known only in words, that *I was a slave*. Deep was this feeling and it preyed upon my heart like a never-dying worm."

Other narrators tend to balance their feelings of being a slave against their desire to escape. Narratives like those written by William Wells Brown, Henry "Box" Brown, and William and Ellen Craft, for example, are almost entirely structured around their methods of escape. For Lane, however, escape is replaced by his talent for business. Lane discovers his talent for trade soon after he realizes his enslavement: "One day, while I was in this state of mind, my father gave me a small basket of peaches. I sold them for thirty cents, which was the first money I ever had in my life. Afterwards I won some marbles, and sold them for sixty cents, and some weeks after, Mr. Hog, from Fayetteville, came to visit my master, and on leaving gave me one dollar. After that, Mr. Bennahan, from Orange county, gave me a dollar, and a son of my master fifty cents. These sums, and the hope that then entered my mind of purchasing at some future time my freedom, made me long for money: and the plans for money-making took the principal possession of my thoughts. . . . Now I began to think seriously of becoming able to buy myself; and cheered by this hope, I went on from one thing to another, laboring 'at dead of night,' after the long weary day's toil for my master was over, till I found I had collected one hundred dollars." With his father's help, Lane developed a process for preparing smoking tobacco that allowed him "to manufacture a good article out of a very indifferent material."

His financial success allowed him, even as a slave, to marry in 1828, start a family, and begin to save funds in hopes of eventually purchasing their freedom. Lane purchased his own freedom on September 9, 1835. Unlike other narratives, where writers often see their lowest point as being when they are beaten and otherwise fully deprived of any sense of humanity, Lane's lowest moment arrived when the cost of providing for his family caused him to exhaust his savings: "So that by the expense of providing for my wife and children, all the money I had earned, and could earn, by my night labor, was consumed, till I found myself reduced to five dollars, and this I lost one day in going to the plantation. My light of hope now went out." Lane's opportunity for financial independence arrived when his master died and his master's widow agreed to allow him to hire himself out: "This was a privilege which comparatively few slaves at the south enjoy; and in this I felt truly blessed." By 1842, Lane had fulfilled the agreement to purchase his family. He relocated them to New England in the hope of starting a new business.

As he promises to do in his preface to the *Narrative*, Lane resolutely describes the "bright" side of his experiences. He does, however, enigmatically indicate that for the person so inclined, parts of his narrative "might be twisted to convey an idea more than should be expressed." As William L. Andrews observes, this dual narrative role is precisely the role Lane chooses for himself throughout the *Narrative*. While a slave, Lane hid both his prosperity and his intelligence from fellow slaves and slaveholders alike. Similarly, as a narrator, he has obscured the bite of his social critique by claiming in his preface to present "only a simple narration of such facts connected with my own case, as I thought would be most interesting and instructive to readers generally."[1]

The *Narrative* reprinted here is from the third edition of the text, originally published in 1845. The first edition of the *Narrative* was published in 1842.

Further Reading

Andrews, William. *To Tell a Free Story: The First Century of Afro-American Autobiography, 1760–1865*. Urbana: University of Illinois Press, 1986; Starling, Marion Wilson. *The Slave Narrative: Its Place in American History*. 2nd ed. Washington, D.C.: Howard University Press, 1988; Wilentz, Gay. "Authenticating Experience: North Carolina Slave Narratives and the Politics of Race." *North Carolina Literary Review* 1 (Summer 1992): 115–37.

THE NARRATIVE OF LUNSFORD LANE, FORMERLY OF RALEIGH, N. C.

EMBRACING AN ACCOUNT OF HIS EARLY LIFE, THE REDEMPTION BY PURCHASE OF HIMSELF AND FAMILY FROM SLAVERY, AND HIS BANISHMENT FROM THE PLACE OF HIS BIRTH FOR THE CRIME OF WEARING A COLORED SKIN.

PUBLISHED BY HIMSELF.

THIRD EDITION.

BOSTON:
PRINTED FOR THE PUBLISHER:
HEWES AND WATSON'S PRINT.
No. 60. . . . Congress St.
1845.

Entered according to Act of Congress, in the year 1842,
BY LUNSFORD LANE,

In the Clerk's Office of the District Court of Massachusetts.

NOTE TO THE THIRD EDITION

The rapidity with which the first and second editions of this work has been sold, renders it necessary to put another edition to press, without any enlargement or material alteration.

Thanks to those friends who have aided me in the sale of the former editions,—to those editors who have so favorably noticed the work,—and to those who have so freely purchased. May I not justly hope for a continuance of the same kind regards?

L. L.
BOSTON, JULY 4, 1845.

TO THE READER

The following Narrative has been prepared at the solicitation of very many friends. Whatever my own judgment might be, I should yield to theirs. In the hope that these pages may produce an impression favorable to my countrymen in bondage; also that I may realize something from the sale of my work towards the support of a numerous family, I have committed this publication to press. It might have been made two or three, or even six times larger, without diminishing from the interest of any one of its pages—*indeed with an increased interest*—but the want of the pecuniary means, and other considerations, have induced me to present it as here seen.

I have not, in this publication, attempted or desired to argue anything. It is only a simple narration of such facts connected with my own case, as I thought would be most interesting and instructive to readers generally. The facts will, I think, cast some light upon the policy of a slave-holding community, and the effect on the minds of the more enlightened, the more humane, and the *Christian* portion of the southern people, of holding and trading in the bodies and souls of men.

I have said in the following pages, that my condition as a slave was comparatively a happy, indeed a highly favored one; and to this circumstance is it owing that I have been able to come up from bondage and relate the story to the public; and that my wife, my mother, and my seven children, are here with me this day. If for anything this side the invisible world I bless Heaven, it is that I was not born a plantation slave, nor even a house servant under what is termed a hard and cruel master.

It has not been any part of my object to describe slavery generally, and in the narration of my own case I have dwelt as little as possible upon the dark side—have spoken mostly of the bright. In whatever I have been obliged to say unfavorable to others, I have endeavored not to overstate, but have chosen rather to come short of giving the full picture—omitting much which it did not seem important to my object to relate. And yet I would not venture to say that this publication does not contain a single period which might be twisted to convey an idea more than should be expressed.

Those of whom I have had occasion to speak, are regarded, where they are known, as among the most kind men to their slaves. Mr. Smith, some of whose conduct will doubtless seem strange to the reader, is sometimes taunted with being an abolitionist, in consequence of the interest he manifests towards the colored people. If to any his character appear like a riddle, they should remember that men, like other things, have "two sides," and often a top and a bottom in addition.

While in the South, I succeeded, by stealth, in learning to read and write a little, and since I have been in the North I have learned more. But I need not say that I have been obliged to employ the services of a friend, in bringing this Narrative into shape for the public eye. And it should perhaps be said on the part of the writer, that it has been hastily compiled, with little regard to style, only to express the ideas accurately, and in a manner to be understood.

LUNSFORD LANE.
BOSTON, JULY 4, 1845.

NARRATIVE

The small city of Raleigh, North Carolina, it is known, is the capital of the State, situated in the interior, and containing about thirty-six hundred inhabitants. Here lived Mr. SHERWOOD HAYWOOD, a man of considerable respectability, a planter, and the cashier of a bank. He owned three plantations, at the distances, respectively, of seventy-five, thirty, and three miles from his residence in Raleigh. He owned in all about two hundred and fifty slaves, among the rest my mother, who was a house servant to her master, and of course a resident in the city. My father was a slave to a near neighbor. The apartment where I was born and where I spent my childhood and youth, was called "the kitchen," situated some fifteen or twenty rods[2] from the "great house." Here the house servants lodged and lived, and here the meals were prepared for the people in the mansion. The "field hands," of course, reside upon the plantation.

On the 30th of May, 1803, I was ushered into the world; but I did not begin to see the rising of its dark clouds, nor fancy how they might be broken and dispersed, until some time afterwards. My infancy was spent upon the floor, in a rough cradle, or sometimes in my mother's arms; my early boyhood, in playing with the other boys and girls, colored and white, in the yard, and occasionally doing such little matters of labor as one of so young years could. I knew no difference between myself and the white children: nor did they seem to know any in turn. Sometimes my master would come out and give a biscuit to me, and another to one of his own white boys; but I did not perceive the difference between us. I had no brothers or sisters, but there were other colored families living in the same kitchen, and the children playing in the same yard, with me and my mother.

When I was ten or eleven years old, my master set me regularly to cutting wood, in the yard, in the winter, and working in the garden in the summer. And when I was fifteen years of age, he gave me the care of the pleasure horses, and made me his carriage driver: but this did not exempt me from other labor, especially in the summer. Early in the morning, I used to take his three horses to the plantation, and turn them into the pasture to graze, and myself into the cotton or cornfield, with a hoe in my hand, to work through the day: and after sunset I would take these horses back to the city, a distance of three miles, feed them, and then attend to any other business my master or any of his family had for me to do, until bed time, when, with my blanket in my hand, I would go into the dining room to rest through the night. The next day the same round of labor would be repeated, unless some of the family wished to ride out, in which case I must be on hand with the horses to wait upon them, and in the meantime to work about the yard. On Sunday I had to drive to church twice, which, with other things necessary to be done, took the whole day. So my life went wearily on from day to day, from night to night, and from week to week.

When I began to work, I discovered the difference between myself and my master's white children. They began to order me about, and were told to do so by my master and mistress. I found, too, that they had learned to read, while I was not permitted to have a book in my hand. To be in the possession of anything written or printed, was regarded as an offence. And then there was the fear that I might be sold away from those who were dear to me, and conveyed to the far south. I had learned, that, being a slave, I was subject to this worst (to us) of all calamities; and I knew of others in similar situations to myself, thus sold away. My friends were not numerous; but in proportion as they were few they were dear; and the thought that I might be separated from them forever, was like that of having the heart torn from its socket; while the idea of being conveyed to the far south seemed infinitely worse than the terrors of death. To know, also, that I was never to consult my own will, but was, while I lived, to be entirely under the control of another, was another state of mind hard for me to bear. Indeed all things now made me *feel*, what I had before known only in words, that *I was a slave*. Deep was this feeling, and it preyed upon my heart like a never-dying worm. I saw no prospect that my condition would ever be changed. Yet I used to plan in my mind from day to day, and from night to night, how I might be free.

One day, while I was in this state of mind, my father gave me a small basket of peaches. I sold them for thirty cents, which was the first money I ever had in my life. Afterwards I won some marbles, and sold them for sixty cents, and some weeks after, Mr. Hog, from Fayetteville, came to visit my master, and on leaving gave me one dollar. After that, Mr. Bennahan, from Orange county, gave me a dollar, and a son of my master fifty cents. These sums, and the hope that then entered my mind of purchasing at some future time my freedom, made me long for money: and plans for money-making took the principal possession of my thoughts. At night I would steal away with my axe, get a load of wood to cut for twenty-five cents, and the next morning hardly escape a whipping for the offence. But I persevered until I had obtained twenty dollars. Now I began to think seriously of becoming able to buy myself; and cheered by this hope, I went on from one thing to another, laboring "at dead of night," after the long weary day's toil for my master was over, till I found I had collected one hundred dollars. This sum I kept hid, first in one place and then in another, as I dare not put it out, for fear I should lose it.

After this, I lit upon a plan which proved of great advantage to me. My father suggested a mode of preparing smoking tobacco, different from any then or since employed. It had the double advantage of giving the tobacco a peculiarly pleasant flavor, and of enabling me to manufacture a good article out of a very indifferent material. I improved somewhat upon his suggestion, and commenced the manufacture, doing, as I have before said, all my work in the night. The tobacco I put up in papers of about a quarter of a pound each, and sold them at fifteen cents. But the tobacco could not be smoked without a pipe, and as I had given the former a flavor peculiarly grateful, it occurred to me that I might so construct a pipe as to cool the smoke in passing through it, and thus meet the wishes of those who are more fond of smoke than heat. This I effected by means of a reed, which grows plentifully in that region: I made a passage through the reed with a hot wire, polished it, and attached a clay pipe to the end, so that the smoke should be cooled in flowing through the stem, like whiskey or rum in passing from the boiler through the worm of the still. These pipes I sold at ten cents a-piece. In the early part of the night I would sell my tobacco and pipes, and manufacture them in the latter part. As the Legislature sat in Raleigh every year, I sold these articles considerably to the members, so that I became known not only in the city, but in many parts of the State, as a *tobacconist*.

Perceiving that I was getting along so well, I began, slave as I was, to think about taking a wife. So I fixed my mind upon Miss Lucy Williams, a slave of Thomas Devereaux, Esq., an eminent lawyer in the place; but failed in my undertaking. Then I thought I never would marry; but at the end of two or three years my resolution began to slide away, till finding I could not keep it longer, I set out once more in pursuit of a wife. So I fell in with her to whom I am now united, Miss MARTHA CURTIS, and the bargain between *us* was completed. I next went to her master, Mr. Boylan, and asked him, according to the custom, if I might "marry his woman." His reply was, "Yes, if you will behave yourself." I told him I would. "And make her behave herself?" To this I also assented: and then proceeded to ask the approbation of my master, which was granted. So in May, 1828, I was bound as fast in wedlock as a slave can be. God may at any time sunder that band in a freeman; either master may do the same at pleasure in a slave. The bond is not recognized in law. But in my case it has never been broken; and now it cannot be, except by a higher power.

When we had been married nine months and one day, we were blessed with a son, and two years afterwards with a daughter. My wife also passed from the hands of Mr. Boylan, into those of Mr. BENJAMIN B. SMITH, a merchant, a member and class-leader in the methodist church, and in much repute for his deep piety and devotion to religion. But grace (of course,) had not wrought in the same *manner* upon the heart of Mr. Smith, as nature had done upon that of Mr. Boylan, who made no religious profession. This latter gentleman used to give my wife, who was a favorite slave, (her mother nursed every one of his own children,) sufficient food and clothing to render her comfortable, so that I had to spend for her but little, except to procure such small articles of extra comfort as I was prompted to from time to time. Indeed, Mr. Boylan was regarded as a very kind master to all the slaves about him,—that is, to his house servants; nor did he personally inflict much cruelty, if any, upon his field hands. The overseer on his nearest plantation (I know but little about the rest,) was a very cruel man; in one instance, as it was said among the slaves, he whipped a man *to death*; but of course he denied that the man died in consequence of the whipping. Still it was the choice of my wife to pass into the hands of Mr. Smith, as she had become attached to him in consequence of belonging to the same church, and receiving his religious instruction and counsel as her class-leader, and in consequence of the peculiar devotedness to the cause of religion for which he was noted, and which he always seemed to manifest. But when she became his slave, he withheld both from her and her children, the needful food and clothing, while he exacted from them to the uttermost all the labor they were able to perform. Almost every article of clothing worn either by my wife or children, especially every article of much value, I had to purchase; while the food he furnished the family amounted to less than a meal a day, and that of the coarser kind. I have no remembrance that he ever gave us a blanket, or any other article of bedding, although it is considered a rule at the south that the master shall furnish each of his slaves with one blanket a year. So that, both as to food and clothing, I had in fact to support both my wife and the children, while he claimed them as his property, and received all their labor. She was a house servant to Mr. Smith, sometimes cooked the food for his family, and usually took it from the table; but her mistress was so particular in giving it out to be cooked, or so watched it, that she always knew whether it was all returned; and when the table was cleared away, the stern old lady would sit by and see that every dish (except the very little she would send into the kitchen,) was put away, and then she would turn the key upon it, so as to be sure her slaves should not die of gluttony. This practise is common with some families in that region, but with others it is not. It was not so in that of her less pious master, Mr. Boylan, nor was it precisely so at my master's. We used to have corn bread enough, and some meat. When I was a boy, the pot-liquor, in which the meat was boiled for the "great house," together with some little cornmeal balls that had been thrown in just before the meat was done, was poured into a tray and set in the middle of the yard, and a clam-shell or pewter spoon given to each of us children, who would fall upon the delicious fare as greedily as pigs. It was not generally so much as we wanted, consequently it was customary for some of the white persons who saw us from the piazza of the house where they were sitting, to order the more stout and greedy ones to eat slower, that those more young and feeble might have a chance. But it was not so with Mr. Smith; such luxuries were more than he could afford, kind and Christian man as he was considered to be. So that by the expense of providing for my wife and children, all the money I had earned, and could earn, by my night labor, was consumed, till I found myself reduced to five dollars, and this I lost one day in going to the plantation. My light of hope now went out. My prop seemed to have given way from under me. Sunk in the very night of despair respecting my freedom, I discovered myself, as though I had never known it before, a husband, the father of two children, a family looking up to me for bread, and I a slave, penniless, and well watched by my master, his wife, and his children, lest I should, perchance, catch the friendly light of the stars to make something in order to supply the cravings of nature in those with whom my soul was bound up; or lest some plan of freedom might lead me to trim the light of diligence after the day's labor was over, while the rest of the world were enjoying the hours in pleasure or sleep.

At this time an event occurred, which, while it cast a cloud over the prospects of some of my fellow slaves, was a rainbow over mine. My master died; and his widow, by the will, became sole executrix of his property. To the surprise of all, the bank of which he had been cashier, presented a claim against the estate for forty thousand dollars. By a compromise, this sum was reduced to twenty thousand dollars: and my mistress, to meet the amount, sold some of her slaves, and hired out others. I hired my time of her,[*] for which I paid her a price varying from one hundred dollars to one hundred and twenty dollars per year. This was a privilege which comparatively few slaves at the south enjoy; and in this I felt truly blessed.

I commenced the manufacture of pipes and tobacco on an enlarged scale. I opened a regular place of business, labelled my tobacco in a conspicuous manner

---

[*] It is contrary to the laws of the State for a slave to have command of his own time in this way, but in Raleigh it is sometimes winked at. I knew one slave-man, who was *doing well for himself*, taken up by the public authorities and hired out for the public good, three times in succession for this offence. The time of hiring in such a case is one year. The master is subject to a fine. But generally, as I have said, if the slave is *orderly*, and appears to be *making nothing*, neither he nor the master is interfered with.

with the names of *"Edward and Lunsford Lane,"* and of some of the persons who sold it for me,—establishing agencies for the sale in various parts of the State, one at Fayetteville, one at Salisbury, one at Chapel Hill, and so on,—sold my articles from my place of business, and about town, also deposited them in stores on commission: and thus, after paying my mistress for my time, and rendering such support as was necessary to my family, I found in the space of some six or eight years, that I had collected the sum of one thousand dollars. During this time I had found it politic to go shabbily dressed, and to appear to be very poor, but to pay my mistress for my services promptly. I kept my money hid, never venturing to put out a penny, nor to let any body but my wife know that I was making any. The thousand dollars was what I supposed my mistress would ask for me, and so I determined now what I would do.

I went to my mistress and inquired what was her price for me. She said a thousand dollars. I then told her that I wanted to be free, and asked her if she would sell me to be made free. She said she would; and accordingly I arranged with her, and with the master of my wife, Mr. Smith, already spoken of, for the latter to take my money* and buy of her my freedom, as I could not legally purchase it, and as the laws forbid emancipation, except for "meritorious services." This done, Mr. Smith endeavored to emancipate me formally, and to get my manumission recorded; I tried also; but the court judged that I had done nothing "meritorious," and so I remained, nominally only, the slave of Mr. Smith for a year; when, feeling unsafe in that relation, I accompanied him to New York, whither he was going to purchase goods, and was there regularly and formally made a freeman, and there my manumission was recorded. I returned to my family in Raleigh, and endeavored to do by them as a freeman should. I had known what it was to be a slave, and I knew what it was to be free.

But I am going too rapidly over my story. When the money was paid to my mistress and the conveyance fairly made to Mr. Smith, I felt that I was free. And a queer and a joyous feeling it is to one who has been a slave. I cannot describe it, only it seemed as though I was in heaven. I used to lie awake whole nights thinking of it. And oh, the strange thoughts that passed through my soul, like so many rivers of light; deep and rich were their waves as they rolled;—these were more to me than sleep, more than soft slumber after long months of watching over the decaying, fading frame of a friend, and the loved one laid to rest in the dust. But I cannot describe my feelings to those who have never been slaves: then why should I attempt it? He who has passed from spiritual death to life, and received the witness within his soul that his sins are forgiven, may possibly form some distant idea,

---

* *Legally,* my money belonged to my mistress; and she could have taken it and refused to grant me my freedom. But she was a very kind woman for a slave owner; and she would under the circumstances scorn to do such a thing. I have known of slaves, however, served in this way.

like the ray of the setting sun from the far off mountain top, of the emotions of an emancipated slave. That opens heavens. To break the bonds of slavery, opens up at once both earth and heaven. Neither can be truly seen by us while we are slaves.

And now will the reader take with me a brief review of the road I had trodden. I cannot here dwell upon its dark shades, though some of these were black as the pencillings of midnight, but upon the light, that had followed my path from my infancy up, and had at length conducted me quite out of the deep abyss of bondage. There is a hymn opening with the following stanza, which very much expresses my feelings:

"When all thy mercies, Oh my God,
   My rising soul surveys,
Transported with the view, I'm lost
   In wonder, love, and praise."

I had endured what a freeman would indeed call hard fare; but my lot, on the whole, had been a favored one for a slave. It is known that there is a wide difference in the situations of what are termed house servants, and plantation hands. I, though sometimes employed upon the plantation, belonged to the former, which is the favored class. My master, too, was esteemed a kind and humane man; and altogether I fared quite differently from many poor fellows whom it makes my blood run chill to think of, confined to the plantation, with not enough of food and that little of the coarsest kind, to satisfy the gnawings of hunger,—compelled oftentimes, to hie away in the night-time, when worn down with work, and *steal*, (if it be stealing,) and privately devour such things as they can lay their hands upon,—made to feel the rigors of bondage with no cessation,—torn away sometimes from the few friends they love, friends doubly dear because they are few, and transported to a climate where in a few hard years they die,—or at best conducted heavily and sadly to their resting place under the sod, upon their old master's plantation,—sometimes, perhaps, enlivening the air with merriment, but a forced merriment, that comes from a stagnant or a stupefied heart. Such as this is the fate of the plantation slaves generally, but such was not my lot. My way was comparatively light, and what is better, it conducted to freedom. And my wife and children were with me. After my master died, my mistress sold a number of her slaves from their families and friends—but not me. She sold several children from their parents—but my children were with me still. She sold two husbands from their wives—but I was still with mine. She sold one wife from her husband—but mine had not been sold from me. The master of my wife, Mr. Smith, had separated members of families by sale—but not of mine. With me and my house, the tenderer tendrils of the heart still clung to where the vine had entwined; pleasant was its shade and delicious its fruits to our taste, though we knew, and what is more, we *felt* that we were slaves.

But all around I could see where the vine had been torn down, and its bleeding branches told of vanished joys, and of new wrought sorrows, such as, slave though I was, had never entered into my practical experience.

I had never been permitted to learn to read; but I used to attend church, and there I received instruction which I trust was of some benefit to me. I trusted, too, that I had experienced the renewing influences of the gospel; and after obtaining from my mistress a written *permit*, (a thing *always* required in such a case,) I had been baptised and received into fellowship with the Baptist denomination. So that in religious matters, I had been indulged in the exercise of my own conscience—a favor not always granted to slaves. Indeed I, with others, was often told by the minister how good God was in bringing us over to this country from dark and benighted Africa, and permitting us to listen to the sound of the gospel. To me, God also granted temporal freedom, which man without God's consent, had stolen away.

I often heard select portions of the scriptures read. And on the Sabbath there was one sermon preached expressly for the colored people which it was generally my privilege to hear. I became quite familiar with the texts, "Servants be obedient to your masters."[3]—"Not with eye service as men pleasers."[4]—"He that knoweth his master's will and doeth it not, shall be beaten with many stripes,"[5] and others of this class: for they formed the basis of most of these public instructions to us. The first commandment impressed upon our minds was to obey our masters, and the second was like unto it, namely, to do as much work when they or the overseers were not watching us as when they were. But connected with these instructions there was more or less that was truly excellent; though mixed up with much that would sound strangely in the ears of freedom. There was one very kind hearted Episcopal minister whom I often used to hear; he was very popular with the colored people. But after he had preached a sermon to us in which he argued from the Bible that it was the will of heaven from all eternity we should be slaves, and our masters be our owners, most of us left him; for like some of the faint hearted disciples in early times we said,—"This is a hard saying, who can bear it?"[6]

My manumission, as I shall call it—that is, the bill of sale conveying me to Mr. Smith, was dated Sept. 9th, 1835. I continued in the tobacco and pipe business as already described, to which I added a small trade in a variety of articles; and some two years before I left Raleigh, I entered also into a considerable business in wood, which I used to purchase by the acre standing, cut it, haul it into the city, deposit it in a yard and sell it out as I advantageously could. Also I was employed about the office of the Governor, as I shall hereafter relate. I used to keep one or two horses, and various vehicles, by which I did a variety of work at hauling about town. Of course I had to hire more or less help, to carry on my business.

In the manufacture of tobacco I met with considerable competition, but none that materially injured me. The method of preparing it having originated with me and my father, we found it necessary, in order to secure the advantage of the invention, to keep it to ourselves, and decline, though often solicited, going into partnership with others. Those who undertook the manufacture could neither give the article a flavor so pleasant as ours, nor manufacture it so cheaply, so they either failed in it, or succeeded but poorly.

Not long after obtaining my own freedom, I began seriously to think about purchasing the freedom of my family. The first proposition was that I should buy my wife, and that we should jointly labor to obtain the freedom of the children afterwards, as we were able. But that idea was abandoned when her master, Mr. Smith, refused to sell her to me for less than one thousand dollars, a sum which then appeared too much for me to raise.

Afterwards, however, I conceived the idea of purchasing at once the entire family. I went to Mr. Smith to learn his price, which he put at *three thousand dollars* for my wife and six children, the number we then had. This seemed a large sum, both because it was a great deal for me to raise, and also because Mr. Smith, when he bought my wife and *two* children, had actually paid but five hundred and sixty dollars for them, and had received, ever since, their labor, while I had almost entirely supported them, both as to food and clothing. Altogether, therefore, the case seemed a hard one, but as I was entirely in his power I must do the best I could. At length he concluded, perhaps partly of his own motion, and partly through the persuasion of a friend, to sell the family for $2,500, as I wished to free them, though he contended still that they were worth three thousand dollars. Perhaps they would at that time have brought this larger sum, if sold for the Southern market. The arrangement with Mr. Smith was made in December, 1838. I gave him five notes of five hundred dollars each, the first due in January, 1840, and one in January each succeeding year; for which he transferred my family into my own possession, with a *bond* to give me a bill of sale when I should pay the notes. With this arrangement, we found ourselves living in our own house,—a house which I had previously purchased,—in January, 1839.

After moving my family, my wife was for a short time sick, in consequence of her labor and the excitement in moving, and her excessive joy. I told her that it reminded me of a poor shoemaker in the neighborhood, who purchased a ticket in a lottery; but not expecting to draw, the fact of his purchasing it had passed out of his mind. But one day as he was at work on his last, he was informed that his ticket had drawn the liberal prize of ten thousand dollars; and the poor man was so overjoyed, that he fell back on his seat, and immediately expired.

In this new and joyful situation we found ourselves getting along very well, until September, 1840, when, to my surprise, as I was passing the street one day, engaged in my business, the following note was handed me. "Read it," said the officer, "or if you cannot read, get some white man to read it to you." Here it is, *verbatim*:

To Lunsford Lane, a free man of Color:
Take notice, that whereas complaint has been made to us, two Justices of the Peace for the county of Wake and State of North Carolina, that you are a free negro

from another State, who has migrated into this State contrary to the provisions of the act of assembly concerning free negroes and mulattoes, now notice is given you that unless you leave and remove out of this State within twenty days, that you will be proceeded against for the penalty prescribed by said act of assembly, and be otherwise dealt with as the law directs. Given under our hands and seals this the 5th Sept. 1840.

WILLIS SCOTT, JP (Seal)
JORDAN WOMBLE, JP (Seal).

This was a terrible blow to me, for it prostrated at once all my hopes in my cherished object of obtaining the freedom of my family, and led me to expect nothing but a separation from them forever.

In order that the reader may understand the full force of the foregoing notice, I will copy the law of the State under which it was issued:

SEC. 65. It shall not be lawful for any free negro or mulatto to migrate into this State: and if he or she shall do so, contrary to the provisions of this act, and being thereof informed, shall not, within twenty days thereafter, remove out of the State, he or she being thereof convicted in the manner hereafter directed, shall be liable to a penalty of five hundred dollars; and upon failure to pay the same, within the time prescribed in the judgment awarded against such person or persons, he or she shall be liable to be held in servitude and at labor a term of time not exceeding ten years, in such manner and upon such terms as may be provided by the court awarding such sentence, and the proceeds arising therefrom shall be paid over to the county trustee for county purposes: Provided, that in case any free negro or mulatto shall pay the penalty of five hundred dollars, according to the provisions of this act, it shall be the duty of such free negro or mulatto to remove him or herself out of this State within twenty days thereafter, and for every such failure, he or she shall be subject to the like penalty as is prescribed for a failure to remove in the first instance.—*Revised Statutes North Carolina, chap.* 111.

The next section provides that if the free person of color so notified, does not leave within the twenty days after receiving the notice, he may be arrested on a warrant from any Justice, and be held to bail for his appearance at the next county court, when he will be subject to the penalties specified above; or in case of his failure to give bonds, he may be sent to jail.

I made known my situation to my friends, and after taking legal counsel, it was determined to induce, if possible, the complainants to prosecute no farther at present, and then as the Legislature of the State was to sit in about two months, to petition that body for permission to remain in the State until I could complete the purchase of my family; after which I was willing, if necessary, to leave.

From January 1st, 1837, I had been employed, as I have mentioned, in the office of the Governor of the State, principally under the direction of his private Secretary, in keeping the office in order, taking the letters to the Post Office, and doing such other duties of the sort as occurred from time to time. This circumstance, with the fact of the high standing in the city of the family of my former master, and of the former masters of my wife, had given me the friendship of the first people in the place generally, who from that time forward acted towards me the friendly part.

Mr. BATTLE, then private Secretary to Governor Dudley, addressed the following letter to the prosecuting attorney in my behalf:

RALEIGH, Nov. 3, 1840.
DEAR SIR:—Lunsford Lane, a free man of color, has been in the employ of the State under me since my entering on my present situation. I understand that under a law of the State, he has been notified to leave, and that the time is now at hand.

In the discharge of the duties I had from him, I have found him prompt, obedient and faithful. At this particular time, his absence to me would be much regretted, as I am now just fixing up my books and other papers in the new office, and I shall not have time to learn another what he can already do so well. With me the period of the Legislature is a very busy one, and I am compelled to have a servant who understands the business I want done, and one I can trust. I would not wish to be an obstacle in the execution of any law, but the enforcing of the one against him will be doing me a serious inconvenience, and the object of this letter is to ascertain whether I could not procure a suspension of the sentence till after the adjournment of the Legislature, say about 1st January, 1841,

I should feel no hesitation in giving my word that he will conduct himself orderly and obediently.

I am, most respectfully,
Your obedient servant,
C. C. BATTLE.

G. W. HAYWOOD, Esq.,
Attorney at Law, Raleigh, N. C.

To the above letter the following reply was made:

RALEIGH, Nov. 3, 1840.
MY DEAR SIR:—I have no objection, so far as I am concerned, that all further proceedings against Lunsford should be postponed until after the adjournment of the Legislature.

The process now out against him is one issued by two magistrates, Messrs. Willis Scott and Jordan Womble, over which I have no control. You had better see them today, and perhaps, at your request, they will delay further action on the subject.

Respectfully yours,
GEO. W. HAYWOOD.

Mr. Battle then enclosed the foregoing correspondence to Messrs. Scott and Womble, requesting their "favorable consideration." They returned the correspondence, but neglected to make any reply.

In consequence, however, of this action on the part of my friends, I was permitted to remain without further interruption, until the day the Legislature commenced its session. On that day a warrant was served upon me, to appear before the county court, to answer for the sin of having remained in the place of my birth for the space of twenty days and more after being warned out. I escaped going to jail through the kindness of Mr. Haywood, a son of my former master, and Mr. Smith, who jointly became security for my appearance at court.

This was on Monday; and on Wednesday I appeared before the court; but as my prosecutors were not ready for the trial, the case was laid over three months, to the next term.

I then proceeded to get up a petition to the Legislature. It required much hard labor and persuasion on my part to start it; but after that, I readily obtained the signatures of the principal men in the place. Then I went round to the members, many of whom were known to me, calling upon them at their rooms, and urging them for my sake, for humanity's sake, for the sake of my wife and little ones, whose hopes had been excited by the idea that they were even now free; I appealed to them as husbands, fathers, brothers, sons, to vote in favor of my petition, and allow me to remain in the State long enough to purchase my family. I was doing well in business, and it would be but a short time before I could accomplish the object. Then, if it was desired, I and my wife and children, redeemed from bondage, would together seek a more friendly home, beyond the dominion of slavery. The following is the petition presented, endorsed as the reader will see:

To the Hon. General Assembly of the State of North Carolina.
GENTLEMEN:—The petition of Lunsford Lane humbly shews—That about five years ago, he purchased his freedom from his mistress, Mrs. Sherwood Haywood, and by great economy and industry has paid the purchase money; that he has a wife and seven children whom he has agreed to purchase, and for whom he has paid a part of the purchase money; but not having paid in full, is not yet able to leave the State, without parting with his wife and children.

Your petitioner prays your Honorable Body to pass a law, allowing him to remain a limited time within the State, until he can remove his family also. Your petitioner will give bond and good security for his good behavior while he remains.

> Your petitioner will ever pray, &c.
> —LUNSFORD LANE.

The undersigned are well acquainted with Lunsford Lane, the petitioner, and join in his petition to the Assembly for relief.

Charles Manly,	Drury Lacy,
R. W. Haywood,	Will. Peck,
Eleanor Haywood,	W. A. Stith,
William Hill,	A. B. Stith,
R. Smith,	J. Brown,
William Peace,	William White,
Jos. Peace,	George Simpson,
William M'Pheeters,	Jno. I. Christophers,
William Boylan,	John Primrose,
Fabius J. Haywood,	Hugh M'Queen,
D. W. Stone,	Alex. J. Lawrence,
T. Merideth,	C. L. Hinton.
A. J. Battle,	

Lunsford Lane, the petitioner herein, has been servant to the Executive Office since the 1st of January, 1837, and it gives me pleasure to state that, during the whole time, without exception, I have found him faithful and obedient, in keeping every thing committed to his care in good condition. From what I have seen of his conduct and demeanor, I cheerfully join in the petition for his relief.

C. C. BATTLE, *P. Secretary to Gov. Dudley*.
RALEIGH, Nov. 20, 1840.

The foregoing petition was presented to the Senate. It was there referred to a committee. I knew when the committee was to report, and watched about the State House that I might receive the earliest news of the fate of my petition. I should have gone within the senate chamber, but no colored man has that permission. I do not know why, unless for fear he may hear the name of *Liberty*. By and by a member came out, and as he passed me, said, *"Well, Lunsford, they have laid you out; the nigger bill is killed."* I need not tell the reader that my feelings did not enter into the merriment of this honorable senator. To me, the fate of my petition was the last blow to my hopes. I had done all I could do, had said all I could say, laboring night and day, to obtain a favorable reception to my petition;

but all in vain. Nothing appeared before me but I must leave the State, and leave my wife and my children, never to see them more. My friends had also done all they could for me.

And why must I be banished? Ever after I entertained the first idea of being free, I had endeavored so to conduct myself as not to become obnoxious to the white inhabitants, knowing as I did their power, and their hostility to the colored people. The two points necessary in such a case I had kept constantly in mind. First, I had made no display of the little property or money I possessed, but in every way I wore as much as possible the aspect of poverty. Second, I had never appeared to be even so intelligent as I really was. This all colored people at the south, free and slaves, find it peculiarly necessary to their own comfort and safety to observe.

I should, perhaps, have mentioned that on the same day I received the notice to leave Raleigh, similar notices were presented to two other free colored people, who had been slaves; were trying to purchase their families; and were otherwise in a like situation to myself. And they took the same course I did to endeavor to remain a limited time. ISAAC HUNTER, who had a family with five children, was one; and WALLER FREEMAN, who had six children, was the other. Mr. Hunter's petition went before mine; and a bill of some sort passed the Senate, which was so cut down in the Commons, as to allow him only *twenty days* to remain in the State. He has since, however, obtained the freedom of his family, who are living with him in Philadelphia.

Mr. Freeman's petition received no better fate than mine. His family were the property of Judge BADGER, who was afterwards made a member of Mr. Harrison's cabinet. When Mr. Badger removed to Washington, he took with him among other slaves this family; and Freeman removed also to that city. After this, when Mr. B. resigned his office, with the other members of the cabinet under President Tyler, he entered into some sort of contract with Freeman, to sell him this family, which he left at Washington, while he took the rest of his slaves back to Raleigh. Freeman is now endeavoring to raise money to make the purchase.

It was now between two and three months to the next session of the court; and I knew that before or at that time I must leave the State. I was bound to appear before the court; but it had been arranged between my lawyer and the prosecuting attorney, that if I would leave the State, and pay the costs of court, the case should be dropped, so that my bondsmen should not be involved. I therefore concluded to stay as long as I possibly could, and then leave. I also determined to appeal to the kindness of the friends of the colored man in the north, for assistance, though I had but little hope of succeeding in this way. Yet it was the only course I could think of, by which I could see any possible hope of accomplishing the object.

I had paid Mr. Smith six hundred and twenty dollars, and had a house and lot worth five hundred dollars, which he had promised to take when I had raised the balance. He gave me also a bill of sale of one of my children, Laura, in consideration of two hundred and fifty dollars of the money already paid; and her I determined to take with me to the north. The costs of court, which I had to meet, amounted to between thirty and forty dollars, besides the fee of my lawyer.

On the 18th of May, 1841, three days after the court commenced its session, I bid adieu to my friends in Raleigh, and set out for the city of New York. I took with me a letter of introduction and recommendation from Mr. John Primrose, a very estimable man, a recommendatory certificate from Mr. Battle, and a letter from the church of which I was a member, together with such papers relating to the affair as I had in my possession. Also I received the following:

RALEIGH, N. C., May, 1841.
The bearer, Lunsford Lane, a free man of color, for some time a resident in this place, being about to leave North Carolina in search of a more favorable location to pursue his trade, has desired us to give him a certificate of his good conduct heretofore.

We take pleasure in saying that his habits are temperate and industrious, that his conduct has been orderly and proper, and that he has for these qualities been distinguished among his caste.

William Hall,	R. Smith,
Weston R. Gales,	C. Dewey.
C. L. Hinton,	

The above was certified to officially in the usual form, by the clerk of the Court of Common Pleas and Quarter Sessions.

My success in New York was at first small; but at length I fell in with two friends who engaged to raise for me three hundred dollars, provided I should first obtain from other sources the balance of the sum required, which balance would be one thousand and eighty dollars. Thus encouraged, I proceeded to Boston; and in the city and vicinity the needful sum was contributed by about the 1st of April, 1842. My thanks I have endeavored to express in my poor way to the many friends who so kindly and liberally assisted me. I cannot reward them; I hope they will receive their reward in another world. If the limits of this publication would permit, I should like to record the names of many to whom I am very especially indebted for their kindness and aid, not only in contributing, but in introducing me, and opening various ways of access, to others.

On the 5th of February, 1842, finding that I should soon have in my possession the sum necessary to procure my family, and fearing that there might be danger in visiting Raleigh for that purpose, in consequence of the strong opposition of many of the citizens against colored people, their opposition to me, and their previously persecuting me from the city, I wrote to Mr. Smith, requesting him to see the Governor, and obtain, under his hand, a permit to visit the State for a sufficient time to accomplish this business. I requested Mr. Smith to publish the permit in one or two of the city papers, and then to enclose the original to me. This letter he answered, under date of Raleigh, 19th Feb. 1842, as follows:

LUNSFORD:—Your letter of the 5th inst. came duly to hand, and in reply I have to inform you, that owing to the absence of Gov. Morehead, I cannot send you the permit you requested, but this will make no difference, for you can come home, and after your arrival you can obtain one to remain long enough to settle up your affairs. You ought of course to apply to the Governor immediately on your arrival, before any malicious person would have time to inform against you; I don't think by pursuing this course you need apprehend any danger. * * * *

We are all alive at present in Raleigh on the subjects of temperance and religion. We have taken into the temperance societies about five hundred members, and about fifty persons have been happily converted. * * * The work seems still to be spreading, and such a time I have never seen before in my life. Glorious times truly.

Do try to get all the religion in your heart you possibly can, for it is the only thing worth having after all.

Your, &c.
B. B. SMITH.

The way now appeared to be in a measure open; also I thought that the religious and temperance interest mentioned in the latter portion of Mr. Smith's letter, augured a state of feeling which would be a protection to me. But fearing still that there might be danger in visiting Raleigh without the permit from the Governor, or at least wishing to take every possible precaution, I addressed another letter to Mr. Smith, and received under date of March 12th, a reply, from which I copy as follows:

"The Governor has just returned, and I called upon him to get the permit, as you requested, but he said he had no authority by law to grant one; and *he told me to say to you that you might in perfect safety come home* in a quiet manner, and remain twenty days without being interrupted. I also consulted Mr. Manly, (a lawyer,) and he *told me the same thing.* * * * *Surely you need not fear any thing under these circumstances. You had therefore better come on just as soon as possible.*"

I need not say, what the reader has already seen, that my life so far had been one of joy succeeding sorrow, and sorrow following joy; of hope, of despair, of bright prospects, of gloom; and of as many hues as ever appear on the varied sky, from the black of midnight, or of the deep brown of a tempest, to the bright warm glow of a clear noon day. On the 11th of April, it was noon with me; I left Boston on my way for Raleigh with high hopes, intending to pay over the money for my family and return with them to Boston, which I designed should be my future home; for there I had found friends, and there I would find a grave. The visit I was making to the south was to be a farewell one; and I did not dream that my old cradle, hard as it once had jostled me, would refuse to rock me a pleasant, or even an affectionate good bye. I thought, too, that the assurances I had received from the Governor, through Mr. Smith, and the assurances of other friends, were a sufficient guaranty that I might visit the home of my boyhood, of my youth, of my manhood, in peace, especially as I was to stay but for a few days and then to return. With these thoughts, and with the thoughts of my family and freedom, I pursued my way to Raleigh, and arrived there on the 23d of the month. It was Saturday, about four o'clock, P.M., when I found myself once more in the midst of my family. With them I remained over the Sabbath, as it was sweet to spend a little time with them after so long an absence, an absence filled with so much of interest to us, and as I could not do any business until the beginning of the week. On Monday morning, between eight and nine o'clock, while I was making ready to leave the house for the first time after my arrival, to go to the store of Mr. Smith, where I was to transact my business with him, two constables, Messrs. Murray and Scott, entered, accompanied by two other men, and summoned me to appear immediately before the police. I accordingly accompanied them to the City Hall, but as it was locked and the officers could not at once find the key, we were told that the court would be held in Mr. Smith's store, a large and commodious room. This was what is termed in common phrase, in Raleigh, a "call court." The Mayor, Mr. Loring, presided, assisted by William Boylan and Jonathan Busbye, Esqs., Justices of the Peace. There were a large number of people together—more than could obtain admission to the room—and a large company of mobocratic spirits crowded around the door. Mr. Loring read the writ, setting forth that I had been guilty of *delivering abolition lectures in the State of Massachusetts*. He asked me whether I was guilty or not guilty. I told him I did not know whether I had given abolition lectures or not, but if it pleased the court, I would relate the course I had pursued during my absence from Raleigh. He then said that I was at liberty to speak.

The circumstances under which I left Raleigh, said I, are perfectly familiar to you. It is known that I had no disposition to remove from this city, but resorted to every lawful means to remain. After I found that I could not be permitted to stay, I went away, leaving behind everything I held dear, with the exception of one child, whom I took with me, after paying two hundred and fifty dollars for her. It is also known to you and to many other persons here present, that I had engaged to purchase my wife and children of their master, Mr. Smith, for the sum of twenty-five hundred dollars, and that I had paid of this sum (including my house and lot,) eleven hundred and twenty dollars, leaving a balance to be made up of thirteen hundred and eighty dollars. I had previously to that lived in Raleigh, a slave, the property of Mr. Sherwood Haywood, and had purchased my freedom by paying the sum of one thousand dollars. But being driven away,—no longer permitted to live in this city to raise the balance of the money due on my family,—my last resort was to call upon the friends of humanity in other places, to assist me.

I went to the city of Boston, and there I related the story of my persecutions here, the same as I have now stated to you. The people gave ear to my statements; and one of them, Rev. Mr. Neale, wrote back, unknown to me, to Mr. Smith, inquiring of him whether the statements made by me were correct. After Mr. Neale received the answer, he sent for me, informed me of his having written, and read to me the reply. The letter fully satisfied Mr. Neale and his friends. He placed it in my hands, remarking that it would, in a great measure, do away the necessity of using the other documents in my possession. I then, with that letter in my hands, went out from house to house, from place of business to place of business, and from church to church, relating, where I could gain an ear, the same heart-rending and soul-trying story which I am now repeating to you. In pursuing that course, the people, first one and then another, contributed, until I had succeeded in raising the amount alluded to, namely, thirteen hundred and eighty dollars. I may have had contributions from abolitionists; but I did not stop to ask those who assisted me whether they were anti-slavery or pro-slavery, for I considered that the money coming from either would accomplish the object I had in view. These are the facts; and now, sir, it remains for you to say, whether I have been giving abolition lectures or not.

In the course of my remarks, I presented the letter of Mr. Smith to Mr. Neale, showing that I had acted the open part while in Massachusetts; also I referred to my having written to Mr. Smith, requesting him to obtain for me the permit of the Governor; and I showed to the court Mr. Smith's letters in reply, in order to satisfy them that I had reason to believe I should be unmolested in my return.

Mr. Loring then whispered to some of the leading men; after which he remarked that he saw nothing in what I had done, according to my statements, implicating me in a manner worthy of notice. He called upon any present who might be in possession of information tending to disprove what I had said, or to show any wrong on my part, to produce it, otherwise I should be set at liberty. No person appeared against me; so I was discharged.

I started to leave the house; but just before I got to the door I met Mr. James Litchford, who touched me on the shoulder, and I followed him back. He observed to me that if I went out of that room I should in less than five minutes be a dead man; for there was a mob outside waiting to drink my life. Mr. Loring then spoke to me again, and said that notwithstanding I had been found guilty of nothing, yet public opinion was law; and he advised me to leave the place the next day, otherwise he was convinced I should have to suffer death. I replied, "not to-morrow, but to-day." He answered that I could not go that day, because I had not done my business. I told him that I would leave my business in his hands and in those of other such gentlemen as himself, who might settle it for me and send my family to meet me at Philadelphia. This was concluded upon, and a guard appointed to conduct me to the depot. I took my seat in the cars, when the mob that had followed us surrounded me, and declared that the cars should not go, if I were permitted to go in them. Mr. Loring inquired what they wanted of me; he told them that there had been an examination, and nothing had been found against me; that they were at the examination invited to speak if they knew aught to condemn me, but they had remained silent, and that now it was but right I should be permitted to leave in peace. They replied that they wanted a more thorough investigation, that they wished to search my trunks (I had but one trunk) and see if I was not in possession of abolition papers. It now became evident that I should be unable to get off in the cars; and my friends advised me to go the shortest way possible to jail, for my safety. They said they were persuaded that what the rabble wanted was to get me into their possession, and then to murder me. The mob looked dreadfully enraged, and seemed to lap for blood. The whole city was in an uproar. But the first men and the more wealthy were my friends; and they did everything in their power to protect me. Mr. Boylan, whose name has repeatedly occurred in this publication, was more than a father to me; and Mr. Smith and Mr. Loring, and so many other gentlemen, whose names it would give me pleasure to mention, were exceedingly kind.

The guard then conducted me through the mob to the prison; and I felt joyful that even a prison could protect me. Looking out from the prison window, I saw my trunk in the hands of Messrs. Johnson, Scott, and others, who were taking it to the City Hall for examination. I understood afterwards that they opened my trunk; and as the lid flew up, Lo! a paper! a paper!! Those about seized it, three or four at once, as hungry dogs would a piece of meat after forty days famine. But the meat quickly turned to a stone; for the paper it happened, was one *printed in Raleigh*, and edited by Weston R. Gales, a nice man to be sure, but no abolitionist. The only other printed or written things in the trunk were some business cards of a firm in Raleigh—not incendiary.

Afterwards I saw from the window Mr. Scott, accompanied by Mr. Johnson, lugging my carpet-bag in the same direction my trunk had gone. It was opened at the City Hall, and found actually to contain a pair of old shoes, and a pair of old boots!—but they did not conclude that these were incendiary.

Mr. Smith now came to the prison and told me that the examination had been completed, and nothing found against me; but that it would not be safe for me to leave the prison immediately. It was agreed that I should remain in prison until after nightfall, and then steal secretly away, being let out by the keeper, and pass unnoticed to the house of my old and tried friend Mr. Boylan. Accordingly I was discharged between nine and ten o'clock. I went by the back way leading to

Mr. Boylan's; but soon and suddenly a large company of men sprang upon me, and instantly I found myself in their possession. They conducted me sometimes high above ground and sometimes dragging me along, but as silently as possible, in the direction of the gallows, which is always kept standing upon the Common, or as it is called "the pines," or "piny old field." I now expected to pass speedily into the world of spirits; I thought of that unseen region to which I seemed to be hastening; and then my mind would return to my wife and children, and the labors I had made to redeem them from bondage. Although I had the money to pay for them according to a bargain already made, it seemed to me some white man would get it, and they would die in slavery, without benefit from my exertions and the contributions of my friends. Then the thought of my own death, to occur in a few brief moments, would rush over me, and I seemed to bid adieu in spirit to all earthly things, and to hold communion already with eternity. But at length I observed those who were carrying me away, changed their course a little from the direct line to the gallows, and hope, a faint beaming, sprung up within me; but then as they were taking me to the woods, I thought they intended to murder me there, in a place where they would be less likely to be interrupted than in so public a spot as where the gallows stood. They conducted me to a rising ground among the trees, and set me down. "Now," said they, "tell us the truth about those abolition lectures you have been giving at the north." I replied that I had related the circumstances before the court in the morning; and could only repeat what I had then said. "But that was not the truth—tell us the truth." I again said that any different story would be false, and as I supposed I was in a few minutes to die, I would not, whatever they might think I would say under other circumstances, pass into the other world with a lie upon my lips. Said one, "you were always, Lunsford, when you were here, a clever fellow, and I did not think you would be engaged in such business as giving abolition lectures." To this and similar remarks, I replied, that the people of Raleigh had always said the abolitionists did not believe in buying slaves, but contended that their masters ought to free them without pay. I had been laboring to buy my family; and how then could they suppose me to be in league with the abolitionists?

After other conversation of this kind, and after they seemed to have become tired of questioning me, they held a consultation in a low whisper among themselves. Then a bucket was brought and set down by my side; but what it contained, or for what it was intended, I could not divine. But soon, one of the number came forward with a pillow, and then hope sprung up, a flood of light and joy within me. The heavy weight on my heart rolled off; death had passed by and I unharmed. They commenced stripping me till every rag of clothes was removed; and then the bucket was set near, and I discovered it to contain tar. One man,—I will do him the honor to record his name,—Mr. WILLIAM ANDRES, a journeyman printer, when he is anything except a tar-and-featherer, put his hands the first into the bucket, and was about passing them to my face. "Don't put any in his face or eyes," said one.* So he desisted; but he, with three other "gentlemen," whose names I should be happy to record if I could recall them, gave me as nice a coat of tar all over, face only excepted, as any one would wish to see. Then they took the pillow and ripped it open at one end, and with the open end commenced the operation at the head and so worked downwards, of putting a coat of its contents over that of the contents of the bucket. A fine escape from the hanging this will be, thought I, provided they do not with a match set fire to the feathers. I had some fear they would. But when the work was completed they gave me my clothes, and one of them handed me my watch, which he had carefully kept in his hands; they all expressed great interest in my welfare, advised me how to proceed with my business the next day, told me to stay in the place as long as I wished, and with other such words of consolation they bid me good night.

After I had returned to my family, to their inexpressible joy, as they had become greatly alarmed for my safety, some of the persons who had participated in this outrage, came in, (probably influenced by a curiosity to see how the tar and feathers would be got off,) and expressed great sympathy for me. They said they regretted that the affair had happened,—that they had no objections to my living in Raleigh,—I might feel perfectly safe to go out and transact my business preparatory to leaving,—I should not be molested.

Meanwhile, my friends, understanding that I had been discharged from prison, and perceiving I did not come to them, had commenced a regular search for me, on foot and on horseback, everywhere; and Mr. Smith called upon the Governor to obtain his official interference; and after my return, a guard came to protect me; but I chose not to risk myself at my own house, and so went to Mr. Smith's, where this guard kept me safely until morning. They seemed friendly indeed, and were regaled with a supper during the night by Mr. Smith. My friend, Mr. Battle, (late Private Secretary to the Governor,) was with them; and he made a speech to them, setting forth the good qualities I had exhibited in my past life, particularly in my connection with the Governor's office.

In the morning, Mr. Boylan, true as ever, and unflinching in his friendship, assisted me in arranging my business,† so that I should start with my family *that*

---

* I think this was Mr. Burns, a blacksmith in the place, but I am not certain. At any rate, this man was my *friend* (if so he may be called,) on this occasion; and it was fortunate for me that the company generally seemed to look up to him for wisdom.

† Of course I was obliged to sacrifice much on my property, leaving in this hurried manner. And while I was in the north, a kind *friend* had removed from the wood-lot wood that I had cut and corded, for which I expected to receive over one hundred dollars; thus saving me the trouble of making sale of it, or of being burdened with the money it would bring. I suppose I have no redress. I might add other things as bad.

day for the north. He furnished us with provisions more than sufficient to sustain the family to Philadelphia, where we intended to make a halt; and sent his own baggage wagon to convey our baggage to the depot, offering also to send his carriage for my family. But my friend, Mr. Malone, had been before him in this kind offer, which I had agreed to accept.

Brief and sorrowful was the parting from my kind friends; but the worst was the thought of leaving my mother. The cars were to start at ten o'clock in the morning. I called upon my old mistress, Mrs. Haywood, who was affected to weeping by the considerations that naturally came to her mind. She had been kind to me; the day before, she and her daughter, Mrs. Hogg, now present, had jointly transmitted a communication to the court, representing that in consequence of my good conduct from my youth, I could not be supposed to be guilty of any offence. And now, "with tears that ceased not flowing," they gave me their parting blessing. My mother was still Mrs. Haywood's slave, and I her only child. Our old mistress could not witness the sorrow that would attend the parting with my mother. She told her to go with me; and said that if I ever became able to pay two hundred dollars for her, I might; otherwise it should be her loss. She gave her the following paper, which is in the ordinary form of a *pass*:

RALEIGH, N. C., April 26, 1842.
Know all Persons by these Presents, That the bearer of this, Clarissa, a slave, belonging to me, hath my permission to visit the city of New York with her relations, who are in company with her; and it is my desire that she may be protected and permitted to pass without molestation or hindrance, on good behavior. Witness my hand this 26th April, 1842.

ELEANOR HAYWOOD.

Witness—J. A. CAMPBELL.

On leaving Mrs. Haywood's, I called upon Mrs. Badger, another daughter, and wife of Judge Badger, previously mentioned. She seemed equally affected; she wept as she gave me her parting counsel. She and Mrs. Hogg, and I, had been children together, playing in the same yard, while yet none of us had learned that they were of a superior and I of a subject[7] race. And in those infant years there were pencillings made upon the heart, which time and opposite fortunes could not all efface. May these friends never be slaves as I have been; nor their bosom companions and their little ones be slaves like mine.

When the cars were about to start, the whole city seemed to be gathered at the depot; and, among the rest, the mobocratic portion, who appeared to be determined still that I should not go peaceably away. Apprehending this, it had been arranged with my friends and the conductor, that my family should be put in the cars and that I should go a distance from the city on foot, and be taken up as they passed. The mob, therefore, supposing that I was left behind, allowed the cars to start.

Mr. Whiting, known as the agent of the rail-road company, was going as far as Petersburg, Va.; and he kindly assisted in purchasing our tickets, and enabling us to pass on unmolested. After he left, Capt. Guyan, of Raleigh, performed the same kind office as far as Alexandria, D. C., and then he placed us in the care of a citizen of Philadelphia, whose name I regret to have forgotten, who protected us quite out of the land of slavery. But for this we should have been liable to be detained at several places on our way, much to our embarrassment, at least, if nothing had occurred of a more serious nature.

One accident only had happened; we lost at Washington a trunk containing most of our valuable clothing. This we have not recovered; but our lives have been spared to bless the day that conferred freedom upon us. I felt when my feet struck the pavements in Philadelphia, as though I had passed into another world. I could draw in a full long breath, with no one to say to the ribs, "why do ye so?"

On reaching Philadelphia we found that our money had all been expended, but kind friends furnished us with the means of proceeding as far as New-York; and thence we were with equal kindness aided on to Boston.

In Boston and in the vicinity, are persons almost without number, who have done me favors more than I can express. The thought that I was now in my loved, though recently acquired home—that my family were with me where the stern, cruel, hated hand of slavery could never reach us more—the greetings of friends—the interchange of feeling and sympathy—the kindness bestowed upon us, more grateful than rain to the thirsty earth—the reflections of the past that would rush into my mind,—these and more almost overwhelmed me with emotion, and I had deep and strange communion with my own soul. Next to God from whom every good gift proceeds, I feel under the greatest obligations to my kind friends in Massachusetts. To be rocked in their cradle of Liberty,—oh, how unlike being stretched on the pillory of slavery! May that cradle rock forever; may many a poor care-worn child of sorrow, many a spirit-bruised (worse than lash-mangled) victim of oppression, there sweetly sleep to the lullaby of Freedom, sung by Massachusetts' sons and daughters.

A number of meetings have been held at which friends have contributed to our temporal wants, and individuals have sent us various articles of provision and furniture and apparel, so that our souls have been truly made glad. There are now ten of us in the family, my wife, my mother, and myself, with seven children, and we expect soon to be joined by my father, who several years ago received his freedom by legacy. The wine fresh from the clustering grapes never filled so sweet a cup as mine. May I and my family be permitted to drink it, remembering whence it came!

I suppose such of my readers as are not accustomed to trade in human beings, may be curious to see the Bills of Sale, by which I have obtained the right to my wife and children. They are both in the hand writing of Mr. Smith. The first—that for Laura—is as follows:

State of North Carolina, Wake County.

Know all Men by these Presents, That for and in consideration of the sum of two hundred and fifty dollars, to me in hand paid, I have this day bargained and sold, and do hereby bargain, sell and deliver, unto Lunsford Lane, a free man of color, a certain negro girl by the name of Laura, aged about seven years, and hereby warrant and defend the right and title of the said girl to the said Lunsford and his heirs forever, free from the claims of all persons whatsoever.

In Witness whereof, I have hereunto set my hand and seal, at Raleigh, this 17th May, 1841.

B. B. SMITH, [Seal.]

Witness—Robt. W. Haywood.

Below is the Bill of Sale for my wife and other six children, to which the papers that follow are attached:

State of North Carolina, Wake County.

Know all Men by these Presents, That for and in consideration of the sum of eighteen hundred and eighty dollars, to me in hand paid, the receipt of which is hereby acknowledged, I have this day bargained, sold and delivered, unto Lunsford Lane, a free man of color, one dark mulatto woman named Patsy, one boy named Edward, one boy also named William, one boy also named Lunsford, one girl named Maria, one boy also named Ellick, and one girl named Lucy, to have and to hold the said negroes free from the claims of all persons whatsoever.

In Witness whereof, I have hereunto affixed my hand and seal, this 25th day of April, 1842.

B. B. SMITH, [Seal.]

Witness—Th. L. West.

State of North Carolina, Wake County.
Office of Court of Pleas &. Quarter Sessions, Apr. 26, 1842.
The execution of the within Bill of Sale was this day duly acknowledged before me, by B. B. Smith, the executor of the same.

In Testimony whereof, I have hereunto affixed the seal of said Court, and subscribed my name at Office, in Raleigh, the date above.

JAS. T. MARRIOTT, *Clerk.*

State of North Carolina, Wake County.
I, William Boylan, presiding magistrate of the Court of Pleas and Quarter Sessions for the County aforesaid, certify that Jas. T. Marriott, who has written and

signed the above certificate, is Clerk of the Court aforesaid, that the same is in due form, and full faith and credit are due to such his official acts.

Given under my hand and private seal, (having no seal of office,) this 26th day of April, 1842.

WM. BOYLAN, P. M. [Seal.]

THE STATE OF NORTH CAROLINA.

To all to whom these Presents shall come—Greeting:

Be it Known, That William Boylan, whose signature appears in his own proper hand writing to the annexed certificate, was, at the time of signing the same, and now is, a Justice of the Peace and the Presiding Magistrate for the County of Wake, in the State aforesaid, and as such he is duly qualified and empowered to give such certificate, which is here done in the usual and proper manner; and full faith and credit are due to the same, and ought to be given to all the official acts of the said William Boylan, as Presiding Magistrate aforesaid.

In Testimony whereof, I, J. M. Morehead, Governor, Captain General and Commander in Chief, have caused the Great Seal of the State to be hereunto affixed, and signed the same, at the city of Raleigh, on the 26th day of April, in the year of our Lord one thousand eight hundred and forty-two, and in the sixty-sixth year of the Independence of the United States.

J. M. MOREHEAD.

By the Governor.
P. REYNOLDS, *Private Secretary*.

NOTES

1. William Andrews, *To Tell a Free Story: The First Century of Afro-American Autobiography, 1760–1865* (Urbana: University of Illinois Press, 1986), 115–18.

2. A measure containing 5 1/2 yards or 16 1/2 feet.

3. Titus 2:9–10, "Exhort servants to be obedient unto their own masters, and to please them well in all things; not answering again; Not purloining, but shewing all good fidelity; that they may adorn the doctrine of God our Saviour in all things"; Ephesians 6:5, "Servants, be obedient to them that are your masters according to the flesh, with fear and trembling, in singleness of your heart, as unto Christ."

4. Ephesians 6:6, "Not with eyeservice, as menpleasers; but as the servants of Christ, doing the will of God from the heart."

5. Luke 12:47, "And that servant, which knew his lord's will, and prepared not himself, neither did according to his will, shall be beaten with many stripes."

6. John 6:60, "Many therefore of his disciples, when they had heard this, said, This is an hard saying; who can hear it?"

7. Subordinate or inferior.

■ CHAPTER 3
William Wells Brown (1814–1884)

NARRATIVE OF WILLIAM W. BROWN, A FUGITIVE SLAVE

William Wells Brown (1814–1884) is widely regarded as an abolitionist, a novelist, a playwright, and a travel writer. It is a testament to Brown's talents and interests that, beginning just thirteen years after his escape from slavery, he was able to publish an account of his experiences that was widely successful and highly influential.

William was born in Lexington, Kentucky, in 1814. According to available records, William's father was named George Higgins. Higgins was the cousin of Dr. John Young, who was William's owner.[1] There is certainly no irony to the fact that one of William's subsequent accomplishments was his work as a travel writer. His *Narrative* describes the experiences of a slave who was remarkably mobile and not, like many slave narrative writers, primarily confined to a plantation during his formative years. William's fair complexion undoubtedly contributed to his being chosen to work in the house. Early in his life, William relocated with his owner to Saint Charles County in the Missouri Territory and then to St. Louis in 1816. He stayed primarily in the area until he escaped slavery in 1834. As he acquired skills and education, William was hired out to a slave trader named James Walker. Walker's work required many trips on the Mississippi River between New Orleans and St. Louis. These outings exposed William firsthand to the widespread abuses of the slave system.

William began his escape from slavery in 1834. He departed from Cincinnati, Ohio, with the intention of reaching Canada. He added "Wells Brown" to his name as a way of acknowledging the support he received from a Quaker ally of the same name.[2] Though Brown never reached Canada, he did achieve his freedom by reaching Cleveland, Ohio, where he used his job aboard a steamboat to help other blacks escape. Brown eventually moved to Buffalo, New York, and continued to actively help slaves escape to Canada. He was introduced to organized abolitionist political activity when he met Frederick Douglass in August 1843 and was persuaded, like Douglass, to serve the abolitionist movement as a platform speaker. Brown lectured for three years on behalf of the Western New York Anti-Slavery Society. He moved to Boston in the summer of 1847, near the time of the publication of the *Narrative*.[3]

In terms of style and structure, Brown's *Narrative* employs many of the elements most frequently associated with the abolitionist-sponsored fugitive slave narrative form: a title page asserting authorship ("Written by Himself"); prefaces from abolitionist supporters who attest to the truth of the narrative, the understatement of description, and the character of the author; an account of parentage that includes a white father; descriptions of cruelty; a description of a slave who refuses to be beaten (and who, in some ways foreshadows the future resistance of the narrator); reports of various barriers to literacy; the emptiness of slaveholding religion; accounts of auctions; unsuccessful escape attempts; report of the successful escape attempt and the narrator's decision to select a new name reflecting the narrator's new identity; and concluding descriptions of the narrator's abolitionist activities.[4] Brown's rhetorical style in the *Narrative* is consistently spare and direct throughout. As J. C. Hathaway, president of the Western New York Anti-Slavery Society, notes in his preface to the *Narrative*, "Many harrowing scenes are graphically portrayed; and yet with that simplicity and ingenuousness which carries with it a conviction of the truthfulness of the picture." There is in Brown's writing an attempt to use a straightforward, seemingly artless method of address as a way of realistically evoking the experiences of individuals within the broader oppressive realities of the slave system.

Since Brown and Frederick Douglass were part of the same antislavery organizations, were each successful lecturers, and published popular narratives of their experiences as slaves, comparisons between the two are inevitable. Four years after Douglass, Brown followed Douglass's visit to Great Britain. By all accounts, Brown was warmly accepted and highly effective in spreading abroad the message of enslaved African Americans. Brown's supporters purchased his freedom for him as a way of safeguarding his return to the United States in the wake of the Fugitive Slave Act of 1850. After publishing the *Narrative*, Brown published, among a remarkably large and various body of writing, *Clotel; or, The President's Daughter* (1853), which is often identified as the first novel written by an African American; *The Escape; or, A Leap for Freedom: A Drama in Five Acts* (1858); and *The Black Man, His Antecedents, His Genius, and His Achievements* (1863). Like Douglass, Brown's activity and influence continued during and after the Civil War. Brown actively campaigned with other black leaders to allow African Americans to fight in the Civil War and in the years following the war published *The Rising Son; or, The Antecedents and Advancement of the Colored Race* (1873). He continued his work as a lecturer, largely on behalf of the temperance cause; published *My Southern Home, or The South and Its People* (1880); and even practiced as a physician.[5] He died in Boston in 1884.

Narrative of William W. Brown, a Fugitive Slave is reprinted here from the second edition. This edition was initially published in 1848 by the Boston Office of the American Antislavery Society. The first edition of the *Narrative* was published in 1847.

Further Reading

Abramson, Doris M. "William Wells Brown: America's First Negro Playwright." *Educational Theatre Journal* 20 (1968): 370–75; Andrews, William L., ed. *From Fugitive Slave to Free Man: The Autobiographies of William Wells Brown.* New York: Mentor Books, 1993; Andrews, William L. "Mark Twain, William Wells Brown, and the Problem of Authority in New South Writing." In *Southern Literature and Literary Practice*, edited by Jefferson Humphries. Athens: University of Georgia Press, 1990, 1–21; Andrews, William L. *To Tell a Free Story: The First Century of Afro-American Autobiography, 1760–1865.* Urbana: University of Illinois Press, 1986; Andrews, William L., ed. *Two Biographies by African-American Women.* New York: Oxford University Press, 1991; Barbour, James. "Nineteenth Century Black Novelists: A Checklist." *Minority Voices* 3 (1980): 27–43; Brown, William Wells. *The American Fugitive in Europe: Sketches of Places and People Abroad.* New York: Negro Universities Press, 1969; Brown, William Wells. *Clotel; or, The President's Daughter.* Edited by Joan E. Cashin. Armonk, NY: M. E. Sharpe, 1996; Brown, William Wells. *The Rising Son; or, The Antecedents and Advancement of the Colored Race.* New York: Johnson Reprint Corp., 1970; Castronovo, Russ. "Radical Configurations of History in the Era of American Slavery." *American Literature* 65 (September 1993): 523–47; David, Jay, ed. *Black Defiance: Black Profiles in Courage.* New York: Morrow, 1972; Dorsey, Peter A. "De-Authorizing Slavery: Realism in Stowe's *Uncle Tom's Cabin* and Brown's *Clotel*." *ESQ* 41 (1995): 256–88; Emmeluth, Nancy Elizabeth. "William Wells Brown's *My Southern Home* and the African-American Literary Tradition." PhD dissertation, State University of New York at Albany, 1995; Ernest, John. "The Reconstruction of Whiteness: William Wells Brown's *The Escape; or, A Leap for Freedom*." *PMLA* 113 (October 1998): 1108–21; Fabi, M. Giulia. "Representing Slavery in Nineteenth-Century Britain: The Anxiety of Non/Fictional Authorship in Charles Dickens' *American Notes* (1842) and William Wells Brown's *Clotel* (1853)." In *Images of America: Through the European Looking-Glass*, edited by William L. Chew III, 125–40. Brussels, Belgium: VUB University Press, 1997; Fabi, M. Giulia. "The 'Unguarded Expressions of the Feelings of the Negroes': Gender, Slave Resistance, and William Wells Brown's Revisions of *Clotel*." *African American Review* 27 (Winter 1993): 639–54; Farrison, William Edward. "Clotel, Thomas Jefferson, and Sally Hemings." *College Language Association Journal* 17 (December 1973): 147–74; Farrison, William Edward. "The Kidnapped Clergyman and Brown's Experience." *College Language Association Journal* 18 (1975): 507–15; Farrison, William Edward. *William Wells Brown: Author and Reformer.* Chicago: University of Chicago Press, 1969; Gilmore, Paul. "'De Genewine Artekil': William Wells Brown, Blackface Minstrelsy, and

Abolitionism." *American Literature* 69 (December 1997): 743–80; Haskett, Norman D. "Afro-American Images of Africa: Four Antebellum Authors." *Ufahamu* 3 (1972): 29–40; Heermance, J. Noel. *William Wells Brown and Clotelle: A Portrait of the Artist in the First Negro Novel*. Hamden, CT: Archon, 1969; Heller, Murray. "The Names of Slaves and Masters: Real and Fictional." *Literary Onomastics Studies* 6 (1979): 130–48; Levine, Robert S. "'Whiskey, Blacking, and All': Temperance and Race in William Wells Brown's *Clotel*." In *The Serpent in the Cup: Temperance in American Literature*, edited by David S. Reynolds and Debra J. Rosenthal, 93–114. Amherst: University of Massachusetts Press, 1997; Lewis, Richard O. "Irony in the Fiction of William Wells Brown and Charles Waddell Chesnutt." PhD dissertation, State University of New York at Buffalo, 1978; Lewis, Richard O. "Literary Conventions in the Novels of William Wells Brown." *College Language Association Journal* 29 (December 1985): 129–56; MacKethan, Lucinda H. "Huck Finn and the Slave Narratives: Lighting Out as Design." *Southern Review* 20 (Spring 1984): 247–64; MacKethan, Lucinda H. "Metaphors of Mastery in the Slave Narratives." In *The Art of Slave Narrative: Original Essays in Criticism and Theory*, edited by John Sekora and Darwin T. Turner, 55–69. Macomb: Western Illinois University, 1982; Miller, Ruth, and Peter J. Katopes. "Modern Beginnings: William Wells Brown, Charles Waddell Chesnutt, Martin R. Delany, Paul Laurence Dunbar, Sutton E. Griggs, Frances Ellen Watkins Harper, and Frank J. Webb." In *Black American Writers: Bibliographical Essays, I: The Beginnings through the Harlem Renaissance and Langston Hughes*, edited by M. Thomas Inge, Maurice Duke, and Jackson R. Bryer, 133–60. New York: St. Martin's, 1978; Mitchell, Angelyn. "Her Side of His Story: A Feminist Analysis of Two Nineteenth-Century Antebellum Novels—William Wells Brown's *Clotel* and Harriet E. Wilson's *Our Nig*." *American Literary Realism* 24 (Spring 1992): 7–21; Mitchell, Verner D. "To Steal Away Home: Tracing Race, Slavery, and Difference in Selected Writings of Thomas Jefferson, David Walker, William Wells Brown, Ralph Waldo Emerson, and Pauline Elizabeth Hopkins." PhD dissertation, Rutgers University, 1995; Mulvey, Christopher. "The Fugitive Self and the New World of the North: William Wells Brown's Discovery of America." In *The Black Columbiad: Defining Moments in African American Literature and Culture*, edited by Werner Sollors and Maria Diedrich, 99–111. Cambridge, MA: Harvard University Press, 1994; Osofsky, Gilbert. *Puttin' on Ole Massa: The Slave Narratives of Henry Bibb, William Wells Brown, and Solomon Northrup*. New York: Harper and Row, 1969; Rosselot, Gerald S. "*Clotel*, a Black Romance." *College Language Association Journal* 23 (1980): 296–302; Ruff, Loren K. "William Wells Brown: Dramatic Apostle Abolition." *New England Theatre Journal* 2 (1991): 73–83; Sengupta, Ashis. "William Wells Brown's *Clotel*: A Critique of Slave Life in America." In *Indian Views on American Literature*, edited by Desai A. A. Mutalik, 117–25. New Delhi, India: Prestige, 1998; Simson, Rennie. "Christianity: Hypocrisy and Honesty in the Afro-American Novel of the Mid-Nineteenth Century." *University of Dayton Review* 15 (Spring 1982): 11–16; Sloss, Phyllis Ann. "Hierarchy, Irony, and the Thesis of Death in William Wells Brown's *Clotel; or, The President's Daughter*." PhD dissertation, State University of New York at Buffalo, 1976; Sollors, Werner. "A

British Mercenary and American Abolitionists: Literary Retellings from 'Inkle and Yarico' and John Gabriel Stedman to Lydia Maria Child and William Wells Brown." In *(Trans)Formations of Cultural Identity in the English-Speaking World*, edited by Jochen Achilles and Carmen Birkle, 95–123. Heidelberg, Germany: Carl Winter Universitatsverlag, 1998; Warner, Lucille Schulberg. *From Slave to Abolitionist: The Life of William Wells Brown*. New York: Dial Press, 1976.

NARRATIVE
OF
WILLIAM W. BROWN,
A
FUGITIVE SLAVE,

WRITTEN BY HIMSELF

———Is there not some chosen curse,
Some hidden thunder in the stores of heaven,
Red with uncommon wrath, to blast the man
Who gains his fortune from the blood of souls?

Cowper[6]

Second Edition, Enlarged

BOSTON:
PUBLISHED AT THE ANTI-SLAVERY
OFFICE,
No. 21 Cornhill
1848

NOTE TO THE SECOND EDITION

The first edition, of three thousand copies, of this little work was sold in less than six months from the time of its publication. Encouraged by the rapid sale of the first, and by a demand for a second edition, the author has been led to enlarge the work by the addition of matter which, he thinks, will add materially to its value.

And if it shall be instrumental in helping to undo the heavy burdens, and letting the oppressed go free, he will have accomplished the great desire of his heart in publishing this work.

LETTER FROM EDMUND QUINCY, ESQ.[7]

Dedham, July 1, 1847.

To William W. Brown

My Dear Friend:—I heartily thank you for the privilege of reading the manuscript of your Narrative. I have read it with deep interest and strong emotion. I am much mistaken if it be not greatly successful and eminently useful. It presents a different phase of the infernal slave-system from that portrayed in the admirable story of Mr. Douglass[8] and gives us a glimpse of its hideous cruelties in other portions of its domain.

Your opportunities of observing the workings of this accursed system have been singularly great. Your experiences in the Field, in the House, and especially on the River in the service of the slave-trader, Walker, have been such as few individuals have had;—no one, certainly, who has been competent to describe them. What I have admired, and marvelled at, in your Narrative, is the simplicity and calmness with which you describe scenes and actions which might well "move the very stones to rise and mutiny" against the National Institution which makes them possible.

You will perceive that I have made very sparing use of your flattering permission to alter what you had written. To correct a few errors, which appeared to be merely clerical ones, committed in the hurry of composition under unfavorable circumstances, and to suggest a few curtailments, is all that I have ventured to do. I should be a bold man, as well as a vain one, if I should attempt to improve your descriptions of what you have seen and suffered. Some of the scenes are not unworthy of De Foe himself.[9]

I trust and believe that your Narrative will have a wide circulation. I am sure it deserves it. At least, a man must be differently constituted from me, who can rise from the perusal of your Narrative without feeling that he understands slavery better, and hates it worse, than he ever did before.

I am, very faithfully and respectfully,

Your friend,
EDMUND QUINCY

PREFACE

The friends of freedom may well congratulate each other on the appearance of the following Narrative. It adds another volume to the rapidly increasing anti-slavery literature of the age. It has been remarked by a close observer of human nature, "Let me make the songs of a nation, and I care not who makes its laws;" and it may with equal truth be said, that, among a reading people like our own, their books will at least give character to their laws. It is an influence which goes forth noiselessly upon its mission, but fails not to find its way to many a warm heart, to kindle on the altar thereof the fires of freedom, which will one day break forth in a living flame to consume oppression.

This little book is a voice from the prison-house, unfolding the deeds of darkness which are there perpetrated. Our cause has received efficient aid from this source. The names of those who have come from thence, and battled manfully for the right, need not to be recorded here. The works of some of them are an enduring monument of praise, and their perpetual record shall be found in the grateful hearts of the redeemed bondman.

Few persons have had greater facilities for becoming acquainted with slavery, in all its horrible aspects, than WILLIAM W. BROWN. He has been behind the curtain. He has visited its secret chambers. Its iron has entered his own soul. The dearest ties of nature have been riven in his own person. A mother has been cruelly scourged before his own eyes. A father—alas! slaves have no father. A brother has been made the subject of its tender mercies. A sister has been given up to the irresponsible control of the pale-faced oppressor. This nation looks on approvingly. The American Union sanctions the deed. The constitution shields the criminals. American religion sanctifies the crime. But the tide is turning. Already, a mighty under-current is sweeping onward. The voice of warning, of remonstrance, of rebuke, of entreaty, has gone forth. Hand is linked in hand, and heart mingles with heart, in this great work of the slave's deliverance.

The convulsive throes of the monster, even now, give evidence of deep wounds.

The writer of this Narrative was hired by his master to a *"soul-driver,"* and has witnessed all the horrors of the traffic, from the buying up of human cattle in the slave-breeding states, which produced a constant scene of separating the victims from all those whom they loved, to their final sale in the southern market, to be worked up in seven years, or given over to minister to the lust of southern *Christians*.

Many harrowing scenes are graphically portrayed; and yet with that simplicity and ingenuousness which carries with it a conviction of the truthfulness of the picture.

This book will do much to unmask those who have "clothed themselves in the livery of the court of heaven" to cover up the enormity of their deeds.

During the past three years, the author has devoted his entire energies to the anti-slavery cause. Laboring under all the disabilities and disadvantages growing out of his education in slavery—subjected, as he had been from his birth, to all the wrongs and deprivations incident to his condition—he yet went forth, impelled to the work by a love of liberty—stimulated by the remembrance of his own sufferings—urged on by the consideration that a mother, brothers, and sister, were still grinding in the prison-house of bondage, in common with three millions of our Father's children—sustained by an unfaltering faith in the omnipotence of truth and the final triumph of justice—to plead the cause of the slave; and by the eloquence of earnestness carried conviction to many minds, and enlisted the sympathy and secured the cooperation of many to the cause.

His labors have been chiefly confined to Western New York, where he has secured many warm friends, by his untiring zeal, persevering energy, continued fidelity, and universal kindness.

Reader, are you an Abolitionist? What have you done for the slave? What are you doing in his behalf? What do you purpose to do? There is a great work before us! Who will be an idler now? This is the great humanity movement of the age, swallowing up, for the time being, all other questions, comparatively speaking. The course of human events, in obedience to the unchangeable laws of our being, is fast hastening the final crisis, and

> "Have ye chosen, O my people, on whose party ye shall stand,
> Ere the Doom from its worn sandal shakes the dust against our land?"

Are you a Christian? This is the carrying out of practical Christianity; and there is no other. Christianity is *practical* in its very nature and essence. It is a life, springing out of a soul imbued with its spirit. Are you a friend of the missionary cause? This is the greatest missionary enterprise of the day. Three millions of *Christian*, law-manufactured heathen are longing for the glad tidings of the gospel of freedom. Are you a friend of the Bible? Come, then, and help us to restore to these millions, whose eyes have been bored out by slavery, their sight, that they may see or read the Bible. Do you love God whom you have not seen? Then manifest that love, by restoring to your brother whom you have seen his rightful inheritance, of which he has been so long and so cruelly deprived.

It is not for a single generation alone, numbering three millions—sublime as would be that effort—that we are working. It is for Humanity, the wide world over, not only now, but for all coming time, and all future generations:

> "For he who settles Freedom's principles,
> Writes the death-warrant of all tyranny."

It is a vast work—a glorious enterprise—worthy the unswerving devotion of the entire life-time of the great and the good.

Slaveholding and slaveholders must be rendered disreputable and odious. They must be stripped of their respectability and Christian reputation. They must be treated as "MEN-STEALERS—guilty of the highest kind of theft, and sinners of the first rank." Their more guilty accomplices in the persons of *northern apologists*, both in Church and State, must be placed in the same category. Honest men must be made to look upon their crimes with the same abhorrence and loathing with which they regard the less guilty robber and assassin, until

> "The common damned shun their society,
> And look upon themselves as fiends less foul."

When a just estimate is placed upon the crime of slave-holding, the work will have been accomplished, and the glorious day ushered in—

> "When man nor woman in all our wide domain,
> Shall buy, or sell, or hold, or be a slave."

J. C. HATHAWAY

Farmington, N.Y., 1847.

CHAPTER 1

I was born in Lexington, Ky. The man who stole me as soon as I was born, recorded the births of all the infants which he claimed to be born his property, in a book which he kept for that purpose. My mother's name was Elizabeth. She had seven children, viz.: Solomon, Leander, Benjamin, Joseph, Millford, Elizabeth, and myself. No two of us were children of the same father. My father's name, as I learned from my mother, was George Higgins. He was a white man, a relative of my master, and connected with some of the first families in Kentucky.

My master owned about forty slaves, twenty-five of whom were field hands. He removed from Kentucky to Missouri when I was quite young, and settled thirty or forty miles above St. Charles, on the Missouri, where, in addition to his practice as a physician, he carried on milling, merchandizing and farming. He had a large farm, the principal productions of which were tobacco and hemp. The slave cabins were situated on the back part of the farm, with the house of the overseer, whose name was Grove Cook, in their midst. He had the entire charge of the farm, and having no family, was allowed a woman to keep house for him, whose business it was to deal out the provisions for the hands.

A woman was also kept at the quarters to do the cooking for the field hands, who were summoned to their unrequited toil every morning at four o'clock, by the ringing of a bell, hung on a post near the house of the overseer. They were allowed half an hour to eat their breakfast, and get to the field. At half past four a horn was blown by the overseer, which was his signal to commence work; and every one that was not on the spot at the time, had to receive ten lashes from the negro-whip, with which the overseer always went armed. The handle was about three feet long, with the butt-end filled with lead, and the lash, six or seven feet in length, made of cow-hide, with platted wire on the end of it. This whip was put in requisition very frequently and freely, and a small offence on the part of a slave furnished an occasion for its use. During the time that Mr. Cook was overseer, I was a house servant—a situation preferable to that of a field hand, as I was better fed, better clothed, and not obliged to rise at the ringing of the bell, but about half an hour after. I have often laid and heard the crack of the whip, and the screams of the slave. My mother was a field hand, and one morning was ten or fifteen minutes behind the others in getting into the field. As soon as she reached the spot where they were at work, the overseer commenced whipping her. She cried, "Oh! pray—Oh! pray—Oh! pray"—these are generally the words of slaves, when imploring mercy at the hands of their oppressors. I heard her voice, and knew it, and jumped out of my bunk, and went to the door. Though the field was some distance from the house I could hear every crack of the whip, and every groan and cry of my poor mother. I remained at the door, not daring to venture any further. The cold chills ran over me, and I wept aloud. After giving her ten lashes, the sound of the whip ceased, and I returned to my bed, and found no consolation but in my tears. Experience has taught me that nothing can be more heart-rending than for one to see a dear and beloved mother or sister tortured, and to hear their cries, and not be able to render them assistance. But such is the position which an American slave occupies.

My master, being a politician, soon found those who were ready to put him into office, for the favors he could render them; and a few years after his arrival in Missouri he was elected to a seat in the legislature. In his absence from home everything was left in charge of Mr. Cook, the overseer, and he soon became more tyrannical and cruel. Among the slaves on the plantation was one by the name of Randall. He was a man about six feet high, and well-proportioned, and known as a man of great strength and power. He was considered the most valuable and able-bodied slave on the plantation; but no matter how good or useful a slave may be, he seldom escapes the lash. But it was not so with Randall. He had been on the plantation since my earliest recollection, and I had never known of his being flogged. No thanks were due to the master or overseer for this. I have often heard him declare that no white man should ever whip him—that he would die first.

Cook, from the time that he came upon the plantation, had frequently declared that he could and would flog any nigger that was put into the field to work under him. My master had repeatedly told him not to attempt to whip Randall, but he was determined to try it. As soon as he was left sole dictator, he thought the time had come to put his threats into execution. He soon began to find fault with Randall, and threatened to whip him if he did not do better. One day he gave him a very hard task—more than he could possibly do; and at night, the task not being performed, he told Randall that he should remember him the next morning. On the following morning, after the hands had taken breakfast, Cook called out to Randall, and told him that he intended to whip him, and ordered him to cross his hands and be tied. Randall asked why he wished to whip him. He answered, because he had not finished his task the day before. Randall said that the task was too great, or he should have done it. Cook said it made no difference—he should whip him. Randall stood silent for a moment, and then said, "Mr. Cook, I have always tried to please you since you have been on the plantation, and I find you are determined not to be satisfied with my work, let me do as well as I may. No man has laid hands on me, to whip me, for the last ten years, and I have long since come to the conclusion not to be whipped by any man living." Cook, finding by Randall's determined look and gestures, that he would resist, called three of the hands from their work, and commanded them to seize Randall, and tie him. The hands stood still;—they knew Randall—and they also knew him to be a powerful man, and were afraid to grapple with him. As soon as Cook had ordered the men to seize him, Randall turned to them, and said—"Boys, you all know me; you know that I can handle any three of you, and the man that lays hands on me shall die. This white man can't whip me himself, and therefore he has called you to help him." The overseer was unable to prevail upon them to seize and secure Randall, and finally ordered them all to go to their work together.

    Nothing was said to Randall by the overseer for more than a week. One morning, however, while the hands were at work in the field, he came into it, accompanied by three friends of his, Thompson, Woodbridge and Jones. They came up to where Randall was at work, and Cook ordered him to leave his work, and go with them to the barn. He refused to go; whereupon he was attacked by the overseer and his companions, when he turned upon them, and laid them, one after another, prostrate on the ground. Woodbridge drew out his pistol, and fired at him, and brought him to the ground by a pistol ball. The others rushed upon him with their clubs, and beat him over the head and face, until they succeeded in tying him. He was then taken to the barn, and tied to a beam. Cook gave him over one hundred lashes with a heavy cowhide, had him washed with salt and water, and left him tied during the day. The next day he was untied, and taken to a blacksmith's shop, and had a ball and chain attached to his leg. He was compelled to labor in the field, and perform the same amount of work that the other hands did. When his master returned home, he was much pleased to find that Randall had been subdued in his absence.

CHAPTER II

Soon afterwards, my master removed to the city of St. Louis, and purchased a farm four miles from there, which he placed under the charge of an overseer by the name of Friend Haskell. He was a regular Yankee from New England. The Yankees are noted for making the most cruel overseers.

My mother was hired out in the city, and I was also hired out there to Major Freeland, who kept a public house. He was formerly from Virginia, and was a horse-racer, cock-fighter, gambler, and withal an inveterate drunkard. There were ten or twelve servants in the house, and when he was present, it was cut and slash—knock down and drag out. In his fits of anger, he would take up a chair, and throw it at a servant; and in his more rational moments, when he wished to chastise one, he would tie them up in the smoke-house, and whip them; after which, he would cause a fire to be made of tobacco stems, and smoke them. This he called *"Virginia play."*

I complained to my master of the treatment which I received from Major Freeland; but it made no difference. He cared nothing about it, so long as he received the money for my labor. After living with Major Freeland five or six months, I ran away, and went into the woods back of the city; and when night came on, I made my way to my master's farm, but was afraid to be seen, knowing that if Mr. Haskell, the overseer, should discover me, I should be again carried back to Major Freeland; so I kept in the woods. One day, while in the woods, I heard the barking and howling of dogs, and in a short time they came so near that I knew them to be the bloodhounds of Major Benjamin O'Fallon. He kept five or six, to hunt runaway slaves with.

As soon as I was convinced that it was them, I knew there was no chance of escape. I took refuge in the top of a tree, and the hounds were soon at its base, and there remained until the hunters came up in a half or three quarters of an hour afterwards. There were two men with the dogs, who, as soon as they came up, ordered me to descend. I came down, was tied, and taken to St. Louis jail. Major Freeland soon made his appearance, and took me out, and ordered me to follow him, which I did. After we returned home, I was tied up in the smoke-house, and was very severely whipped. After the major had flogged me to his satisfaction, he sent out his son Robert, a young man eighteen or twenty years of age, to see that I was well smoked. He made a fire of tobacco stems, which soon set me to coughing and sneezing. This, Robert told me, was the way his father used to do to his slaves in Virginia. After giving me what they conceived to be a decent smoking, I was untied and again set to work.

Robert Freeland was a "chip of the old block." Though quite young, it was not unfrequently that he came home in a state of intoxication. He is now, I believe, a popular commander of a steamboat on the Mississippi river. Major Freeland soon after failed in business, and I was put on board the steamboat Missouri, which plied between St. Louis and Galena. The commander of the boat was William B. Culver.

I remained on her during the sailing season, which was the most pleasant time for me that I had ever experienced. At the close of navigation I was hired to Mr. John Colburn, keeper of the Missouri Hotel. He was from one of the free states; but a more inveterate hater of the negro I do not believe ever walked God's green earth. This hotel was at that time one of the largest in the city, and there were employed in it twenty or thirty servants, mostly slaves.

Mr. Colburn was very abusive, not only to the servants, but to his wife also, who was an excellent woman, and one from whom I never knew a servant to receive a harsh word; but never did I know a kind one to a servant from her husband. Among the slaves employed in the hotel was one by the name of Aaron, who belonged to Mr. John F. Darby, a lawyer. Aaron was the knife-cleaner. One day, one of the knives was put on the table, not as clean as it might have been. Mr. Colburn, for this offence, tied Aaron up in the wood-house, and gave him over fifty lashes on the bare back with a cow-hide, after which, he made me wash him down with rum. This seemed to put him into more agony than the whipping. After being untied he went home to his master, and complained of the treatment which he had received. Mr. Darby would give no heed to anything he had to say, but sent him directly back. Colburn, learning that he had been to his master with complaints, tied him up again, and gave him a more severe whipping than before. The poor fellow's back was literally cut to pieces; so much so, that he was not able to work for ten or twelve days.

There was, also, among the servants, a girl whose master resided in the country. Her name was Patsey. Mr. Colburn tied her up one evening, and whipped her until several of the boarders came out and begged him to desist. The reason for whipping her was this. She was engaged to be married to a man belonging to Major William Christy, who resided four or five miles north of the city. Mr. Colburn had forbid her to see John Christy. The reason of this was said to be the regard which he himself had for Patsey. She went to meeting that evening, and John returned home with her. Mr. Colburn had intended to flog John, if he came within the inclosure; but John knew too well the temper of his rival, and kept at a safe distance:—so he took vengeance on the poor girl. If all the slave-drivers had been called together, I do not think a more cruel man than John Colburn—and he too a northern man—could have been found among them.

While living at the Missouri hotel, a circumstance occurred which caused me great unhappiness. My master sold my mother, and all her children, except myself. They were sold to different persons in the city of St. Louis.

CHAPTER III

I was soon after taken from Mr. Colburn's, and hired to Elijah P. Lovejoy,[10] who was at that time publisher and editor of the "St. Louis Times." My work, while with him, was mainly in the printing office, waiting on the hands, working the press, &c. Mr. Lovejoy was a very good man, and decidedly the best master that I had ever had. I am chiefly indebted to him, and to my employment in the printing office, for what little learning I obtained while in slavery.

Though slavery is thought, by some, to be mild in Missouri, when compared with the cotton, sugar and rice growing states, yet no part of our slaveholding country is more noted for the barbarity of its inhabitants than St. Louis. It was here that Col. Harney, a United States officer, whipped a slave woman to death. It was here that Francis McIntosh, a free colored man from Pittsburg, was taken from the steamboat Flora and burned at the stake. During a residence of eight years in this city, numerous cases of extreme cruelty came under my own observation; to record them all would occupy more space than could possibly be allowed in this little volume. I shall, therefore, give but a few more in addition to what I have already related.

Capt. J. B. Brant, who resided near my master, had a slave named John. He was his body servant, carriage driver, &c. On one occasion, while driving his master through the city—the streets being very muddy, and the horses going at a rapid rate—some mud spattered upon a gentleman by the name of Robert More. More was determined to be revenged. Some three or four months after this occurrence, he purchased John, for the express purpose, as he said, "to tame the d———d nigger." After the purchase he took him to a blacksmith's shop, and had a ball and chain fastened to his leg, and then put him to driving a yoke of oxen, and kept him at hard labor, until the iron around his leg was so worn into the flesh, that it was thought mortification would ensue. In addition to this, John told me that his master whipped him regularly three times a week for the first two months:—and all this to "*tame him*." A more noble looking man than he was not to be found in all St. Louis, before he fell into the hands of More; and a more degraded and spirit-crushed looking being was never seen on a southern plantation, after he had been subjected to this "*taming*" process for three months. The last time that I saw him, he had nearly lost the entire use of his limbs.

While living with Mr. Lovejoy, I was often sent on errands to the office of the "Missouri Republican," published by Mr. Edward Charles. Once, while returning to the office with type, I was attacked by several large boys, sons of slave-holders, who pelted me with snow-balls. Having the heavy form of type in my hands, I could not make my escape by running; so I laid down the type and gave them battle. They gathered around me, pelting me with stones and sticks, until they overpowered me, and would have captured me, if I had not resorted to my heels. Upon my retreat they took possession of the type; and what to do to regain it I could not devise. Knowing Mr. Lovejoy to be a very humane man, I went to the office and laid the case before him. He told me to remain in the office. He took one of the apprentices with him and went after the type, and soon returned with it; but on his return informed me that Samuel McKinney had told him he would whip me, because I had hurt his boy. Soon after, McKinney was seen making his way to the office by one of the printers, who informed me of the fact, and I made my escape through the back door.

McKinney not being able to find me on his arrival, left the office in a great rage, swearing that he would whip me to death. A few days after, as I was walking along Main street, he seized me by the collar, and struck me over the head five or six times with a large cane, which caused the blood to gush from my nose and ears in such a manner that my clothes were completely saturated with blood. After beating me to his satisfaction he let me go, and I returned to the office so weak from the loss of blood that Mr. Lovejoy sent me home to my master. It was five weeks before I was able to walk again. During this time it was necessary to have some one to supply my place at the office, and I lost the situation.

After my recovery, I was hired to Capt. Otis Reynolds, as a waiter on board the steamboat Enterprise, owned by Messrs. John and Edward Walsh, commission merchants at St. Louis. This boat was then running on the upper Mississippi. My employment on board was to wait on gentlemen, and the captain being a good man, the situation was a pleasant one to me;—but in passing from place to place, and seeing new faces every day, and knowing that they could go where they pleased, I soon became unhappy, and several times thought of leaving the boat at some landing-place, and trying to make my escape to Canada, which I had heard much about as a place where the slave might live, be free, and be protected.

But whenever such thoughts would come into my mind, my resolution would soon be shaken by the remembrance that my dear mother was a slave in St. Louis, and I could not bear the idea of leaving her in that condition. She had often taken me upon her knee, and told me how she had carried me upon her back to the field when I was an infant—how often she had been whipped for leaving her work to nurse me—and how happy I would appear when she would take me into her arms. When these thoughts came over me, I would resolve never to leave the land of slavery without my mother. I thought that to leave her in slavery, after she had undergone and suffered so much for me, would be proving recreant to the duty which I owed to her. Besides this, I had three brothers and a sister there—two of my brothers having died.

My mother, my brothers Joseph and Millford, and my sister Elizabeth, belonged to Mr. Isaac Mansfield, formerly from one of the free states, (Massachusetts, I believe.) He was a tinner by trade, and carried on a large manufacturing establishment. Of all my relatives, mother was first, and sister next. One evening, while visiting them, I made some allusion to a proposed journey to Canada, and sister took her seat by my side, and taking my hand in hers, said, with tears in her eyes—

"Brother, you are not going to leave mother and your dear sister here without a friend, are you?"

I looked into her face, as the tears coursed swiftly down her cheeks, and bursting into tears myself, said—

"No, I will never desert you and mother!"

She clasped my hand in hers, and said—

"Brother, you have often declared that you would not end your days in slavery. I see no possible way in which you can escape with us; and now, brother, you are on a steamboat where there is some chance for you to escape to a land of liberty. I beseech you not to let us hinder you. If we cannot get our liberty, we do not wish to be the means of keeping you from a land of freedom."

I could restrain my feelings no longer, and an outburst of my own feelings caused her to cease speaking upon that subject. In opposition to their wishes, I pledged myself not to leave them in the hand of the oppressor. I took leave of them, and returned to the boat, and laid down in my bunk; but "sleep departed from mine eyes, and slumber from mine eyelids."[11]

A few weeks after, on our downward passage, the boat took on board, at Hannibal, a drove of slaves, bound for the New Orleans market. They numbered from fifty to sixty, consisting of men and women from eighteen to forty years of age. A drove of slaves on a southern steamboat, bound for the cotton or sugar regions, is an occurrence so common, that no one, not even the passengers, appear to notice it, though they clank their chains at every step. There was, however, one in this gang that attracted the attention of the passengers and crew. It was a beautiful girl, apparently about twenty years of age, perfectly white, with straight light hair and blue eyes. But it was not the whiteness of her skin that created such sensation among those who gazed upon her—it was her almost unparalleled beauty. She had been on the boat but a short time, before the attention of all the passengers, including the ladies, had been called to her, and the common topic of conversation was about the beautiful slave-girl. She was not in chains. The man who claimed this article of human merchandise was a Mr. Walker—a well known slave-trader, residing in St. Louis. There was a general anxiety among the passengers and crew to learn the history of the girl. Her master kept close by her side, and it would have been considered impudent for any of the passengers to have spoken to her, and the crew were not allowed to have any conversation with them. When we reached St. Louis, the slaves were removed to a boat bound for New Orleans, and the history of the beautiful slave-girl remained a mystery.

I remained on the boat during the season, and it was not an unfrequent occurrence to have on board gangs of slaves on their way to the cotton, sugar and rice plantations of the south.

Toward the latter part of the summer Captain Reynolds left the boat, and I was sent home. I was then placed on the farm, under Mr. Haskell, the overseer. As I had been some time out of the field, and not accustomed to work in the burning sun, it was very hard; but I was compelled to keep up with the best of the hands.

I found a great difference between the work in the steamboat cabin and that in a corn-field.

My master, who was then living in the city, soon after removed to the farm, when I was taken out of the field to work in the house as a waiter. Though his wife was very peevish, and hard to please, I much preferred to be under her control than the overseer's. They brought with them Mr. Sloane, a Presbyterian minister; Miss Martha Tulley, a niece of theirs from Kentucky; and their nephew William. The latter had been in the family a number of years, but the others were all newcomers.

Mr. Sloane was a young minister, who had been at the south but a short time, and it seemed as if his whole aim was to please the slaveholders, especially my master and mistress. He was intending to make a visit during the winter, and he not only tried to please them, but I think he succeeded admirably. When they wanted singing, he sung; when they wanted praying, he prayed; when they wanted a story told, he told a story. Instead of his teaching my master theology, my master taught theology to him. While I was with Captain Reynolds my master "got religion," and new laws were made on the plantation. Formerly we had the privilege of hunting, fishing, making splint brooms, baskets, &c., on Sunday; but this was all stopped. Every Sunday we were all compelled to attend meeting. Master was so religious that he induced some others to join him in hiring a preacher to preach to the slaves.

CHAPTER IV

My master had family worship, night and morning. At night the slaves were called in to attend; but in the mornings they had to be at their work, and master did all the praying. My master and mistress were great lovers of mint julep,[12] and every morning, a pitcher-full was made, of which they all partook freely, not excepting little master William. After drinking freely all round, they would have family worship, and then breakfast. I cannot say but I loved the julep as well as any of them, and during prayer was always careful to seat myself close to the table where it stood, so as to help myself when they were all busily engaged in their devotions. By the time prayer was over, I was about as happy as any of them. A sad accident happened one morning. In helping myself, and at the same time keeping an eye on my old mistress, I accidentally let the pitcher fall upon the floor, breaking it in pieces, and spilling the contents. This was a bad affair for me; for as soon as prayer was over, I was taken and severely chastised.

My master's family consisted of himself, his wife, and their nephew, William Moore. He was taken into the family when only a few weeks of age. His name being that of my own, mine was changed for the purpose of giving precedence to his, though I was his senior by ten or twelve years. The plantation being four miles from the city, I had to drive the family to church. I always dreaded the approach of the Sabbath; for, during service, I was obliged to stand by the horses in the hot, broiling sun, or in the rain, just as it happened.

One Sabbath, as we were driving past the house of D. D. Page, a gentleman who owned a large baking establishment, as I was sitting upon the box of the carriage, which was very much elevated, I saw Mr. Page pursuing a slave around the yard with a long whip, cutting him at every jump. The man soon escaped from the yard, and was followed by Mr. Page. They came running past us, and the slave, perceiving that he would be overtaken, stopped suddenly, and Page stumbled over him, and falling on the stone pavement, fractured one of his legs, which crippled him for life. The same gentleman, but a short time previous, tied up a woman of his, by the name of Delphia, and whipped her nearly to death; yet he was a deacon in the Baptist church, in good and regular standing. Poor Delphia! I was well acquainted with her, and called to see her while upon her sick bed; and I shall never forget her appearance. She was a member of the same church with her master.

Soon after this, I was hired out to Mr. Walker, the same man whom I have mentioned as having carried a gang of slaves down the river on the steamboat Enterprise. Seeing me in the capacity of a steward on the boat, and thinking that I would make a good hand to take care of slaves, he determined to have me for that purpose; and finding that my master would not sell me, he hired me for the term of one year.

When I learned the fact of my having been hired to a negro speculator, or a "soul driver," as they are generally called among slaves, no one can tell my emotions. Mr. Walker had offered a high price for me, as I afterwards learned, but I suppose my master was restrained from selling me by the fact that I was a near relative of his. On entering the service of Mr. Walker, I found that my opportunity of getting to a land of liberty was gone, at least for the time being. He had a gang of slaves in readiness to start for New Orleans, and in a few days we were on our journey. I am at a loss for language to express my feelings on that occasion. Although my master had told me that he had not sold me, and Mr. Walker had told me that he had not purchased me, I did not believe them; and not until I had been to New Orleans, and was on my return, did I believe that I was not sold.

There was on the boat a large room on the lower deck, in which the slaves were kept, men and women, promiscuously[13]—all chained two and two, and a strict watch kept that they did not get loose; for cases have occurred in which slaves have got off their chains, and made their escape at landing-places, while the boats were taking in wood;—and with all our care, we lost one woman who had been taken from her husband and children, and having no desire to live without them, in the agony of her soul jumped overboard, and drowned herself. She was not chained.

It was almost impossible to keep that part of the boat clean.

On landing at Natchez, the slaves were all carried to the slave-pen, and there kept one week, during which time several of them were sold. Mr. Walker fed his slaves well. We took on board at St. Louis several hundred pounds of bacon (smoked meat) and corn-meal, and his slaves were better fed than slaves generally were in Natchez, so far as my observation extended.

At the end of a week, we left for New Orleans, the place of our final destination, which we reached in two days. Here the slaves were placed in a negro-pen, where those who wished to purchase could call and examine them. The negro-pen is a small yard, surrounded by buildings, from fifteen to twenty feet wide, with the exception of a large gate with iron bars. The slaves are kept in the building during the night, and turned out into the yard during the day. After the best of the stock was sold at private sale at the pen, the balance were taken to the Exchange Coffee-House Auction Rooms, kept by Isaac L. McCoy, and sold at public auction. After the sale of this lot of slaves, we left New Orleans for St. Louis.

CHAPTER V

On our arrival at St. Louis I went to Dr. Young, and told him that I did not wish to live with Mr. Walker any longer. I was heart-sick at seeing my fellow-creatures bought and sold. But the Dr. had hired me for the year, and stay I must. Mr. Walker again commenced purchasing another gang of slaves. He bought a man of Colonel John O'Fallon, who resided in the suburbs of the city. This man had a wife and three children. As soon as the purchase was made, he was put in jail for safe keeping, until we should be ready to start for New Orleans. His wife visited him while there, several times, and several times when she went for that purpose was refused admittance.

In the course of eight or nine weeks Mr. Walker had his cargo of human flesh made up. There was in this lot a number of old men and women, some of them with gray locks. We left St. Louis in the steamboat Carlton, Captain Swan, bound for New Orleans. On our way down, and before we reached Rodney, the place where we made our first stop, I had to prepare the old slaves for market. I was ordered to have the old men's whiskers shaved off, and the grey hairs plucked out where they were not too numerous, in which case he had a preparation of blacking to color it, and with a blacking brush we would put it on. This was new business to me, and was performed in a room where the passengers could not see us. These slaves were also taught how old they were by Mr. Walker, and after going through the blacking process they looked ten or fifteen years younger; and I am sure that some of those who purchased slaves of Mr. Walker were dreadfully cheated, especially in the ages of the slaves which they bought.

We landed at Rodney, and the slaves were driven to the pen in the back part of the village. Several were sold at this place, during our stay of four or five days, when we proceeded to Natchez. There we landed at night, and the gang were put in the warehouse until morning, when they were driven to the pen. As soon as the slaves are put in these pens, swarms of planters may be seen in and about them. They knew when Walker was expected, as he always had the time advertised beforehand when he would be in Rodney, Natchez, and New Orleans. These were the principal places where he offered his slaves for sale.

When at Natchez the second time, I saw a slave very cruelly whipped. He belonged to a Mr. Broadwell, a merchant who kept a store on the wharf. The slave's name was Lewis. I had known him several years, as he was formerly from St. Louis. We were expecting a steamboat down the river, in which we were to take passage for New Orleans. Mr. Walker sent me to the landing to watch for the boat, ordering me to inform him on its arrival. While there I went into the store to see Lewis. I saw a slave in the store, and asked him where Lewis was. Said he, "They have got Lewis hanging between the heavens and the earth." I asked him what he meant by that. He told me to go into the warehouse and see. I went in, and found Lewis there. He was tied up to a beam, with his toes just touching the floor. As there was no one in the warehouse but himself, I inquired the reason of his being in that situation. He said Mr. Broadwell had sold his wife to a planter six miles from the city, and that he had been to visit her—that he went in the night, expecting to return before daylight, and went without his master's permission. The patrol had taken him up before he reached his wife. He was put in jail, and his master had to pay for his catching and keeping, and that was what he was tied up for.

Just as he finished his story, Mr. Broadwell came in, and inquired what I was doing there. I knew not what to say, and while I was thinking what reply to make he struck me over the head with the cowhide, the end of which struck me over my right eye, sinking deep into the flesh, leaving a scar which I carry to this day. Before I visited Lewis he had received fifty lashes. Mr. Broadwell gave him fifty lashes more after I came out, as I was afterwards informed by Lewis himself.

The next day we proceeded to New Orleans, and put the gang in the same negro-pen which we occupied before. In a short time the planters came flocking to the pen to purchase slaves. Before the slaves were exhibited for sale, they were dressed and driven out into the yard. Some were set to dancing, some to jumping, some to singing, and some to playing cards. This was done to make them appear cheerful and happy. My business was to see that they were placed in those situations before the arrival of the purchasers, and I have often set them to dancing when their cheeks were wet with tears. As slaves were in good demand at that time, they were all soon disposed of, and we again set out for St. Louis.

On our arrival, Mr. Walker purchased a farm five or six miles from the city. He had no family, but made a housekeeper of one of his female slaves. Poor Cynthia! I knew her well. She was a quadroon, and one of the most beautiful women I ever saw. She was a native of St. Louis, and bore an irreproachable character for virtue and propriety of conduct. Mr. Walker bought her for the New Orleans market, and took her down with him on one of the trips that I made with him. Never shall I forget the circumstances of that voyage! On the first night that we were on board the steamboat, he directed me to put her into a state-room he had provided for her, apart from the other slaves. I had seen too much of the workings of slavery not to know what this meant. I accordingly watched him into the state-room, and listened to hear what passed between them. I heard him make his base offers, and her reject them. He told her that if she would accept his vile proposals, he would take her back with him to St. Louis, and establish her as his housekeeper on his farm. But if she persisted in rejecting them, he would sell her as a field hand on the worst plantation on the river. Neither threats nor bribes prevailed, however, and he retired, disappointed of his prey.

The next morning poor Cynthia told me what had passed, and bewailed her sad fate with floods of tears. I comforted and encouraged her all I could; but I foresaw but too well what the result must be. Without entering into any further particulars, suffice it to say that Walker performed his part of the contract at that time. He took her back to St. Louis, established her as his mistress and housekeeper at his farm, and before I left, he had two children by her. But, mark the end! Since I have been at the North, I have been credibly informed that Walker has been married, and, as a previous measure, sold poor Cynthia and her four children (she having had two more since I came away) into hopeless bondage!

He soon commenced purchasing to make up the third gang. We took steamboat, and went to Jefferson City, a town on the Missouri river. Here we landed, and took stage for the interior of the state. He bought a number of slaves as he passed the different farms and villages. After getting twenty-two or twenty-three men and women, we arrived at St. Charles, a village on the banks of the Missouri. Here he purchased a woman who had a child in her arms, appearing to be four or five weeks old.

We had been travelling by land for some days, and were in hopes to have found a boat at this place for St. Louis, but were disappointed. As no boat was expected for some days, we started for St. Louis by land. Mr. Walker had purchased two horses. He rode one, and I the other. The slaves were chained together, and we took up our line of march, Mr. Walker taking the lead, and I bringing up the rear. Though the distance was not more than twenty miles, we did not reach it the first day. The road was worse than any that I have ever travelled.

Soon after we left St. Charles the young child grew very cross, and kept up a noise during the greater part of the day. Mr. Walker complained of its crying several times, and told the mother to stop the child's d——d noise, or he would. The woman tried to keep the child from crying, but could not. We put up at night with an acquaintance of Mr. Walker, and in the morning, just as we were about to start, the child again commenced crying. Walker stepped up to her, and told her to give the child to him. The mother tremblingly obeyed. He took the child by one arm, as you would a cat by the leg, walked into the house, and said to the lady:

"Madam, I will make you a present of this little nigger; it keeps such a noise that I can't bear it."

"Thank you, sir," said the lady.

The mother, as soon as she saw that her child was to be left, ran up to Mr. Walker, and falling upon her knees, begged him to let her have her child: she clung around his legs, and cried, "Oh, my child! my child! master, do let me have my child! oh, do, do, do! I will stop its crying if you will only let me have it again." When I saw this woman crying for her child so piteously, a shudder—a feeling akin to horror—shot through my frame. I have often since in imagination heard her crying for her child:—

> "O, master, let me stay to catch
> My baby's sobbing breath,
> His little glassy eye to watch,
> And smooth his limbs in death,
>
> And cover him with grass and leaf,
> Beneath the large oak tree:
> It is not sullenness, but grief—
> O, master, pity me!
>
> The morn was chill—I spoke no word,
> But feared my babe might die,
> And heard all day, or thought I heard,
> My little baby cry.
>
> At noon, oh, how I ran and took
> My baby to my breast!
> I lingered—and the long lash broke
> My sleeping infant's rest.
>
> I worked till night—till darkest night,
> In torture and disgrace;
> Went home and watched till morning light,
> To see my baby's face.
>
> Then give me but one little hour—
> O! do not lash me so!
> One little hour—one little hour—
> And gratefully I'll go."

Mr. Walker commanded her to return into the ranks with the other slaves. Women who had children were not chained, but those that had none were. As soon as her child was disposed of she was chained in the gang.

The following song I have often heard the slaves sing, when about to be carried to the far south. It is said to have been composed by a slave.

"See these poor souls from Africa
Transported to America;
We are stolen, and sold to Georgia—
Will you go along with me?
We are stolen, and sold to Georgia—
Come sound the jubilee!

See wives and husbands sold apart,
Their children's screams will break my heart;—
There's a better day a coming—
Will you go along with me?
There's a better day a coming,
Go sound the jubilee!

O, gracious Lord! when shall it be,
That we poor souls shall all be free?
Lord, break them slavery powers—
Will you go along with me?
Lord, break them slavery powers,
Go sound the jubilee!

Dear Lord, dear Lord, when slavery 'll cease,
Then we poor souls will have our peace;—
There's a better day a coming—
Will you go along with me?
There's a better day a coming,
Go sound the jubilee!"

We finally arrived at Mr. Walker's farm. He had a house built during our absence to put slaves in. It was a kind of domestic jail. The slaves were put in the jail at night, and worked on the farm during the day. They were kept here until the gang was completed, when we again started for New Orleans, on board the steamboat North America, Capt. Alexander Scott. We had a large number of slaves in this gang. One, by the name of Joe, Mr. Walker was training up to take my place, as my time was nearly out, and glad was I. We made our first stop at Vicksburg, where we remained one week and sold several slaves.

Mr. Walker, though not a good master, had not flogged a slave since I had been with him, though he had threatened me. The slaves were kept in the pen, and he always put up at the best hotel, and kept his wines in his room, for the accommodation of those who called to negotiate with him for the purchase of slaves.

One day, while we were at Vicksburg, several gentlemen came to see him for that purpose, and as usual the wine was called for. I took the tray and started around with it, and having accidentally filled some of the glasses too full, the gentlemen spilled the wine on their clothes as they went to drink. Mr. Walker apologized to them for my carelessness, but looked at me as though he would see me again on this subject.

After the gentlemen had left the room, he asked me what I meant by my carelessness, and said that he would attend to me. The next morning he gave me a note to carry to the jailer, and a dollar in money to give to him. I suspected that all was not right, so I went down near the landing, where I met with a sailor, and, walking up to him, asked him if he would be so kind as to read the note for me. He read it over, and then looked at me. I asked him to tell me what was in it. Said he,

"They are going to give you hell."

"Why?" said I.

He said, "This is a note to have you whipped, and says that you have a dollar to pay for it."

He handed me back the note, and off I started. I knew not what to do, but was determined not to be whipped. I went up to the jail—took a look at it, and walked off again. As Mr. Walker was acquainted with the jailer, I feared that I should be found out if I did not go, and be treated in consequence of it still worse.

While I was meditating on the subject, I saw a colored man about my size walk up, and the thought struck me in a moment to send him with my note. I walked up to him, and asked him who he belonged to. He said he was a free man, and had been in the city but a short time. I told him I had a note to go into the jail, and get a trunk to carry to one of the steamboats; but was so busily engaged that I could not do it, although I had a dollar to pay for it. He asked me if I would not give him the job. I handed him the note and the dollar, and off he started for the jail.

I watched to see that he went in, and as soon as I saw the door close behind him, I walked around the corner, and took my station, intending to see how my friend looked when he came out. I had been there but a short time, when a colored man came around the corner, and said to another colored man with whom he was acquainted—

"They are giving a nigger scissors in the jail."

"What for?" said the other. The man continued,

"A nigger came into the jail, and asked for the jailer. The jailer came out, and he handed him a note, and said he wanted to get a trunk. The jailer told him to go with him, and he would give him the trunk. So he took him into the room, and told the nigger to give up the dollar. He said a man had given him the dollar to pay for getting the trunk. But that lie would not answer. So they made him strip himself, and then they tied him down, and are now whipping him."

I stood by all the while listening to their talk, and soon found out that the person alluded to was my customer. I went into the street opposite the jail, and concealed myself in such a manner that I could not be seen by any one coming out. I had been there but a short time, when the young man made his appearance, and looked around for me. I, unobserved, came forth from my hiding place, behind a pile of brick, and he pretty soon saw me, and came up to me complaining bitterly, saying that I had played a trick upon him. I denied any knowledge of what the note contained, and asked him what they had done to him. He told me in substance what I heard the man tell who had come out of the jail.

"Yes," said he, "they whipped me and took my dollar, and gave me this note."

He showed me the note which the jailer had given him, telling him to give it to his master. I told him I would give him fifty cents for it—that being all the money I had. He gave it to me and took his money. He had received twenty lashes on his bare back, with the negro-whip.

I took the note and started for the hotel where I had left Mr. Walker. Upon reaching the hotel, I handed it to a stranger whom I had not seen before, and requested him to read it to me. As near as I can recollect, it was as follows:—

"Dear Sir:—By your direction, I have given your boy twenty lashes. He is a very saucy boy, and tried to make me believe that he did not belong to you, and I put it on to him well for lying to me.

"I remain

"Your obedient servant."

It is true that in most of the slave-holding cities, when a gentleman wishes his servants whipped, he can send him to the jail and have it done. Before I went in where Mr. Walker was, I wet my cheeks a little, as though I had been crying. He looked at me, and inquired what was the matter. I told him that I had never had such a whipping in my life, and handed him the note. He looked at it and laughed;— "And so you told him that you did not belong to me?" "Yes, sir," said I. "I did not know that there was any harm in that." He told me I must behave myself, if I did not want to be whipped again.

This incident shows how it is that slavery makes its victims lying and mean; for which vices it afterwards reproaches them, and uses them as arguments to prove that they deserve no better fate. Had I entertained the same views of right and wrong which I now do, I am sure I should never have practised the deception upon that poor fellow which I did. I know of no act committed by me while in slavery which I have regretted more than that; and I heartily desire that it may be at some time or other in my power to make him amends for his vicarious sufferings in my behalf.

CHAPTER VI

In a few days we reached New Orleans, and arriving there in the night, remained on board until morning. While at New Orleans this time, I saw a slave killed; an account of which has been published by Theodore D. Weld, in his book entitled "Slavery as it is."[14] The circumstances were as follows. In the evening, between seven and eight o'clock, a slave came running down the levee, followed by several men and boys. The whites were crying out, "Stop that nigger! stop that nigger!" while the poor panting slave, in almost breathless accents, was repeating, "I did not steal the meat—I did not steal the meat." The poor man at last took refuge in the river. The whites who were in pursuit of him, run on board of one of the boats to see if they could discover him. They finally espied him under the bow of the steam-boat Trenton. They got a pike-pole, and tried to drive him from his hiding place. When they would strike at him he would dive under the water. The water was so cold, that it soon became evident that he must come out or be drowned.

While they were trying to drive him from under the bow of the boat or drown him, he would in broken and imploring accents say, "I did not steal the meat; I did not steal the meat. My master lives up the river. I want to see my master. I did not steal the meat. Do let me go home to master." After punching him, and striking him over the head for some time, he at last sunk in the water, to rise no more alive.

On the end of the pike-pole with which they were striking him was a hook, which caught in his clothing, and they hauled him up on the bow of the boat. Some said he was dead; others said he was *"playing possum;"* while others kicked him to make him get up; but it was of no use—he was dead.

As soon as they became satisfied of this, they commenced leaving, one after another. One of the hands on the boat informed the captain that they had killed the man, and that the dead body was lying on the deck. The captain came on deck, and said to those who were remaining, "You have killed this nigger; now take him off of my boat." The captain's name was Hart. The dead body was dragged on shore and left there. I went on board of the boat where our gang of slaves were, and during the whole night my mind was occupied with what I had seen. Early in the morning I went on shore to see if the dead body remained there. I found it in the same position that it was left the night before. I watched to see what they would do with it. It was left there until between eight and nine o'clock, when a cart, which takes up the trash out of the streets, came along, and the body was thrown in, and in a few minutes more was covered over with dirt which they were removing from the streets. During the whole time, I did not see more than six or seven persons around it, who, from their manner, evidently regarded it as no uncommon occurrence.

During our stay in the city I met with a young white man with whom I was well acquainted in St. Louis. He had been sold into slavery, under the following circumstances. His father was a drunkard, and very poor, with a family of five or six children. The father died, and left the mother to take care of and provide for the children as best she might. The eldest was a boy, named Burrill, about thirteen years of age, who did chores in a store kept by Mr. Riley, to assist his mother in procuring a living for the family. After working with him two years, Mr. Riley took him to New Orleans to wait on him while in that city on a visit, and when he returned to St. Louis, he told the mother of the boy that he had died with the yellow fever. Nothing more was heard from him, no one supposing him to be alive. I was much astonished when Burrill told me his story. Though I sympathized with him I could not assist him. We were both slaves. He was poor, uneducated, and without friends; and, if living, is, I presume, still held as a slave.

After selling out his cargo of human flesh, we returned to St. Louis, and my time was up with Mr. Walker. I had served him one year, and it was the longest year I ever lived.

CHAPTER VII

I was sent home, and was glad enough to leave the service of one who was tearing the husband from the wife, the child from the mother, and the sister from the brother—but a trial more severe and heart-rending than any which I had yet met with awaited me. My dear sister had been sold to a man who was going to Natchez, and was lying in jail awaiting the hour of his departure. She had expressed her determination to die, rather than go to the far south, and she was put in jail for safekeeping. I went to the jail the same day that I arrived, but as the jailer was not in I could not see her.

I went home to my master, in the country, and the first day after my return he came where I was at work, and spoke to me very politely. I knew from his appearance that something was the matter. After talking to me about my several journeys to New Orleans with Mr. Walker, he told me that he was hard pressed for money, and as he had sold my mother and all her children except me, he thought it would be better to sell me than any other one, and that as I had been used to living in the city, he thought it probable that I would prefer it to country life. I raised up my head, and looked him full in the face. When my eyes caught his he immediately looked to the ground. After a short pause, I said,

"Master, mother has often told me that you are a near relative of mine, and I have often heard you admit the fact; and after you have hired me out, and received, as I once heard you say, nine hundred dollars for my services—after receiving this large sum, will you sell me to be carried to New Orleans or some other place?"

"No," said he, "I do not intend to sell you to a negro trader. If I had wished to have done that, I might have sold you to Mr. Walker for a large sum, but I would not sell you to a negro trader. You may go to the city, and find you a good master."

"But," said I, "I cannot find a good master in the whole city of St. Louis."

"Why?" said he.

"Because there are no good masters in the state."

"Do you not call me a good master?"

"If you were you would not sell me."

"Now I will give you one week to find a master in, and surely you can do it in that time."

The price set by my evangelical master upon my soul and body was the trifling sum of five hundred dollars. I tried to enter into some arrangement by which I might purchase my freedom; but he would enter into no such arrangement.

I set out for the city with the understanding that I was to return in a week with some one to become my new master. Soon after reaching the city, I went to the jail, to learn if I could once more see my sister; but could not gain admission. I then went to mother, and learned from her that the owner of my sister intended to start for Natchez in a few days.

I went to the jail again the next day, and Mr. Simonds, the keeper, allowed me to see my sister for the last time. I cannot give a just description of the scene at that parting interview. Never, never can be erased from my heart the occurrences of that day! When I entered the room where she was, she was seated in one corner, alone. There were four other women in the same room, belonging to the same man. He had purchased them, he said, for his own use. She was seated with her face towards the door where I entered, yet she did not look up until I walked up to her. As soon as she observed me she sprung up, threw her arms around my neck, leaned her head upon my breast, and, without uttering a word, burst into tears. As soon as she recovered herself sufficiently to speak, she advised me to take mother, and try to get out of slavery. She said there was no hope for herself—that she must live and die a slave. After giving her some advice, and taking from my finger a ring and placing it upon hers, I bade her farewell forever, and returned to my mother, and then and there made up my mind to leave for Canada as soon as possible.

I had been in the city nearly two days, and as I was to be absent only a week, I thought best to get on my journey as soon as possible. In conversing with mother, I found her unwilling to make the attempt to reach a land of liberty, but she counselled me to get my liberty if I could. She said, as all her children were in slavery, she did not wish to leave them. I could not bear the idea of leaving her among those pirates, when there was a prospect of being able to get away from them. After much persuasion I succeeded in inducing her to make the attempt to get away.

The time fixed for our departure was the next night. I had with me a little money that I had received, from time to time, from gentlemen for whom I had done errands. I took my scanty means and purchased some dried beef, crackers and cheese, which I carried to mother, who had provided herself with a bag to carry it in. I occasionally thought of my old master, and of my mission to the city to find a new one. I waited with the most intense anxiety for the appointed time to leave the land of slavery, in search of a land of liberty.

The time at length arrived, and we left the city just as the clock struck nine. We proceeded to the upper part of the city, where I had been two or three times during the day, and selected a skiff to carry us across the river. The boat was not mine, nor did I know to whom it did belong; neither did I care. The boat was fastened with a small pole, which, with the aid of a rail, I soon loosened from its moorings. After hunting round and finding a board to use as an oar, I turned to the city, and bidding it a long farewell, pushed off my boat. The current running very swift, we had not reached the middle of the stream before we were directly opposite the city.

We were soon upon the Illinois shore, and, leaping from the boat, turned it adrift, and the last I saw of it it was going down the river at good speed. We took the main road to Alton, and passed through just at daylight, when we made for the woods, where we remained during the day. Our reason for going into the woods was, that we expected that Mr. Mansfield (the man who owned my mother) would start in pursuit of her as soon as he discovered that she was missing. He also knew that I had been in the city looking for a new master, and we thought probably he would go out to my master's to see if he could find my mother, and in so doing, Dr. Young might be led to suspect that I had gone to Canada to find a purchaser.

We remained in the woods during the day, and as soon as darkness over-shadowed the earth, we started again on our gloomy way, having no guide but the NORTH STAR.[15] We continued to travel by night, and secrete ourselves in the woods by day; and every night, before emerging from our hidingplace, we would anxiously look for our friend and leader—the NORTH STAR. And in the language of Pierpont we might have exclaimed,

> "Star of the North! while blazing day
> Pours round me its full tide of light,
> And hides thy pale but faithful ray,
> I, too, lie hid, and long for night.
> For night;—I dare not walk at noon,
> Nor dare I trust the faithless moon,
> Nor faithless man, whose burning lust
> For gold hath riveted my chain;
> No other leader can I trust
> But thee, of even the starry train;
> For, all the host around thee burning,
> Like faithless man, keep turning, turning.
>
> In the dark top of southern pines
> I nestled, when the driver's horn

Called to the field, in lengthening lines,
My fellows, at the break of morn.
And there I lay, till thy sweet face
Looked in upon my 'hiding place,'
Star of the North!
Thy light, that no poor slave deceiveth,
Shall set me free."

CHAPTER VIII

As we travelled towards a land of liberty, my heart would at times leap for joy. At other times, being, as I was, almost constantly on my feet, I felt as though I could travel no further. But when I thought of slavery, with its democratic whips—its republican chains—its evangelical blood-hounds, and its religious slave-holders—when I thought of all this paraphernalia of American democracy and religion behind me, and the prospect of liberty before me, I was encouraged to press forward, my heart was strengthened, and I forgot that I was tired or hungry.

On the eighth day of our journey, we had a very heavy rain, and in a few hours after it commenced we had not a dry thread upon our bodies. This made our journey still more unpleasant. On the tenth day, we found ourselves entirely destitute of provisions, and how to obtain any we could not tell. We finally resolved to stop at some farmhouse, and try to get something to eat. We had no sooner determined to do this, than we went to a house, and asked them for some food. We were treated with great kindness, and they not only gave us something to eat, but gave us provisions to carry with us. They advised us to travel by day and lie by at night. Finding ourselves about one hundred and fifty miles from St. Louis, we concluded that it would be safe to travel by daylight, and did not leave the house until the next morning. We travelled on that day through a thickly settled country, and through one small village. Though we were fleeing from a land of oppression, our hearts were still there. My dear sister and two beloved brothers were behind us, and the idea of giving them up, and leaving them forever, made us feel sad. But with all this depression of heart, the thought that I should one day be free, and call my body my own, buoyed me up, and made my heart leap for joy. I had just been telling my mother how I should try to get employment as soon as we reached Canada, and how I intended to purchase us a little farm, and how I would earn money enough to buy sister and brothers, and how happy we would be in our own FREE HOME—when three men came up on horseback, and ordered us to stop.

I turned to the one who appeared to be the principal man, and asked him what he wanted. He said he had a warrant to take us up. The three immediately dismounted, and one took from his pocket a handbill, advertising us as runaways, and offering a reward of two hundred dollars for our apprehension and delivery in the city of St. Louis. The advertisement had been put out by Isaac Mansfield and John Young.

While they were reading the advertisement, mother looked me in the face, and burst into tears. A cold chill ran over me, and such a sensation I never experienced before, and I hope never to again. They took out a rope and tied me, and we were taken back about six miles, to the house of the individual who appeared to be the leader. We reached there about seven o'clock in the evening, had supper, and were separated for the night. Two men remained in the room during the night. Before the family retired to rest, they were all called together to attend prayers. The man who but a few hours before had bound my hands together with a strong cord, read a chapter from the Bible, and then offered up prayer, just as though God had sanctioned the act he had just committed upon a poor, panting, fugitive slave.

The next morning a blacksmith came in, and put a pair of handcuffs on me, and we started on our journey back to the land of whips, chains, and Bibles. Mother was not tied, but was closely watched at night. We were carried back in a wagon, and after four days' travel, we came in sight of St. Louis. I cannot describe my feelings upon approaching the city.

As we were crossing the ferry, Mr. Wiggins, the owner of the ferry, came up to me, and inquired what I had been doing that I was in chains. He had not heard that I had run away. In a few minutes we were on the Missouri side, and were taken directly to the jail. On the way thither, I saw several of my friends, who gave me a nod of recognition as I passed them. After reaching the jail, we were locked up in different apartments.

CHAPTER IX

I had been in jail but a short time when I heard that my master was sick, and nothing brought more joy to my heart than that intelligence. I prayed fervently for him—not for his recovery, but for his death. I knew he would be exasperated at having to pay for my apprehension, and knowing his cruelty, I feared him. While in jail, I learned that my sister Elizabeth, who was in prison when we left the city, had been carried off four days before our arrival.

I had been in jail but a few hours when three negro-traders, learning that I was secured thus for running away, came to my prison-house and looked at me, expecting that I would be offered for sale. Mr. Mansfield, the man who owned mother, came into the jail as soon as Mr. Jones, the man who arrested us, informed him that he had brought her back. He told her that he would not whip her, but would sell her to a negro-trader, or take her to New Orleans himself. After being in jail about one week, master sent a man to take me out of jail, and send me home. I was taken out and carried home, and the old man was well enough to sit up. He had me brought into the room where he was, and as I entered, he asked me where I had been? I told him I had acted according to his orders. He had told me to look for a master, and I had been to look for one. He answered that he did not tell me to go to Canada to look for a master. I told him that as I had served him faithfully, and had been the means of putting a number of hundreds of dollars into his pocket, I thought I had a right to my liberty. He said he had promised my father that I should not be sold to supply the New Orleans market, or he would sell me to a negro-trader.

I was ordered to go into the field to work, and was closely watched by the overseer during the day, and locked up at night. The overseer gave me a severe whipping on the second day that I was in the field. I had been at home but a short time, when master was able to ride to the city; and on his return he informed me that he had sold me to Samuel Willi, a merchant tailor. I knew Mr. Willi. I had lived with him three or four months some years before, when he hired me of my master.

Mr. Willi was not considered by his servants as a very bad man, nor was he the best of masters. I went to my new home, and found my new mistress very glad to see me. Mr. Willi owned two servants before he purchased me—Robert and Charlotte. Robert was an excellent white-washer, and hired his time from his master, paying him one dollar per day, besides taking care of himself. He was known in the city by the name of Bob Music. Charlotte was an old woman, who attended to the cooking, washing, &c. Mr. Willi was not a wealthy man, and did not feel able to keep many servants around his house; so he soon decided to hire me out, and as I had been accustomed to service in steamboats, he gave me the privilege of finding such employment.

I soon secured a situation on board the steamer Otto, Capt. J. B. Hill, which sailed from St. Louis to Independence, Missouri. My former master, Dr. Young, did not let Mr. Willi know that I had run away, or he would not have permitted me to go on board a steamboat. The boat was not quite ready to commence running, and therefore I had to remain with Mr. Willi. But during this time, I had to undergo a trial for which I was entirely unprepared. My mother, who had been in jail since her return until the present time, was now about being carried to New Orleans, to die on a cotton, sugar, or rice plantation!

I had been several times to the jail, but could obtain no interview with her. I ascertained, however, the time the boat in which she was to embark would sail, and as I had not seen mother since her being thrown into prison, I felt anxious for the hour of sailing to come. At last, the day arrived when I was to see her for the first time after our painful separation, and, for aught that I knew, for the last time in this world!

At about ten o'clock in the morning I went on board of the boat, and found her there in company with fifty or sixty other slaves. She was chained to another woman. On seeing me, she immediately dropped her head upon her heaving bosom. She moved not, neither did she weep. Her emotions were too deep for tears.

I approached, threw my arms around her neck, kissed her, and fell upon my knees, begging her forgiveness, for I thought myself to blame for her sad condition; for if I had not persuaded her to accompany me, she would not then have been in chains.

She finally raised her head, looked me in the face, (and such a look none but an angel can give!) and said, *"My dear son, you are not to blame for my being here. You have done nothing more nor less than your duty. Do not, I pray you, weep for me. I cannot last long upon a cotton plantation. I feel that my heavenly Master will soon call me home, and then I shall be out of the hands of the slave-holders!"*

I could bear no more—my heart struggled to free itself from the human form. In a moment she saw Mr. Mansfield coming toward that part of the boat, and she whispered into my ear, *"My child, we must soon part to meet no more this side of the grave. You have ever said that you would not die a slave; that you would be a freeman. Now try to get your liberty! You will soon have no one to look after but yourself!"* and just as she whispered the last sentence into my ear, Mansfield came up to me, and with an oath, said, "Leave here this instant; you have been the means of my losing one hundred dollars to get this wench back"—at the same time kicking me with a heavy pair of boots. As I left her, she gave one shriek, saying, "God be with you!" It was the last time that I saw her, and the last word I heard her utter.

I walked on shore. The bell was tolling. The boat was about to start. I stood with a heavy heart, waiting to see her leave the wharf. As I thought of my mother, I could but feel that I had lost

"——the glory of my life,
My blessing and my pride!
I half forgot the name of slave,
When she was by my side."

The love of liberty that had been burning in my bosom had well-nigh gone out. I felt as though I was ready to die. The boat moved gently from the wharf, and while she glided down the river, I realized that my mother was indeed

"Gone—gone—sold and gone,
To the rice swamp, dank and lone!"

After the boat was out of sight I returned home; but my thoughts were so absorbed in what I had witnessed, that I knew not what I was about half of the time. Night came, but it brought no sleep to my eyes.

In a few days, the boat upon which I was to work being ready, I went on board to commence. This employment suited me better than living in the city, and I remained until the close of navigation; though it proved anything but pleasant. The captain was a drunken, profligate, hard-hearted creature, not knowing how to treat himself, or any other person.

The boat, on its second trip, brought down Mr. Walker, the man of whom I have spoken in a previous chapter, as hiring my time. He had between one and two hundred slaves, chained and manacled. Among them was a man that formerly belonged to my old master's brother, Aaron Young. His name was Solomon. He was a preacher, and belonged to the same church with his master. I was glad to see the old man. He wept like a child when he told me how he had been sold from his wife and children.

The boat carried down, while I remained on board, four or five gangs of slaves. Missouri, though a comparatively new state, is very much engaged in raising slaves to supply the southern market. In a former chapter, I have mentioned that I was once in the employ of a slave-trader, or driver, as he is called at the south. For fear that some may think that I have misrepresented a slave-driver, I will here give an extract from a paper published in a slave-holding state, Tennessee, called the "Millennial Trumpeter."

"Droves of negroes, chained together in dozens and scores, and hand-cuffed, have been driven through our country in numbers far surpassing any previous year, and these vile slave-drivers and dealers are swarming like buzzards around a carrion. Through this county, you cannot pass a few miles in the great roads without having every feeling of humanity insulted and lacerated by this spectacle, nor can you go into any county or any neighborhood, scarely, without seeing or hearing of some of these despicable creatures, called negro-drivers.

"Who is a negro-driver? One whose eyes dwell with delight on lacerated bodies of helpless men, women and children; whose soul feels diabolical raptures at the chains, and hand-cuffs, and cart-whips, for inflicting tortures on weeping mothers torn from helpless babes, and on husbands and wives torn asunder forever!"

Dark and revolting as is the picture here drawn, it is from the pen of one living in the midst of slavery. But though these men may cant about negro-drivers, and tell what despicable creatures they are, who is it, I ask, that supplies them with the human beings that they are tearing asunder? I answer, as far as I have any knowledge of the state where I came from, that those who raise slaves for the market are to be found among all classes, from Thomas H. Benton down to the lowest political demagogue who may be able to purchase a woman for the purpose of raising stock, and from the doctor of divinity down to the most humble lay member in the church.

It was not uncommon in St. Louis to pass by an auction-stand, and behold a woman upon the auction-block, and hear the seller crying out, *"How much is offered for this woman? She is a good cook, good washer, a good obedient servant. She has got religion!"* Why should this man tell the purchasers that she has religion? I answer, because in Missouri, and as far as I have any knowledge of slavery in the other states, the religious teaching consists in teaching the slave that he must never strike a white man; that God made him for a slave; and that, when whipped, he must not find fault—for the Bible says, "He that knoweth his master's will and doeth it not, shall be beaten with many stripes!"[16] And slaveholders find such religion very profitable to them.

After leaving the steamer Otto, I resided at home, in Mr. Willi's family, and again began to lay my plans for making my escape from slavery. The anxiety to be a freeman would not let me rest day or night. I would think of the northern cities that I had heard so much about;—of Canada, where so many of my acquaintances had found a refuge. I would dream at night that I was in Canada, a freeman, and on waking in the morning, weep to find myself so sadly mistaken.

> "I would think of Victoria's domain,
> And in a moment I seemed to be there!
> But the fear of being taken again,
> Soon hurried me back to despair."

Mr. Willi treated me better than Dr. Young ever had; but instead of making me contented and happy, it only rendered me the more miserable, for it enabled me better to appreciate liberty. Mr. Willi was a man who loved money as most men do, and without looking for an opportunity to sell me, he found one in the offer of Captain Enoch Price, a steamboat owner and commission merchant, living in the city of St. Louis. Captain Price tendered seven hundred dollars, which was two hundred more than Mr. Willi had paid. He therefore thought best to accept the offer. I was wanted for a carriage driver, and Mrs. Price was very much pleased with the captain's bargain. His family consisted besides of one child. He had three servants besides myself—one man and two women.

Mrs. Price was very proud of her servants, always keeping them well dressed, and as soon as I had been purchased, she resolved to have a new carriage. And soon one was procured, and all preparations were made for a turn-out in grand style, I being the driver.

One of the female servants was a girl some eighteen or twenty years of age, named Maria. Mrs. Price was very soon determined to have us united, if she could so arrange matters. She would often urge upon me the necessity of having a wife, saying that it would be so pleasant for me to take one in the same family! But getting married, while in slavery, was the last of my thoughts; and had I been ever so inclined, I should not have married Maria, as my love had already gone in another quarter. Mrs. Price soon found out that her efforts at this match-making between Maria and myself would not prove successful. She also discovered (or thought she had) that I was rather partial to a girl named Eliza, who was owned by Dr. Mills. This induced her at once to endeavor the purchase of Eliza, so great was her desire to get me a wife!

Before making the attempt, however, she deemed it best to talk to me a little upon the subject of love, courtship, and marriage. Accordingly, one afternoon she called me into her room—telling me to take a chair and sit down. I did so, thinking it rather strange, for servants are not very often asked thus to sit down in the same room with the master or mistress. She said that she had found out that I did not care enough about Maria to marry her. I told her that was true. She then asked me if there was not a girl in the city that I loved. Well, now, this was coming into too close quarters with me! People, generally, don't like to tell their love stories to everybody that may think fit to ask about them, and it was so with me. But, after blushing a while and recovering myself, I told her that I did not want a wife. She then asked me if I did not think something of Eliza. I told her that I did. She then said that if I wished to marry Eliza, she would purchase her if she could.

I gave but little encouragement to this proposition, as I was determined to make another trial to get my liberty, and I knew that if I should have a wife, I should not be willing to leave her behind; and if I should attempt to bring her with me, the chances would be difficult for success. However, Eliza was purchased, and brought into the family.

CHAPTER X

But the more I thought of the trap laid by Mrs. Price to make me satisfied with my new home, by getting me a wife, the more I determined never to marry any woman on earth until I should get my liberty. But this secret I was compelled to keep to myself, which placed me in a very critical position. I must keep upon good terms with Mrs. Price and Eliza. I therefore promised Mrs. Price that I would marry Eliza; but said that I was not then ready. And I had to keep upon good terms with Eliza, for fear that Mrs. Price would find out that I did not intend to get married.

I have here spoken of marriage, and it is very common among slaves themselves to talk of it. And it is common for slaves to be married; or at least to have the marriage ceremony performed. But there is no such thing as slaves being lawfully married. There has been never yet a case occurred where a slave has been tried for bigamy. The man may have as many women as he wishes, and the women as many men; and the law takes no cognizance of such acts among slaves. And in fact some masters, when they have sold the husband from the wife, compel her to take another.

There lived opposite Captain Price's, Doctor Farrar, well known in St. Louis. He sold a man named Ben, to one of the traders. He also owned Ben's wife, and in a few days he compelled Sally (that was her name) to marry Peter, another man belonging to him. I asked Sally "why she married Peter so soon after Ben was sold." She said, "because master made her do it."

Mr. John Calvert, who resided near our place, had a woman named Lavinia. She was quite young, and a man to whom she was about to be married was sold, and carried into the country near St. Charles, about twenty miles from St. Louis. Mr. Calvert wanted her to get a husband; but she had resolved not to marry any other man, and she refused. Mr. Calvert whipped her in such a manner that it was thought she would die. Some of the citizens had him arrested, but it was soon hushed up. And that was the last of it. The woman did not die, but it would have been the same if she had.

Captain Price purchased me in the month of October, and I remained with him until December, when the family made a voyage to New Orleans, in a boat owned by himself, and named the "Chester." I served on board as one of the stewards. On arriving at New Orleans, about the middle of the month, the boat took in freight for Cincinnati; and it was decided that the family should go up the river in her, and what was of more interest to me, I was to accompany them.

The long looked for opportunity to make my escape from slavery was near at hand.

Captain Price had some fears as to the propriety of taking me near a free state, or a place where it was likely I could run away, with a prospect of liberty. He asked me if I had ever been in a free state. "Oh yes," said I, "I have been in Ohio; my master carried me into that state once, but I never liked a free state."

It was soon decided that it would be safe to take me with them, and what made it more safe, Eliza was on the boat with us, and Mrs. Price, to try me, asked if I thought as much as ever of Eliza. I told her that Eliza was very dear to me indeed, and that nothing but death should part us. It was the same as if we were married. This had the desired effect. The boat left New Orleans, and proceeded up the river.

I had at different times obtained little sums of money, which I had reserved for a "rainy day." I procured some cotton cloth, and made me a bag to carry provisions in. The trials of the past were all lost in hopes for the future. The love of liberty, that had been burning in my bosom for years, and had been well-nigh extinguished, was now resuscitated. At night, when all around was peaceful, I would walk the decks, meditating upon my happy prospects.

I should have stated, that, before leaving St. Louis, I went to an old man named Frank, a slave, owned by a Mr. Sarpee. This old man was very distinguished (not only among the slave population, but also the whites) as a fortune-teller. He was about seventy years of age, something over six feet high, and very slender. Indeed, he was so small around his body, that it looked as though it was not strong enough to hold up his head.

Uncle Frank was a very great favorite with the young ladies, who would go to him in great numbers to get their fortunes told. And it was generally believed that he could really penetrate into the mysteries of futurity. Whether true or not, he had the *name*, and that is about half of what one needs in this gullible age. I found Uncle Frank seated in the chimney corner, about ten o'clock at night. As soon as I entered, the old man left his seat. I watched his movement as well as I could by the dim light of the fire. He soon lit a lamp, and coming up, looked me full in the face, saying, "Well, my son, you have come to get uncle to tell your fortune, have you?" "Yes," said I. But how the old man should know what I came for, I could not tell. However, I paid the fee of twenty-five cents, and he commenced by looking into a gourd, filled with water. Whether the old man was a prophet, or the son of a prophet, I cannot say; but there is one thing certain, many of his predictions were verified.

I am no believer in soothsaying; yet I am sometimes at a loss to know how Uncle Frank could tell so accurately what would occur in the future. Among the many things he told was one which was enough to pay me for all the trouble of hunting him up. It was that I *should be free!* He further said, that in trying to get my liberty I would meet with many severe trials. I thought to myself any fool could tell me that!

The first place in which we landed in a free state was Cairo, a small village at the mouth of the Ohio river. We remained here but a few hours, when we proceeded to Louisville. After unloading some of the cargo, the boat started on her upward trip. The next day was the first of January. I had looked forward to New Year's day as the commencement of a new era in the history of my life. I had decided upon leaving the peculiar institution[17] that day.

During the last night that I served in slavery I did not close my eyes a single moment. When not thinking of the future, my mind dwelt on the past. The love of a dear mother, a dear sister, and three dear brothers, yet living, caused me to shed many tears. If I could only have been assured of their being dead, I should have felt satisfied; but I imagined I saw my dear mother in the cotton-field, followed by a merciless taskmaster, and no one to speak a consoling word to her! I beheld my dear sister in the hands of a slave-driver, and compelled to submit to his cruelty! None but one placed in such a situation can for a moment imagine the intense agony to which these reflections subjected me.

CHAPTER XI

At last the time for action arrived. The boat landed at a point which appeared to me the place of all others to start from. I found that it would be impossible to carry anything with me but what was upon my person. I had some provisions, and a single suit of clothes, about half worn. When the boat was discharging her cargo, and the passengers engaged carrying their baggage on and off shore, I improved the opportunity to convey myself with my little effects on land. Taking up a trunk, I went up the wharf, and was soon out of the crowd. I made directly for the woods, where I remained until night, knowing well that I could not travel, even in the state of Ohio, during the day, without danger of being arrested.

I had long since made up my mind that I would not trust myself in the hands of any man, white or colored. The slave is brought up to look upon every white man as an enemy to him and his race; and twenty-one years in slavery had taught me that there were traitors, even among colored people. After dark, I emerged from the woods into a narrow path, which led me into the main travelled road. But I knew not which way to go. I did not know north from south, east from west. I looked in vain for the North Star; a heavy cloud hid it from my view. I walked up and down the road until near midnight, when the clouds disappeared, and I welcomed the sight of my friend—truly the slave's friend—the North Star!

As soon as I saw it, I knew my course, and before daylight I travelled twenty or twenty-five miles. It being in the winter, I suffered intensely from the cold; being without an overcoat, and my other clothes rather thin for the season. I was provided with a tinder-box, so that I could make up a fire when necessary. And but for this, I should certainly have frozen to death; for I was determined not to go to any house for shelter. I knew of a man belonging to Gen. Ashly, of St. Louis, who had run away near Cincinnati, on the way to Washington, but had been caught and carried back into slavery; and I felt that a similar fate awaited me, should I be seen by any one. I travelled at night, and lay by during the day.

On the fourth day my provisions gave out, and then what to do I could not tell. Have something to eat I must; but how to get it was the question! On the first night after my food was gone, I went to a barn on the road-side and there found some ears of corn. I took ten or twelve of them, and kept on my journey. During the next day, while in the woods, I roasted my corn and feasted upon it, thanking God that I was so well provided for.

My escape to a land of freedom now appeared certain, and the prospects of the future occupied a great part of my thoughts. What should be my occupation, was a subject of much anxiety to me; and the next thing what should be my name? I have before stated that my old master, Dr. Young, had no children of his own, but had with him a nephew, the son of his brother, Benjamin Young. When this boy was brought to Dr. Young, his name being William, the same as mine, my mother was ordered to change mine to something else. This, at the time, I thought to be one of the most cruel acts that could be committed upon my rights; and I received several very severe whippings for telling people that my name was William, after orders were given to change it. Though young, I was old enough to place a high appreciation upon my name. It was decided, however, to call me "Sandford," and this name I was known by, not only upon my master's plantation, but up to the time that I made my escape. I was sold under the name of Sandford.

But as soon as the subject came to my mind, I resolved on adopting my old name of William, and let Sandford go by the board, for I always hated it. Not because there was anything peculiar in the name; but because it had been forced upon me. It is sometimes common, at the south, for slaves to take the name of their masters. Some have a legitimate right to do so. But I always detested the idea of being called by the name of either of my masters. And as for my father, I would rather have adopted the name of "Friday," and been known as the servant of some Robinson Crusoe, than to have taken his name. So I was not only hunting for my liberty, but also hunting for a name; though I regarded the latter as of little consequence, if I could but gain the former. Travelling along the road, I would sometimes speak to myself, sounding my name over, by way of getting used to it, before I should arrive among civilized human beings. On the fifth or six day, it rained very fast, and froze about as fast as it fell, so that my clothes were one glare of ice. I travelled on at night until I became so chilled and benumbed—the wind blowing into my face—that I found it impossible to go any further, and accordingly took shelter in a barn, where I was obliged to walk about to keep from freezing.

I have ever looked upon that night as the most eventful part of my escape from slavery. Nothing but the providence of God and that old barn, saved me from freezing to death. I received a very severe cold, which settled upon my lungs, and from time to time my feet had been frostbitten, so that it was with difficulty I could walk. In this situation I travelled two days, when I found that I must seek shelter somewhere, or die.

The thought of death was nothing frightful to me, compared with that of being caught, and again carried back into slavery. Nothing but the prospect of enjoying liberty could have induced me to undergo such trials, for

"Behind I left the whips and chains,
Before me were sweet Freedom's plains!"

This, and this alone, cheered me onward. But I at last resolved to seek protection from the inclemency of the weather, and therefore I secured myself behind some logs and brush, intending to wait there until some one should pass by; for I thought it probable that I might see some colored person, or, if not, some one who was not a slave-holder; for I had an idea that I should know a slave-holder as far as I could see him.

The first person that passed was a man in a buggy-wagon. He looked too genteel for me to hail him. Very soon another passed by on horseback. I attempted to speak to him, but fear made my voice fail me. As he passed, I left my hidingplace and was approaching the road, when I observed an old man walking towards me, leading a white horse. He had on a broad-brimmed hat and a very long coat, and was evidently walking for exercise. As soon as I saw him, and observed his dress, I thought to myself, "You are the man that I have been looking for!" Nor was I mistaken. He was the very man!

On approaching me, he asked me, "if I was not a slave." I looked at him some time, and then asked him "if he knew of any one who would help me, as I was sick." He answered that he would; but again asked, if I was not a slave. I told him I was. He then said that I was in a very pro-slavery neighborhood, and if I would wait until he went home, he would get a covered wagon for me. I promised to remain. He mounted his horse, and was soon out of sight.

After he was gone, I meditated whether to wait or not; being apprehensive that he had gone for some one to arrest me. But I finally concluded to remain until he should return; removing some few rods to watch his movements. After a suspense of an hour and a half or more, he returned with a two-horse covered wagon, such as are usually seen under the shed of a Quaker meetinghouse on Sundays and Thursdays; for the old man proved to be a Quaker of the George Fox stamp.[18]

He took me to his house, but it was some time before I could be induced to enter it; not until the old lady came out, did I venture into the house. I thought I saw something in the old lady's cap that told me I was not only safe, welcome, in her house. I was not, however, prepared to receive their hospitalities. The only fault I found with them was their being too kind. I had never had a white man treat me as an equal, and the idea of a white lady waiting on me at the table was still worse! Though the table was loaded with the good things of this life, I could not eat. I thought if I could only be allowed the privilege of eating in the kitchen I should be more than satisfied!

Finding that I could not eat, the old lady, who was a "Thompsonian,"[19] made me a cup of "composition," or "number six;" but it was so strong and hot, that I called it *"number seven!"* However, I soon found myself at home in this family. On different occasions, when telling these facts, I have been asked how I felt upon finding myself regarded as a man by a white family; especially just having run away from one. I cannot say that I have ever answered the question yet.

The fact that I was in all probability a freeman, sounded in my ears like a charm. I am satisfied that none but a slave could place such an appreciation upon liberty as I did at that time. I wanted to see mother and sister, that I might tell them "I was free!" I wanted to see my fellow-slaves in St. Louis, and let them know that the chains were no longer upon my limbs. I wanted to see Captain Price, and let him learn from my own lips that I was no more a chattel, but a man! I was anxious, too, thus to inform Mrs. Price that she must get another coachman. And I wanted to see Eliza more than I did either Mr. or Mrs. Price!

The fact that I was a freeman—could walk, talk, eat and sleep, as a man, and no one to stand over me with the blood-clotted cow-hide—all this made me feel that I was not myself.

The kind friend that had taken me in was named Wells Brown. He was a devoted friend of the slave; but was very old, and not in the enjoyment of good health. After being by the fire awhile, I found that my feet had been very much frozen. I was seized with a fever, which threatened to confine me to my bed. But my Thompsonian friends soon raised me, treating me as kindly as if I had been one of their own children. I remained with them twelve or fifteen days, during which time they made me some clothing, and the old gentleman purchased me a pair of boots.

I found that I was about fifty or sixty miles from Dayton, in the State of Ohio, and between one and two hundred miles from Cleaveland, on Lake Erie, a place I was desirous of reaching on my way to Canada. This I know will sound strangely to the ears of people in foreign lands, but it is nevertheless true. An American citizen was fleeing from a democratic, republican, Christian government, to receive protection under the monarchy of Great Britain. While the people of the United States boast of their freedom, they at the same time keep three millions of their own citizens in chains; and while I am seated here in sight of Bunker Hill Monument, writing this narrative, I am a slave, and no law, not even in Massachusetts, can protect me from the hands of the slaveholder!

Before leaving this good Quaker friend, he inquired what my name was besides William. I told him that I had no other name. "Well," said he, "thee must have another name. Since thee has got out of slavery, thee has become a man, and men always have two names."

I told him that he was the first man to extend the hand of friendship to me, and I would give him the privilege of naming me.

"If I name thee," said he, "I shall call thee Wells Brown, after myself."

"But," said I, "I am not willing to lose my name of William. As it was taken from me once against my will, I am not willing to part with it again upon any terms."

"Then," said he, "I will call thee William Wells Brown."

"So be it," said I; and I have been known by that name ever since I left the house of my first white friend, Wells Brown.

After giving me some little change, I again started for Canada. In four days I reached a public house, and went in to warm myself. I there learned that some fugitive slaves had just passed through the place. The men in the bar-room were talking about it, and I thought that it must have been myself they referred to, and I was therefore afraid to start, fearing they would seize me; but I finally mustered courage enough, and took my leave. As soon as I was out of sight, I went into the woods, and remained there until night, when I again regained the road, and travelled on until next day.

Not having had any food for nearly two days, I was faint with hunger, and was in a dilemma what to do, as the little cash supplied me by my adopted father, and which had contributed to my comfort, was now all gone. I however concluded to go to a farm-house, and ask for something to eat. On approaching the door of the first one presenting itself, I knocked, and was soon met by a man who asked me what I wanted. I told him that I would like something to eat. He asked me where I was from, and where I was going. I replied that I had come some way, and was going to Cleaveland.

After hesitating a moment or two, he told me that he could give me nothing to eat, adding, "that if I would work, I could get something to eat."

I felt bad, being thus refused something to sustain nature, but did not dare tell him that I was a slave.

Just as I was leaving the door, with a heavy heart, a woman, who proved to be the wife of this gentleman, came to the door, and asked her husband what I wanted. He did not seem inclined to inform her. She therefore asked me herself. I told her that I had asked for something to eat. After a few other questions, she told me to come in, and that she would give me something to eat.

I walked up to the door, but the husband remained in the passage, as if unwilling to let me enter.

She asked him two or three times to get out of the way, and let me in. But as he did not move, she pushed him on one side, bidding me walk in! I was never before so glad to see a woman push a man aside! Ever since that act, I have been in favor of "woman's rights!"[20]

After giving me as much food as I could eat, she presented me with ten cents, all the money then at her disposal, accompanied with a note to a friend, a few miles further on the road. Thanking this angel of mercy from an overflowing heart, I pushed on my way, and in three days arrived at Cleaveland, Ohio.

Being an entire stranger in this place, it was difficult for me to find where to stop. I had no money, and the lake being frozen, I saw that I must remain until the opening of the navigation, or go to Canada by way of Buffalo. But believing myself to be somewhat out of danger, I secured an engagement at the Mansion House, as a table waiter, in payment for my board. The proprietor, however, whose name was E. M. Segur, in a short time, hired me for twelve dollars a month; on which terms I remained until spring, when I found good employment on board a lake steamboat.

I purchased some books, and at leisure moments perused them with considerable advantage to myself. While at Cleaveland, I saw for the first time, an anti-slavery newspaper. It was the *"Genius of Universal Emancipation,"* published by Benjamin Lundy,[21] and though I had no home, I subscribed for the paper. It was my great desire, being out of slavery myself, to do what I could for the emancipation of my brethren yet in chains, and while on Lake Erie, I found many opportunities of "helping their cause along."

It is well known that a great number of fugitives make their escape to Canada, by way of Cleaveland; and while on the lakes, I always made arrangement to carry them on the boat to Buffalo or Detroit, and thus effect their escape to the "promised land." The friends of the slave, knowing that I would transport them without charge, never failed to have a delegation when the boat arrived at Cleaveland. I have sometimes had four or five on board at one time.

In the year 1842, I conveyed, from the first of May to the first of December, sixty-nine fugitives over Lake Erie to Canada. In 1843, I visited Malden, in Upper Canada, and counted seventeen in that small village, whom I had assisted in reaching Canada. Soon after coming north I subscribed for the Liberator, edited by that champion of freedom, William Lloyd Garrison.[22] I had heard nothing of the anti-slavery movement while in slavery, and as soon as I found that my enslaved countrymen had friends who were laboring for their liberation, I felt anxious to join them, and give what aid I could to the cause.

I early embraced the temperance cause,[23] and found that a temperance reformation was needed among my colored brethren. In company with a few friends, I commenced a temperance reformation among the colored people in the city of Buffalo, and labored three years, in which time a society was built up, numbering over five hundred out of a population of less than seven hundred.

In the autumn, 1843, impressed with the importance of spreading anti-slavery truth, as a means to bring about the abolition of slavery, I commenced lecturing as an agent of the western New York Anti-Slavery Society, and have ever since devoted my time to the cause of my enslaved countrymen.

NOTES

1. Edward Farrison, *William Wells Brown: Author and Reformer* (Chicago: University of Chicago Press, 1969), 4–6.
2. Farrison, *William Wells Brown*, 8.
3. Jefferson, ed., *The Travels of William Wells Brown*, 1–5.
4. James Olney, "'Was Born': Slave Narratives, Their Status as Autobiography and as Literature," in *The Slave's Narrative*, edited by Charles T. Davis and Henry Louis Gates Jr. (New York: Oxford University Press, 1985), 152–54.
5. Farrison, *William Wells Brown*, 399–401; Jefferson, ed., *The Travels of William Wells Brown*, 5–6.
6. William Cowper (1731–1800) was an English poet known for poems about nature and rural life. Brown misattributes this verse, which was actually written by Joseph Addison (1672–1719) in his patriotic verse tragedy *Cato*. Addison, an English writer and politician, is best known for *The Spectator*, a series of essays published in 1711 and 1712, and his contributions to the periodical *The Tatler*, published 1709–1711.
7. Edmund Quincy (1808–1877) was an antislavery activist and supporter.
8. Frederick Douglass (1818?–1895) was the most prominent African American leader in the nineteenth century. After escaping slavery in Maryland, Douglass, in 1841, became a speaker for the Massachusetts Anti-Slavery Society. He published his *Narrative* (1845) and briefly went to England to escape possible recapture. While he was away, his supporters purchased his freedom. In 1847, he began to publish the *North Star*, an antislavery newspaper based in Rochester, NY. In 1855, he published an expanded narrative of his experiences entitled *My Bondage and My Freedom*. Douglass recruited blacks for the Civil War, served as recorder of deed in Washington, D.C. (1881–1886), and was appointed minister to Haiti (1889–1891). His final autobiography, *Life and Times of Frederick Douglass*, was published in 1881 and in an expanded edition in 1892.
9. Daniel Defoe (1660–1731) was an English novelist and journalist known for his novels *Robinson Crusoe* (1719) and *Moll Flanders* (1722). His writing helped define the new genre of novel writing. Crusoe is a merchant-adventurer marooned on a desert island

off the northern coast of South America. After living alone for twenty-six years, he rescues a black man, whom he names Friday, from cannibals. They are eventually rescued and taken to England.

10. Elijah Parish Lovejoy (1802–1837) was a clergyman and antislavery activist. Lovejoy edited a religious newspaper, the *St. Louis Observer*, which was very critical of slavery, until he relocated across the Mississippi River in 1837. From his new location, Lovejoy published the *Alton Observer* and helped organize the Illinois Anti-Slavery Society. He was killed in November 1837 by rioters intending to destroy his press. See Paul Simon, *Freedom's Champion: Elijah Lovejoy* (Carbondale: Southern Illinois University Press, 1994), 77–135; Paul Simon, *Lovejoy: Martyr to Freedom* (St. Louis: Concordia Publishing House, 1964), 77–135. Merton L. Dillon, *Elijah P. Lovejoy, Abolitionist Editor* (Urbana: University of Illinois Press, 1961), 159–70; Chris Padgett, "Comeouterism and Antislavery Violence in Ohio's Western Reserve," in *Antislavery Violence: Sectional, Racial, and Cultural Conflict in Antebellum America*, edited by John R. McKivigan and Stanley Harrold (Knoxville: University of Tennessee Press, 1999), 193–214.

11. Psalms 132:4, "I will not give sleep to mine eyes, or slumber to mine eyelids"; Proverbs 6:4, "Give not sleep to thine eyes, nor slumber to thine eyelids."

12. A beverage popular in the South. It is composed of brandy or whiskey, sugar, ice, and sprigs of mint.

13. Indiscriminately combining men and women.

14. Theodore Dwight Weld (1803–1895) was the author of *American Slavery As It Is: Testimony of a Thousand Witnesses* (1839).

15. The star in the Northern Hemisphere to which the axis of the earth nearly points. Because of this, it appears stationary. The star was used by escaping slaves as a point of reference.

16. Luke 12:47, "And that servant, which knew his lord's will, and prepared not himself, neither did according to his will, shall be beaten with many stripes."

17. Black slavery, more fully called "peculiar domestic institution of the South."

18. George Fox (1624–1691) was an English religious leader who founded the Society of Friends (Quakers) circa 1647. Their beliefs encourage humanitarianism, racial equality, prison reform, and quality education.

19. Samuel Thomson (1769–1843) was a naturalist. He prescribed mixtures of herbs and vegetables to treat illness and disease. See Packard, *History of Medicine in the United States*, vol. 2 (New York: Hafner Publishing, 1963), 1233–39.

20. Lucretia Mott and Elizabeth Cady Stanton organized a women's rights convention in 1848. The convention adopted a Declaration of Sentiments demanding equal rights for women in all areas, including education, property, and suffrage.

21. *The Genius of Universal Emancipation* was an abolitionist newspaper edited in Baltimore, Maryland, by Benjamin Lundy, a Quaker antislavery organizer. Lundy advocated using persuasion to end slavery rather than direct government intervention.

22. William Lloyd Garrison (1805–1879) was a journalist and reformer. Garrison edited the *National Philanthropist* and, in 1828, began working with Benjamin Lundy. In 1831, Garrison began editing his own antislavery newspaper, *The Liberator*, which continued to be published until 1865. Garrison advocated immediate abolition.

23. The temperance cause to which Brown refers was a movement whose objective it was to eliminate the sale of alcoholic beverages. The cause organized itself into the Women's Christian Temperance Union. The organization's influence contributed to the passing of the Eighteenth Amendment to the Constitution in 1919, which prohibited the manufacture and sale of alcohol. The amendment was repealed in 1933.

■ CHAPTER 4
Henry "Box" Brown (1816–?)

NARRATIVE OF HENRY BOX BROWN

Henry Brown, who was unrelated to William Wells Brown, was born in Louisa County, Virginia, (approximately forty-five miles away from Richmond) in 1816. He escaped slavery in 1849 at the age of thirty-three. His descriptions of slavery are punctuated by extended digressions on true Christianity versus the hypocrisy of slaveholding religion; the difficulties slaves faced in maintaining familial connection; descriptions of slaveholders who encouraged their slaves to steal from others; and criticisms of a slave system that allowed slaveholders to routinely promise eventual freedom to slaves from whom they extorted additional labor and money (sometimes forcing their slaves to pay for their freedom several times over) without ever granting the freedom initially promised.

Brown was eventually taken to Richmond, Virginia, to work in a tobacco factory owned by his master's son. His parents remained behind on the plantation. Brown worked diligently and avoided the kinds of whippings routinely inflicted upon other slaves: "I tried extremely hard to perform what I thought was my duty, and escaped the lash almost entirely; although the overseer would oftentimes have liked to have given me a severe whipping; but fear of both me and my master deterred him from so doing."

Brown married, fathered three children, and, because he was able to hire himself out as a tobacconist, was able to assist in purchasing his wife. His goal was to prevent having her sold away from him. Brown contributed $50.00 toward her purchase, paid $50.00 a year for her time, and $72.00 rent for their house. His wife took in washing to help support their family. At a superficial level, Brown's life looked deceptively free. That illusion was temporary. In August 1848, Brown's family was sold away from him. Without his family, Brown resolved to escape:

> The first thing that occurred to me, after the cruel separation of my wife and children from me, and I had recovered my senses, so as to know how to act, was, thoughts of freeing myself from slavery's iron yoke. I had suffered enough under its heavy

weight, and I determined I would endure it no longer; and those reasons which often deter the slave from attempting to escape, no longer existed in reference to me, for my family were gone, and slavery now had no mitigating circumstances, to lessen the bitterness of its cup of woe.

Brown hired a carpenter to build a crate measuring three feet one inch long, two feet six inches deep, and two feet wide. Brown packed himself fetus-like into the box and arranged to have his six-foot, 200-pound frame sent from Baltimore to Philadelphia. The 350-mile trip took twenty-seven hours. Brown subsisted on several biscuits and water he carried in a small bladder. He endured long periods of time when the box was placed upside down.

His middle name was given him by abolitionists eager to commemorate and exploit his daring and ingenious escape. In an address delivered on May 31, 1849, at Faneuil Hall in Boston, the abolitionist Samuel J. May remarked that "Never will the story be forgotten in our country, or throughout the world, of the man—whom I trust you will all be permitted to see—who, that he might escape from Southern oppression, consented to a living entombment. He entered the box with the determination to be free or die: and as he heard the nails driven in, his fear was that death was to be his portion; yet, said he, let death come in preference to slavery."[1]

By 1850, Brown's story was well-known among abolitionists and, like many slaves who had recently escaped the South with no true marketable skills, Brown involved himself with the abolitionist lecture circuit. Brown's image appeared in periodicals in North America and Great Britain. Brown's narrative, published in 1849, served as a way of situating the particularities of the African American experience within the larger context of America's history and revolutionary spirit.

Brown's work continued in the United States until the passage of the Fugitive Slave Act, which was contained in the Compromise of 1850. In September 1850, Brown relocated to England in an effort to avoid being captured and returned to the South. He prospered as an entrepreneur and quasi entertainer who specialized in exposing the injustices of the North American slave system. Brown eventually married a British woman and seems to have lived abroad for the remainder of his life.[2]

Narrative of Henry Box Brown is reprinted here from the first edition. This edition was initially published in Boston in 1849.

Further Reading

Blackett, R. J. M. *Building an Antislavery Wall*. Baton Rouge: Louisiana State University Press, 1983; Olney, James. "'Was Born': Slave Narratives, Their Status as Autobiography and as Literature." In *The Slave's Narrative*, edited by Charles T. Davis and Henry Louis Gates Jr., 148–75. New York: Oxford University Press, 1985;

Wolff, Cynthia Griffin. "Passing Beyond the Middle Passage: Henry 'Box' Brown's Translations of Slavery." *Massachusetts Review* 37 (Spring 1996): 23–44; Wood, Marcus. "'All Right!': The Narrative of Henry Box Brown as a Test Case for the Racial Prescription of Rhetoric and Semiotics." *Proceedings of the American Antiquarian Society* 107 (April 1997): 65–104.

NARRATIVE
OF
HENRY BOX BROWN,
WHO ESCAPED FROM SLAVERY ENCLOSED IN A BOX 3 FEET LONG AND 2 WIDE.

Written from a
Statement of Facts Made by Himself.
With Remarks Upon the Remedy for Slavery
by Charles Stearns.

Boston:
PUBLISHED BY BROWN & STEARNS.
For Sale by Bela Marsh, 25 Cornhill.

Abner Forbes, Printer.
37 Cornhill

The Christian Reformer and Workingmen's advocate, Is published monthly at 25 Cornhill, Boston, by CHARLES STEARNS, *at 50 Cents per annum.*

The object of this journal is two-fold. First, to expose the rotten systems of error, which usurp the place upon which should stand the beautiful temple of "pure and undefiled religion." Secondly, to erect on the spot now occupied by these temples of sin, or adjacent thereto, a broad and stately tabernacle of perfect love to God and man, into which all the human race may crowd, and find a heaven for their souls, by *developing and perfecting their mental, moral, and physical faculties.*

The object of this paper is to redeem man from all bondage to his fellow men, and from all slavery to wrongdoing, and to present him a "perfect man in Christ Jesus." *Subscriptions received at No. 25 Cornhill.*

BELA MARSH, No. 25 Cornhill, keeps constantly on hand a large supply of all kinds of REFORMATORY PUBLICATIONS, which he will sell at Wholesale or Retail, at the lowest prices. Works on Prenology, Physiology, Diseases of Women, and *Physical Science* in general, for sale by him.

Also, a new work on Epidemics, or "the Science of Man," embracing moral as well as physical epidemics, and abounding in important instructions in reference to diet, cure of diseases without a physician, &c., &c., by Lewis S. Hough, A. M.

PREFACE

Not for the purpose of administering to a prurient desire to "hear and see some new thing," nor to gratify any inclination on the part of the hero of the following story to be honored by man, is this simple and touching narrative of the perils of a seeker after the "boon of liberty," introduced to the public eye; but that the people of this country may be made acquainted with the horrid sufferings endured by one as, in a *portable prison*, shut out from the light of heaven, and nearly deprived of its balmy air, he pursued his fearful journey directly through the heart of a country making its boasts of liberty and freedom to all, and that thereby a chord of human sympathy may be touched in the hearts of those who listen to his plaintive tale, which may be the means of furthering the spread of those principles, which under God, shall yet prove "mighty to the pulling down of the strong-holds" of slavery.

O reader, as you peruse this heart-rending tale, let the tear of sympathy roll freely from your eyes, and let the deep fountains of human feeling, which God has implanted in the breast of every son and daughter of Adam, burst forth from their enclosure, until a stream shall flow therefrom on to the surrounding world, of so invigorating and purifying a nature, as to arouse from the "death of the sin" of slavery, and cleanse from the pollutions thereof, all with whom you may be connected. As Henry Box Brown's thrilling escape is portrayed before you, let it not be perused by you as an idle tale, while you go away "forgetting what manner of persons you are;" but let truth find an avenue through your sensibilities, by which it can reach the citadel of your soul, and there dwell in all its life-giving power, expelling the whole brotherhood of pro-slavery errors, which politicians, priests, and selfish avarice, have introduced to the acquaintance of your intellectual faculties. These faculties are oftener blinded by selfishness, than are imbecile of themselves, as the powerful intellect of a Webster[3] is led captive to the inclinations of a not unselfish heart; so that that which should be the ruling power of every man's nature, is held in degrading submission to the inferior feelings of his heart. If man is blinded to the appreciation of the good, by a mass of selfish sensibilities, may he not be induced to surrender his will to the influence of truth, by *benevolent* feelings being caused to spring forth in his heart? That this may be the case with all whose eyes gaze upon the picture here drawn of misery, and of endurance, worthy of a Spartan, and such as a hero of olden times might be proud of, and transmit to posterity, along with the armorial emblazonry of his ancestors, is the ardent desire of all connected with the publication of this work. A word in regard to the literary character of the tale before you. The narrator is freshly from a land where books and schools are forbidden under severe penalties, to all in his former condition, and of course knoweth not letters, having never learned them; but of his capabilities otherwise, no one can doubt, when they recollect that if the records of all nations, from the time when Adam and Eve first placed their free feet upon the soil of Eden, until the conclusion of the scenes depicted by Hildreth and Macaulay,[4] should be diligently searched, a parallel instance of heroism, in behalf of personal liberty, could not be found. Instances of fortitude for the defence of religious freedom, and in cases of a violation of conscience being required; and for the sake of offspring, of friends and of one's country are not uncommon; but whose heroism and ability to contrive, united, have equalled our friend's whose story is now before you?*

A William and an Ellen Craft[5] indeed performed an almost equally hazardous undertaking, and one which, as a devoted admirer of human daring has said, far exceeded any thing recorded by Macaulay, and will yet be made the ground-work for a future Scott to build a more intensely interesting tale upon than "the author of Waverly" ever put forth, but they had the benefit of their eyes and ears—they were not entirely helpless; enclosed in a moving tomb, and as utterly destitute of power to control your movements as if death had fastened its icy arm upon you, and yet possessing all the full tide of gushing sensibilities, and a complete

---

*Hugo Grotius was, in the year 1620, sent from prison, confined in a small chest of drawers, by the affectionate hands of a faithful wife, but he was taken by *friends* on horseback and carried to the house of a friend, without undergoing much suffering or running the terrible risk which our friend ran.

knowledge of your existence, as was the case with our friend. We read with horror of the burial of persons before life has entirely fled from them, but here is a man who voluntarily assumed a condition in which he well knew all the chances were against him, and when his head seemed well-nigh severed from his body, on account of the concussion occasioned by the rough handling to which he was subject, see the Spartan firmness of his soul. Not a groan escaped from his agonized heart, as the realities of his condition were so vividly presented before him. Death stared him in the face, but like Patrick Henry,[6] only when the alternative was more a matter of fact than it was to that patriot, he exclaims, "Give me liberty or give me death;" and death seemed to say, as quickly as the lion seizes the kid cast into its den, "You are already mine," and was about to wrap its sable mantle around the form of our self-martyred hero—bound fast upon the altars of freedom, as the Hindoo widow is bound upon the altar of a husband's love; when the bright angel of liberty, whose dazzling form he had so long and so anxiously watched, as he pored over the scheme hid in the recesses of his own fearless brain, while yet a slave, and whose shining eyes had bewitched his soul, until he had said in the language of one of old to Jesus, "I will follow thee whithersoever thou goest;"[7] when this blessed goddess stood at his side, and, as Jesus said to one lying cold in death's embrace, "I say unto thee, arise," said to him, as she took him by the hand and lifted him from his travelling tomb, "thy warfare is over, thy work is accomplished, a free man art thou, my guidance has availed thee, arise and breathe the air of freedom."[8]

Did Lazarus[9] astonish his weeping sisters, and the surrounding multitude, as he emerged from his house of clay, clad in the habiliments of the grave, and did joy unfeigned spread throughout that gazing throng? How much more astonishing seemed the birth of Mr. Brown, as he "came forth" from a box, clothed not in the habiliments of the grave, but in those of slavery, worse than the "silent house of death," as his acts had testified; and what greater joy thrilled through the wondering witnesses, as the lid was removed from the travelling carriage of our friend's electing, and straightway arose therefrom a living man, a being made in God's own image, a son of Jehovah, whom the piety and republicanism of this nation had doomed to pass through this terrible ordeal, before the wand of the goddess of liberty could complete his transformation from a slave to a free man! But we will desist from further comments. Here is the plain narrative of our friend, and is it asking too much of you, whose sympathies may be aroused by the recital which follows, to continue to peruse these pages until the cause of all his sufferings is depicted before you, and your duty under the circumstances is clearly pointed out?

Here are the identical words uttered by him as soon as he inhaled the fresh air of freedom, after the faintness occasioned by his sojourn in his temporary tomb had passed away.

Hymn of Thanksgiving, Sung By Henry Box Brown, *After Being Released From His Confinement in the Box, At Philadelphia.*

I waited patiently, I waited patiently for the Lord, for the Lord,
And he inclined unto me, and heard my calling;
I waited patiently, I waited patiently for the Lord,
And he inclined unto me, and heard my calling;
And he hath put a new song in my mouth,
Ev'n a thanksgiving, Ev'n a thanksgiving, Ev'n a thanksgiving unto our God.

Blessed, Blessed, Blessed, Blessed is the man, Blessed is the man,
Blessed is the man that hath set his hope, his hope in the Lord;
O Lord my God, Great, Great, Great,
Great are the wondrous works which thou hast done,
Great are the wondrous works which thou hast done, which thou hast done,
Great are the wondrous works,
Great are the wondrous works,
Great are the wondrous works, which thou hast done.

If I should declare them and speak of them, they should be more, more, more than I am able to express.
I have not kept back thy loving kindness and truth from the great congregation,
I have not kept back thy loving kindness and truth from the great congregation.

Withdraw not thou thy mercy from me,
Withdraw not thou thy mercy from me, O Lord,
Let thy loving kindness and thy truth always preserve me,
Let all those that seek thee be joyful and glad,
Let all those that seek thee, be joyful and glad, be joyful, be glad, be joyful and glad, be joyful, be joyful, be joyful, be joyful, be joyful and glad, be glad in thee.

And let such as love thy salvation,
And let such as love thy salvation, say always,
The Lord be praised,
The Lord be praised:
Let all those that seek thee be joyful and glad,
And let such as love thy salvation, say always,
The Lord be praised,
The Lord be praised,
The Lord be praised.

Boston, Sept. 1, 1849.

NARRATIVE

I AM not about to harrow the feelings of my readers by a terrific representation of the untold horrors of that fearful system of oppression, which for thirty-three long years entwined its snaky folds about my soul, as the serpent of South America coils itself around the form of its unfortunate victim. It is not my purpose to descend deeply into the dark and noisome caverns of the hell of slavery, and drag from their frightful abode those lost spirits who haunt the souls of the poor slaves, daily and nightly with their frightful presence, and with the fearful sound of their terrific instruments of torture; for other pens far abler than mine have effectually performed that portion of the labor of an exposer of the enormities of slavery. Slavery, like the shield discovered by the knights of olden time, has two diverse sides to it; the one, on which is fearfully written in letters of blood, the character of the mass who carry on that dreadful system of unhallowed bondage; the other, touched with the pencil of a gentler delineator, and telling the looker on, a tale of comparative freedom, from the terrible deprivations so vividly portrayed on its opposite side.

My book will present, if possible, the beautiful side of the picture of slavery; will entertain you with stories of partial kindness on the part of my master, and of comparative enjoyment on my own part, as I grew up under the benign influence of the blessed system so closely connected with our "republican institutions," as Southern politicians tell us.

From the time I first breathed the air of human existence, until the hour of my escape from bondage, I did not receive but one whipping. I never suffered from lack of food, or on account of too extreme labor; nor for want of sufficient clothing to cover my person. My tale is not, therefore, one of horrid inflictions of the lash upon my naked body; of cruel starvings and of insolent treatment; but is the very best representation of slavery which can be given; therefore, reader, allow me to inform you, as you, for aught I know, may be one of those degraded mortals who fancy that if no blows are inflicted upon the slave's body, and a plenty of "bread and bacon" is dealed out to him, he is therefore no sufferer, and slavery is not a cruel institution; allow me to inform you, that I did not escape from such deprivations. It was not for fear of the lash's dreaded infliction, that I endured that fearful imprisonment, which you are waiting to read concerning; nor because of destitution of the necessaries of life, did I enclose myself in my travelling prison, and traverse your boasted land of freedom, a portion of the time with my head in an inverted position, as if it were a terrible crime for me to endeavor to escape from slavery.

Far beyond, in terrible suffering, all outward cruelties of the foul system, are those inner pangs which rend the heart of fond affection, when the "bone of your bone, and the flesh of your flesh" is separated from your embrace, by the ruthless hand of the merciless tyrant, as he plucks from your heart of love, the one whom

God hath given you for a "help-meet" through the journey of life; and more fearful by far than all the blows of the bloody lash, or the pangs of cruel hunger are those lashings of the *heart*, which the best of slaveholders inflict upon their happy and "well off" slaves, as they tear from their grasp the pledges of love, smiling at the side of devoted attachment. Tell me not of kind masters under slavery's hateful rule! There is no such thing as a person of that description; for, as you will see, my master, one of the most distinguished of this uncommon class of slaveholders, hesitated not to allow the wife of my love to be torn from my fond embrace, and the darling idols of my heart, my little children, to be snatched from my arms, and thus to doom them to a separation from me, more dreadful to all of us than a large number of lashes, inflicted on us daily. And yet to this fate I was continually subject, during a large portion of the time, when heaven *seemed* to smile propitiously above me; and no black clouds of fearful character lowered over my head. Heaven save me from kind masters, as well as from those called more cruel; for even their "tender mercies are cruel," and what no freeman could endure for a moment. My tale necessarily lacks that thrilling interest which is attached to the more than romantic, although perfectly true descriptions of a life in slavery, given by my numerous forerunners in the work of sketching a slave's personal experience; but I shall endeavor to intermingle with it other scenes which came under my own observation, which will serve to convince you, that if I was spared a worse fate than actually fell to my lot, yet my comrades around me were not so fortunate; but were the victims of the ungovernable rage of those men, of whose characters one cannot be informed, without experiencing within his soul, a rushing of overflowing emotions of pity, indignation and horror.

I first drew the breath of life in Louisa County, Va., forty-five miles from the city of Richmond, in the year 1816. I was born a slave. Not because at the moment of my birth an angel stood by, and declared that such was the will of God concerning me; although in a country whose most honored writings declare that all men have a right to liberty, given them by their Creator, it seems strange that I, or any of my brethren, could have been born without this inalienable right, unless God had thus signified his departure from his usual rule, as described by our fathers.[10] Not, I say, on account of God's willing it to be so, was I born a slave, but for the reason that nearly all the people of this country are united in legislating against heaven, and have contrived to vote down our heavenly father's rules, and to substitute for them, that cruel law which binds the chains of slavery upon one sixth part of the inhabitants of this land. I was born a slave! and wherefore? Tyrants, remorseless, destitute of religion and principle, stood by the couch of my mother, as heaven placed a pure soul, in the infantile form, there lying in her arms—a new being, never having breathed earth's atmosphere before; and fearlessly, with no compunctions of remorse, stretched forth their bloody arms and pressed the life of God from me, baptizing my soul and body as their own property; goods and chattels in their hands! Yes, they robbed me of myself, before I could know the nature of their wicked acts; and for ever afterwards, until I took possession of my own soul and body, did they retain their stolen property. This was why I was born a slave. Reader, can you understand the horrors of that fearful name? Listen, and I will assist you in this difficult work. My father, and my *mother* of course, were slaves before me;[11] but both of them are now enjoying the invaluable boon of liberty, having purchased themselves, in this land of freedom! At an early age, my mother would take me on her knee, and pointing to the forest trees adjacent, now being stripped of their thick foliage by autumnal winds, would say to me, "my son, as yonder leaves are stripped from off the trees of the forest, so are the children of slaves swept away from them by the hands of cruel tyrants;" and her voice would tremble, and she would seem almost choked with her deep emotions, while the big tears would find their way down her saddened cheeks, as she fondly pressed me to her heaving bosom, as if to save me from so dreaded a calamity. I was young then, but I well recollect the sadness of her countenance, and the mournfulness of her words, and they made a deep impression upon my youthful mind. Mothers of the North, as you gaze upon the free forms of your idolized little ones, as they playfully and confidently move around you, O if you knew that the lapse of a few years would infallibly remove them from your affectionate care, not to be laid in the silent grave, "where the wicked cease from troubling," but to be the sport of cruel men, and the victims of barbarous tyrants, who would snatch them from your side, as the robber seizes upon the bag of gold in the traveller's hand; O, would not your life then be rendered a miserable one indeed? Who can trace the workings of a slave mother's soul, as she counts over the hours, the departure of which, she almost knows, will rob her of her darling children, and consign them to a fate more horrible than death's cold embrace! O, who can hear of these cruel deprivations, and not be aroused to action in the slave's behalf?

My mother used to instruct me in the principles of morality, as much as she was able; but I was deplorably ignorant on religious subjects, for what ideas can a slave have of religion, when those who profess it around him, are demons in human shape oftentimes, as you will presently see was the case with my master's overseer? My mother used to tell me not to steal, and not to lie, and to behave myself properly in other respects. She took a great deal of pains with me and my brother; which resulted in our endeavors to conduct ourselves with propriety. As a specimen of the religious knowledge of the slaves, I will state here my ideas in regard to my master; assuring the reader that I am not joking, but stating what was the opinion of all the slave children on my master's plantation; and I have often talked it over with my early associates, and my mother, and enjoyed hearty laughs at the absurdity of our youthful ideas.

I really believed my old master was Almighty God, and that his son, my young master, was Jesus Christ.* One reason I had for this belief was, that when it was about to thunder, my old master would approach us, if we were in the yard, and say, "All you children run into the house now, for it is going to thunder," and after the shower was over, we would go out again, and he would approach us smilingly, and say, "What a fine shower we have had," and bidding us look at the flowers in the garden, would say, "how pretty the flowers look now." We thought that *he* thundered, and caused the rain to fall; and not until I was eight years of age, did I get rid of this childish superstition. Our master was uncommonly kind, and as he moved about in his dignity, he seemed like a god to us, and probably he did not dislike our reverential feelings towards him. All the slaves called his son, our Saviour, and the way I was enlightened on this point was as follows. One day after returning from church, my mother told father of a woman who wished to join the church. She told the preacher she had been baptized by one of the slaves, who was called from his office, "John the Baptist;" and on being asked by the minister if she believed "that our Saviour came into the world, and had died for the sins of man," she replied, that she "knew he had come into the world," but she "had not heard he was dead, as she lived so far from the road, she did not learn much that was going on in the world." I then asked mother, if young master was dead. She said it was not him they were talking about; it was "our Saviour in heaven." I then asked her if there were two Saviours, when she told me that young master was not "our Saviour," which filled me with astonishment, and I could not understand it at first. Not long after this, my sister became anxious to have her soul converted, and shaved the hair from her head, as many of the slaves thought they could not be converted without doing this. My mother reproved her, and began to tell her of God who dwelt in heaven, and that she must pray to him to convert her. This surprised me still more, and I asked her if old master was not God; to which she replied that he was not, and began to instruct me a little in reference to the God of heaven. After this, I believed there was a God who ruled the world, but I did not previously, have the least idea of any such being. And why should not my childish fancy be correct, according to the blasphemous teachings of the heathen system of slavery? Does not every slaveholder assume exclusive control over all the actions of his unfortunate victims? Most assuredly he does, as this extract from the laws of a slaveholding State will show you. "A slave is one who is in the power of his master, to whom he belongs. A slave owes to his master and all his family, *respect without bounds and absolute obedience*." How tallies this with the unalterable law of Jehovah, "Thou shalt have no other gods before me?"[12] Does not the system of slavery effectually shut

---

*The reader may be disposed to doubt the truth of the above assertion, but I once asked a girl in Ky., whose mistress was a Methodist church member, if she could tell me "who Jesus Christ was?" "Yes," said she, "he is the bad man." C. S.

out from the slave's heart, all true knowledge of the eternal God, and doom him to grope his perilous way, amid the thick darkness of unenlightened heathenism, although he dwells in a land professing much religion, and an entire freedom from the superstitions of paganism?

Let me tell you my opinion of the slaveholding religion of this land. I believe in a hell, where the wicked will forever dwell, and knowing the character of slaveholders and slavery, it is my settled belief, as it was while I was a slave, even though I was treated kindly, that *every* slaveholder will infallibly go to that hell, unless he repents. I do not believe in the religion of the Southern churches, nor do I perceive any great difference between them, and those at the North, which uphold them.

While a young lad, my principal employment was waiting upon my master and mistress, and at intervals taking lessons in what is the destiny of most of the slaves, the cultivation of the plantation. O how often as the hot sun sent forth its scorching rays upon my tender head, did I look forward with dismay, to the time, when I, like my fellow slaves, should be driven by the task-master's cruel lash, to the performance of unrequited toil upon the plantation of my master. To this expectation is the slave trained. Like the criminal under sentence of death, he notches upon his wooden stick, as Sterne's captive did,[13] the days, after the lapse of which he must be introduced to his dreaded fate; in the case of the criminal, merely death—a cessation from the pains and toils of life; but in our cases, the commencement of a living death; a death never ending, second in horror only to the eternal torment of the wicked in a future state. Yea, even worse than that, for there, a God of love and mercy holds the rod of punishment in his own hand; but in our case, it is held by men from whom almost the last vestige of goodness has departed, and in whose hearts there dwells hardly a spark of humanity, certainly not enough to keep them from the practice of the most inhuman crimes. Imagine, reader, a fearful cloud, gathering blackness as it advances towards you, and increasing in size constantly; hovering in the deep blue vault of the firmament above you, which cloud seems loaded with the elements of destruction, and from the contents of which you are certain you cannot escape. You are sailing upon the now calm waters of the broad and placid deep, spreading its "unadorned bosom" before you, as far as your eye can reach,

"Calm as a slumbering babe,
Tremendous Ocean lays:"

and on its "burnished waves," gracefully rides your little vessel, without fear or dismay troubling your heart. But this fearful cloud is pointed out to you, and as it gathers darkness, and rushes to the point of the firmament overhanging your fated vessel, O what terror then seizes upon your soul, as hourly you expect your little bark to be deluged by the contents of the cloud, and riven by the fierce lightnings enclosed in that mass of angry elements. So with the slave, only that he knows his chances of escape are exceedingly small, while you may very likely outlive the storm.

To this terrible apprehension we are all constantly subject. To-day, master may smile lovingly upon us, and the sound of the cracking whip may be hushed, but the dread uncertainty of our future fate still hangs over us, and to-morrow may witness a return of all the elements of fearful strife, as we emphatically "know not what a day may bring forth." The sweet songsters of the air, as it were, may warble their musical notes ever so melodiously, harmonizing with the soft blowing of the western winds which invigorates our frames, and the genial warmth of the early sun may fill us with pleasurable emotions; but we know that ere long, this sweet singing must be silenced by the fierce cracking of the bloody lash, falling on our own shoulders, and that the cool breezes and the gentle heat of early morn, must be succeeded by the hot winds and fiery rays of Slavery's meridian day. The slave has *no certainty* of the enjoyment of *any privilege whatever!* All his fancied blessings, without a moment's warning being granted to him, may be swept forever from his trembling grasp. Who will then say that "disguise itself" as Slavery will, it is not "a bitter cup," the mixture whereof is gall and wormwood?

My brother and myself, were in the practice of carrying grain to mill, a few times a year, which was the means of furnishing us with some information respecting other slaves. We often went twenty miles, to a mill owned by a Col. Ambler, in Yansinville county, and used to improve our opportunities for gaining information. Especially desirous were we, of learning the condition of slaves around us, for we knew not how long we should remain in as favorable hands as we were then. On one occasion, while waiting for our grain, we entered a house in the neighborhood, and while resting ourselves there, we saw a number of forlorn-looking beings pass the door, and as they passed, we noticed that they turned and gazed earnestly upon us. Afterwards, about fifty performed the same act, which excited our minds somewhat, as we overheard some of them say, "Look there, and see those two colored men with shoes, vests and hats on," and we determined to obtain an interview with them. Accordingly, after receiving some bread and meat from our hosts, we followed these abject beings to their quarters;—and such a sight we had never witnessed before, as we had always lived on our master's plantation, and this was about the first of our journeys to the mill. They were dressed with shirts made of coarse bagging, such as coffee-sacks are made from, and some kind of light substance for pantaloons, and *no other clothing whatever*. They had on no shoes, hats, vests, or coats, and when my brother asked them why they spoke of our being dressed with those articles of clothing, they said they had "never seen negroes dressed in that way before." They looked very hungry, and we divided our bread and meat among them, which furnished them only a mouthful each. They never had any meat, they said, given them by their masters. My brother put various questions to them, such as, "if they had wives?" "did they go to church?" "had they any sisters?" &c. The one who gave us the information, said they had wives, but were obliged to marry on their own plantation. Master would not allow them to go away from home to marry, consequently he said they were all related to each other, and master made them marry, *whether related or not*. My brother asked this man to show him his sisters; he said he could not tell them from the rest, *they were all his sisters*; and here let me state, what is well known by many people, that no such thing as real marriage is allowed to exist among the slaves. Talk of marriage under such a system! Why, the owner of a Turkish harem, or the keeper of a house of ill-fame, might as well allow the inmates of their establishments to marry as for a Southern slaveholder to do the same. Marriage, as is well known, is the voluntary and perfect union of one man with one woman, without depending upon the will of a third party. This never can take place under slavery, for the moment a slave is allowed to form such a connection as he chooses, the spell of slavery is dissolved. The slave's wife is his, only at the will of her master, who may violate her chastity with impunity. It is my candid opinion that one of the strongest motives which operate upon the slaveholders, and induce them to retain their iron grasp upon the unfortunate slave, is because it gives them such unlimited control in this respect over the female slaves. The greater part of slaveholders are licentious men, and the most respectable and the kindest of masters, keep some of their slaves as mistresses. It is for their pecuniary interest to do so in several respects. Their progeny is so many dollars and cents in their pockets, instead of being a bill of expense to them, as would be the case if their slaves were free; and mulatto slaves command a higher price than dark colored ones; but it is too horrid a subject to describe. Suffice it to say, that no slave has the least certainty of being able to retain his wife or her husband a single hour; so that the slave is placed under strong inducements not to form a union of *love*, for he knows not how soon the chords wound around his heart would be snapped asunder, by the hand of the brutal slave-dealer. Northern people sustain slavery, knowing that it is a system of perfect licentiousness, and yet go to church and boast of their purity and holiness!

On this plantation, the slaves were never allowed to attend church, but managed their religious affairs in their own way. An old slave, whom they called Uncle John, decided upon their piety, and would baptize them during the silent watches of the night, while their master was "taking his rest in sleep." Thus is the slave under the necessity of ever "saving his soul" in the hours when the eye of his master, who usurps the place of God over him, is turned from him. Think of it, ye who contend for the necessity of these rites, to constitute a man a Christian! By night must the poor slave steal away from his bed of straw, and leaving his miserable hovel, must drag his weary limbs to some adjacent stream of water, where a fellow slave as ignorant as himself, proceeds to administer the ordinance of baptism; and as he plunges his comrades into the water, in imitation of the Baptist of old,[14] how he trembles, lest the footsteps of his master should be heard, advancing to their

Bethesda,[15] knowing that if such should be the case, the severe punishment that awaits them all. Baptists, are ye striking hands with Southern churches, which thus exclude so many slaves from the "waters of salvation?"

But we were obliged to cut short our conversation with these slaves, by beholding the approach of the overseer, who was directing his steps towards us, like a bear seeking its prey. We had only time to ask this man, "if they were often whipped?" to which he replied, that not a day passed over their heads, without some of their number being brutally punished; "and," said he, "we shall have to suffer for this talk with you." He then told us, that many of them had been severely whipped that very morning, for having been baptized the night before. After we left them, we looked back, and heard the screams of these poor creatures, suffering under the blows of the hard-hearted overseer, for the crime of talking with us;—which screams sounded in our ears for some time. We felt thankful that we were exempted from such terrible treatment; but still, we knew not how soon we should be subject to the same cruel fate. By this time we had returned to the mill, where we met a young man, (a relation of the owner of this plantation,) who for some time appeared to be eyeing us quite attentively. At length he asked me if I had "ever been whipped," and when I told him I had not, he replied, "Well, you will neither of you ever be of any value, then;" so true is it that whipping is considered a necessary part of slavery. Without this practice, it could not stand a single day. He expressed a good deal of surprise that we were allowed to wear hats and shoes,—supposing that a slave had no business to wear such clothing as his master wore. We had brought our fishing-lines with us, and requested the privilege to fish in his stream, which he roughly denied us, saying, "we do not allow niggers to fish." Nothing daunted, however, by this rebuff, my brother went to another place, and was quite successful in his undertaking, obtaining a plentiful supply of the finny tribe;[16] but as soon as this youngster perceived his good luck, he ordered him to throw them back into the stream, which he was obliged to do, and we returned home without them.

We finally abandoned visiting this mill, and carried our grain to another, a Mr. Bullock's, only ten miles distant from our plantation. This man was very kind to us, took us into his house and put us to bed, took charge of our horses, and carried the grain himself into the mill, and in the morning furnished us with a good breakfast. I asked my brother why this man treated us so differently from our old miller. "Oh," said he, "this man is not a slaveholder!" Ah, that explained the difference; for there is nothing in the southern character averse to gentleness. On the contrary, if it were not for slavery's withering touch, the Southerners would be the kindest people in the land. Slavery possesses the power attributed to one of old, of changing the nature of all who drink of its vicious cup.

"———Which, as they taste,
Soon as the potion works, their *human* countenance,
The express resemblance of the gods, is changed

Into some brutish form of wolf, or bear,
Or ounce, or tiger, hog, or bearded goat;
And they, so perfect is their misery,
Not once perceive their foul disfigurement,
But boast themselves more comely than before."

Under the influence of slavery's polluting power, the most gentle women become the fiercest viragos,[17] and the most benevolent men are changed into inhuman monsters. It is true of the northern man who goes South also.

"*Whoever* tastes, loses his upright shape,
And downward falls, into a *grovelling swine.*"

This non-slaveholder also allowed us to catch as many fish as we pleased, and even furnished us with fishing implements. While at this mill, we became acquainted with a colored man from another part of the country; and as our desire was strong to learn how our brethren fared in other places, we questioned him respecting his treatment. He complained much of his hard fate,—said he had a wife and one child, and begged for some of our fish to carry to his wife; which my brother gladly gave him. He said he was expecting to have some money in a few days, which would be *"the first he ever had in his life!"* He had sent a thousand hickory-nuts to market, for which he afterwards informed us he had received thirty-six cents, which he gave to his wife, to furnish her with some little article of comfort. This was the sum total of all the money he had ever been the possessor of! Ye northern pro-slavery men, do you regard this as robbery, or not? The whole of this man's earnings had been robbed from him during his entire life, except simply his coarse food and miserable clothing, the whole expense of which, for a plantation slave, does not exceed twenty dollars a year. This is one reason why I think every slaveholder will go to hell; for my Bible teaches me that no *thief* shall enter heaven,[18] and I know every slaveholder is a thief; and I rather think you would all be of my opinion if you had ever been a slave. But now, assisting these thieves, and being made rich by them, you say they are not robbers; just as wicked men generally shield their abettors.

On our return from this place, we met a colored man and woman, who were very cross to each other. We inquired as to the cause of their trouble, and the man told us, that "women had such tongues!" that some of them had stolen a sheep, and this woman, after eating of it, went and told their master, and they all had to receive a severe whipping. And here follows a specimen of slaveholding morality, which will show you how much many of the masters care for their slaves' stealing. This man enjoined upon his slaves never to steal from him again, but to *steal from his neighbors*, and he would keep them from punishment, if they would furnish him with a portion of the meat! And why not? For is it any worse for the slaveholders to steal from one another, than it is to steal from their helpless slaves? Not long after, these slaves availed themselves of their master's assistance, and stole an animal from a neighboring plantation, and according to agreement, furnished their master with his share. Soon the owner of the missing animal came rushing into the man's house, who had just eaten of the stolen food, and, in a very excited manner, demanded reparation from him, for the beast stolen, as he said, by this man's slaves. The villain, hardly able to stand after eating so bountifully of his neighbor's pork, exclaimed loudly, "my servants know no more about your hogs than I do!" which was strictly true; and the loser of the swine went away satisfied. This man told his slaves that it was a sin to steal from him, but none to steal from his neighbors! My brother told the slave we were conversing with, that it was as much of a sin in God's sight, for him to steal from one, as from the other. "Oh," said the slave, "master says *negroes have nothing to do with God!*" He further informed us that his master and mistress lived very unhappily together, on account of the maid who waited upon them. She had no husband, but had several yellow children. After we left them, they went to a fodder-stack, and took out a jug, and drank of its contents. My brother's curiosity was excited to learn the nature of their drink; and watching his opportunity, unobserved by them, he slipped up to the stack, and ascertained that the jug was nearly full of Irish whiskey. He carried it home with him, and the next time we visited the mill, he returned the jug to its former place, filled with molasses, purchased with his own money, instead of the fiery drink which it formerly contained. Some time after this, the master of this man discovered a great falling off in the supply of stolen meat furnished him by the slaves, and questioned this man in reference to the cause of such a lamentable diminution in the supply of hog-meat in particular. The slave told him the story of the jug, and that he had ceased drinking, which was sad news for the pork-loving gentleman.

I will now return to my master's affairs. My young master's brother was a very benevolent man, and soon became convinced that it was wrong to hold men in bondage; which belief he carried into practice by emancipating forty slaves at one time, and paying the expenses of their transportation to a free state. But old master, although naturally more kind-hearted than his neighbors, could not always remain as impervious to the assaults of the pro-slavery demon; and as stated previously, that all who drank of this hateful cup were transformed into some vile animal, so he became a perfect brute in his treatment of his slaves. I cannot account for this change, only on the supposition, that experience had convinced him that kind treatment was not as well adapted to the production of crops, as a severer kind of discipline. Under the elating influence of freedom's inspiring sound, men will labor much harder, than when forced to perform unpleasant tasks, the accomplishment of which will be of no value to themselves; but while the slave is held as such, it is difficult for him to feel as he would feel, if he was a free man, however light may be his tasks, and however kind may be his master. The lash is still held above his head, and *may* fall upon him, even if its blows are for a longtime withheld. This the slave realizes; and hence no kind treatment can destroy the depressing influence of a consciousness of his being a slave,—no matter how lightly the yoke of slavery may rest upon his shoulders. He knows the yoke is there; and that at any time its weight may be made heavier, and his form almost sink under its weary burden; but give him his liberty, and new life enters into him immediately. The iron yoke falls from his chafed shoulders; the collar, even if it was a silken one, is removed from his enslaved person; and the chains, although made of gold, fall from his bound limbs, and he walks forth with an elastic step, to enjoy the realities of his new existence. Now he is ready to perform irksome tasks; for the avails of his labor will be of value to himself, and with them he can administer comfort to those near and dear to him, and to the world at large, as well as provide for his own intellectual welfare; whereas before, however kind his treatment, all his earnings more than his expenses went to enrich his master. It is on this account, probably, that those who have undertaken to carry out some principles of humanity in their treatment of their slaves, have been generally frowned upon by their neighbors; and they have been forced either to emancipate their slaves, or to return to the cruel practices of those around them. My young master preferred the former alternative; my old master adopted the latter. We now began to taste a little of the horrors of slavery; so that many of the slaves ran away, which had not been the case before. My master employed an overseer also, about this time, which he always refused to do previously, preferring to take charge of us himself; but the clamor of the neighbors was so great at his mild treatment of his slaves, that he at length yielded to the popular will around him, and went "with the multitude to do evil," and hired an overseer. This was an end of our favorable treatment; and there is no telling what would have been the result of this new method among slaves so unused to the whip as we were, if in the midst of this experiment, old master had not been called upon to pay "the debt of nature," and to "go the way of all the earth." As he was about to expire, he sent for me and my brother, to come to his bedside. We ran with beating hearts, and highly elated feelings, not doubting that he was about to confer upon us the boon of freedom, as we expected to be set free when he died; but imagine my deep disappointment, when the old man called me to his side and said to me, "Henry, you will make a good plough-boy, or a good gardener; now you must be an honest boy, and never tell an untruth. I have given you to my son William, and you must obey him." Thus did this old gentleman deceive us by his former kind treatment, and raise expectations in our youthful minds, which were thus doomed to be fatally overthrown. Poor man! he has gone to a higher tribunal than man's, and doubtless ere this, earnestly laments that he did not give us all our liberty at this favorable moment; but sad as was our disappointment, we were constrained to submit to it, as we best were able. One old negro openly expressed his wish that master would die, because he had not released him from his bondage.

If there is any one thing which operates as an impetus to the slave in his toilsome labors and buoys him up, under all the hardships of his severe lot, it is this hope of future freedom, which lights up his soul and cheers his desolate heart in the midst of all the fearful agonies of the varied scenes of his slave life, as the soul of the tempest-tossed mariner is stayed from complete despair, by the faint glimmering of the far-distant light which the kindness of man has placed in a lighthouse, so as to be perceived by him at a long distance. Old ocean's tempestuous waves beat and roar against his frail bark, and the briny deep seems ready to enclose him in its wide open mouth, but "ever and anon" he perceives the glimmering of this feeble light in the distance, which keeps alive the spark of hope in his bosom, which kind heaven has placed within every man's breast. So with the slave. Freedom's fires are dimly burning in the far distant future, and ever and anon a fresh flame appears to arise in the direction of this sacred altar, until at times it seems to approach so near, that he can feel its melting power dissolving his chains, and causing him to emerge from his darkened prison, into the full light of freedom's glorious liberty. O the fond anticipations of the slave in this respect! I cannot correctly describe them to you, but I can recollect the thrills of exulting joy which the name of freedom caused to flow through my soul.

Freedom, the dear and joyful sound,
'Tis music in the sad slave's ear.

How often this hope is destined to fade away, as the early dew before the rising sun! Not unseldom, does the slave labor intensely to obtain the means to purchase his freedom, and after having paid the required sum, is still held a slave, while the master retains the money! This *very often* transpires under the slave system. A good many slaves have in this way paid for themselves several times, and not received their freedom then! And masters often hold out this inducement to their slaves, to labor more than they otherwise would, when they have no intention of fulfilling their promise. O the ineffable meanness of the slave system! Instead of our being set free, a far different fate awaited us; and here you behold, reader, the closing scene of the kindest treatment which a man can bestow upon his slaves.

It mattered not how benign might have been our master's conduct to us, it was to be succeeded by a harrowing scene, the inevitable consequence of our being left slaves. We must now be separated and divided into different lots, as we were inherited by the four sons of my master. It is no easy matter to amicably divide even the old furniture and worn-out implements of husbandry, and sometimes the very clothing of a deceased person, and oftentimes a scene of shame ensues at the opening of the will of a departed parent, which is enough to cause humanity to blush at the meanness of man. What then must be the sufferings of those persons, who are to be the objects of this division and strife? See the heirs of a departed slaveholder, disputing as to the rightful possession of human beings, many of them their old nurses, and their playmates in their younger days! The scene which took place at the division of my master's human property, baffles all description. I was then only thirteen years of age, but it is as fresh in my mind as if but yesterday's sun had shone upon the dreadful exhibition. My mother was separated from her youngest child, and not until she had begged and pleaded most piteously for its restoration to her, was it again placed in her hands. Turning her eyes fondly upon me, who was now to be carried from her presence, she said, "You now see, my son, the fulfilment of what I told you a great while ago, when I used to take you on my knee, and show you the leaves blown from the trees by the fearful winds." Yes, I now saw that one after another were the slave mother's children torn from her embrace, and John was given to one brother, Sarah to another, and Jane to a third, while Samuel fell into the hands of the fourth. It is a difficult matter to satisfactorily divide the slaves on a plantation, for no person wishes for *all* children, or for all old people; while both old, young, and middle aged ones are to be divided. There is no equitable way of dividing them, but by allowing each one to take his portion of both children, middle aged and old people; which necessarily causes heart-rending separations; but "slaves have no feelings," I am sometimes told. "You get used to these things; it would not do for us to experience them, but you are not constituted as we are;" to which I reply, that a slave's friends are *all* he possesses that is of value to him. He cannot read, he has no property, he cannot be a teacher of truth, or a politician; he cannot be very religious, and all that remains to him, aside from the hope of freedom, that ever present deity, forever inspiring him in his most terrible hours of despair, is the society of his friends. We love our friends more than white people love theirs, for we risk more to save them from suffering. Many of our number who have escaped from bondage ourselves, have jeopardized our own liberty, in order to release our friends, and sometimes we have been retaken and made slaves of again, while endeavoring to rescue our friends from slavery's iron jaws.

But does not the slave love his friends! What mean then those frantic screams, which every slave-auction witnesses, where the scalding tears rush in agonizing torrents down the sorrow-stricken cheeks of the bereaved slave mother; and where clubs are sometimes used to drive apart two fond friends who cling to each other, as the merciless slave-trader is to separate them forever. O, to talk of our not having feelings for our friends, is to mock that Being who has created us in his own image, and implanted deep in every human bosom, a gushing fount of tender sensibilities, which no life of sin can ever fully erase. Talk of our not having feelings, and then calmly look on the scene described as taking place when my master died! Have you any feeling? Does this recital arouse those sympathetic feelings in your bosom which you make your boast of? How can white people have hearts *of tenderness*, and allow such scenes to daily transpire at the South? All over the blackened and marred surface of the whole slave territory do these heart-rending transactions continually occur. Not a day inscribes its departing hours upon the dial of human existence, but it marks the overthrow of more than one family altar, and the sundering of numerous family ties; and yet the hot blood of Southern oppression is allowed to find its way into the hearts of the Northern people, who politically and religiously are doing their utmost to sustain the dreadful system; yea, competing with the South in their devotion to the evil genius of their country's choice. Slavery reigns and rules the councils of this nation, as Satan presides over Pandemonium, and the loud and clear cry of the anti-slavery host, calling upon the people of the land to cease their connection with the tyrannical system, is universally unheeded. It falls upon the closed ears of the people of this nation like the noise of the random shots of a vessel at sea, upon the ears of the captain of the opposing squadron, but to arouse them to action in *opposition* to the utterance of the voice of warning.

What though the plaintive cries of three millions of heart-broken and dejected captives, are wafted on every Southern gale to the ears of our Northern brethren, and the hot winds of the South reach our fastnesses amid the mountains and hills of our rugged land, loaded with the stifled cries and choking sobs of poor desolate woman, as her babes are torn one by one from her embrace; yet no Northern voice is heard to sound loudly enough among our hills and dales, to startle from their sleep of indifference, those who have it in their power to break the chains of the suffering bondmen *to-day*, saying to all who hear its clear sounding voice, "Come out from all connection with this terrible system of cruelty and blood, and form a government and a union free from this hateful curse." The Northern people have it in their power to-day, to cause all this suffering of which I have been speaking to cease, and to cause one loud and triumphant anthem of praise to ascend from the millions of panting, bleeding slaves, now stretched upon the plains of Southern oppression; and yet they talk of our being destitute of feeling. "O shame, where is thy blush!"

My father and mother were left on the plantation, and I was taken to the city of Richmond, to work in a tobacco manufactory, owned by my master's son William, who now became my only master. Old master, although he did not give me my freedom, yet left an especial charge with his son to take good care of me, and not to whip me, which charge my master endeavored to act in accordance with. He told me if I would behave well he would take good care of me, and would give me money to spend, &c. He talked so kindly to me that I determined I would exert myself to the utmost to please him, and would endeavor to do just what he wished me to, in every respect. He furnished me with a new suit of clothes, and gave me money to buy things with, to send to my mother. One day I overheard him telling the overseer that his father had raised me, and that I was a smart boy, and he must never whip me. I tried extremely hard to perform what I thought was my duty, and escaped the lash almost entirely; although the overseer would oftentimes have liked to have given me a severe whipping; but fear of both me and my master deterred him from so doing. It is true, my lot was still comparatively easy; but reader, imagine not that others were so fortunate as myself, as I will presently describe to you the character of our overseer; and you can judge what kind of treatment, persons wholly in his power might expect from such a man. But it was some time before I became reconciled to my fate, for after being so constantly with my mother, to be torn from her side, and she on a distant plantation, where I could not see or but seldom hear from her, was exceedingly trying to my youthful feelings, slave though I was. I missed her smiling look when her eye rested upon my form; and when I returned from my daily toil, weary and dejected, no fond mother's arms were extended to meet me, no one appeared to sympathize with me, and I felt I was indeed alone in the world. After the lapse of about a year and a half from the time I commenced living in Richmond, a strange series of events transpired. I did not then know precisely what was the cause of these scenes, for I could not get any very satisfactory information concerning the matter from my master, only that some of the slaves had undertaken to kill their owners; but I have since learned that it was the famous Nat Turner's insurrection[19] that caused all the excitement I witnessed. Slaves were whipped, hung, and cut down with swords in the streets, if found away from their quarters after dark. The whole city was in the utmost confusion and dismay; and a dark cloud of terrific blackness, seemed to hang over the heads of the whites. So true is it, that "the wicked flee when no man pursueth."[20] Great numbers of the slaves were locked in the prison, and many were "half hung," as it was termed; that is, they were suspended to some limb of a tree, with a rope about their necks, so adjusted as not to quite strangle them, and then they were pelted by the men and boys with rotten eggs. This half-hanging is a refined species of cruelty, peculiar to slavery, I believe.

Among the cruelties occasioned by this insurrection, which was however some distance from Richmond, was the forbidding of as many as five slaves to meet together, except they were at work, and the silencing of all colored preachers. One of that class in our city, refused to obey the imperial mandate, and was severely whipped; but his religion was too deeply rooted to be thus driven from him, and no promise could be extorted from his resolute soul, that he would not proclaim what he considered the glad tidings of the gospel. (Query. How many white preachers would continue their employment, if they were served in the same way?) It is strange that more insurrections do not take place among the slaves; but their masters have impressed upon their minds so forcibly the fact, that the United States Government is pledged to put them down, in case they should attempt any such movement, that they have no heart to contend against such fearful odds; and yet the slaveholder lives in constant dread of such an event.*

---

*In proof of this, I would state that during my residence at the South, a whole town was once thrown into an uproar by my entering a slave hut, about Christmas time, and talking and praying with the inmates about an hour. I was told that it would not be safe for me to remain in the town over night. C. S.

The rustling of

"———the lightest leaf,
That quivers to the passing breeze,"

fills his timid soul with visions of flowing blood and burning dwellings; and as the loud thunder of heaven rolls over his head, and the vivid lightning flashes across his pale face, straightway his imagination conjures up terrible scenes of the loud roaring of an enemy's cannon, and the fierce yells of an infuriated slave population, rushing to vengeance.* There is no doubt but this would be the case, if it were not for the Northern people, who are ready, as I have been often told, to shoot us down, if we attempt to rise and obtain our freedom. I believe that if the slaves could do as they wish, they would throw off their heavy yoke immediately, by rising against their masters; but ten millions of Northern people stand with their feet on their necks, and how can they arise? How was Nat Turner's insurrection suppressed, but by a company of United States troops, furnished the governor of Virginia at his request, according to your Constitution?

About this time, I began to grow alarmed respecting my future welfare, as a great eclipse of the sun had recently taken place; and the cholera reaching the country not long after, I thought that perhaps the day of judgment was not far distant, and I must prepare for that dreaded event. After praying for about three months, it pleased Almighty God, as I believe, to pardon my sins, and I was received into the Baptist Church, by a minister who thought it was wicked to hold slaves. I was obliged to obtain permission from my master, however, before I could join. He gave me a note to carry to the preacher, saying that I had *his permission* to join the church!

I shall now make you acquainted with the manner in which affairs were conducted in my master's tobacco manufactory, after which I shall introduce you to the heart-rending scenes which give the principal interest to my narrative.

My master carried on a large tobacco manufacturing establishment in Richmond, which was almost wholly under the supervision of one of those low, miserable, cruel, barbarous, and sometimes religious beings, known under the name of overseers, with which the South abounds. These men hardly deserve the name of men, for they are lost to all regard for decency, truth, justice and humanity, and are so far gone in human depravity, that before they can be saved, Jesus Christ, or some other Saviour, will have to die a second time. I pity them sincerely, but as my mind recurs to the wicked conduct I so often witnessed on the part of this one,

---

*While at the South, a gentleman came one day to a friend of mine, and in a very excited manner said to him, "Why, are you not afraid to have that man about you? Do you not fear that your house will be burned? I cannot sleep nights lest the slaves should rise and burn all before them." C. S.

I cannot prevent these indignant feelings from arising in my soul. O reader, if you had seen the perfect recklessness of conduct so often exhibited by this man, as I witnessed it, you would not blame me for expressing myself so strongly. I know that even this man is my brother, but he is a very wicked brother, whose soul I commend to Almighty God, hoping that his sovereign grace may find its way, if it is a possible thing, to his sin-hardened soul; *and yet he was a pious man*. His name was *John F. Allen*, and I suppose he still lives in Richmond. After reading about his character, I apprehend your judgment of him will coincide with mine. The other overseers, however, were very different men, for hell could hardly spare more than one such man, for one tobacco manufactory; as it is not overstocked with such vile reprobates.

But before proceeding to speak farther of him, I will inform you a little respecting our business—as not many of you have ever seen the inside of a tobacco manufactory. The building I worked in was about 300 feet in length, and three stories high, and afforded room for 200 people to work in, but only 150 persons were employed, 120 of whom were slaves, and the remainder free colored people. We were obliged to work *fourteen* hours a day, in the summer, and *sixteen* in the winter.

This work consisted in removing the stems from the leaves of tobacco, which was performed by women and boys, after which the tobacco was moistened with a liquor made from liquorice and sugar, which gives the tobacco that sweetish taste which renders it not perfectly abhorrent to those who chew it. After being thus moistened, the tobacco was taken by the men and twisted into hands, and pressed into lumps, when it was sent to the machine-house, and pressed into boxes and casks. After remaining in what was called the "sweat-house" about thirty days, it was shipped for the market.

Mr. Allen was a thorough going Yankee in his mode of doing business. He was by no means one of your indolent, do-nothing Southerners, so effeminate as to be hardly able to wield his hands to administer to his own necessities, but he was a savage-looking, dare-devil sort of a man, ready apparently for any emergency to which Beelzebub might call him, a real servant of the bottomless pit. He understood how to turn a penny as well as any Yankee pedlar who ever visited our city. Whether he derived his skill from associating with that class of individuals, or whether it was the natural production of his own cunning mind, I know not. He used often to boast, that by his shrewdness in managing the negroes, he made enough to support his family, which cost him $1000, without touching a farthing of his salary, which was $1500 per annum. Of the probability of this assertion, I can bear witness; for I know he was very skilful in another department of cunning and cheatery. Like many other servants of the evil one, he was an early riser; not for the purpose of improving his health, or that he might enjoy sweet communion with his heavenly Father, at his morning orisons, but that "while the master slept"[21] he might more easily transact his nefarious business. At whatever hour of the morning I might arrive at the factory, I seldom anticipated the seemingly industrious steps of Mr. Allen, who by his punctuality in this respect, obtained a good reputation as a faithful and devoted overseer. But mark the conduct of the pious gentleman, for he was a member of an Episcopalian church. One would have supposed from observing the transactions around him, that Mr. Allen took time by the forelock,[22] emphatically, for long before the early rays of the rising sun had gilded the eastern horizon, was this man busily engaged in loading a wagon with coal, oil, sugar, wood, &c., &c., which always found a place of deposit at *his own door*, entirely unknown to my master. This practice Mr. Allen carried on during my stay there, and yet he was a very pious man.

This man enjoyed the unlimited confidence of my master, so that he would never listen to a word of complaint on the part of any of the workmen. No matter how cruel or how *unjust* might be the punishment inflicted upon any of the hands, master would never listen to their complaints; so that this barbarous man was our master in reality. At one time a colored man, who had been in the habit of singing religious songs quite often, was taken sick and did not make his appearance at the factory. For two or three days no notice whatever was taken of him, no medicine provided for him, and no physician sent to heal him. At the end of that time, Mr. Allen ordered three strongmen to go to the man's house, and bring him to the factory. This order being obeyed, the man, pale and hardly able to stand, was stripped to his waist, his hands tied together, and the rope fastened to a large post. The overseer then questioned him about his singing, told him that it consumed too much time, and that he was going to give him some medicine which would cure him. The poor trembling man made no reply, when the pious Mr. Allen, for no crime except that of sickness, inflicted 200 lashes upon the quivering flesh of the invalid, and he would have continued his "apostolic blows," if the emaciated form of the languishing man, had not sunken under their heavy weight; and Mr. Allen was obliged to desist.[*] I witnessed this transaction with my own eyes; but what could I do, for I was a slave, and any interference on my part would only have brought the same punishment upon me. This man was sick a month afterwards, during which time the weekly allowance of seventy-five cents for the hands to board themselves with, was withheld from him, and his wife was obliged to support him by washing for others; and yet Northern people tell me that a slave is better off than a free man, because when he is sick his master provides for him! Master knew all the circumstances of this case, but never uttered one word of reproof to the overseer,

---

[*] While in Kentucky I knew of a case where a preacher punished a female slave in this way, and his wife stood by, throwing cold water into the slave's face, to keep her from fainting. In endeavoring to escape afterwards, the poor creature became faint from loss of blood, and her body was found partly devoured by the buzzards. C. S.

that I could learn; at any rate, he did not interfere at all with this cruel treatment of him, as his motto was, "Mr. Allen is always right."

Mr. Allen, although a church member, was much addicted to the habit of *profane swearing*, a vice which church members there, indulged in as frequently as non-professors did. He used particularly to expend his swearing breath, in denunciation of the whole race of negroes, calling us "d——d hogs, dogs, pigs," &c. At one time, he was busily engaged in reading in *the Bible*, when a slave came in who had absented himself from work the enormous length of ten minutes! The overseer had been cheated out of ten minutes' precious time; and as he depended upon the punctuality of the slave to support his family in the manner mentioned previously, his desire perhaps not to violate that precept, "he that provideth not for his family is worse than an infidel,"[23] led him to indulge in quite an outbreak of boisterous anger. "What are you so late for, you black scamp?" said he to the delinquent. "I am only ten minutes behind the time, sir," quietly responded the slave, when Mr. Allen exclaimed, "You are a d——d liar," and remembering, for aught that I can say to the contrary, that "he that converteth a *sinner* from the error of his ways, shall save a soul from death,"[24] he proceeded to try the effect of the Bible upon the body of the "liar," striking him a heavy blow in the face, with the sacred book. But that not answering his purpose, and the man remaining incorrigible, he caught up a stick and beat him with that. The slave complained to master, but he would take no notice of him, and directed him back to the overseer.

Mr. Allen, although a superintendent of the Sabbath school, and very fervid in his exhortations to the slave children, whom he endeavored to instruct in reference to their duties to their masters, that they must never disobey them, or lie, or steal, and if they did they would assuredly "go to hell," yet was not wholly destitute of "that fear which hath torment," for always when a heavy thunder storm came up, would he shut himself up in a little room where he supposed the lightning would not harm him; and I frequently overheard him praying earnestly to God to spare his life. He evidently had not that "perfect *love* which casteth out Fear."[25] The same day on which he had beaten the poor sick man, did such a scene transpire; but generally after the storm had abated he would laugh at his own conduct, and say he did not believe the Lord had any thing to do with the thunder and lightning.

As I have stated, Mr. A. was a devout attendant upon public worship, and prayed much with the pupils in the Sabbath school, and was indefatigable in teaching them to repeat the catechism after him, although he was very particular never to allow them to hold the book in their hands. But let not my readers suppose on this account, that he desired the salvation of these slaves. No, far from that; for very soon after thus exhorting them, he would tell his visiters, that it was "a d——d lie that colored people were ever converted," and that they could "not go to heaven," for they had no souls; but that it was his duty to talk to them as he did. The reader can learn from this account of how much value the religious teaching of the slaves is, when such men are its administerers; and also for what purpose this instruction is given them.

This man's liberality to white people, was coextensive with his denunciation of the colored race. A white man, he said, could not be lost, let him do what he pleased—rob the slaves, which he said was not wrong, lie, swear, or any thing else, provided he *read the Bible and joined the Church.*[*]

One word concerning the religion of the South. I regard it as all delusion, and that there is not a particle of religion in their slaveholding churches. The great end to which religion is there made to minister, is to keep the slaves in a docile and submissive frame of mind, by instilling into them the idea that if they do not obey their masters, they will infallibly "go to hell;" and yet some of the miserable wretches who teach this doctrine, do not themselves believe it. Of course the slave prefers obedience to his master, to an abode in the "lake of fire and brimstone." It is true in more senses than one, that slavery rests upon hell! I once heard a minister declare in public, that he had preached six years before he was converted; and that he was then in the habit of taking a glass of "mint julep"[26] directly after prayers, which wonderfully refreshed him, soul and body. This dram he would repeat three or four times during the day; but at length an old slave persuaded him to abstain a while from his potations, the following of which advice, resulted in his conversion. I believe his second conversion, was nearer a true one, than his first, because he said his conscience reproved him for having sold slaves; and he finally left that part of the country, on account of slavery, and went to the North.

But as time passed along, I began to think seriously of entering into the matrimonial state, as much as a person can, who can "make no contract whatever," and whose wife is not his, only so far as her master allows her to be. I formed an acquaintance with a young woman by the name of Nancy—belonging to a Mr. Lee, a clerk in the bank, and a pious man; and our friendship having ripened into mutual love, we concluded to make application to the powers that ruled us, for *permission* to be married, as I had previously applied for permission to join the church. I went to Mr. Lee, and made known to him my wishes, when he told me, he never meant to sell Nancy, and if my master would agree never to sell me, then I might marry her. This man was a member of a Presbyterian church in Richmond, and pretended to me, to believe it wrong to separate families; but after I had been married to my wife one year, his conscientious scruples vanished, and she was sold to a saddler living in Richmond, who was one of Dr. Plummer's church members. Mr. Lee gave me a note to my master, and they afterwards discussed the matter over, and I was allowed to marry the chosen one of my heart. Mr. Lee, as I have said, soon sold my wife, contrary to his promise, and she fell into the hands of a

---

[*] Will not this be considered a sufficient exhibition of that *charity*, which pro-slavery divines exhort abolitionists to practice? C. S.

very cruel mistress, the wife of the saddler above mentioned, by whom she was much abused. This woman used to wish for some great calamity to happen to my wife, because she stayed so long when she *went to nurse her child*; which calamity came very near happening afterwards to herself. My wife was finally sold, on account of the solicitations of this woman; but four months had hardly elapsed, before she insisted upon her being purchased back again.

During all this time, my mind was in a continual agitation, for I knew not one day, who would be the owner of my wife the next. O reader, have you no heart to sympathize with the injured slave, as he thus lives in a state of perpetual torment, the dread uncertainty of his wife's fate, continually hanging over his head, and poisoning all his joys, as the naked sword hung by a *hair*, over the head of an ancient king's guest, as he was seated at a table loaded with all the luxuries of an epicure's devising?[27] This sword, unlike the one alluded to, did often pierce my breast, and when I had recovered from the wound, it was again hung up, to torture me. This is slavery, a natural and concomitant part of the accursed system!

The saddler who owned my wife, whose name I suppress for particular reasons, was at one time taken sick, but when *his minister*, the Rev. (so called) Dr. Plummer came to pray with him, he would not allow him to perform that rite, which strengthened me in the opinion I entertained of Dr. Plummer, that he was *as wicked a man* as this saddler, and you will presently see, how bad a man he was. The saddler sent for *his slaves to pray* for him, and afterwards for me, and when I repaired to his bed-side, he beseeched me to pray for him, saying that he would live a much better life than he had done, if the Lord would only spare him. I and the other slaves prayed *three nights* for him, after our work was over, and we needed rest in sleep; but the earnest desire of this man, induced us to forego our necessary rest; and yet one of the first things he did after his recovery, was to *sell my wife*. When he was reminded of my praying for his restoration to health, he angrily exclaimed, that it was "all d——d lies" about the Lord restoring him to health in consequence of the negroes praying for him,—and that if any of them mentioned that they had prayed for him, he "would *whip them for it.*"

The last purchaser of my wife, was Mr. Samuel S. Cartrell, also a member of Dr. Plummer's church.*

He induced me to pay him $50.00 in order to assist him in purchasing my companion, so as to prevent her being sold away from me. I also paid him $50 a year, for her time, although she would have been of but little value to him, for she had young children and could not earn much for him,—and rented a house for which I paid $72, and she took in washing, which with the remainder of my earnings, after deducting master's "lion's share," supported our family. Our bliss, as far as the term bliss applies to a slave's situation, was now complete in this respect, for a

---

*Reader, do you wonder at abolitionists calling such churches the brotherhood of thieves? C. S.

season; for never had we been so pleasantly situated before; but, reader, behold its cruel termination. O the harrowing remembrance of those terrible, terrible scenes! May God spare you from ever enduring what I then endured.

It was on a pleasant morning, in the month of August, 1848, that I left my wife and three children safely at our little home, and proceeded to my allotted labor. The sun shone brightly as he commenced his daily task, and as I gazed upon his early rays, emitting their golden light upon the rich fields adjacent to the city, and glancing across the abode of my wife and family, and as I beheld the numerous companies of slaves, hieing their way to their daily labors, and reflected upon the difference between their lot and mine, I felt that, although I was a slave, there were many alleviations to my cup of sorrow. It was true, that the greater portion of my earnings was taken from me, by the unscrupulous hands of my dishonest master,— that I was entirely at his mercy, and might at any hour be snatched from what sources of joy were open to me—that he might, if he chose, extend his robber hand, and demand a still larger portion of my earnings,—and above all, that intellectual privileges were entirely denied me; but as I imprinted a parting kiss upon the lips of my faithful wife, and pressed to my bosom the little darling cherubs, who followed me saying, in their childish accents, "Father, come back soon," I felt that life was not all a blank to me; that there were some pure joys yet my portion. O, how my heart would have been riven with unutterable anguish, if I had then realized the awful calamity which was about to burst upon my unprotected head! Reader, are you a husband, and can you listen to my sad story, without being moved to cease all your connection with that stern power, which stretched out its piratical arm, and basely robbed me of all dear to me on earth!

The sun had traced his way to mid-heaven, and the hour for the laborers to turn from their tasks, and to seek refreshment for their toil-worn frames,—and when I should take my prattling children on my knee,—was fast approaching; but there burst upon me a sound so dreadful, and so sudden, that the shock well nigh overwhelmed me. It was as if the heavens themselves had fallen upon me, and the everlasting hills of God's erecting, like an avalanche, had come rolling over my head! And what was it? "Your wife and smiling babes are gone; in prison they are locked, and to-morrow's sun will see them far away from you, on their way to the distant South!" Pardon the utterance of my feelings here, reader, for surely a man may feel, when all that he prizes on earth is, at one fell stroke, swept from his reach! O God, if there is a moment when vengeance from thy righteous throne should be hurled upon guilty man, and hot thunderbolts of wrath, should burst upon his wicked head, it surely is at such a time as this! And this is Slavery; its certain, necessary and constituent part. Without this terrific pillar to its demon walls, it falls to the ground, as a bridge sinks, when its buttresses are swept from under it by the rushing floods. This is Slavery. No kind master's indulgent care can guard his chosen slave, his petted chattel, however fond he may profess to be of such a piece of property, from so fearful a calamity. My master treated me as kindly as he could, and retain me in slavery; but did that keep me from experiencing this terrible deprivation? The sequel will show you even his care for me. What could I do? I had left my fond wife and prattling children, as happy as slaves could expect to be; as I was not anticipating their loss, for the pious man who bought them last, had, as you recollect, received a sum of money from me, under the promise of not selling them. My first impulse, of course, was to rush to the jail, and behold my family once more, before our final separation. I started for this infernal place, but had not proceeded a great distance, before I met a gentleman, who stopped me, and beholding my anguish of heart, as depicted on my countenance, inquired of me what the trouble was with me. I told him as I best could, when he advised me not to go to the jail, for the man who had sold my wife, had told my master some falsehoods about me, and had induced him to give orders to the jailor to seize me, and confine me in prison, if I should appear there. He said I would undoubtedly be sold separate from my wife, and he thought I had better not go there. I then persuaded a young man of my acquaintance to go to the prison, and sent by him, to my wife, some money and a message in reference to the cause of my failure to visit her. It seems that it would have been useless for me to have ventured there, for as soon as this young man arrived, and inquired for my wife, he was seized and put in prison,—the jailor mistaking him for me; but when he discovered his mistake, he was very angry, and vented his rage upon the innocent youth, by kicking him out of prison. I then repaired to my Christian master, and three several times, during the ensuing twenty-four hours, did I beseech and entreat him to purchase my wife; but no tears of mine made the least impression upon his obdurate heart. I laid my case before him, and reminded him of the faithfulness with which I had served him, and of my utmost endeavors to please him, but this *kind* master—recollect reader—utterly refused to advance a small portion of the $5,000 I had paid him, in order to relieve my sufferings; and he was a member, in good and regular standing, of an Episcopal church in Richmond! His reply to me was worthy of the morality of Slavery, and shows just how much religion, the kindest and most pious of Southern slaveholders have. "*You can get another wife*," said he; but I told him the Bible said, "What God has joined together, let not man put asunder,"[28] and that I did not want any other wife but my own lawful one, whom I loved so much. At the mention of this passage of Scripture, he drove me from his house, saying, he did not wish to hear that!

I now endeavored to persuade two gentlemen of my acquaintance, to buy my wife; but they told me they did not think it was right to hold slaves, or else they would gladly assist me, for they sincerely pitied me, and advised me to go to my master again; but I knew this would be useless. My agony was now complete. She with whom I had travelled the journey of life, for the space of twelve years, with three little pledges of domestic affection, must now be forever separated from me—I must remain alone and desolate. O God, shall my wife and children never more greet my sight, with their cheerful looks and happy smiles? Far, far away, in Carolina's swamps are they now, toiling beneath the scorching rays of the hot sun, with no husband's voice to soothe the hardships of my wife's lot, and no father's kind look to gladden the heart of my disconsolate little ones.*

I call upon you, Sons of the North, if your blood has not lost its bright color of liberty, and is not turned to the blackened gore which surrounds the slaveholder's polluted hearts, to arise in your might, and demand the liberation of the slaves. If you do not, at the day of final account, I shall bear witness against you, as well as against the slaveholders themselves, as the cause of my and my brethren's bereavement. Think you, at that dread hour, you can escape the scrutinizing look of the Judge of all the earth, as he "maketh inquisition for the blood of the innocents?" Oh, no; but equally with the Southern slaveholders, will your character be condemned by the Ruler of the universe.

The next day, I stationed myself by the side of the road, along which the slaves, amounting to three hundred and fifty, were to pass. The purchaser of my wife was a *Methodist* minister, who was about starting for North Carolina. Pretty soon five waggonloads of little children passed, and looking at the foremost one, what should I see but a little child, pointing its tiny hand towards me, exclaiming, "There's my father; I knew he would come and bid me good-bye." It was my eldest child! Soon the gang approached in which my wife was chained. I looked, and beheld her familiar face; but O, reader, that glance of agony! may God spare me ever again enduring the excruciating horror of that moment! She passed, and came near to where I stood. I seized hold of her hand, *intending* to bid her farewell; but words failed me; the gift of utterance had fled, and I remained speechless. I followed her for some distance, with her hand grasped in mine, as if to save her from her fate, but I could not speak, and I was obliged to turn away in silence.

This is not an imaginary scene, reader; it is not a fiction, but an every-day reality at the South; and all I can say more to you, in reference to it is, that if you will not, after being made acquainted with these facts, consecrate your all to the slaves' release from bondage, you are utterly unworthy the name of a man, and should go and hide yourself, in some impenetrable cave, where no eye can behold your demon form.

One more scene occurs in the tragical history of my life, before the curtain drops, and I retire from the stage of observation, as far as past events are concerned; not, however, to shrink from public gaze, as if ashamed of my perilous adventures, or to retire into private life, lest the bloodhounds of the South should

---

*I would here state, that Mr. Brown is endeavoring to raise money to purchase his family. Twelve hundred dollars being the sum demanded for them. Any person wishing to assist him in this laudable purpose, can enclose donations to him, directing No. 21 Cornhill, Boston.

scent my steps, and start in pursuit of their missing property. No, reader, for as long as three millions of my countrymen pine in cruel bondage, on Virginia's exhausted soil, and in Carolina's pestilential rice swamps; in the cane-breaks of Georgia, and on the cotton fields of Louisiana and Mississippi, and in the insalubrious climate of Texas; as well as suffer under the slave-driver's cruel lash, all over the almost God-forsaken South; I shall never refuse to advocate their claims to your sympathy, whenever a fitting occasion occurs to speak in their behalf.

But you are eager to learn the particulars of my journey from freedom to liberty. The first thing that occurred to me, after the cruel separation of my wife and children from me, and I had recovered my senses, so as to know how to act, was, thoughts of freeing myself from slavery's iron yoke. I had suffered enough under its heavy weight, and I determined I would endure it no longer; and those reasons which often deter the slave from attempting to escape, no longer existed in reference to me, for my family were gone, and slavery now had no mitigating circumstances, to lessen the bitterness of its cup of woe. It is true, as my master had told me, that I could "get another wife;" but no man, excepting a brute below the human species, would have proposed such a step to a person in my circumstances; and as I was not such a degraded being, I did not dream of so conducting. Marriage was not a thing of personal convenience with me, to be cast aside as a worthless garment, whenever the slaveholder's will required it; but it was a sacred institution binding upon me, as long as the God who had "joined us together," refrained from untying the nuptial knot. What! leave the wife of my bosom for another! and while my heart was leaping from its abode, to pour its strong affections upon the kindred soul of my devoted partner, could I receive a stranger, another person to my embrace, as if the ties of love existed only in the presence of the object loved! Then, indeed, should I have been a traitor to that God, who had linked our hearts together in fond affection, and cemented our union, by so many additional cords, twining around our hearts; as a tree and an arbor are held together by the clinging of the tendrils of the adhering vine, which winds itself about them so closely. Slavery, and slavery abettors, seize hold of these tender scions, and cut and prune them away from both tree and arbor, as remorselessly as a gardener cuts down the briars and thorns which disturb the growth of his fair plants; but all humane, and every virtuous man, must instinctively recoil from such transactions, as they would from soul murder, or from the commission of some enormous deed of villany.

Reader, in the light of these scenes you may behold, as in a glass, your true character. Refined and delicate you may pretend to be, and may pass yourself off as a pure and virtuous person; but if you refuse to exert yourself for the overthrow of a system, which thus tramples human affection under its bloody feet, and demands of its crushed victims, the sacrifice of all that is noble, virtuous and pure, upon its smoking altars; you may rest assured, that if the balances of *purity* were extended before you, He who "searcheth the hearts, and trieth the reins," would say to you, as your character underwent his searching scrutiny, "Thou art weighed in the balance and found wanting."

I went to Mr. Allen, and requested of him permission to refrain from labor for a short time, in consequence of a disabled finger; but he refused to grant me this permission, on the ground that my hand was not lame enough to justify him in so doing. Nothing daunted by this rebuff, I took some oil of vitriol,[29] intending to pour a few drops upon my finger, to make it sufficiently sore, to disable me from work, which I succeeded in, beyond my wishes; for in my hurry, a larger quantity than it was my purpose to apply to my finger, found its way there, and my finger was soon eaten through to the bone. The overseer then was obliged to allow me to absent myself from business, for it was impossible for me to work in that situation. But I did not waste my precious furlough in idle mourning over my fate. I armed myself with determined energy, for action, and in the words of one of old, in the name of God, "I leaped over a wall, and run through a troop" of difficulties. After searching for assistance for some time, I at length was so fortunate as to find a friend, who promised to assist me, for one half the money I had about me, which was one hundred and sixty-six dollars. I gave him eighty-six, and he was to do his best in forwarding my scheme. Long did we remain together, attempting to devise ways and means to carry me away from the land of separation of families, of whips and thumbscrews, and auction blocks; but as often as a plan was suggested by my friend, there would appear some difficulty in the way of its accomplishment. Perhaps it may not be best to mention what these plans were, as some unfortunate slaves may thereby be prevented from availing themselves of these methods of escape.

At length, after praying earnestly to Him, who seeth afar off, for assistance, in my difficulty, suddenly, as if from above, there darted into my mind these words, "Go and get a box, and put yourself in it." I pondered the words over in my mind. "Get a box?" thought I; "what can this mean?" But I was "not disobedient unto the heavenly vision," and I determined to put into practice this direction, as I considered it, from my heavenly Father.* I went to the depot, and there noticed the size of the largest boxes, which commonly were sent by the cars, and returned with their dimensions. I then repaired to a carpenter, and induced him to make me a box of such a description as I wished, informing him of the use I intended to make of it. He assured me I could not live in it; but as it was dear liberty I was in pursuit of, I thought it best to make the trial.

When the box was finished, I carried it, and placed it before my friend, who had promised to assist me, who asked me if that was to "put my clothes in?" I replied

---

*Reader, smile not at the above idea, for if there is a God of love, we must believe that he suggests steps to those who apply to him in times of trouble, by which they can be delivered from their difficulty. I firmly believe this doctrine, and know it to be true from frequent experience. C. S.

that it was not, but to *"put Henry Brown in!"* He was astonished at my temerity; but I insisted upon his placing me in it, and nailing me up, and he finally consented.

After corresponding with a friend in Philadelphia, arrangements were made for my departure, and I took my place in this narrow prison, with a mind full of uncertainty as to the result. It was a critical period of my life, I can assure you, reader; but if you have never been deprived of your liberty, as I was, you cannot realize the power of that hope of freedom, which was to me indeed, "an anchor to the soul, both sure and steadfast."

I laid me down in my darkened home of three feet by two, and like one about to be guillotined, resigned myself to my fate. My friend was to accompany me, but he failed to do so; and contented himself with sending a telegraph message to his correspondent in Philadelphia, that such a box was on its way to his care.

I took with me a bladder filled with water to bathe my neck with, in case of too great heat; and with no access to the fresh air, excepting three small gimblet holes, I started on my perilous cruise. I was first carried to the express office, the box being placed on its end, so that I started with my head downwards, although the box was directed, "this side up with care." From the express office, I was carried to the depot, and from thence tumbled roughly into the baggage car, where I *happened* to fall "right side up," but no thanks to my transporters. But after a while the cars stopped, and I was put aboard a steamboat, *and placed on my head.* In this dreadful position, I remained the space of an hour and a half, it seemed to me, when I began to feel of my eyes and head, and found to my dismay, that my eyes were almost swollen out of their sockets, and the veins on my temple seemed ready to burst. I made no noise however, determining to obtain *"victory or death,"* but endured the terrible pain, as well as I could, sustained under the whole by the thoughts of sweet liberty. About half an hour afterwards, I attempted again to lift my hands to my face, but I found I was not able to move them. A cold sweat now covered me from head to foot. Death seemed my inevitable fate, and every moment I expected to feel the blood flowing over me, which had burst from my veins. One half hour longer and my sufferings would have ended in that fate, which I preferred to slavery; but I lifted up my heart to God in prayer, believing that he would yet deliver me, when to my joy, I overheard two men say, "We have been here *two* hours and have travelled twenty miles, now let us sit down, and rest ourselves." They suited the action to the word, and turned the box over, containing my soul and body, thus delivering me from the power of the grim messenger of death, who a few moments previously, had aimed his fatal shaft at my head, and had placed his icy hands on my throbbing heart. One of these men inquired of the other, what he supposed that box contained, to which his comrade replied, that he guessed it was the mail. "Yes," thought I, "it is a *male*, indeed, although not the *mail* of the United States."

Soon after this fortunate event, we arrived at Washington, where I was thrown from the wagon, and again as my luck would have it, fell on my head. I was then rolled down a declivity, until I reached the platform from which the cars were to start. During this short but rapid journey, my neck came very near being dislocated, as I felt it crack, as if it had snapped asunder. Pretty soon, I heard some one say, "there is no room for this box, it will have to remain behind." I then again applied to the Lord, my help in all my difficulties, and in a few minutes I heard a gentleman direct the hands to place it aboard, as "it came with the mail and must go on with it." I was then tumbled into the car, my head downwards again, as I seemed to be destined to escape on my head; a sign probably, of the opinion of American people respecting such bold adventurers as myself; that our heads should be held downwards, whenever we attempt to benefit ourselves. Not the only instance of this propensity, on the part of the American people, towards the colored race. We had not proceeded far, however, before more baggage was placed in the car, at a stopping place, and I was again turned to my proper position. No farther difficulty occurred until my arrival at Philadelphia. I reached this place at three o'clock in the morning, and remained in the depot until six o'clock, A. M., at which time, a waggon drove up, and a person inquired for a box directed to such a place, "right side up." I was soon placed on this waggon, and carried to the house of my friend's correspondent, where quite a number of persons were waiting to receive me. They appeared to be some afraid to open the box at first, but at length one of them rapped upon it, and with a trembling voice, asked, "Is all right within?" to which I replied, "All right." The joy of these friends was excessive, and like the ancient Jews, who repaired to the rebuilding of Jerusalem,[30] each one seized hold of some tool, and commenced opening my grave. At length the cover was removed, and I arose, and shook myself from the lethargy into which I had fallen; but exhausted nature proved too much for my frame, and I swooned away.

After my recovery from this fainting fit, the first impulse of my soul, as I looked around, and beheld my friends, and was told that I was safe, was to break out in a song of deliverance, and praise to the most high God, whose arm had been so signally manifest in my escape. Great God, was I a freeman! Had I indeed succeeded in effecting my escape from the human wolves of Slavery? O what extatic joy thrilled through every nerve and fibre of my system! My labor was accomplished, my warfare was ended, and I stood erect before my equal fellow men;[*] no longer a crouching slave, forever at the look and nod of a whimsical and tyrannical slave-owner. Long had seemed my journey, and terribly hazardous had been my attempt to gain my birth-right;[31] but it all seemed a comparatively light price to pay for the precious boon of *Liberty*. O ye, who know not the value of this "pearl of great price," by having been all your life shut out from its life-giving presence; learn of how much importance its possession is regarded, by the panting fugitive,

---

[*] For a corroboration of this part of Mr. Brown's narrative, the reader is referred to the close of this book.

as he traces his way through the labyrinths of snares, placed between him and the object of his fond desires! Sympathize with the three millions of crushed and mangled ones who this day pine in cruel bondage, and arouse yourself to action in their behalf! This you will do, if you are not traitors to your God and to humanity. Aid not in placing in high offices, *baby-stealers and women-whippers*; and if these wicked men, all covered with the clotted gore of their mangled victims, come among you, scorn the idea of bowing in homage to them, whatever may be the character of their claims to your regard. No matter, if they are called presidents of your nation, still utterly refuse to honor them; which *you will most certainly do*, if you are true to the Slave!

After remaining a short time in Philadelphia, it was thought expedient that I should proceed to Massachusetts, and accordingly funds sufficient to carry me there, were raised by some anti-slavery friends, and I proceeded to Boston. After remaining a short time in that city, I concluded to go to New Bedford, in which place I remained a few weeks, under the care of Mr. Joseph Rickerston of that place, who treated me very kindly. At length hearing of a large anti-slavery meeting to be held in Boston, I left New Bedford, and found myself again in that city, so famous for its devotion to liberty in the days of the American revolution; and here, in the presence of several thousand people, did I first relate in public, the story of my sufferings, since which time I have repeated my simple tale in different parts of Massachusetts, and in the State of Maine.

I now stand before you as a free man, but since my arrival among you, I have been informed that your laws require that I should still be held as a slave; and that if my master should espy me in any nook or corner of the free states, according to the constitution of the United States, he could secure me and carry me back into Slavery;[32] so that I am confident I am not safe, even here, if what I have heard concerning your laws is true. I cannot imagine why you should uphold such strange laws. I have been told that every time a man goes to the polls and votes, he virtually swears to sustain them, frightful as they are. It seems to me to be a hard case, for a man to endure what I have endured in effecting my escape, and then to be continually exposed to be seized by my master, and carried back into that horrid pit from which I have escaped. I have been told, however, that the people here would not allow me to be thus returned, that they would break their own laws in my behalf, which seems quite curious to me; for why should you make laws, and swear to uphold them, and then break them? I do not understand much about laws, to be sure, as the law of my master is the one I have been subject to all my life, but some how, it looks a little singular to me, that wise people should be obliged to break their own laws, or else do a very wicked act. I have been told that there are twice as many voters at the North as there are at the South, and much more wealth, as well as other things of importance, which makes me study much, why the Northern people live under such laws. If I was one of them, and had any influence among them, it appears to me, I should advocate the overthrow of such laws, and the establishment of better ones in their room. Many people tell me besides, that if the slaves should rise up, and do as they did in Nat Turner's time, endeavor to fight their way to freedom, that the Northern people are pledged to shoot them down, and keep them in subjection to their masters. Now I cannot understand this, for almost all the people tell me, that they "are opposed to Slavery," and yet they swear to prevent the slaves from obtaining their liberty! If these things could be made clear to my mind, I should be glad; but a fog hangs over my eyes at present in reference to this matter.

I now wish to introduce to your hearing, a friend of mine, who will tell you more about these things than I can, until I have had more time to examine this curious subject. What he shall have to say to you, may not be as interesting as the account of my sufferings, but if you really wish to help my brethren in bondage, you will not be unwilling to hear what he may say to you, in reference to the way to abolish slavery, as you cannot be opposed to my sufferings, unless you are willing to exert yourselves for the overthrow of the cruel system which caused them.

CURE FOR THE EVIL OF SLAVERY

Dear Friends,—You have listened with eager ears, and with tearful eyes, to the recital of Mr. Brown. He has alluded to the laws which many of you uphold, when you go to the polls and vote, but he has not informed you of your duty at the present crisis. What I have to say at this time, will be mainly directed to the remedy for this terrible evil, so strikingly portrayed in his eventful life. As one of those who desire the abolition of Slavery, it is my earnest desire to be made acquainted with a true and proper remedy for this dreadful disease. I apprehend that no moral evil exists, for the cure of which there cannot be found some specific, the application of which, will effectually eradicate the disorder. I am not a politician, and cannot write as politicians do. Still I may be pardoned for entering a little into their sphere of action, for the purpose of plucking some choice fruit from the overhanging boughs of that fruitful arena. I am not *afraid* of politics, for I do not regard them as too sacred, or as too profane, for me to handle. I believe that the people of this country are not ready for a truly Christian government; therefore, although I cannot unite myself with any other, yet I should be rejoiced, at beholding the faintest resemblance to such an one, in opposition to our present pro-slavery government.

I would like to see all men perfect Christians, but as I do not expect to witness this sight very soon, I am gratified as their becoming anti-slavery, or even temperance men. Any advance from the old corruptions of the past, is hailed with delight by me.

The point I would now urge upon your attention is, the immediate formation of *a new government at the North*, at all events, and at all hazards! I do not say,

"Down with this Union" merely, but I do say, up with an Anti-Slavery government, in the free States. Our object should be the establishment of a form of government, directly in opposition to the one we at present live under. The stars and stripes of our country's flag, should be trodden into the dust, and a white banner, with the words, "Emancipation to the Slaves" inscribed upon it, should be unfurled to the breeze, in the room of the old emblem of despotic servitude. Too long have we been dilatory upon this point; but the period I believe has now arrived, for us to strike for freedom, in earnest. Let us see first, what we have to accomplish; and then the means whereby we can bring about the desired end; our capabilities for such a work; and the reasons why we should adopt this plan; and what will be the consequences of such a course of action. First. What have we to accomplish? A great and an important end truly, which is nothing less, than the establishment of a new government, right in the midst of our present pro-slavery one.

A government, is a system of authority sustained by either the rulers, or the ruled, or by both conjointly. If it depends on the will of the rulers, then they can change it at pleasure; but if the people are connected with it, their consent must be gained, before its character can be altered. If, as is the case with our government, it is the *people* who "ordain and establish" laws, then it lies with them to change those laws, and to remodel that government. Let this fact be distinctly understood; for the majority of the people of this land, seem to labor under the delusion, that our government is sustained by some other power than their own; and are very much in the situation of those heathen nations, condemned by one of the ancient prophets, who manufactured their deities, and then fell down and worshipped the work of their own hands. The people make laws for their own guidance, and then offer as an excuse for their bad conduct, that the *laws* require them to do so! The government appears to be yet surrounded with a halo of glory, as it was in the days of kingly authority, when "the powers that be" were supposed to have been approvingly "ordained of God," and men fear to touch the sacred structure of their own erecting, as if God's throne would be endangered thereby. This is not the only manifestation of self-esteem connected with their movement.

The people also fancy, that what their fathers created is divine, when their fathers have departed, and left them to do as they elect, without any obligation resting upon them to follow in their steps; but so great is the self-esteem of the people, as manifested in their pride of ancestry, that they seem to suppose, that God would cast them off forever, if they should cease to be children, and become men, casting from them, the doctrines and political creeds of their fathers; and yet they boast of their spirit of progress! They fear to act for themselves, lest they should mar the reputation of their ancestors and be deprived of their feeling of self-adulation, in consequence of the perfection of their worthy sires. But we must humble our pride, and cease worshipping, either our own, or our father's handiwork,—in reference to the laws, of which we are speaking. What we want is, a very simple thing. Our fathers proclaimed themselves free and independent of the British government, and proceeded to establish a new one, in its room. They threw off the British yoke! We can do the same, in reference to the United States government! We can put forth *our* "declaration of independence,"[33] and issue our manifesto of grievances; and as our fathers did, can pledge to one another, "our lives, our property and our sacred honor," in promoting the accomplishment of this end. We can *immediately organize* a new government, independent of the present one under which we live. We may be deemed traitors for so doing; but were not Samuel Adams and John Hancock traitors?[34] and did not our forefathers inscribe on their banners, "resistance to tyrants is obedience to God?" Are we more faint-hearted than they were? Are not our and the slave's grievances more unendurable than were their wrongs? A new government is what we want; and the sound should go forth from all these free hills, echoing across the plains of the far distant West, that New England and the whole North, are ready to do battle with the myrmidons of the slave power, not with the sword of steel, but with the spirit of patient submission to robbery and death, in defence of our principles. We are not obliged to muster our squadrons in "hot haste," to the "sound of the cannon's deafening roar," nor to arm ourselves for physical combat; for there is more power in suffering death, for truth's sake, than in fighting with swords of steel, and with cannon balls. A new government we must have; and now let us consider, Secondly, how we shall bring this end about, and some reasons why we should adopt this course.

Step by step, do we progress in all improvements designed for man's well being. At first the people in a semi-barbarous state, are satisfied with a rude code of laws, similar to that given by a military commander, to the rough bandits under his direction; but as science unfolds its truthful wings, and spreads over the minds of the race, a mantle of wisdom, which covers their rude imperfections, and shuts out from the eye of man, their inelegant barbarities, a regard for the good opinion of others more civilized than they, induces such a people to demand the overthrow of their savage code, which they have become ashamed of acknowledging. The ancient Jews were supposed to stand in need of laws of this character; which hungover their heads, threatening the most severe punishments for the commission of, sometimes, very light crimes; as Sinai's burning mountain flashed its fierce lightnings in their awe-stricken faces, and sent forth its terrible thunders, sounding in their superstitious ears, like the voice of Deity. This people had just emerged from the depths of Egyptian slavery,[35] and might have stood in need of such severe and terrible laws, so Draconic in their nature;[36] but the refined inhabitants of polished Greece and Rome, needed not such barbarous enactments. The advancing spirit of civilization had swept along in its effacing train, all the necessity for such brutal ferocity, by destroying the ferocious character of the people; as it opened to them more refined sources of enjoyment, in the erection of works of art, and in mental cultivation. The muses too, had purified and rendered delicate their tastes, so that outward barbarity seemed no longer attractive; although their ancestors had indulged in such scenes with great gusto. Our Druidical, Saxon and Norman ancestry,[37] might have needed as cruel laws as those we now live under. At least such laws would have been more appropriate to their semi-barbarous condition, than they are to our improved state; but surely, we of the nineteenth century, having outlived the errors of the past, and having reached a point, from which we can cast our eyes far back into the distant past, and behold with utter astonishment, the absurd practices of our cruel and ignorant ancestors; are not obliged, out of regard for the memory of those not so far removed from us, in point of time, as those whose memories we do not hesitate to execrate, to retain as objectionable laws as ever disgraced the statute book of England, in the days of the bloody Jeffreys, or when the unalterable "Star chamber" decisions,[38] were the law of the land. For a country to make its boast of civilization, and to call itself a refined nation, while it tenaciously grasps the worst errors of its ancestors, and plunges into a fit of madness, at the least allusion to an alteration of its cannibal laws, seems somewhat astonishing. It makes one think of a man, who should propose joining a church, and when asked to give up dram-drinking and gambling, should break forth in a torrent of abuse, against those who made the proposition to him; for those practices are no more contrary to the sweet spirit of heavenly religion, than is slaveholding in opposition to true civilization, and perfect refinement. It is a remnant of that spirit of barbarity, which formerly induced men to fight for conquest and territory, in the palmiest days of the ancient Eastern empires, when the fields of the earth, fair mother of our existence, were made fertile by the rich streams of blood, flowing from the mangled corpses, strewn upon its surface, by the fiendish barbarity of a Sennacherib, a Cyrus, a Xerxes, and an Alexander.[39]

    An alteration of our present laws is demanded; but who will agitate this subject, where it must be agitated, in order to accomplish the end so ardently desired? It is well known, that a simple majority of votes in Congress, can never affect the alteration proposed,—that three fourths of the States of this Union must be penetrated with the spirit of repentance, in reference to slavery, and bring forth the legitimate fruit thereof, by consenting to this alteration, before it can be accomplished; and who will go to the South, that "valley of the shadow of death,"[40] in regard to all subjects having reference to man's improvement, and urge this course upon its darkened inhabitants? But this step must be taken, before the Constitution can be altered, or its meaning rendered unequivocal, so as not to be misunderstood by the authorities of this nation; for it is not to be expected that the South will ever repent of their own accord, and change the laws of the Union, because we demand it, unless the alternative is presented them, of such change, or disunion on our part.

    But the time expended in converting the people of the *North* to a willingness to alter the Constitution, would amply suffice to persuade them to organize a new government; for the Northern people are as ready to go for a dissolution of the Union, as they are for an alteration of the Constitution; for much advance has already been made in indoctrinating them in reference to the former idea, and thousands and tens of thousands are probably converts to this doctrine, while but little or nothing has been said in reference to the latter alternative. No party has yet proposed this step; but a large and increasing one, embodying a great portion of the talent of the nation, is now earnestly engaged in advocating the former. Which would be the easiest of accomplishment then, the conversion of the North to disunion principles, or to a willingness to alter the Constitution? Every one at all versed in political affairs, must be aware, that an alteration of the Constitution, without the consent of the South, would be a virtual dissolution of the Union, even if such a step were possible; so that converting the Northern people to the doctrine of an alteration of the Constitution, would be, in fact, only another phase of conversion to disunion; for, of course, the South will never consent to such an alteration, only as an alternative, in opposition to dissolution. To be sure, if the Northern people would act as a body, and boldly say to the South, "give us an alteration of the 'three-fifths representation' clause of the Constitution[41] a change of that in reference to 'domestic insurrection;' and an entire destruction of the one requiring 'persons held to service, under the laws of a state,' to be given up to 'those to whom *such* service or labor may be due,' or we will break away from your polluting embrace;" there would probably be no need of our ever dissolving the Union, if the South believed the North was speaking truly; for, a petted and indulged child, rendered effeminate by parental fondness and neglect of all discipline, would be in no more danger of leaving forever its parent's abode, without a farthing in its pocket, or the ability to walk a single step alone, because of its parents' refusal to gratify its whims any longer; than would the "spoiled child" of the South, who has been fed on the richest viands our Northern pantry could supply, and drank of the costliest wines our free cellars could furnish, be in danger of leaving its well-supplied table of Northern spreading, and spring from the soft lap of Northern indulgence, to go forth to its own poverty-stricken lands, obliged to earn its coarse bread and clear water, by the hard toil of its own delicate hands.

But will the Northern people ever be ready to say this to the South? Not until years of patient toil in cultivating the pro-slavery soil of their hearts, have been expended by those whose office it seems to be to labor for the slaves' release; and even then, it is questionable whether, after having been supported by the North so long, and so patiently, the South would believe all our affirmations; and we after all might be obliged to withdraw from her. But if the plan we propose, should be adopted, it would save all this uncertainty, for the South would then know we meant what we said, and would be frightened at our movements; as a woman is filled with dismay, when her only protector, talks of leaving her and her helpless babes, to the cold charities of an unfeeling world.

It is certain the South never would consent to an alteration of the Constitution, unless she was driven to it by the North, which object has not yet been proposed by any Northern party; and before any great progress could be made in the reception of such a doctrine, a little knot of patriots, armed with the invincible resolution of him, whose narrative has been presented to you, or with that of our revolutionary fathers; could have erected the standard of revolt, and have formed the basis of a new and powerful government. It is not a reform in our government that we need, but a *revolution—an overthrow of the present one*, and the establishment of a new one. Supposing a few individuals should be hung as traitors, would not that create a sympathy for us among the governments of the old world? and would not the universal voice of all civilized nations cry out against our immolation? Let but as many individuals unite, as signed the famous manifesto of our fathers, and armed with their Spartan spirit, *pledge our lives and fortunes* to the accomplishment of this end! Let our *declaration of independence* be sent forth to all the world, and our grievances be stated in the hearing of mankind! Let a new Continental Congress meet, at some favorable point, draft a new Constitution, and all who drink of the spirit of liberty, which flowed into the hearts of our fathers, be requested to annex their names to the document! Let it go forth to the whole land as *our* Constitution! Let immediate measures be taken for an active and efficient agitation of the whole subject; our orators to go forth, and in the streets and lanes of our cities and villages, proclaim the object we have in view; or, if a more silent way of proceeding shall be deemed the most expedient, let committees visit every house and shop in our land, and see who will gird on this armor, and resolve to perish in an attempt to rescue the bleeding slave, from the hands of his cruel master, by refusing all support to this government, even to the deprivation of the necessaries of life.

And now comes the period of our proposed bloodless revolution, which will try men's souls. Let us do as our fathers did, and *refuse to pay taxes to the general government.* "Millions for defence, but not one cent for tribute," cried our ancestors, in order to save their descendants from the oppressive spirit of England's grasping avarice. They at first were ridiculed, and it is stated that when John Warren, one of the aristocracy of Boston, made an inflammatory speech, at a rebel meeting, that he was denounced by the leading citizens of this place, and a copy of a letter is still preserved, written by some of them in reference to the transaction, in which they state, that "one Dr. Warren, had indeed made a rebellious speech, but he was applauded only by *a few rowdies.*" Shall not we be as willing to sacrifice our property and lives, as were our ancestors? Did not John Hancock hand the keys of his stores and dwelling to the authorities of the city, saying to them, "this is all of my property, but if the good of Boston requires its destruction, I freely yield it to you?" To pay taxes is to support the government, under which we live, for without this support it could not exist. These taxes are not paid of course directly, but still we eat, drink, and wear those things, on which a duty is paid, which gives the general government all its power. For instance. The Mexican War has left a large debt resting on our shoulders.[42] The only way in which it will be paid probably is, by an increased tariff on particular articles of consumption. Now if an entire cessation of such consumption should take place, would not the government be left destitute of the means to pay this debt? Who pays the salaries of the officers of this government, but the consumer of the articles taxed by it? If the consumption of all such articles can be prevented, would not our government be obliged to cease operations, for want of oil to grease its machinery with? It moves only as money is furnished it. Our navy and army, the protectors of the South, can only be supported by large sums of money, derived from the revenue of the nation, which revenue we help to create by our consumption of these things. If sugar pays a large duty, or tea and coffee, or silks and satins, broadcloths and cassimeres, by refusing to use those articles, and inducing others to do the same, would not the revenue of the nation be affected? and when the actual tax-gatherer in the shape of the merchant, holds out his seductive wares for our purchase, could we not exhibit to him our pledge to "totally abstain" from the use of such articles; as the temperance man shows his ticket, as a reason why he should not partake of the intoxicating cup?

Another step could also be taken. A president could be chosen by us, and other necessary officers, and we could go on with our government, just as if no other existed, "beating for recruits" all the while, and offering no physical resistance to those who molest us.

Have we not a right so to do?

"Children of the glorious dead!
Who for freedom fought and bled,"

have you become bond slaves to a power fully as oppressive of you, as that of Britain's tyrannical king, against whom your ancestors lifted their stout arms in rebellion, and unfurled their banner of revolt, on which was gloriously inscribed, "victory or death?" Have you forever lost all that portion of your ancestral fire, which armed three millions of poor and feeble men to engage in deadly combat with the richest and most powerful nation in Christendom? Ah, has God forsaken you so entirely, that no pulse of gladness beats in your frame, as you listen to the stirring notes of the wild, clarion sound of freedom, coming over these hills, and echoing from the far-distant prairies of the wide West? Oh is there not, friends, any deep fountain of sorrow gushing up from the inmost depths of your secret souls, for the sufferings and woes of the three millions of your Southern brethren? Ah, is there not any remnant of the spark of divinity which our Father in heaven has placed in every human heart, left to warm up your frigid souls? Say, breathes there not a particle of indignant life in your moral nature, as you listen to the mad agonies of shrieking mothers, the victims of remorseless tyrants who now stand defacing

God's image and stamping in the dust the lineaments of their Creator? Oh, is there none of manhood left in you, that the shrieks of trampled upon and bleeding innocence, should not move you to contend with Slavery's cruel power? But is not your own safety a reason why you should cease to doff your beavers to the South, and should refuse to pay homage to her any longer? Listen a moment while I exhibit to you some more personal and selfish arguments. At the last election, the Southern States were allowed one electoral vote for every 7,500 voters, while at the North, it took 12,000 voters to entitle us to *one* elector. The number of electors, of which we were thus deprived, was about 100, which was the same as excluding from the privilege of the elective franchise, 750,000 voters, about the number in all New England and Pennsylvania! Now are not these persons taxed equally with those who have the privilege of voting? Do not all the citizens of the North pay taxes? Yes, and much more than their true proportion, for by far the greater portion of duty-paying goods, are consumed at the North. Then, is not the principle which our fathers died to oppose, fully carried out by our government, *taxation without representation?*[43] and yet we tamely submit to this plucking our substance from us, by the fierce beak of our country's eagle; while our fathers would not so much as listen to the slight growling of the English lion, as he shook his shaggy mane in their faces, and touched them with but the extremities of his bloody paw! Robbery, if committed by a bird of prey, the American eagle, is to be patiently submitted to, and indeed we call it but the tickling of an affectionate friend or child; but let the valiant lion of Old England take the value of a pin's point, or a few old pine trees and worthless rocks from us, and how the welkin rings with the sound of our abhorrence of such depredations. We are like the slaveholder, spoken of in our friend's narrative, who told the slaves it was a crime to steal from him, but none to rob his neighbors, because he reaped the benefits of the theft. So with us. We are *rewarded* for our submission to this robbery, by the paltry trade of the South, and as long as a few of us can make more money than we lose otherwise by our connection with the South, we care not for our principles, although every fourth of July we laud our fathers for fighting in behalf of them; or for the losses of the mass of the people. *Taxation without representation!* This practice deluged the fields of our country, with our ancestor's and Briton's son's blood; and caused our prosperity, as a nation, to be stricken to the ground, and we magnify our fathers for their boldness, in reference to it; yet we cherish the same principle, and press it to our bosoms as a part of our religion!

Great Britain *tried* our fathers, accused of crime, away from their homes, across the waters of the ocean, and we call it a great oppression; but let one of our sons be guilty of an act in violation of Southern law, or be even suspected of it, and there is *no* law by which he can be tried. All law is trampled under foot, and he is doomed to waste away his life, in a gloomy prison, or to be whipped almost to death. Which is the worst, being tried across the sea, by an impartial court, or being strung up by Lynch law[44] between the heavens and the earth, and left dangling on the limb of a tree, or else doomed to wear out a miserable existence in some foul dungeon?

But to make the case still more parallel. Great Britain, our fathers complained, quartered soldiers upon them in times of peace, who eat out their substance and corrupted the people. For what other earthly purpose is the army of the United States continued in existence, but to watch the bidding of the monster Slavery, and be ready to fly at a moment's warning to her assistance, in case the least attempt should be made by their victims to regain their freedom? That this is a true statement, may be seen from the fact, that all our wars for the last thirty-five years, have been waged in behalf of Slavery, and even our last war with Great Britain, is attributed by many persons to the demands of the slave power. It is certain, that no war will ever be allowed by the South, except in behalf of Slavery, for it would be detrimental to their interests; and it is well known that she rules over the destinies of this country, and guides its affairs of state, as effectually as Alexander or Napoleon ruled the countries they had conquered.[45] Slavery rules this nation, did we say? It can hardly be called ruling, for we are so submissive to the faintest manifestation of her will, that she has but to glance her glowing eye towards our craven souls, and we will prostrate our abject forms lowly on the ground, with our faces hid in the dust, which we are truly unworthy to touch; as submissively and reverentially, as the devout Mussulman kisses the ground when the hour of prayer arrives, crying, "God is great." Our God is emphatically Slavery. To him we address our early matins, and in his ear are uttered our evening orisons.[46] More devoutly do we render homage to our god, Slavery, than the most pious of us adore the God of heaven, which proves that we are a very religious people, worshipping, not crocodiles, leeks and onions, snakes, and images of wood and stone, but a god, whose service is infinitely more disgusting than that of any heathen idol, but one who *pays* us well, for our obeisance, as we imagine.

In this matter of a standing army, we go beyond our fathers in suffering oppression. They were not obliged to fight for England, when the object of the war was to enslave themselves; but it is well known that the great object the South has in view, in all her wars, is the aggrandizement of herself and the subjection of the North to her complete dictation; and we are called upon to engage in these wars, and after they are fought, we are compelled to foot the heavy bills.

But when our fathers were oppressed, they could plead in their own behalf. If they placed their feet on England's shores, no harm could befal them, as long as they were guilty of no crime. They could defend their own cause; and the thunders of a Burke's eloquence,[47] shook the walls of Parliament to their foundation, and made the tyrants of England tremble and quake with fear, as he poured forth the fervor of his vehement eloquence in strong condemnation of the oppression of the colonies. A William Pitt too,[48] could frighten the British minister from his unhallowed security, amid the multitude of fawning sycophants surrounding him, in the height of his political power, by the thunders of his voice, uttered in faithful rebuke of the war measures of the government. This noble Earl, was allowed to plead in behalf of American freedom, until his earnest spirit was claimed by the grim messenger death, as he arose in his place in the House of Lords, to speak in our behalf. But suffer what we may, is there any redress for us at the hands of our government? Our property may be injured by spoliations on our commerce, such as imprisoning our seamen, as well as by the crime of seizing our free citizens and depriving them of their liberty; and can we obtain the least redress? O the ignominy of our puerile connection with the South!

It is well known that under the system of Slavery, the three great blessings of republicanism are denied to a large portion of our citizens. These are, freedom of the press, of speech and of locomotion. And will we allow ourselves to be deprived of what even Europe's despotic kings have been bestowing upon their subjects? Are we more base and abject in our submission to the South, than are the oppressed millions of the old world, in their subjection to their kingly oppressors? O what falsifiers of our own professions, and truants to our own dearly prized principles, we are! Can an abolitionist travel unexposed at the South? I have had some little experience in the matter, and know that such is not the case. Men have pursued me with relentless hate, and implements of death have been brought into requisition against me, for no crime, only for exposing Slavery, in its own dominions. Can we send to any part of the South those newspapers we may wish to send there? While at the South, I was advised by a friend to conceal a paper I had received, because of its being opposed to Slavery; and it is in only particular portions of that ill-fated country, that anti-slavery publications, can be introduced. It is not many years, since a man was publicly whipped, for having an anti-slavery newspaper wrapped around a bible, which he was offering for sale. As to liberty of speech, not half the freedom is allowed the opponents of Slavery on the floors of Congress, that the British Parliament allowed the opposers of the American War. In Boston, on the day which ushered the famous *stamp act*[49] into existence, the bells were tolled, and a funeral procession passed through the streets, bearing a coffin, on which the word *Liberty* was inscribed. "During the movement of the procession, minute guns were fired, and an oration was pronounced in favor of the *deceased*. Similar expressions of grief and indignation occurred in many parts of the land;" but friends, no funeral procession passed through our streets when Liberty died the second time—no muffled bells sounded their melancholy peals in the ears of a mourning people; no liberty-loving orator was found to pronounce a requiem for the departed goddess; and yet she was slain—and slain too, not by foreign hands, nor by the natural allies of human oppressors, but, shall I tell the sad and dismal tale? by those, who twenty-five years before, had shrouded their faces in mantles of mourning, and rent the air with their expressions of grief, at the destruction of one of liberty's little fingers, by the passage of the stamp act; but when Liberty lay a full length corpse, on the floors of that Congress, which sold her to the South, as Judas betrayed the Son of God,[50] and for almost as small a boon, viz.: "the carrying trade" of the South; not only were there *no* lamentations made over her complete departure, but she was taken by night and buried hastily; while

"Not a drum was heard nor a funeral note,"

as her corpse was deposited without a "winding sheet," or even "a soldier's cloak" to wrap around her bleeding form. Clandestinely was she hurried out of the sight of the men who murdered her; and instead of songs of sorrow, being heard throughout the land, pæans of praise ascended from its every corner, and honors were heaped on the heads of her murderers. But Liberty as truly died then, as if loud lamentations had been made in her behalf, and the descendants of those very men, who in 1765 followed the coffin of liberty to its place of deposit, because no business was deemed lawful unless the records of it were made on *stamped paper*; the descendants of these very mourners of liberty, now, do what is infinitely worse than to use the stamped paper of a British king; they swear to support that sacrifice of Liberty upon the altar of Southern slavery, whenever they are admitted to any offices of trust and renown. Is not this oppressive, when we may not administer justice to our fellow men, or exercise the most common authority, without renewing the thrust at the departed spirit of liberty, as our fathers actually slew her fair form?

O liberty! didst thou draw thy keen sword
For those, whom av'rice sought to rob, and slay,
And sent its minions far, to seek its prey,
That glittering gold might its coffers fill;
While they their foes should crush, and seek to kill,
That England's lords, their gold could steal, and hoard?

Goddess celestial, and divine, and pure,
Wert thou, the champion brave, the soldier true,
Who fought with youthful vigor, with the few,
Of Columbia's sons, who stood, a sturdy band,
And bade their country's foes to leave their land,
While they, to thee didst vow allegiance sure?

Insulted nymph! thy fair form shone so bright,
That kings, as thee they saw, could not reject
That face, alive with claims to their respect;
E'en they, besotted with the lust of power,
Could not refuse to yield to thee thy dower,
But ceased at thy command, their foes to fight.

But ah! the men who thee so loud did call,
The souls, whom thou hadst saved from bondage dread,
O fearful! tale! *themselves on thee did tread*;
And thy fair robe was pierced with traitorous thrusts.
As Caesar groaning fell and kissed the dust,
When ingrate Brutus' blows on him did fall.

On the 5th of March, 1775, the Boston massacre occurred[51]—the fearful tragedy of State Street! All Boston was aroused, murders dreadful had been committed by the British troops, and it was a difficult task to allay the excitement occasioned thereby. What was the amount of this terrible massacre? Why, three Boston citizens had been shot in the heat of an affray with the British soldiery! What horror seemed to seize upon the hearts of the people! Why, "our brothers are being shot down in the face of open day, and our turn may come next." Terrible was the indignation of our fathers! And yet we, their descendants, calmly allow the South to slay our citizens at their leisure. The blood of a murdered Lovejoy,[52] still cries out from the ground for vengeance! A Baltimore prison, still contains the impress of a departed spirit's feet, which left an impression on its gloomy pavement, as he fled from an earthly prison-house to the mansions of the blest. A C. C. Torrey still calls for redress for his wrongs at the hands of Southern tyrants. The jail of our own capital if it could speak, would tell of him who pined away within its noisome walls, as he lay in that republican enclosure, a victim to Southern tyranny. Yes, Dr. Crandall's blood has not yet been atoned for, by the wicked South. Here are, at least three victims who have been slain, at the cruel dictation of Slavery's dreadful power. But time would fail me, to tell of a Van Zandt, of a Fairbanks, and of numerous others, whose lives have been forfeited to the South. And yet we submit to her dictation. Our own citizens slain, imprisoned, and cruelly beaten, but yet we have no heart to break away from this degrading alliance with our Southern man-stealing brethren.

But, I must bring this expostulation to a close, and proceed to show the *consequences* of this event, the formation of a new government. Of these it may be said; they could not be more disastrous to the North than Slavery has been; for like the "horse-leech's two daughters," she continually cries "give, give," and never seems to have enough. Hardly through with the digestion of the tremendous morsel just administered to her gormandizing appetite, she commences to lick her lips, and daintily ask for a dessert, with which to finish the full meal which she has already made of California and New Mexico, and as her mother deems it her duty, never to deny any of her darling daughter's reasonable requests, probably the Island of Cuba, will soon be placed at her side, for her to nibble upon at leisure.

Many persons deprecate our plan, for fear of a civil war; and terrific ideas of rivers of blood rolling across our fields, and piles of bones heaped on our shores, startle them in their slumbers, as the rustling of a leaf fills the slaveholder's heart with fear. In the first place, how very absurd is this idea of a civil war being the result of disunion. Can any one seriously urge it, as an objection to this movement? Look at the vast extent of territory open to the incursions of an enemy, if the North should withdraw from the South. There are the Islands of the West Indies, filled with emancipated slaves, ready, some of them to join in an effort to redeem the Southern slaves from bondage. Then there is the longline of seaboard, entirely unprotected, which even in the last war was devastated in part by the British army, and the capital of our country reduced to ashes. On the Northern frontier, runs that talismanic line,[53] over which a slave has but to place his foot, and glorious liberty becomes his possession. Here stand, twelve millions of freemen, ready to fight in behalf of the panting fugitive, while nearly 20,000 sturdy hearts beat quick to the sound of the trumpet of freedom, and are ready to leave their homes in *Canada*, to assist their brethren. Then, there is ill-treated and insulted Mexico, burning under a sense of the wrongs inflicted upon her, and watching an opportunity to redress those wrongs. Last of all, are the numerous Indian tribes, smarting under a deep sense of the wrongs they have received at our hands. Now will any sensible person assert that five millions of Southerners, allowing all her white population to be in favor of Slavery, with an intestine foe, ready to spring upon her, as soon as the last chance of freedom presents itself, will be in danger of fighting twelve millions of free Northerners, who can call to their aid all these, and numerous other allies? Why, the idea is preposterous, and none but an insane man, can seriously entertain it. Who would fight the North, if war should be declared? At the first sound of the trumpet of war, every slave would be instantly free; for never could the Southerners leave their homes exposed to the fury of an insurgent population, as they would be obliged to, if an army should be organized to fight the North.

But who are those persons who cry out "civil war, and bloodshed?" Are they not mostly those who believe the revolutionary war to have been right? If Slavery is wrong, to be consistent, they ought to hail any movement which will hasten an insurrection among the Slaves. What is a civil war of a few years' continuance, in comparison to the seven years' war we waged with Great Britain? *Then* our resources were limited, our treasury light, and we were only three millions strong. But *now*, we abound in resources, have become plethoric on account of our riches, and are twelve millions strong, while our enemy is less than half that number. We coped with twenty millions of British subjects, when we numbered but three millions, can we not now with twelve millions cope with five? Then has our glory departed indeed, and we are the veriest slaves in existence. But would our trade be endangered? Ah, that is *the* question. Said a person to me not long since, "I acknowledge there would be benefits in a dissolution of the Union, but there are also disadvantages." And what are they? we inquired. "Why, our trade would be injured." Let it perish then! Every mother's son of us, had better pack up and on board our numerous vessels go on a begging expedition to England or France, or we had better "tie millstones about our necks, and drown ourselves in the depths of the sea;" or, we had better lay down in the streets and perish with hunger, than to allow Slavery to continue its existence.

The moment it is granted that a dissolution of the Union would abolish Slavery quicker than any other course, then I think our point is gained, and there is no necessity of proving that we shall not lose the sale of a few hats and boots, or *slave whips*. It seems almost an insult to the character of the Northern people to answer such an argument as this, and yet I fear that it is the "strong reason" why this question meets with so much opposition.

If slavery is abolished, no one can deny that our *trade*, so important to Northern men, and for which they are ready to barter the welfare of three millions of human beings, would be materially increased; but for one I care not, whether this will be the case or not. I cannot, I will not argue this question. It is a sin against the Holy Ghost, to dream of balancing the matter in this way. Northern men, you are too much actuated by this spirit of Avarice! You must be converted from this accursed love for gold; for it will sink you into the lowest degradation of a life afar from Deity. You cannot be the friends of God, while it reigns in your hearts! You must arise, and cast it from you! You must be converted from your selfishness, and then you will have no objections to offer against a dissolution of the Union! If your eyes can only be anointed with the eye-salve of humanity, and be washed in the waters of benevolence, you will see the folly of all your objections, and will be ready to sink all your ships with their rich cargoes, into the depths of the sea, and to burn your well-filled stores, rather than to cause Slavery to continue another day! O, men of the North, can ye not be aroused to action in the slave's behalf? Shall the purple streams of the slave's blood, flow ceaselessly and rapidly o'er our land, gushing forth from every hill-side of the South, and coloring all the fair fields of Southern industry, on account of your sustaining power? O that I could utter some word in your ear, which would quicken your dormant sensibilities and arouse you to action in the slave's cause! Shall I tell you of God, of heaven, and of hell? There is a God, and as he descends from his abode among the stars, and essays to find an entrance into your soul, by which he may make you "a joint heir with Christ to an inheritance, incorruptible and undefiled and which fadeth not away," depend upon it, that he will be frustrated in his benevolent purpose, if the demon of pro-slavery, lies coiled up in your heart. Whatever may be said of religion, it is true that God can never approve of any person, in league with slaveholders; for a just God is forever opposed to all forms of robbery and oppression. If God's favor then is of any value, flee, I beseech thee, to the arms of liberty, and be encircled by her protecting power; so that all approach to Slavery may be dreaded by thee, as an angel dreads the polluting touch of sin.

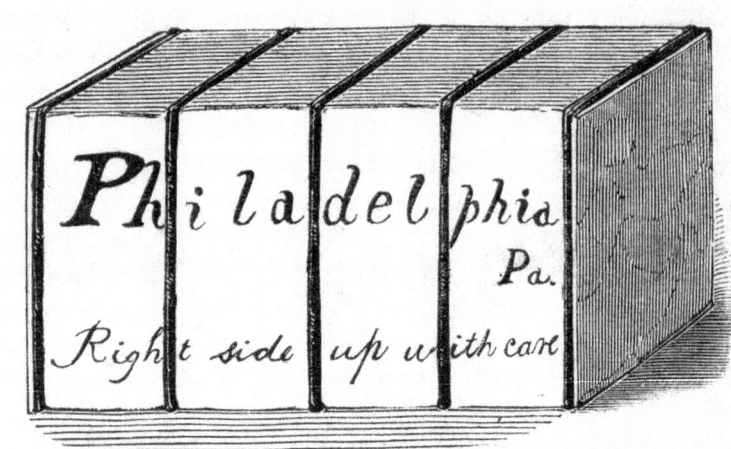

Henry "Box" Brown's box. (Library of Congress)

Extract of an Address of Sam'l J. May, Unitarian Clergyman, in Syracuse, N.Y., Delivered in Faneuil Hall.

Never will the story be forgotton in our country, or throughout the world, of the man—whom I trust you will all be permitted to see—who, that he might escape from Southern oppression, consented to a living entombment. He entered the box with the determination to be free or die: and as he heard the nails driven in, his fear was that death was to be his portion; yet, said he, let death come in preference to slavery! I happened to be in the City of Philadelphia—I have told the story to the convention already, but I will tell it again—in the midst of an excitement that was caused by the arrival of a man in a box. I measured it myself; *three feet one inch long, two feet wide, and two feet six inches deep.* IN THAT BOX A MAN WAS ENTOMBED FOR TWENTY SEVEN HOURS.

The box was placed in the express car in Richmond, Va., and subjected to all the rough treatment ordinarily given to boxes of merchandise; for, notwithstanding the admonition of *"this side up with care,"* the box was tumbled over, so that he was sometimes on his head; yes, at one time, for nearly two hours, as it seemed to him, *on his head*, and momentarily expecting that life would become extinct, from the terrible pressure of blood that poured upon his brain. Twenty-seven hours was this man subjected to this imminent peril, that he might, for one moment, at least, breathe the air of liberty. Does not such a man deserve to be free? Is there a heart here, that does not bid him welcome? Is there a heart here, that can doubt that there must be in him not merely the heart and soul of a deteriorated man—a degraded, inferior man—but the heart and soul of a noble man? Not a *nobleman*, sir, but a NOBLE MAN? Who can doubt it?

NOTES

1. This is taken from an address by the Unitarian minister Samuel J. May, which he delivered in Boston's Faneuil Hall. Brown includes an extract from May's address at the conclusion of his *Narrative*.

2. Cynthia Griffin Wolff, "Passing beyond the Middle Passage: Henry 'Box' Brown's Translations of Slavery," *Massachusetts Review* 37 (Spring 1996): 41; R. J. M. Blackett, *Building an Antislavery Wall* (Baton Rouge: Louisiana State University Press, 1983), 25.

3. Daniel Webster (1782–1852) was an American lawyer and statesman. He served in the United States House of Representatives 1813–1817 and in the Senate beginning in 1827. Webster also served as secretary of state for Presidents William Henry Harrison, John Tyler, and Millard Fillmore. Though he was personally opposed to slavery, Webster strongly believed in preserving the Union. Webster further believed that the federal government should avoid interfering with policies established within individual states. Webster drew the criticism of antislavery supporters when he sponsored the Compromise of 1850, which contained the Fugitive Slave Act requiring the North to return escaped slaves to the South.

4. Richard Hildreth (1807–1865) was an American antislavery historian, journalist, and novelist. His novel *The Slave; or, Memoirs of Archie Moore* (1836) was one of the first antislavery novels. His most important work is the six-volume *History of the United States* (1849–1852). Thomas Babington Macaulay 1st Baron (1800–1859) was a British essayist, historian, and statesman. His father, Zachary Macaulay, was a businessman who opposed slavery and edited the *Christian Observer*. He served in several political positions before being elected to Parliament in 1839. His greatest literary work is his six-volume *History of England* (1848–1861).

5. William and Ellen Craft received national and international notoriety when they escaped from slavery in Macon, Georgia. In their escape ruse, Ellen, who had a very fair complexion, posed as a white slaveholder traveling North and accompanied by "his" trusted slave, William.

6. Patrick Henry (1736–1799) was a Virginia statesman, lawyer, and orator who is best known for the words "Give me liberty or give me death," which he used in a speech given before the Virginia Provincial Convention in 1775. He spoke in favor of calling the Virginia militia to defend the colony against the British.

7. Matthew 8:19, "And a certain scribe came, and said unto him, Master, I will follow thee whithersoever thou goest."

8. Luke 5:24, "But that ye may know that the Son of man hath power upon earth to forgive sins, (he said unto the sick of the palsy,) I say unto thee, Arise, and take up thy couch, and go into thine house."

9. Lazarus was a citizen of Bethany whom Jesus raised from the dead in John 11.

10. A reference to the Declaration of Independence, "We hold these truths to be self-evident, that all men are created equal, that they are endowed by their Creator with certain unalienable Rights, that among these are Life, Liberty, and the Pursuit of Happiness."

11. According to the conventions of Southern slavery, children followed the condition of their mother. Thus, a slave mother could only produce a slave child, even if the father of the child was free.

12. Exodus 20:3, "Thou shalt have no other god before me"; Deuteronomy 5:7, "Thou shalt have none other gods before me."

13. Laurence Sterne (1713–1768) was an English clergyman most well-known for his novel *The Life and Opinions of Tristram Shandy, Gentleman* (1760–1767). In it, Tristram attempts to tell the story of his life. He is, however, unable to complete the work because of his obsessive need to incorporate all details, beginning with the events leading to his conception. Because of his captivation with telling the entire story, Tristram, at the conclusion of the novel, has only reached the point where he is about five years old.

14. John the Baptist was a first-century Jewish prophet who is seen as a precursor to Jesus. His ministry involved preaching social justice and baptizing. He was arrested, imprisoned, and executed by Herod Antipas in AD 28 or AD 29.

15. John 5:2, "Now there is at Jerusalem by the sheep market a pool, which is called in the Hebrew tongue Bethesda, having five porches." Jesus healed an impotent man in the pool.

16. Fish.

17. A woman with great stature and strength, and often possessing masculine qualities.

18. Brown here misquotes Matthew 19:23–24, "Then said Jesus unto his disciples, Verily I say unto you, That a rich man shall hardly enter into the kingdom of heaven. And again I say unto you, It is easier for a camel to go through the eye of a needle, than for a rich man to enter into the kingdom of heaven"; Mark 10:23–25, "And Jesus looked round about, and saith unto his disciples, How hardly shall they that have riches enter into the kingdom of God! And the disciples were astonished at his words. But Jesus answereth again, and saith unto them, Children, how hard is it for them that trust in riches to enter into the kingdom of God! It is easier for a camel to go through the eye of a needle than for a rich man to enter into the kingdom of God"; and Luke 18:24–25, "And when Jesus saw that he was very sorrowful, he said, How hardly shall they that have riches enter into the kingdom of God! For it is easier for a camel to go through a needle's eye, than for a rich man to enter into the kingdom of God."

19. Nat Turner's insurrection occurred August 21–23, 1831, in Southampton, Virginia. At least fifty-five white people were killed.

20. Proverbs 28:1, "The wicked flee when no man pursueth: but the righteous are bold as a lion."

21. Brown's biblical reference here is unclear. He could possibly be misquoting Matthew 13:25, "But while men slept, his enemy came and sowed tares among the wheat, and went his way."

22. A lock of hair that grows from the front part of the head.

23. 1 Timothy 5:8, "But if any provide not for his own, and specially for those of his own house, he hath denied the faith, and is worse than an infidel."

24. James 5:20, "Let him know, that he which converteth the sinner from the error of his way, shall save a soul from death, and shall hide a multitude of sins."

25. 1 John 4:18, "There is no fear in love; but perfect love casteth out fear: because fear hath torment. He that feareth is not made perfect in love."

26. A beverage popular in the South. It is composed of brandy or whiskey, sugar, ice, and sprigs of mint.

27. Damocles (?–?) was a member of the court of Dionysius II, ruler of Syracuse, Sicily (367–344 BC). Because of Dionysius's immense wealth and prosperity, Damocles had observed that Dionysius must be wonderfully happy. Dionysius arranged a lavish banquet and seated Damocles beneath a sword suspended by a single hair as a way of showing Damocles what that kind of happiness felt like. The term now refers to imminent danger.

28. Matthew 19:6, "Wherefore they are no more twain, but one flesh. What therefore God hath joined together, let not man put asunder"; and Mark 10:9, "What therefore God hath joined together, let not man put asunder."

29. Sulfuric acid.

30. After King David captured the city of Jerusalem for the Israelites, King Solomon, his successor, built a temple there, which has come to be known as the First Temple. In 587 or 586 BC, the Babylonians captured Judah and took many Jews into captivity. This period became known as the Babylonian Exile. In 539 BC, the Persians conquered the Babylonians and eventually allowed the Jews to return to Judah. The Jews who returned rebuilt the temple in Jerusalem. That temple has come to be known as the Second Temple.

31. In Genesis 25:29–34, Esau sold his birthright to his younger brother, Jacob, for a bowl of stew. Later, his mother, Rebecca, urged Jacob to pretend to be Esau to his blind father, Isaac. Isaac blessed Jacob, thinking him Esau. When Esau discovered what had happened, his anger caused Jacob to flee for his life.

32. The Fugitive Slave Act was part of the Compromise of 1850. It imposed substantial penalties on those who failed to participate in the recovery of, or aided, runaway slaves.

33. The document by which American colonists declared their independence from British rule. The Second Continental Congress adopted the Declaration on July 4, 1776.

34. Samuel Adams (1722–1803) was an American patriot and politician. (He was the cousin of John Adams, who became the second president of the United States.) Adams served as governor of Massachusetts (1793–1797). John Hancock (1737–1793) served as president of the Continental Congress (1775–1777) and was the first signer of the Declaration of Independence. He served as governor of Massachusetts from 1780 to 1785, and from 1787 until his death.

35. Jacob's son Joseph was sold into slavery in Egypt. As a reward for correctly interpreting pharaoh's dreams, Joseph was appointed prime minister to the pharaoh. When famine arrived in Canaan, Joseph invited the Israelites to come to Egypt. They lived peacefully until a new pharaoh enslaved them. Moses led the Israelites in their exodus. The Israelites were eventually able to successfully return to their homeland in Canaan.

36. Harsh or severe. Draco framed a series of laws circa 621 BC in Athens for which the penalties for most infractions was death.

37. Generally speaking, Germanic people who invaded Britain circa AD 500. These groups helped establish the Anglo-Saxon kingdom, which lasted until the Norman Conquest of 1066.

38. A secretly oppressive or capricious tribunal. In England, until 1641 when it was abolished, the Star Chamber was a high court exercising wide civil and criminal powers. It could proceed on rumors alone and could rule in favor of torture.

39. Xerxes (519?–465 BC) ruled the Persian Empire from 486 BC until his death. After surviving revolts from the provinces of Babylon and Egypt, Xerxes led his forces in a number of confrontations with the Greeks. Alexander the Great (356–323 BC) was a Macedonian general who conquered the Persian Empire. Under Alexander, the Greek empire stretched from the Mediterranean Sea to India and included much of the Middle East.

40. Psalm 23:4, "Yea, though I walk through the valley of the shadow of death, I will fear no evil: for thou art with me; thy rod and thy staff they comfort me."

41. A reference to Article I, Section 2, of the Constitution, which allows only three-fifths of the total number of slaves to be counted when determining the size of states' delegations to the House of Representatives.

42. The Mexican War (1846–1848) was fought to resolve the dispute concerning the boundary between Mexico and the United States. According to the Treaty of Guadalupe Hidalgo, the United States acquired a region that included what is now California, Nevada, Utah, and parts of Arizona, New Mexico, Colorado, and Wyoming. Many saw the war as an unnecessary attack by the United States on a weaker country.

43. The slogan used by colonists to rally support against the British Stamp Act of 1765.

44. Probably originally named after Charles Lynch (1736–1796), a planter and justice of the peace in Virginia, who employed extralegal methods of trying and punishing Tories. The term basically refers to the infliction of punishment by individuals or groups without due process of law.

45. Alexander the Great (356–323 BC) was a Macedonian general who conquered the Persian Empire. Under Alexander, the Greek empire stretched from the Mediterranean Sea to India and included much of the Middle East. Napoleon I (also known as Napoleon Bonaparte) (1769–1821) crowned himself emperor of France and established an empire that included much of western and central Europe. His ambition contributed to his eventual downfall.

46. Early matins are an early morning choral service, usually sung between midnight and dawn. Evening orisons are prayers.

47. Edmund Burke (1727–1797) was a British statesman and political writer. Burke served in Parliament from 1765 to 1794. His political essays were widely influential. During the American Revolution, Burke advised the British government to allow the colonists to share all the rights accorded to British citizens.

48. William Pitt (1708–1778) was a powerful British statesman. He helped expand the British empire and defended the rights of American colonists.

49. The Stamp Act was an act of the British Parliament in 1765. It required a tax on all paper used in the colonies. This tax included deeds, mortgages, licenses, and paper used by printers for periodicals and other reading material. The slogan used to gain public support against the tax was "No taxation without representation." The tax was repealed in 1766 due to colonial protest.

50. The disciple, called Iscariot, who betrayed Jesus. See Matthew 26:14–16, Mark 14:10–11, and Luke 22:3–6.

51. The date given here is incorrect. The disturbance actually occurred in 1770, when a British soldier fired into a crowd. Three people were killed immediately. Several others died afterward as a result of their wounds.

52. Elijah Parish Lovejoy (1802–1837) was a clergyman and antislavery activist. Lovejoy edited a religious newspaper, the *St. Louis Observer*, which was very critical of slavery, until he relocated across the Mississippi River in 1837. From his new location, Lovejoy published the *Alton Observer* and helped organize the Illinois Anti-Slavery Society. He was killed in November 1837 by rioters intending to destroy his press. See Simon, *Freedom's Champion*, 77–136; Simon, *Lovejoy*, 66–117; Dillon, *Elijah P. Lovejoy, Abolitionist Editor*, 159–70; Padgett, "Comeouterism and Antislavery Violence in Ohio's Western Reserve," 193–214.

53. The border between the United States and Canada.

Chapter 5
James W. C. Pennington (1807–1870)

THE FUGITIVE BLACKSMITH

James William Charles Pennington, who was born James Pembroke, is as well known for his abolitionist activities as he is for his work as a Presbyterian minister, his work as a social reformer, and his writings about African Americans and the slave system. Pennington was born on Maryland's eastern shore in 1807. As a child, until he was eleven, Pennington was hired out to a stonemason and then to a blacksmith. He continued this trade until he decided to escape at age twenty. Pennington's escape is punctuated by the "great moral dilemma" he faces when confronted by slave catchers who suspect him to be a runaway slave and question him about where he is from and who is his owner. "The facts here demanded were in my breast. I knew according to the law of slavery, who I belonged to and where I came from, and I must now do one of three things—I must refuse to speak at all, or I must communicate the fact, or I must tell an untruth." According to his thinking, his story is his alone to tell or refrain from telling. He estimates that while his would-be captors will be paid two hundred dollars, his liberty is worth more "than two hundred dollars are to them." Though insisting on his own freedom, Pennington chooses to tell an untruth: "A few weeks ago, I was sold from the eastern shore to a slave-trader, who had a large gang, and set out for Georgia, but when he got to a town in Virginia, he was taken sick, and died with the small-pox. Several of his gang also died with it, so that the people in the town became alarmed, and did not wish the gang to remain among them. No one claimed us, or wished to have anything to do with us; I left the rest and thought I would go somewhere and get work." Though his ruse is successful, Pennington agonizes about having been pressured into a situation by the institution of slavery that made the moral ambiguity of telling a lie his best option for engineering his own escape.[1]

Pennington safely arrived in Philadelphia, where he received assistance from Quaker supporters, and eventually made his way to Long Island. According to his narrative, Pennington found employment and was able to continue his education. Pennington moved to Brooklyn, New York, in 1828, and in 1831 attended the first annual meeting of the Negro Convention. The convention was organized by the Reverend Richard Allen, then bishop of the African Methodist Episcopal church.[2] Between 1840 and 1848, Pennington served as a pastor for congregations in Newtown and Hartford, Connecticut. There, Pennington became involved with the Underground Railroad and, in that capacity, officiated at Frederick Douglass's marriage to Anna Murray. In 1841, Pennington became president of the Union Missionary Society, which organized boycotts against goods produced by slaves and advocated sending African American missionaries to Africa. Pennington remained, however, strongly opposed to African American emigration to Africa (colonization) as a way of establishing an independent, self-governing African American nation.[3] In 1843, Pennington was elected by the Connecticut State Anti Slavery Society to go to London to represent the organization at the second World Anti Slavery Convention. His numerous speaking engagements throughout Britain during the trip were successful and brought him national and international celebrity. Benjamin Quarles, in his book *Black Abolitionists*, credits Pennington with expanding the significance of American slavery beyond its domestic confines.[4] Pennington served as pastor of the First Colored Presbyterian Church in New York City (it later changed its name to Shiloh) from 1847–1855. Pennington published *The Fugitive Blacksmith* in 1849 and soon thereafter, during a trip abroad to avoid recapture under the Fugitive Slave Act, had his freedom purchased on his behalf by supporters.

By July 1850, Pennington's narrative had sold over 6,000 copies and was in its third printing. During his trip abroad in 1849, Pennington was awarded an honorary doctorate from the School of Divinity at the University of Heidelberg. By 1855, Pennington's problems with alcohol had forced him to resign his position at Shiloh and return to the Talcott Street Church in Hartford, Connecticut, and the small church in Newtown where he had earlier officiated. By the end of 1859, Pennington was financially destitute.[5] Pennington remained politically active, however, and by 1865 had relocated to preach in the South.[6]

At a time when African Americans were asserting their own cultural identity and agenda, Pennington's staunch opposition to the African American colonization, as well as the ideas he presented in his book *A Text Book of the Origin and History, &c. &c of Colored People* (1841), place him at the origins of African American social and intellectual thought. Pennington remained socially active through the Civil War. In 1869, Pennington was called by the Presbyterian Committee of Missions for Freedmen to go to Jacksonville, Florida, and found a church and Sabbath school for recently emancipated blacks. His congregation, just out of slavery, could afford to provide only a small salary. It was there that Pennington died in poverty on October 22, 1870.[7]

The Fugitive Blacksmith is reprinted here from the third edition. This edition, which slightly expands the earlier editions, was initially published in 1850 in

London by Charles Gilpin after favorable public response to the first two editions. The first edition of the narrative was published in 1849.

Further Reading

Andrews, William L. "Mark Twain and James W. C. Pennington: Huckleberry Finn's Smallpox Lie." *Studies in American Fiction* 9 (Spring 1981): 103–12; Andrews, William L. *To Tell a Free Story: The First Century of Afro-American Autobiography, 1760–1865*. Urbana: University of Illinois Press, 1986; Bell, Howard Holman. *A Survey of the Negro Convention Movement, 1830–1861*. New York: Arno Press, 1969; Blackett, R. J. M. *Beating Against the Barriers: Biographical Essays in Nineteenth-Century Afro-American History*. Baton Rouge: Louisiana State University Press, 1986; Jugurtha, Lillie Butler. "Point of View in the Afro-American Slave Narratives: A Study of Narratives by Douglass and Pennington." In *The Art of Slave Narrative: Original Essays in Criticism and Theory*, edited by John Sekora and Darwin T. Turner, 110–19. Macomb: Western Illinois University, 1982; Katz, William L. *Eyewitness: The Negro in American History*. New York: Pitman Publishing Corporation, 1967; MacKethan, Lucinda H. "Huck Finn and the Slave Narratives: Lighting Out as Design." *Southern Review* 20 (Spring 1984): 247–64; MacKethan, Lucinda H. "Metaphors of Mastery in the Slave Narratives." In *The Art of Slave Narrative: Original Essays in Criticism and Theory*, edited by John Sekora and Darwin T. Turner, 55–69. Macomb: Western Illinois University, 1982; Pease, Jane H. and William H. Pease. *They Who Would Be Free: Blacks' Search for Freedom, 1830–1861*. New York: Atheneum, 1974; Quarles, Benjamin. *Black Abolitionists*. New York: Oxford University Press, 1969; Swift, David E. *Black Prophets of Justice: Activist Clergy before the Civil War*. Baton Rouge: Louisiana State University Press, 1989; Thomas, Herman E. *James W. C. Pennington: African American Churchman and Abolitionist*. New York: Garland Publishing, 1995; Washington, Joseph R., Jr. *The First Fugitive Foreign and Domestic Doctor of Divinity: Rational Race Rules of Religion and Realism, Revered and Reversed or Revised by the Reverend Doctor James William Charles Pennington*. Lewiston, NY: Edwin Mellen Press, 1990.

THE FUGITIVE BLACKSMITH;
OR,
EVENTS IN THE HISTORY
OF
JAMES W. C. PENNINGTON,

PASTOR OF A PRESBYTERIAN CHURCH, NEW YORK,

FORMERLY A SLAVE IN THE STATE OF MARYLAND, UNITED STATES.

"Let mine outcasts dwell with thee, Moab; be thou a covert to them from the face of the spoiler.
—ISAIAH XVI. 4.

Third Edition.

MR. CHARLES GILPIN,
MY DEAR SIR,
The information just communicated to me by you, that another edition of my little book, "The Fugitive Blacksmith," is called for, has agreeably surprised me. The British public has laid me under renewed obligations by this mark of liberality, which I hasten to acknowledge. I would avail myself of this moment also, to acknowledge the kindness of the gentlemen of the newspaper press for the many favourable reviews which my little book has received. It is to them I am indebted, in no small degree, for the success with which I have been favoured in getting the book before the notice of the public.
Yours truly,
J.W.C. PENNINGTON.
Hoxton, Oct. 15th, 1849.

PREFACE

The brief narrative I here introduce to the public, consists of outline notes originally thrown together to guide my memory when lecturing on this part of the subject of slavery. This will account for its style, and will also show that the work is not full.

The question may be asked, Why I have published anything so long after my escape from slavery?[8] I answer I have been induced to do so on account of the increasing disposition to overlook the fact, that THE SIN of slavery lies in the chattel principle, or relation. Especially have I felt anxious to save professing Christians, and my brethren in the ministry, from falling into a great mistake. My feelings are always outraged when I hear them speak of "kind masters,"—"Christian masters,"—"the mildest form of slavery,"—"well fed and clothed slaves," as extenuations of slavery; I am satisfied they either mean to pervert the truth, or they do not know what they say. The being of slavery, its soul and body, lives and moves in the chattel principle, the property principle, the bill of sale principle; the cartwhip, starvation, and nakedness, are its inevitable consequences to a greater or less extent, warring with the dispositions of men.

There lies a skein of silk upon a lady's work-table. How smooth and hand-some are the threads. But while that lady goes out to make a call, a party of children enter the apartment, and in amusing themselves, tangle the skein of silk, and now who can untangle it? The relation between master and slave is even as delicate as a skein of silk: it is liable to be entangled at any moment.

The mildest form of slavery, if there be such a form, looking at the chattel principle as the definition of slavery, is comparatively the worst form; for it not only keeps the slave in the most unpleasant apprehension, like a prisoner in chains awaiting his trial; but it actually, in a great majority of cases, where kind masters do exist, trains him under the most favourable circumstances the system admits of, and then plunges him into the worst of which it is capable.

It is under the mildest form of slavery, as it exists in Maryland, Virginia, and Kentucky, that the finest specimens of coloured females are reared. There are no mothers who rear, and educate in the natural graces, finer daughters than the Æthiopian women, who have the least chance to give scope to their maternal affections. But what is generally the fact of such female slaves? When they are not raised for the express purpose of supplying the market of a class of economical Louisian and Mississippi gentlemen, who do not wish to incur the expense of rearing legitimate families, they are, nevertheless, on account of their attractions, exposed to the most shameful degradation, by the young masters in the families where it is claimed they are so well off. My master once owned a beautiful girl about twenty-four. She had been raised in a family where her mother was a great favorite. She was her mother's darling child. Her master was a lawyer of eminent abilities and great fame, but owing to habits of intemperance, he failed in business, and my master purchased this girl for a nurse. After he had owned her about a year, one of his sons became attached to her, for no honourable purposes; a fact which was not only well-known among all the slaves, but which became a source of unhappiness to his mother and sisters.

The result was, that poor Rachel had to be sold to "Georgia." Never shall I forget the heart-rending scene, when one day one of the men was ordered to get "the one-horse cart ready to go into town;" Rachel, with her few articles of clothing, was placed in it, and taken into the very town where her parents lived, and there sold to the traders before their weeping eyes. That same son who had degraded her, and who was the cause of her being sold, acted as salesman, and bill of saleman. While this cruel business was being transacted, my master stood aside, and the girl's father, a pious member and exhorter in the Methodist Church, a venerable grey-headed man, with his hat off, besought that he might be allowed to get some one in the place to purchase his child. But no: my master was invincible. His reply was, "She has offended in my family, and I can only restore confidence by sending her out of hearing." After lying in prison a short time, her new owner took her with others to the far South, where her parents heard no more of her.

Here was a girl born and reared under the mildest form of slavery. Her original master was reputed to be even indulgent. He lived in a town, and was a high-bred gentleman, and a lawyer. He had but a few slaves, and had no occasion for an overseer, those negro leeches, to watch and drive them; but when he became embarrassed by his own folly, the chattel principle doomed this girl to be sold at the same sale with his books, house, and horses. With my master she found herself under far more stringent discipline than she had been accustomed to, and finally degraded, and sold where her condition could not be worse, and where she had not the least hope of ever bettering it.

This case presents the legitimate working of the great chattel principle. It is no accidental result—it is the fruit of the tree. You cannot constitute slavery without the chattel principle—and with the chattel principle you cannot save it from these results. Talk not then about kind and christian masters. They are not masters of the system. The system is master of them; and the slaves are their vassals.

These storms rise on the bosom of the calmed waters of the system. You are a slave, a being in whom another owns property. Then you may rise with his pride, but remember the day is at hand when you must also fall with his folly. To-day you may be pampered by his meekness; but to-morrow you will suffer in the storm of his passions.

In the month of September, 1848, there appeared in my study, one morning, in New York City, an aged coloured man of tall and slender form. I saw depicted on his countenance anxiety bordering on despair, still I was confident that he was a man whose mind was accustomed to faith. When I learned that he was a native of my own state, Maryland, having been born in the county of Montgomery, I at once became much interested in him. He had been sent to me by my friend, William Harned, Esq., of the Anti-Slavery Office, 61, John Street. He put into my hand the following bill of distress:—

"Alexander, Virginia, *September 5th*, 1848.

"The bearer, Paul Edmondson, is the father of two girls, Mary Jane and Emily Catherine Edmondson. These girls have been purchased by us, and once sent to the South; and upon the positive assurance that the money for them would be raised if they were brought back, they were returned. Nothing, it appears, has as yet been done in this respect by those who promised, and we are on the very eve of sending them south a second time; and we are candid in saying, that if they go again, we will not regard any promises made in relation to them.

"The father wishes to raise money to pay for them, and intends to appeal to the liberality of the humane and the good to aid him, and has requested us to state in writing *the condition upon which we will sell his daughters.*

"We expect to start our servants to the South in a few days; if the sum of twelve hundred dollars be raised and paid us in fifteen days, or we be assured of that sum, then we will retain them for twenty-five days more, to give an opportunity for raising the other thousand and fifty dollars, otherwise we shall be compelled to send them along with our other servants.

(Signed)   "Bruin and Hill."

The old man also showed me letters from other individuals, and one from the Rev. Matthew A. Turner, pastor of Asbury Chapel, where himself and his daughters were members. He was himself free, but his wife was a slave. Those two daughters were two out of fifteen children he had raised for the owner of his wife. These two girls had been sold, along with four brothers, to the traders, for an attempt to escape to the North, and gain their freedom.

On the next Sabbath evening, I threw the case before my people, and the first fifty dollars of the sum was raised to restore the old man his daughters. Subsequently the case was taken up under the management of a committee of ministers of the Methodist Episcopal Church, consisting of the Rev. G. Peck, D.D., Rev. E. E. Griswold, and Rev. D. Curry, and the entire sum of £2,250 dollars, (£450.) was raised for two girls, fourteen and sixteen years of age!

But why this enormous sum for two mere children? Ah, reader, they were reared under the mildest form of slavery known to the laws of Maryland! The mother is an invalid, and allowed to live with her free husband; but she is a woman of excellent mind, and has bestowed great pains upon her daughters. If you would know, then, why these girls were held at such a price, even to their own father, read the following extract of a letter from one who was actively engaged in behalf of them, and who had several interviews with the traders to induce them to reduce the price, but without success. Writing from Washington, D.C., September 12th, 1848, this gentleman says to William Harned, "The truth is, *and is confessed to be, that their destination is prostitution*; of this you would be satisfied on seeing them; they are of elegant form, and fine faces."

And such, dear reader, is the sad fate of hundreds of my young country-women, natives of my native state. Such is the fate of many who are not only reared under the mildest form of slavery, but of those who have been made acquainted with the milder system of the Prince of Peace.[9]

When Christians, and Christian ministers, then, talk about the "mildest form of slavery,"—"Christian masters," &c., I say my feelings are outraged. It is a great mistake to offer these as an extenuation of the system. It is calculated to mislead the public mind. The opinion seems to prevail, that the negro, after having toiled as a slave for centuries to enrich his white brother, to lay the foundation of his proud institutions, after having been sunk as low as slavery can sink him, needs now only a second-rate civilization, a lower standard of civil and religious privileges than the whites claim for themselves.

During the last year or two we have heard of nothing but revolutions and the enlargements of the eras of freedom, on both sides of the Atlantic. Our white brethren everywhere are reaching out their hands to grasp more freedom. In the place of absolute monarchies they have limited monarchies, and in the place of limited monarchies they have republics: so tenacious are they of their own liberties.

But when we speak of slavery, and complain of the wrong it is doing us, and ask to have the yoke removed, we are told, "O, you must not be impatient, you must not create undue excitement. You are not so badly off, for many of your masters are kind Christian masters." Yes, sirs, many of our masters are professed Christians; and what advantage is that to us? The grey heads of our fathers are brought down in scores to the grave in sorrow, on account of their young and tender sons, who are sold to the far South, where they have to toil without requite to supply the world's market with *cotton, sugar, rice, tobacco, &c*. Our venerable mothers are borne down with poignant grief at the fate of their children. Our sisters, if not by the law, are by common consent made the prey of vile men, who can bid the highest.

In all the bright achievements we have obtained in the great work of emancipation, if we have not settled the fact that the chattel principle is wrong, and cannot be maintained upon Christian ground, then we have wrought and triumphed to little purpose, and we shall have to do our first work over again.

It is this that has done all the mischief connected with slavery; it is this that threatens still further mischief. Whatever may be the ill or favoured condition of the slave in the matter of mere personal treatment, it is the chattel relation that robs him of his manhood, and transfers his ownership in himself to another. It is this that transfers the proprietorship of his wife and children to another. It is this that throws his family history into utter confusion, and leaves him without a single record to which he may appeal in vindication of his character, or honour. And has a man no sense of honour because he was born a slave? Has he no need of character?

Suppose insult, reproach, or slander, should render it necessary for him to appeal to the history of his family in vindication of his character, where will he find that history? He goes to his native state, to his native county, to his native town; but nowhere does he find any record of himself *as a man*. On looking at the family record of his old, kind, Christian, master, there he finds his name on a catalogue with the horses, cows, hogs, and dogs. However humiliating and degrading it may be to his feelings to find his name written down among the beasts of the field, *that* is just the place, and the *only* place assigned to it by the chattel relation. I beg our Anglo-Saxon brethren to accustom themselves to think that we need something more than mere kindness. We ask for justice, truth, and honour as other men do.

My coloured brethren are now widely awake to the degradation which they suffer in having property vested in their persons, and they are also conscious of the deep and corrupting disgrace of having our wives and children owned by other men,—men who have shown to the world that their own virtue is not infallible, and who have given us no flattering encouragement to entrust that of our wives and daughters to them.

I have great pleasure in stating that my dear friend W. W., spoken of in this narrative, to whom I am so deeply indebted, is still living. I have been twice to see him within four years, and have regular correspondence with him. In one of the last letters I had from him, he authorises me to use his name in connection with this narrative in these words,—"As for using my name, by reference or otherwise, in thy narrative, it is at thy service. I know thee so well, James, that I am not afraid of thy making a bad use of it, nor am I afraid or ashamed to have it known that I took thee in and gave thee aid, when I found thee travelling alone and in want.—W. W."

On the second page of the same sheet I have a few lines from his excellent lady, in which she says, "James, I hope thee will not attribute my long silence in writing to indifference. No such feeling can ever exist towards thee in our family. Thy name is mentioned almost every day. Each of the children claims the next letter from thee. It will be for thee to decide which shall have it.—P. W."

In a postscript following this, W. W. says again:—"Understand me, James, that thee is at full liberty to use my name in any way thee wishes in thy narrative. We have a man here from the eastern shore of thy state. He is trying to learn as fast as thee did when here.—W. W."

I hope the reader will pardon me for introducing these extracts. My only apology is, the high gratification I feel in knowing that this family has not only been greatly prospered in health and happiness, but that I am upon the most intimate and pleasant terms with all its members, and that they all still feel a deep and cordial interest in my welfare.

There is another distinguished individual whose sympathy has proved very gratifying to me in my situation—I mean that true friend of the negro, *Gerrit Smith,*

Esq.[10] I was well acquainted with the family in which Mr. Smith married in Maryland. My attention has been fixed upon him for the last ten years, for I have felt confident that God had set him apart for some great good to the negro. In a letter dated Peterborough, November 7th, 1848, he says:—

"J.W.C. PENNINGTON,

"Slight as is my *personal* acquaintance with you, I nevertheless am well acquainted with you. I am familiar with many passages in your history—all that part of your history extending from the time when, a sturdy blacksmith, you were running away from Maryland oppression, down to the present, when you are the successor of my lamented friend, Theodore S. Wright.[11] Let me add that my acquaintance with you has inspired me with a high regard for your wisdom and integrity."

Give us a few more such men in America, and slavery will soon be numbered among the things that were. A few men who will not only have the moral courage to aim the severing blow at the chattel relation between master and slave, without parley, palliation or compromise; but who have also the christian fidelity to brave public scorn and contumely, to seize a coloured man by the hand, and elevate him to the position from whence the avarice and oppression of the whites have degraded him. These men have the right view of the subject. They see that in every case where the relation between master and slave is broken, slavery is weakened, and that every coloured man elevated, becomes a step in the ladder upon which his whole people are to ascend. They would not have us accept of some modified form of liberty, while the old mischief-working chattel relation remains unbroken, untouched and unabrogated.

J.W.C. PENNINGTON.
13, *Princes Square, London,*
August 15*th*, 1849.

PREFACE TO THIRD EDITION

MR. CHARLES GILPIN,

THE rapid sale of the Sixth Thousand of *The Fugitive Blacksmith*, calls upon me for another acknowledgment of gratitude to the British public, and to yourself. In addition to favourable notices taken of the book originally by the news-presses, it has been my happiness to hear the most flattering opinions from all classes of readers. My object was to write an unexceptional book of the kind for children in point of matter, and for the masses in point of price. I believe both of these have been gained. I have been gratified also to find that my book has awakened a deep interest in the cause of the *American slave*. Since the second edition was printed, I have been constantly engaged in preaching and lecturing. I have spoken on an average five evenings weekly on slavery, temperance, missions, and sabbath-schools, and preached on an average three times each sabbath. In almost every instance where I have gone into a place, I have found the way prepared by the book. In some cases a single copy had been handed from one to another in the town, and some minister or leading gentleman has been prepared to speak of it at my meeting.

The fugitive slave question has assumed a painful interest in America within a few months. The masters have been for twenty years exerting themselves with increased vigilance to cut off the escape of the fugitives. Failing in this, and finding the stream regularly increasing, they *now*come out with the broad demand upon the free states to arrest and send back the flying bondman.*[12]* The North will hardly degrade herself by acceding to this. Meanwhile, no power in this world will arrest the exodus of the slaves from the South. Since the day I came out myself, I have ever believed—and I believe it now more firmly than ever—that this is the divinely ordered method for the effectual destruction of American slavery. For this I have been, and shall continue to exert my influence. The masters may legislate, rave like madmen, pursue with bloodhounds, and offer rewards which call to their aid the vile and the murderous. But we fear them not. Things have been shaping for years in favour of a general movement amongst the slaves. The conduct of the masters, the state of the world, the providences of God have all tended to this. We have the right of the question upon Christian principles. We deny utterly and positively their claim to property in us, and if as men they are determined to be so heartless, cruel and barbarous, that we cannot dwell with them in peace—God, the spirit of peace, the love of order, and the spirit of liberty say to us, come out from among them.

---

*In February last, the Honourable Henry Clay, a slaveholder and a senator from Kentucky, a slave-breeding state, offered the following among other resolutions in the Senate of the United States,—"7th, Resolved, That more effectual provisions ought to be made by law, according to the requirement of the constitution, for the restitution and delivery of persons bound to service or labour in any state, who may escape into any other state or territory of this Union." And among other things, he said in support of it, "I do not say, sir, that a private individual is obliged to make the tour of his whole state, in order to assist the owner of a slave to recover his property, but I do say, if he is present when the owner of a slave is about to assert his rights and regain possession of his property, that he, that is every man present, whether officer or agent of the state or government, or private individual, is bound to assist in the execution of the laws of their country."

The Honourable John C. Calhoun, also a slaveholder and a senator, from South Carolina, who has since died, said in a speech, on the occasion—"The North has only to will, to do justice, and perform her duty, in order to accomplish it; to do justice by conceding to the South an equal right in the acquired territory; and to do her duty by causing the stipulations relative to the fugitive slave to be faithfully fulfilled; to cease the agitation of the slave question, and provide for the insertion of a provision in the constitution, by an amendment, which will restore in substance the power she possessed of protecting herself, before the equilibrium between the sections destroyed by the action of the government. There will be no difficulty in devising such a provision—one that will protect the South, and which at the same time will improve and strengthen the government, instead of impairing or weakening it."

This matter has gone so far that the compromise committee of thirteen, of which Mr. Clay was chairman, has empowered him to frame a bill in accordance with the above resolution.

I send forth the third edition of the *Fugitive Blacksmith* as an humble harbinger to prepare and keep the way open; that the world may be acquainted with the question, and that every one may be well aware of the unreasonable claims urged by the American planters, and the utter impossibility of their maintaining them.

J.W.C. PENNINGTON.
London, July 30*th*, 1850.

CHAPTER I

My Birth and Parentage—The Treatment of Slaves Generally in Maryland.

I was born in the state of Maryland, which is one of the smallest and most northern of the slave-holding states; the products of this state are wheat, rye, Indian corn, tobacco, with some hemp, flax, &c. By looking at the map, it will be seen that Maryland, like Virginia her neighbour, is divided by the Chesapeake Bay into eastern and western shores. My birth-place was on the eastern shore, where there are seven or eight small counties; the farms are small, and tobacco is mostly raised.

At an early period in the history of Maryland, her lands began to be exhausted by the bad cultivation peculiar to slave states; and hence she soon commenced the business of breeding slaves for the more southern states. This has given an enormity to slavery, in Maryland, differing from that which attaches to the system in Louisiana, and equalled by none of the kind, except Virginia and Kentucky, and not by either of these in extent.

My parents did not both belong to the same owner: my father belonged to a man named———; my mother belonged to a man named———. This not only made me a slave, but made me the slave of him to whom my mother belonged; as the primary law of slavery is, that the child shall follow the condition of the mother.

When I was about four years of age, my mother, an older brother and myself, were given to a son of my master, who had studied for the medical profession, but who had now married wealthy, and was about to settle as a wheat-planter in Washington County, on the western shore. This began the first of our family troubles that I knew anything about, as it occasioned a separation between my mother and the only two children she then had, and my father, to a distance of about two hundred miles. But this separation did not continue long; my father being a valuable slave, my master was glad to purchase him.

About this time, I began to feel another evil of slavery—I mean the want of parental care and attention. My parents were not able to give any attention to their children during the day. I often suffered much from *hunger* and other similar causes. To estimate the sad state of a slave child, you must look at it as a helpless human being thrown upon the world without the benefit of its natural guardians.

It is thrown into the world without a social circle to flee to for hope, shelter, comfort, or instruction. The social circle, with all its heaven-ordained blessings, is of the utmost importance to the *tender child;* but of this, the slave child, however tender and delicate, is robbed.

There is another source of evil to slave children, which I cannot forbear to mention here, as one which early embittered my life,—I mean the tyranny of the master's children. My master had two sons, about the ages and sizes of my older brother and myself. We were not only required to recognise these young sirs as our young masters, but *they* felt themselves to be such; and, in consequence of this feeling, they sought to treat us with the same air of authority that their father did the older slaves.

Another evil of slavery that I felt severely about this time, was the tyranny and abuse of the overseers. These men seem to look with an evil eye upon children. I was once visiting a menagerie, and being struck with the fact, that the lion was comparatively indifferent to every one around his cage, while he eyed with peculiar keenness a little boy I had; the keeper informed me that such was always the case. Such is true of those human beings in the slave states, called overseers. They seem to take pleasure in torturing the children of slaves, long before they are large enough to be put at the hoe, and consequently under the whip.

We had an overseer, named Blackstone; he was an extremely cruel man to the working hands. He always carried a long hickory whip—a kind of pole. He kept three or four of these, in order that he might not at any time be without one.

I once found one of these hickories lying in the yard, and supposing that he had thrown it away, I picked it up, and boy-like, was using it for a horse; he came along from the field, and seeing me with it, fell upon me with the one he then had in his hand, and flogged me most cruelly. From that, I lived in constant dread of that man; and he would show how much he delighted in cruelty by chasing me from my play with threats and imprecations. I have lain for hours in a wood, or behind a fence, to hide from his eye.

At this time my days were extremely dreary. When I was nine years of age, myself and my brother were hired out from home; my brother was placed with a pump-maker, and I was placed with a stone-mason. We were both in a town some six miles from home. As the men with whom we lived were not slaveholders, we enjoyed some relief from the peculiar evils of slavery. Each of us lived in a family where there was no other negro.

The slaveholders in that state often hire the children of their slaves out to non-slaveholders, not only because they save themselves the expense of taking care of them, but in this way they get among their slaves useful trades. They put a bright slave-boy with a tradesman, until he gets such a knowledge of the trade as to be able to do his own work, and then he takes him home. I remained with the stone-mason until I was eleven years of age: at this time I was taken home. This was another serious period in my childhood; I was separated from my older brother, to whom I was much attached; he continued at his place, and not only learned the trade to great perfection, but finally became the property of the man with whom he lived, so that our separation was permanent, as we never lived nearer after, than six miles. My master owned an excellent blacksmith, who had obtained his trade in the way I have mentioned above. When I returned home at the age of eleven, I was set about assisting to do the mason-work of a new smith's shop. This being done, I was placed at the business, which I soon learned, so as to be called a "first-rate blacksmith." I continued to work at this business for nine years, or until I was twenty-one, with the exception of the last seven months.

In the spring of 1828, my master sold me to a Methodist man, named———, for the sum of seven hundred dollars. It soon proved that he had not work enough to keep me employed as a smith, and he offered me for sale again. On hearing of this, my old master re-purchased me, and proposed to me to undertake the carpentering business. I had been working at this trade six months with a white workman, who was building a large barn when I left. I will now relate the abuses which occasioned me to fly.

Three or four of our farm hands had their wives and families on other plantations. In such cases, it is the custom in Maryland to allow the men to go on Saturday evening to see their families, stay over the Sabbath, and return on Monday morning, not later than "half-an-hour by sun." To overstay their time is a grave fault, for which, especially at busy seasons, they are punished.

One Monday morning, two of these men had not been so fortunate as to get home at the required time: one of them was an uncle of mine. Besides these, two young men who had no families, and for whom no such provision of time was made, having gone somewhere to spend the Sabbath, were absent. My master was greatly irritated, and had resolved to have, as he said, "a general whipping-match among them."

Preparatory to this, he had a rope in his pocket, and a cowhide in his hand, walking about the premises, and speaking to every one he met in a very insolent manner, and finding fault with some without just cause. My father, among other numerous and responsible duties, discharged that of shepherd to a large and valuable flock of Merino sheep. This morning he was engaged in the tenderest of a shepherd's duties;—a little lamb, not able to go alone, lost its mother; he was feeding it by hand. He had been keeping it in the house for several days. As he stooped over it in the yard, with a vessel of new milk he had obtained, with which to feed it, my master came along, and without the least provocation, began by asking, "Bazil have you fed the flock?"

"Yes, sir."

"Were you away yesterday?"

"No, sir."

"Do you know why these boys have not got home this morning yet?"

"No, sir, I have not seen any of them since Saturday night."

"By the Eternal, I'll make them know their hour. The fact is, I have too many of you; my people are getting to be the most careless, lazy, and worthless in the country."

"Master," said my father, "I am always at my post; Monday morning never finds me off the plantation."

"Hush Bazil! I shall have to sell some of you; and then the rest will have enough to do; I have not work enough to keep you all tightly employed; I have too many of you."

All this was said in an angry, threatening, and exceedingly insulting tone. My father was a high-spirited man, and feeling deeply the insult, replied to the last expression,—"If I am one too many, sir, give me a chance to get a purchaser, and I am willing to be sold when it may suit you."

"Bazil, I told you to hush!" and suiting the action to the word, he drew forth the "cowhide" from under his arm, fell upon him with most savage cruelty, and inflicted fifteen, or twenty severe stripes with all his strength, over his shoulders and the small of his back. As he raised himself upon his toes, and gave the last stripe,[13] he said, "By the *** I will make you know that I am master of your tongue as well as of your time!"

Being a tradesman, and just at that time getting my breakfast, I was near enough to hear the insolent words that were spoken to my father, and to hear, see, and even count the savage stripes inflicted upon him.

Let me ask any one of Anglo-Saxon blood and spirit, how would you expect a *son* to feel at such a sight?

This act created an open rupture with our family—each member felt the deep insult that had been inflicted upon our head; the spirit of the whole family was roused; we talked of it in our nightly gatherings, and showed it in our daily melancholy aspect. The oppressor saw this, and with the heartlessness that was in perfect keeping with the first insult, commenced a series of tauntings, threatenings, and insinuations, with a view to crush the spirit of the whole family.

Although it was some time after this event before I took the decisive step, yet in my mind and spirit, I never was a *Slave* after it.

Whenever I thought of the great contrast between my father's employment on that memorable Monday morning, (feeding the little lamb,) and the barbarous conduct of my master, I could not help cordially despising the proud abuser of my sire; and I believe he discovered it, for he seemed to have diligently sought an occasion against me. Many incidents occurred to convince me of this, too tedious to mention; but there is one I will mention, because it will serve to show the state of feeling that existed between us, and how it served to widen the already open breach.

I was one day shoeing a horse in the shop yard. I had been stooping for some time under the weight of the horse, which was large, and was very tired; meanwhile, my master had taken his position on a little hill just in front of me, and stood leaning back on his cane, with his hat drawn over his eyes. I put down the horse's foot, and straightened myself up to rest a moment, and without knowing that he was there, my eye caught his. This threw him into a panic of rage; he would have it that I was watching him. "What are you rolling your white eyes at me for, you lazy rascal?" He came down upon me with his cane, and laid on over my shoulders, arms, and legs, about a dozen severe blows, so that my limbs and flesh were sore for several weeks; and then after several other offensive epithets, left me.

This affair my mother saw from her cottage, which was near; I being one of the oldest sons of my parents, our family was now mortified to the lowest degree. I had always aimed to be trustworthy; and feeling a high degree of mechanical pride, I had aimed to do my work with dispatch and skill; my blacksmith's pride and taste was one thing that had reconciled me so long to remain a slave. I sought to distinguish myself in the finer branches of the business by invention and finish; I frequently tried my hand at making guns and pistols, putting blades in penknives, making fancy hammers, hatchets, sword-canes, &c., &c. Besides I used to assist my father at night in making straw-hats and willow-baskets, by which means we supplied our family with little articles of food, clothing and luxury, which slaves in the mildest form of the system never get from the master; but after this, I found that my mechanic's pleasure and pride were gone. I thought of nothing but the family disgrace under which we were smarting, and how to get out of it.

Perhaps I may as well extend this note a little. The reader will observe that I have not said much about my master's cruel treatment; I have aimed rather to show the cruelties incident to the system. I have no disposition to attempt to convict him of having been one of the most cruel masters—that would not be true—his prevailing temper was kind, but he was a perpetualist.[14] He was opposed to emancipation; thought free negroes a great nuisance, and was, as respects discipline, a thorough slaveholder. He would not tolerate a look or a word from a slave like insubordination. He would suppress it at once, and at any risk. When he thought it necessary to secure unqualified obedience, he would strike a slave with any weapon, flog him on the bare back, and sell. And this was the kind of discipline he also empowered his overseers and sons to use.

I have seen children go from our plantations to join the chained-gang on its way from Washington to Louisiana; and I have seen men and women flogged—I have seen the overseers strike a man with a hay-fork—nay, more, men have been maimed by shooting! Some dispute arose one morning between the overseer and one of the farm hands, when the former made at the slave with a hickory club; the slave taking to his heels, started for the woods; as he was crossing the yard, the overseer turned, snatched his gun which was near, and fired at the flying slave, lodging several shots in the calf of one leg. The poor fellow continued his flight, and got into the woods; but he was in so much pain that he was compelled to come out in the evening, and give himself up to his master, thinking he would not allow him to be punished as he had been shot. He was locked up that night; the next morning the overseer was allowed to tie him up and flog him; his master then took his instruments and picked the shot out of his leg, and told him, it served him just right.

My master had a deeply pious and exemplary slave, an elderly man, who one day had a misunderstanding with the overseer, when the latter attempted to flog him. He fled to the woods; it was noon; at evening he came home orderly. The next morning, my master, taking one of his sons with him, a rope and cowhide in his hand, led the poor old man away into the stable, tied him up, and ordered the son to lay on thirty-nine lashes, which he did, making the keen end of the cowhide lap around and strike him in the tenderest part of his side, till the blood sped out, as if a lance had been used.

While my master's son was thus engaged, the sufferer's little daughter, a child six years of age, stood at the door, weeping in agony for the fate of her father. I heard the old man articulating in a low tone of voice; I listened at the intervals between the stripes, and lo! he was praying!

When the last lash was laid on, he was let down; and leaving him to put on his clothes, they passed out of the door, and drove the man's weeping child away! I was mending a hinge to one of the barn doors; I saw and heard what I have stated. Six months after, this same man's eldest daughter, a girl fifteen years old, was sold to slave-traders, where he never saw her more.

This poor slave and his wife were both Methodists, so was the wife of the young master who flogged him. My old master was an Episcopalian.

These are only a few of the instances which came under my own notice during my childhood and youth on our plantations; as to those which occurred on other plantations in the neighbourhood, I could state any number.

I have stated that my master was watching the movements of our family very closely. Some time after the difficulties began, we found that he also had a confidential slave assisting him in the business. This wretched fellow, who was nearly white, and of Irish descent, informed our master of the movements of each member of the family by day and by night, and on Sundays. This stirred the spirit of my mother, who spoke to our fellow-slave, and told him he ought to be ashamed to be engaged in such low business.

Master hearing of this, called my father, mother, and myself before him, and accused us of an attempt to resist and intimidate his "confidential servant." Finding that only my mother had spoken to him, he swore that if she ever spoke another word to him, he would flog her.

I knew my mother's spirit and my master's temper as well. Our social state was now perfectly intolerable. We were on the eve of a general fraças. This last scene occurred on Tuesday; and on Saturday evening following, without counsel or advice from any one, I determined to fly.

CHAPTER II

The Flight

It was the Sabbath; the holy day which God in his infinite wisdom gave for the rest of both man and beast. In the state of Maryland, the slaves generally have the Sabbath, except in those districts where the evil weed, tobacco, is cultivated; and then, when it is the season for setting the plant, they are liable to be robbed of this only rest.

It was in the month of November, somewhat past the middle of the month. It was a bright day, and all was quiet. Most of the slaves were resting about their quarters; others had leave to visit their friends on other plantations, and were absent. The evening previous I had arranged my little bundle of clothing, and had secreted it at some distance from the house. I had spent most of the forenoon in my workshop, engaged in deep and solemn thought.

It is impossible for me now to recollect all the perplexing thoughts that passed through my mind during that forenoon; it was a day of heartaching to me. But I distinctly remember the two great difficulties that stood in the way of my flight: I had a father and mother whom I dearly loved,—I had also six sisters and four brothers on the plantation. The question was, shall I hide my purpose from them? moreover, how will my flight affect them when I am gone? Will they not be suspected? Will not the whole family be sold off as a disaffected family, as is generally the case when one of its members flies? But a still more trying question was, how can I expect to succeed, I have no knowledge of distance or direction—I know that Pennsylvania is a free state, but I know not where its soil begins, or where that of Maryland ends? Indeed, at this time there was no safety in Pennsylvania, New Jersey, or New York, for a fugitive, except in lurking-places, or under the care of judicious friends, who could be entrusted not only with liberty, but also with life itself.

With such difficulties before my mind, the day had rapidly worn away; and it was just past noon. One of my perplexing questions I had settled—I had resolved to let no one into my secret; but the other difficulty was now to be met. It was to be met without the least knowledge of its magnitude, except by imagination. Yet of one thing there could be no mistake, that the consequences of a failure would be most serious. Within my recollection no one had attempted to escape from my master; but I had many cases in my mind's eye, of slaves of other planters who had failed, and who had been made examples of the most cruel treatment, by flogging and selling to the far South, where they were never to see their friends more. I was not without serious apprehension that such would be my fate. The bare possibility was impressively solemn; but the hour was now come, and the man must act and be free, or remain a slave for ever. How the impression came to be upon my mind I cannot tell; but there was a strange and horrifying belief, that if I did not meet the crisis that day, I should be self-doomed—that my ear would be nailed to the doorpost for ever. The emotions of that moment I cannot fully depict. Hope, fear, dread, terror, love, sorrow, and deep melancholy were mingled in my mind together; my mental state was one of most painful distraction. When I looked at my numerous family—a beloved father and mother, eleven brothers and sisters, &c.; but when I looked at slavery as such; when I looked at it in its mildest form, with all its annoyances; and above all, when I remembered that one of the chief annoyances of slavery, in the most mild form, is the liability of being at any moment sold into the worst form, it seemed that no consideration, not even that of life itself, could tempt me to give up the thought of flight. And then when I considered the difficulties of the way—the reward that would be offered—the human blood-hounds that would be set upon my track—the weariness—the hunger—the gloomy thought, of not only losing all one's friends in one day, but of having to seek and to make new friends in a strange world. But, as I have said, the hour was come, and the man must act, or for ever be a slave.

It was now two o'clock. I stepped into the quarter; there was a strange and melancholy silence mingled with the destitution that was apparent in every part of the house. The only morsel I could see in the shape of food, was a piece of Indian-flour[15] bread. It might be half-a-pound in weight. This I placed in my pocket, and giving a last look at the aspect of the house, and at a few small children who were playing at the door, I sallied forth thoughtfully and melancholy, and after crossing the barn-yard, a few moments' walk brought me to a small cave, near the mouth of which lay a pile of stones, and into which I had deposited my clothes. From this, my course lay through thick and heavy woods and back lands to———town, where my brother lived. This town was six miles distance. It was now near three o'clock, but my object was neither to be seen on the road, or to approach the town by daylight, as I was well-known there, and as any intelligence of my having been seen there would at once put the pursuers on my track. This first six miles of my flight, I not only travelled very slowly, therefore, so as to avoid carrying any daylight to this town; but during this walk another very perplexing question was agitating my mind. Shall I call on my brother as I pass through, and shew him what I am about! My brother was older than I, we were much attached; I had been in the habit of looking to him for counsel.

I entered the town about dark, resolved, all things in view, *not* to shew myself to my brother. Having passed through the town without being recognised, I now found myself under cover of night, a solitary wanderer from home and friends; my only guide was the *north star*,[16] by this I knew my general course northward, but at what point I should strike Penn, or when and where I should find a friend I knew not. Another feeling now occupied my mind,—I felt like a mariner who has gotten his ship outside of the harbour and has spread his sails to the breeze. The cargo is on board—the ship is cleared—and the voyage I must make; besides, this being my first night, almost everything will depend upon my clearing the coast before the day dawns. In order to do this my flight must be rapid. I therefore set forth in sorrowful earnest, only now and then I was cheered by the *wild* hope, that I should somewhere and at some time be free.

The night was fine for the season, and passed on with little interruption for want of strength, until, about three o'clock in the morning, I began to feel the chilling effects of the dew.

At this moment, gloom and melancholy again spread through my whole soul. The prospect of utter destitution which threatened me was more than I could bear, and my heart began to melt. What substance is there in a piece of dry Indian-bread? what nourishment is there in it to warm the nerves of one already chilled to the heart? Will this afford a sufficient sustenance after the toil of the night? But while these thoughts were agitating my mind, the day dawned upon me, in the midst of an open extent of country, where the only shelter I could find, without risking my travel by daylight, was a corn shock, but a few hundred yards from the road, and here I must pass my first day out. The day was an unhappy one; my hiding-place was extremely precarious. I had to sit in a squatting position the whole day, without the least chance to rest. But, besides this, my scanty pittance did not afford me that nourishment which my hard night's travel needed. Night came again to my relief, and I sallied forth to pursue my journey. By this time, not a crumb of my crust remained, and I was hungry and began to feel the desperation of distress.

As I travelled I felt my strength failing and my spirits wavered; my mind was in a deep and melancholy dream. It was cloudy; I could not see my star, and had serious misgivings about my course.

In this way the night passed away, and just at the dawn of day I found a few sour apples, and took my shelter under the arch of a small bridge that crossed the road. Here I passed the second day in ambush.

This day would have been more pleasant than the previous, but the sour apples, and a draught of cold water, had produced any thing but a favourable effect; indeed, I suffered most of the day with severe symptoms of cramp. The day passed away again without any further incident, and as I set out at nightfall I felt quite satisfied that I could not pass another twenty-four hours without nourishment. I made but little progress during the night, and often sat down, and slept frequently fifteen or twenty minutes. At the dawn of the third day I continued my travel. As I had found my way to a public turn-pike road during the night, I came very early in the morning to a toll-gate, where the only person I saw, was a lad about twelve years of age. I inquired of him where the road led to. He informed me it led to Baltimore. I asked him the distance, he said it was eighteen miles.

This intelligence was perfectly astounding to me. My master lived eighty miles from Baltimore. I was now sixty-two miles from home. That distance in the right direction, would have placed me several miles across Mason and Dixon's line, but I was evidently yet in the state of Maryland.

I ventured to ask the lad at the gate another question—Which is the best way to Philadelphia? Said he, you can take a road which turns off about half-a-mile below this, and goes to Getsburgh, or you can go on to Baltimore and take the packet.[17]

I made no reply, but my thought was, that I was as near Baltimore and Baltimore-packets as would answer my purpose.

In a few moments I came to the road to which the lad had referred, and felt some relief when I had gotten out of that great public highway, "The National Turnpike," which I found it to be.

When I had walked a mile on this road, and when it had now gotten to be about nine o'clock, I met a young man with a load of hay. He drew up his horses, and addressed me in a very kind tone, when the following dialogue took place between us.

"Are you travelling any distance, my friend?"

"I am on my way to Philadelphia."

"Are you free?"

"Yes, sir."

"I suppose, then, you are provided with free papers?"

"No, sir. I have no papers."

"Well, my friend, you should not travel on this road: you will be taken up before you have gone three miles. There are men living on this road who are constantly on the look-out for your people; and it is seldom that one escapes them who attempts to pass by day."

He then very kindly gave me advice where to turn off the road at a certain point, and how to find my way to a certain house, where I would meet with an old gentleman who would further advise me whether I had better remain till night, or go on.

I left this interesting young man; and such was my surprise and chagrin at the thought of having so widely missed my way, and my alarm at being in such a dangerous position, that in ten minutes I had so far forgotten his directions as to deem it unwise to attempt to follow them, lest I should miss my way, and get into evil hands.

I, however, left the road, and went into a small piece of wood, but not finding a sufficient hiding-place, and it being a busy part of the day, when persons were at work about the fields, I thought I should excite less suspicion by keeping in the road, so I returned to the road; but the events of the next few moments proved that I committed a serious mistake.

I went about a mile, making in all two miles from the spot where I met my young friend, and about five miles from the toll-gate to which I have referred and I found myself at the twenty-four miles' stone[18] from Baltimore. It was now about ten o'clock in the forenoon; my strength was greatly exhausted by reason of the want of suitable food; but the excitement that was then going on in my mind, left me little time to think of my *need* of food. Under ordinary circumstances as a traveller, I should have been glad to see the "Tavern," which was near the mile-stone; but as the case stood with me, I deemed it a dangerous place to pass, much less to stop at. I was therefore passing it as quietly and as rapidly as possible, when from the lot just opposite the house, or sign-post, I heard a coarse stern voice cry, "Halloo!"

I turned my face to the left, the direction from which the voice came, and observed that it proceeded from a man who was digging potatoes. I answered him politely; when the following occurred:—

"Who do *you* belong to?"

"I am free, sir."

"Have you got papers?"

"No, sir."

"Well, you must stop here."

By this time he had got astride the fence, making his way into the road. I said,

"My business is onward, sir, and I do not wish to stop."

"I will see then if you don't stop, you black rascal."

He was now in the middle of the road, making after me in a brisk walk.

I saw that a crisis was at hand; I had no weapons of any kind, not even a pocket-knife; but I asked myself, shall I surrender without a struggle. The instinctive answer was, "No." What will you do? continue to walk; if he runs after you, get him as far from the house as you can, then turn suddenly and smite him on the knee with a stone; that will render him, at least, unable to pursue you.

This was a desperate scheme, but I could think of no other, and my habits as a blacksmith had given my eye and hand such mechanical skill, that I felt quite sure that if I could only get a stone in my hand, and have time to wield it, I should not miss his knee-pan.

He began to breathe short. He was evidently vexed because I did not halt, and I felt more and more provoked at the idea of being thus pursued by a man to whom I had not done the least injury. I had just began to glance my eye about for a stone to grasp, when he made a tiger-like leap at me. This of course brought us to running. At this moment he yelled out "Jake Shouster!" and at the next moment the door of a small house standing to the left was opened, and out jumped a shoemaker girded up in his leather apron, with his knife in hand. He sprang forward and seized me by the collar, while the other seized my arms behind. I was now in the grasp of two men, either of whom were larger bodied than myself, and one of whom was armed with a dangerous weapon.

Standing in the door of the shoemaker's shop, was a third man; and in the potatoe lot I had passed, was still a fourth man. Thus surrounded by superior physical force, the fortune of the day it seemed to me was gone.

My heart melted away, I sunk resistlessly into the hands of my captors, who dragged me immediately into the tavern which was near. I ask my reader to go in with me, and see how the case goes.

Great Moral Dilemma

A few moments after I was taken into the bar-room, the news having gone as by electricity, the house and yard were crowded with gossippers, who had left their business to come and see "the runaway nigger." This hastily assembled congregation consisted of men, women, and children, each one had a look to give at, and a word to say about the "nigger."

But among the whole, there stood one whose name I have never known, but who evidently wore the garb of a man whose profession bound him to speak for the dumb, but he, standing head and shoulders above all that were round about, spoke the first hard sentence against me. Said he, "That fellow is a runaway I know; put him in jail a few days, and you will soon hear where he came from." And then fixing a fiend-like gaze upon me, he continued, "if I lived on this road, *you* fellows would not find such clear running as you do, I'd trap more of you."

But now comes the pinch of the case, the case of conscience to me even at this moment. Emboldened by the cruel speech just recited, my captors enclosed me, and said, "Come now, this matter may easily be settled without you going to jail; who do you belong to, and where did you come from?"

The facts here demanded were in my breast. I knew according to the law of slavery, who I belonged to and where I came from, and I must now do one of three things—I must refuse to speak at all, or I must communicate the fact, or I must tell an untruth. How would an untutored slave, who had never heard of such a writer as Archdeacon Paley, be likely to act in such a dilemma? The first point decided was, the facts in this case are my private property. These men have no more right to them than a highway robber has to my purse. What will be the consequence if I put them in possession of the facts. In forty-eight hours, I shall have received perhaps one hundred lashes, and be on my way to the Louisiana cotton-fields. Of what service will it be to them. They will get a palty sum of two hundred dollars. Is not my liberty worth more to me than two hundred dollars are to them?

I resolved, therefore, to insist that I was free. This not being satisfactory without other evidence, they tied my hands and set out, and went to a magistrate who lived about half a mile distant. It so happened, that when we arrived at his house he was not at home. This was to them a disappointment, but to me it was a relief; but I soon learned by their conversation, that there was still another magistrate in the neighbourhood, and that they would go to him. In about twenty minutes, and after climbing fences and jumping ditches, we, captors and captive, stood before his door, but it was after the same manner as before—he was not at home. By this time the day had worn away to one or two o'clock, and my captors evidently began to feel somewhat impatient of the loss of time. We were about a mile and a quarter from the tavern. As we set out on our return, they began to parley. Finding it was difficult for me to get over fences with my hands tied, they untied me, and said, "Now John," that being the name they had given me, "if you have run away from any one, it would be much better for you to tell us!" but I continued to affirm that I was free. I knew, however, that my situation was very critical, owing to the shortness of the distance I must be from home: my advertisement might over-take me at any moment.

On our way back to the tavern, we passed through a small skirt of wood, where I resolved to make an effort to escape again. One of my captors was walking on either side of me; I made a sudden turn, with my left arm sweeping the legs of one of my captors from under him; I left him nearly standing on his head, and took to my heels. As soon as they could recover they both took after me. We had to mount a fence. This I did most successfully, and making across an open field towards another wood; one of my captors being a long-legged man, was in advance of the other, and consequently nearing me. We had a hill to rise, and during the ascent he gained on me. Once more I thought of self-defense. I am trying to escape peaceably, but this man is determined that I shall not.

My case was now desperate; and I took this desperate thought: "I will run him a little farther from his coadjutor; I will then suddenly catch a stone, and wound him in the breast." This was my fixed purpose, and I had arrived near the point on the top of the hill, where I expected to do the act, when to my surprise and dismay, I saw the other side of the hill was not only all ploughed up, but we came suddenly upon a man ploughing, who as suddenly left his plough and cut off my flight, by seizing me by the collar, when at the same moment my pursuer seized my arms behind. Here I was again in a sad fix. By this time the other pursuer had come up; I was most savagely thrown down on the ploughed ground with my face downward, the ploughman placed his knee upon my shoulders, one of my captors put his upon my legs, while the other tied my arms behind me. I was then dragged up and marched off with kicks, punches and imprecations.

We got to the tavern at three o'clock. Here they again cooled down, and made an appeal to me to make a disclosure. I saw that my attempt to escape strengthened their belief that I was a fugitive. I said to them, "If you will not put me in jail, I will now tell you where I am from." They promised. "Well," said I, "a few weeks ago, I was sold from the eastern shore to a slave-trader, who had a large gang, and set out for Georgia, but when he got to a town in Virginia, he was taken sick, and died with the small-pox.[19] Several of his gang also died with it, so that the people in the town became alarmed, and did not wish the gang to remain among them. No one claimed us, or wished to have anything to do with us; I left the rest, and thought I would go somewhere and get work."

When I said this, it was evidently believed by those who were present, and notwithstanding the unkind feeling that had existed, there was a murmur of approbation. At the same time I perceived that a panic began to seize some, at the idea that I was one of a small-pox gang. Several who had clustered near me, moved off to a respectful distance. One or two left the bar-room, and murmured, "better let the small-pox nigger go."

I was then asked what was the name of the slave-trader. Without premeditation, I said, "John Henderson."

"John Henderson," said one of my captors, "I knew him; I took up a yaller boy for him about two years ago, and got fifty dollars. He passed out with a gang about that time, and the boy ran away from him at Frederickstown. What kind of a man was he?"

At a venture, I gave a description of him. "Yes," said he, "that is the man." By this time all the gossipers had cleared the coast; our friend, "Jake Shouster," had also gone back to his bench to finish his custom work, after having "lost nearly the whole day, trotting about with a nigger tied," as I heard his wife say as she called him home to his dinner. I was now left alone with the man who first called to me in the morning. In a sober manner, he made this proposal to me: "John, I have a brother living in Risterstown, four miles off, who keeps a tavern; I think you had better go and live with him, till we see what will turn up. He wants an ostler."[20] I at once assented to this. "Well," said he, "take something to eat, and I will go with you."

Although I had so completely frustrated their designs for the moment, I knew that it would by no means answer for me to go into that town, where there were prisons, handbills, newspapers, and travellers. My intention was, to start with him, but not to enter the town alive.

I sat down to eat; it was Wednesday, four o'clock, and this was the first regular meal I had since Sunday morning. This over, we set out, and to my surprise, he proposed to walk. We had gone about a mile and a-half, and were approaching a wood through which the road passed with a bend. I fixed upon that as the spot where I would either free myself from this man, or die in his arms. I had resolved upon a plan of operation—it was this: to stop short, face about, and commence action; and neither ask or give quarters, until I was free or dead!

We had got within six rods[21] of the spot, when a gentleman turned the corner, meeting us on horseback. He came up, and entered into conversation with my captor, both of them speaking in Dutch, so that I knew not what they said. After a few moments, this gentleman addressed himself to me in English, and I then learned that he was one of the magistrates on whom we had called in the morning; I felt that another crisis was at hand. Using his saddle as his bench, he put on an extremely stern and magisterial-like face, holding up his horse not unlike a field-marshal in the act of reviewing troops, and carried me through a most rigid examination in reference to the statement I had made. I repeated carefully all I had said; at the close, he said, "Well, you had better stay among us a few months, until we see what is to be done with you." It was then agreed that we should go back to the tavern, and there settle upon some further plan. When we arrived at the tavern, the magistrate alighted from his horse, and went into the bar-room. He took another close glance at me, and went over some points of the former examination. He seemed quite satisfied of the correctness of my statement, and made the following proposition: that I should go and live with him for a short time, stating that he had a few acres of corn and potatoes to get in, and that he would give me twenty-five cents per day. I most cheerfully assented to this proposal. It was also agreed that I should remain at the tavern with my captor that night, and that he would accompany me in the morning. This part of the arrangement I did not like, but of course I could not say so. Things being thus arranged, the magistrate mounted his horse, and went on his way home.

It had been cloudy and rainy during the afternoon, but the western sky having partially cleared at this moment, I perceived that it was near the setting of the sun.

My captor had left his hired man most of the day to dig potatoes alone; but the waggon being now loaded, it being time to convey the potatoes into the barn, and the horses being all ready for that purpose, he was obliged to go into the potatoe field and give assistance.

I should say here, that his wife had been driven away by the small-pox panic about three o'clock, and had not yet returned; this left no one in the house, but a boy, about nine years of age.

As he went out, he spoke to the boy in Dutch, which I supposed, from the little fellow's conduct, to be instructions to watch me closely, which he certainly did.

The potatoe lot was across the public road, directly in front of the house; at the back of the house, and about 300 yards distant, there was a thick wood. The circumstances of the case would not allow me to think for one moment of remaining there for the night—the time had come for another effort—but there were two serious difficulties. One was, that I must either deceive or dispatch this boy who is watching me with intense vigilance. I am glad to say, that the latter did not for a moment seriously enter my mind. To deceive him effectually, I left my coat and went to the back door, from which my course would be direct to the wood. When I got to the door, I found that the barn, to which the waggon must soon come, lay just to the right, and overlooking the path I must take to the wood. In front of me lay a garden surrounded by a picket fence, to the left of me was a small gate, and that by passing through that gate would throw me into an open field, and give me clear running to the wood; but on looking through the gate, I saw that my captor, being with the team, would see me if I attempted to start before he moved from the position he then occupied. To add to my difficulty the horses had baulked; while waiting for the decisive moment, the boy came to the door and asked me why I did not come in. I told him I felt unwell, and wished him to be so kind as to hand me a glass of water; expecting while he was gone to get it, the team would clear, so that I could start. While he was gone, another attempt was made to start the team but failed; he came with the water and I quickly used it up by gargling my throat and by drinking a part. I asked him to serve me by giving me another glass: he gave me a look of close scrutiny, but went in for the water. I heard him fill the glass, and start to return with it; when the hind end of the waggon cleared the corner of the house, which stood in a range with the fence along which I was to pass in getting to the wood. As I passed out the gate, I "squared my main-yard," and laid my course up the line of fence, I cast a last glance over my right shoulder, and saw the boy just perch his head above the garden picket to look after me; I heard at the same time great confusion with the team, the rain having made the ground slippery, and the horses having to cross the road with a slant and rise to get into the barn, it required great effort after they started to prevent their baulking. I felt some assurance that although the boy might give the alarm, my captor could not leave the team until it was in the barn. I heard the horses' feet on the barn-floor, just as I leaped the fence, and darted into the wood.

The sun was now quite down behind the western horizon, and just at this time a heavy dark curtain of clouds was let down, which seemed to usher in haste the night shade. I have never before or since seen anything which seemed to me to compare in sublimity with the spreading of the night shades at the close of that day. My reflections upon the events of that day, and upon the close of it, since I became acquainted with the Bible, have frequently brought to my mind that beautiful passage in the Book of Job, "He holdeth back the face of His throne, and spreadeth a cloud before it."[22]

Before I proceed to the critical events and final deliverance of the next chapter, I cannot forbear to pause a moment here for reflection. The reader may well imagine how the events of the past day affected my mind. You have seen what was done to me; you have heard what was said to me—you have also seen what I have done, and heard what I have said. If you ask me whether I had expected before I left home, to gain my liberty by shedding men's blood, or breaking their limbs? I answer, No! and as evidence of this, I had provided no weapon whatever; not so much as a penknife—it never once entered my mind. I cannot say that I expected to have the ill fortune of meeting with any human being who would attempt to impede my flight.

If you ask me if I expected when I left home to gain my liberty by fabrications and untruths? I answer, No! my parents, slaves as they were, had always taught me, when they could, that "truth may be blamed but cannot be ashamed;" so far as their example was concerned, I had no habits of untruth. I was arrested, and the demand made upon me, "Who do you belong to?" Knowing the fatal use these men would make of *my* truth, I at once concluded that they had no more right to it than a highwayman has to a traveller's purse.

If you ask me whether I now really believe that I gained my liberty by those lies? I answer, No! I now believe that I should be free, had I told the truth; but, at that moment, I could not see any other way to baffle my enemies, and escape their clutches.

The history of that day has never ceased to inspire me with a deeper hatred of slavery; I never recur to it but with the most intense horror at a system which can put a man not only in peril of liberty, limb, and life itself, but which may even send him in haste to the bar of God[23] with a lie upon his lips.

Whatever my readers may think, therefore, of the history of events of the day, do not admire in it the fabrications; but *see* in it the impediments that often fall into the pathway of the flying bondman. *See* how human bloodhounds gratuitously chase, catch, and tempt him to shed blood and lie; how when he would do good, evil is thrust upon him.

CHAPTER III

A Dreary Night in the Woods—Critical Situation the Next Day

Almost immediately on entering the wood, I not only found myself embosomed in the darkness of the night, but I also found myself entangled in a thick forest of undergrowth, which had been quite thoroughly wetted by the afternoon rain.

I penetrated through the wood, thick and thin, and more or less wet, to the distance I should think of three miles. By this time my clothes were all thoroughly soaked through, and I felt once more a gloom and wretchedness; the recollection of which makes me shudder at this distant day. My young friends in this highly favoured Christian country, surrounded with all the comforts of home and parental care, visited by pastors and Sabbath-school teachers, think of the dreary condition of the blacksmith boy in the dark wood that night; and then consider that thousands of his brethren have had to undergo much greater hardships in their flight from slavery.

I was now out of the hands of those who had so cruelly teased me during the day; but a number of fearful thoughts rushed into my mind to alarm me. It was dark and cloudy, so that I could not see the *north star*. How do I know what ravenous beasts are in this wood? How do I know what precipices may be within its bounds? I cannot rest in this wood to-morrow, for it will be searched by those men from whom I have escaped; but how shall I regain the road? How shall I know when I am on the right road again?

These are some of the thoughts that filled my mind with gloom and alarm.

At a venture I struck an angle northward in search of the road. After several hours of zigzag and laborious travel, dragging through briars, thorns and running vines, I emerged from the wood and found myself wading marshy ground and over ditches.

I can form no correct idea of the distance I travelled, but I came to a road, I should think about three o'clock in the morning. It so happened that I came out near where there was a fork in the road of three prongs.

Now arose a serious query—Which is the right prong for me? I was reminded by the circumstance of a superstitious proverb among the slaves, that "the left-hand turning was unlucky," but as I had never been in the habit of placing faith in this or any similar superstition, I am not aware that it had the least weight upon my mind, as I had the same difficulty with reference to the right-hand turning. After a few moments parley with myself, I took the central prong of the road and pushed on with all my speed.

It had not cleared off, but a fresh wind had sprung up; it was chilly and searching. This with my wet clothing made me very uncomfortable; my nerves began to quiver before the searching wind. The barking of mastiffs, the crowing of fowls, and the distant rattling of market waggons, warned me that the day was approaching.

My British reader must remember that in the region where I was, we know nothing of the long hours of twilight you enjoy here. With us the day is measured more by the immediate presence of the sun, and the night by the prevalence of actual darkness.

The day dawned upon me when I was near a small house and barn, situate close to the road-side. The barn was too near the road, and too small to afford secure shelter for the day; but as I cast my eye around by the dim light, I could see no wood, and no larger barn. It seemed to be an open country to a wide extent. The sun was travelling so rapidly from his eastern chamber, that ten or fifteen minutes would spread broad daylight over my track. Whether *my* deed was evil, *you* may judge, but I freely confess that I did *then* prefer darkness rather than light; I therefore took to the mow of the little barn at a great risk, as the events of the day will shew. It so happened that the barn was filled with corn fodder, newly cured and lately got in. You are aware that however quietly one may crawl into such a bed, he is compelled to make much more noise than if it were a feather-bed; and also considerably more than if it were hay or straw. Besides inflicting upon my own excited imagination the belief that I made noise enough to be heard by the inmates of the house who were likely to be rising at the time, I had the misfortune to attract the notice of a little house-dog, such as we call in that part of the world a "fice," on account of its being not only the smallest species of the canine race, but also, because it is the most saucy, noisy, and teasing of all dogs. This little creature commenced a fierce barking. I had at once great fears that the mischievous little thing would betray me; I fully apprehended that as soon as the man of the house arose, he would come and make search in the barn. It now being entirely daylight, it was too late to retreat from this shelter, even if I could have found another; I, therefore, bedded myself down into the fodder as best I could, and entered upon the annoyances of the day, with the frail hope to sustain my mind.

It was Thursday morning; the clouds that had veiled the sky during the latter part of the previous day and the previous night were gone. It was not until about an hour after the sun rose that I heard any out-door movements about the house. As soon as I heard those movements, I was satisfied there was but one man about the house, and that he was preparing to go some distance to work for the day. This was fortunate for me; the busy movements about the yard, and especially the active preparations in the house for breakfast, silenced my unwelcome little annoyer, the fice, until after the man had gone, when he commenced afresh, and continued with occasional intermissions through the day. He made regular sallies from the house to the barn, and after smelling about, would fly back to the house, barking furiously; thus he strove most skilfully throughout the entire day to raise an alarm. There seemed to be no one about the house but one or two small children and the mother, after the man was gone. About ten o'clock my attention was gravely directed to another trial; how could I pass the day without food. The reader will remember it is Thursday, and the only regular meal I have taken since Sunday, was yesterday in the midst of great agitation, about four o'clock; that since that I have performed my arduous night's travel. At one moment, I had nearly concluded to go and present myself at the door, and ask the woman of the house to have compassion and give me food; but then I feared the consequences might be fatal, and I resolved to suffer the day out. The wind sprang up fresh and cool; the barn being small and the crevices large, my wet clothes were dried by it, and chilled me through and through.

I cannot now, with pen or tongue, give a correct idea of the feeling of wretchedness I experienced; every nerve in my system quivered, so that not a particle of my flesh was at rest. In this way I passed the day till about the middle of the afternoon, when there seemed to be an unusual stir about the public road, which passed close by the barn. Men seemed to be passing in parties on horseback, and talking anxiously. From a word which I now and then overheard, I had not a shadow of doubt that they were in search of me. One I heard say, "I ought to catch such a fellow, the only liberty he should have for one fortnight, would be ten feet of rope." Another I heard say, "I reckon he is in that wood now," Another said, "Who would have thought that rascal was so 'cute?" All this while the little fice was mingling his voice with those of the horsemen, and the noise of the horses' feet. I listened and trembled.

Just before the setting of the sun, the labouring man of the house returned, and commenced his evening duties about the house and barn; chopping wood, getting up his cow, feeding his pigs, &c., attended by the little brute, who continued barking at short intervals. He came several times into the barn below. While matters were passing thus, I heard the approach of horses again, and as they came up nearer, I was led to believe that all I had heard pass were returning in one party. They passed the barn and halted at the house, when I recognized the voice of my old captor; addressing the labourer, he asked, "Have you seen a runaway nigger pass here to-day?"

LABOURER.—"No; I have not been at home since early this morning. Where did he come from?"

CAPTOR.—"I caught him down below here yesterday morning. I had him all day, and just at night he fooled me and got away. A party of us have been after him all day; we have been up to the line, but can't hear or see any thing of him. I heard this morning where he came from. He is a blacksmith, and a stiff reward is out for him—two hundred dollars."

LAB.—"He is worth looking for."

CAP.—I reckon so. If I get my clutches on him again, I'll mosey* him down to———before I eat or sleep."

Reader, you may if you can, imagine what the state of my mind was at this moment. I shall make no attempt to describe it to you; to my great relief, however, the party rode off, and the labourer after finishing his work went into the house. Hope seemed now to dawn for me once more; darkness was rapidly approaching, but the moments of twilight seemed much longer than they did the evening before. At length the sable covering had spread itself over the earth. About eight o'clock I ventured to descend from the mow of the barn into the road. The little dog the while began a furious fit of barking, so much so, that I was sure that with what his master had learned about me, he could not fail to believe I was about his premises. I quickly crossed the road, and got into an open field opposite. After stepping lightly about two hundred yards, I halted, and on listening, I heard the door open. Feeling about on the ground, I picked up two stones, and one in each hand I made off as fast as I could, but I heard nothing more that indicated pursuit, and after going some distance I discharged my encumbrance, as from the reduced state of my bodily strength, I could not afford to carry ballast.

This incident had the effect to start me under great disadvantage to make a good night's journey, as it threw me at once off the road, and compelled me to encounter at once the tedious and laborious task of beating my way across marshy fields, and to drag through woods and thickets where there were no paths.

After several hours I found my way back to the road, but the hope of making any thing like clever speed was out of the question. All I could do was to keep my legs in motion, and this I continued to do with the utmost difficulty. The latter part of the night I suffered extremely from cold. There came a heavy frost; I expected at every moment to fall on the road and perish. I came to a corn-field covered with heavy shocks of Indian corn that had been cut; I went into this and got an ear, and then crept into one of the shocks; ate as much of it as I could, and thought I would rest a little and start again, but weary nature could not sustain the operation of grinding hard corn for its own nourishment, and I sunk to sleep.

When I awoke, the sun was shining around; I started with alarm, but it was too late to think of seeking any other shelter; I therefore nestled myself down, and concealed myself as best I could from the light of day. After recovering a little

---

*An expression which signifies to drive in a hurry.

from my fright, I commenced again eating my whole corn. Grain by grain I worked away at it; when my jaws grew tired, as they often did, I would rest, and then begin afresh. Thus, although I began an early breakfast, I was nearly the whole of the forenoon before I had done.

Nothing of importance occurred during the day, until about the middle of the afternoon, when I was thrown into a panic by the appearance of a party of gunners, who passed near me with their dogs. After shooting one or two birds, however, and passing within a few rods of my frail covering, they went on, and left me once more in hope. Friday night came without any other incident worth naming. As I sallied out, I felt evident benefit from the ear of corn I had nibbled away. My strength was considerably renewed; though I was far from being nourished, I felt that my life was at least safe from death by hunger. Thus encouraged, I set out with better speed than I had made since Sunday and Monday night. I had a presentiment, too, that I must be near free soil. I had not yet the least idea where I should find a home or a friend, still my spirits were so highly elated, that I took the whole of the road to myself; I ran, hopped, skipped, jumped, clapped my hands, and talked to myself. But to the old slaveholder I had left, I said, "Ah! ah! old fellow, I told you I'd fix you."

After an hour or two of such freaks of joy, a gloom would come over me in connexion with these questions, "But where are you going? What are you going to do? What will you do with freedom without father, mother, sisters, and brothers? What will you say when you are asked where you were born? You know nothing of the world; how will you explain the fact of your ignorance?"

These questions made me feel deeply the magnitude of the difficulties yet before me.

Saturday morning dawned upon me; and although my strength seemed yet considerably fresh, I began to feel a hunger somewhat more destructive and pinching, if possible, than I had before. I resolved, at all risk, to continue my travel by daylight, and to ask information of the first person I met.

The events of the next chapter will shew what fortune followed this resolve.

CHAPTER IV

The Good Woman of the Toll-Gate Directs Me to W. W.—My Reception by Him

The resolution of which I informed the reader at the close of the last chapter, being put into practice, I continued my flight on the public road; and a little after the sun rose, I came in sight of a toll-gate again. For a moment all the events which followed my passing a toll-gate on Wednesday morning, came fresh to my recollection, and produced some hesitation; but at all events, said I, I will try again.

On arriving at the gate, I found it attended by an elderly woman, whom I afterwards learned was a widow, and an excellent Christian woman. I asked her if I was in Pennsylvania. On being informed that I was, I asked her if she knew where I could get employ? She said she did not; but advised me to go to W. W., a Quaker, who lived about three miles from her, whom I would find to take an interest in me. She gave me directions which way to take; I thanked her, and bade her good morning, and was very careful to follow her directions.

In about half an hour I stood trembling at the door of W. W. After knocking, the door opened upon a comfortably spread table; the sight of which seemed at once to increase my hunger sevenfold. Not daring to enter, I said I had been sent to him in search of employ. "Well," said he, "Come in and take thy breakfast, and get warm, and we will talk about it; thee must be cold without any coat." *"Come in and take thy breakfast, and get warm!"* These words spoken by a stranger, but with such an air of simple sincerity and fatherly kindness, made an overwhelming impression upon my mind. They made me feel, spite of all my fear and timidity, that I had, in the providence of God, found a friend and a home. He at once gained my confidence; and I felt that I might confide to him a fact which I had, as yet, confided to no one.

From that day to this, whenever I discover the least disposition in my heart to disregard the wretched condition of any poor or distressed persons with whom I meet, I call to mind these words—*"Come in and take thy breakfast, and get warm."* They invariably remind me of what I was at that time; my condition was as wretched as that of any human being can possibly be, with the exception of the loss of health or reason. I had but four pieces of clothing about my person, having left all the rest in the hands of my captors. I was a starving fugitive, without home or friends—a reward offered for my person in the public papers—pursued by cruel man-hunters, and no claim upon him to whose door I went. Had he turned me away, I must have perished. Nay, he took me in, and gave me of his food, and shared with me his own garments. Such treatment I had never before received at the hands of any white man.

A few such men in slaveholding America, have stood, and even now stand, like Abrahams and Lots,[24] to stay its forthcoming and well-earned and just judgment.

The limits of this work compel me to pass over many interesting incidents which occurred during my six months' concealment in that family. I must confine myself only to those which will show the striking providence of God, in directing my steps to the door of W. W., and how great an influence the incidents of that six months has had upon all my subsequent history. My friend kindly gave me employ to saw and split a number of cords of wood, then lying in his yard, for which he agreed with me for liberal pay and board. This inspired me with great encouragement. The idea of beginning to earn something was very pleasant. Next; we confidentially agreed upon the way and means of avoiding surprise, in case any one should come to the house as a spy, or with intention to arrest me. This afforded still further relief, as it convinced me that the whole family would now be on the look out for such persons.

The next theme of conversation was with reference to my education.

"Can thee read or write any, James?" was the question put to me the morning after my arrival, by W. W.

"No, sir, I cannot; my duties as a blacksmith have made me acquainted with the figures on the common mechanics' square. There was a day-book kept in the shop, in which the overseer usually charged the smithwork we did for the neighbours. I have spent entire Sabbaths looking over the pages of that book; knowing the names of persons to whom certain pieces of work were charged, together with their prices, I strove anxiously to learn to write in this way. I got paper, and picked up feathers about the yard, and made ink of———berries. My quills being too soft, and my skill in making a pen so poor, that I undertook some years ago to make a steel pen.* In this way I have learnt to make a few of the letters, but I cannot write my own name, nor do I know the letters of the alphabet."

W. W., (handing a slate and pencil.)—"Let me see how thee makes letters; try such as thou hast been able to make easily."

A. B. C. L. G.

P. W., (wife of W. W.)—"Why, those are better than I can make."

W. W.—"Oh, we can soon get thee in the way, James."

Arithmetic and astronomy became my favourite studies. W. W. was an accomplished scholar; he had been a teacher for some years, and was cultivating a small farm on account of ill-health, which had compelled him to leave teaching. He is one of the most far-sighted and practical men I ever met with. He taught me by familiar conversations, illustrating his themes by diagrams on the slate, so that I caught his ideas with ease and rapidity.

I now began to see, for the first time, the extent of the mischief slavery had done to me. Twenty-one years of my life were gone, never again to return, and I was as profoundly ignorant, comparatively, as a child five years old. This was painful, annoying, and humiliating in the extreme. Up to this time, I recollected to have seen one copy of the New Testament, but the entire Bible I had never seen, and had never heard of the Patriarchs,[25] or of the Lord Jesus Christ. I recollected to have heard two sermons, but had heard no mention in them of Christ, or the way of life by Him. It is quite easy to imagine, then, what was the state of my mind, having been reared in total moral midnight; it was a sad picture of mental and spiritual darkness.

As my friend poured light into my mind, I saw the darkness; it amazed and grieved me beyond description. Sometimes I sank down under the load, and became

---

*This attempt was as early as 1822.

discouraged, and dared not hope that I could ever succeed in acquiring knowledge enough to make me happy, or useful to my fellow-beings.

My dear friend, W. W., however, had a happy tact to inspire me with confidence; and he, perceiving my state of mind, exerted himself, not without success, to encourage me. He cited to me various instances of coloured persons, of whom I had not heard before, and who had distinguished themselves for learning, such as Bannicker, Wheatley, and Francis Williams.[26]

How often have I regretted that the six months I spent in the family of W. W., could not have been six years. The danger of recapture, however, rendered it utterly imprudent that I should remain longer; and early in the month of March, while the ground was covered with the winter's snow, I left the bosom of this excellent family, and went forth once more to try my fortune among strangers.

My dear reader, if I could describe to you the emotions I felt when I left the threshold of W. W.'s door, you could not fail to see how deplorable is the condition of the fugitive slave, often for months and years after he has escaped the immediate grasp of the tyrant. When I left my parents, the trial was great, but I had now to leave a friend who had done more for me than parents could have done as slaves; and hence I felt an endearment to that friend which was heightened by a sense of the important relief he had afforded me in the greatest need, and hours of pleasant and highly profitable intercourse.

About a month previous to leaving the house of W. W., a small circumstance occurred one evening, which I only name to shew the harassing fears and dread in which I lived during most of the time I was there. He had a brother-in-law living some ten miles distant—he was a friend to the slave; he often came unexpectedly and spent a few hours—sometimes a day and a night. I had not however, ever known him to come at night. One night, about nine o'clock, after I had gone to bed, (my lodging being just over the room in which W. W. and his wife were sitting,) I heard the door open and a voice ask, "Where is the boy?" The voice sounded to me like the voice of my master; I was sure it must be his. I sprang and listened for a moment—it seemed to be silent; I heard nothing, and then it seemed to me there was a confusion. There was a window at the head of my bed, which I could reach without getting upon the floor: it was a single sash and opened upon hinges. I quickly opened this window and waited in a perfect tremour of dread for further development. There was a door at the foot of the stairs; as I heard that door open, I sprang for the window, and my head was just out, when the gentle voice of my friend W. W. said, "James?"* "Here," said I. "———has come, and he would like to have thee put up his horse." I drew a breath of relief, but my strength and presence of mind did not return for some hours. I slept none that night; for a moment I could doze away, but the voice would sound in my ears, "Where is that boy?" and

---

* If W. W. had ascended the stairs without calling, I should certainly have jumped out of the window.

it would seem to me it must be the tyrant in quest of his weary prey, and would find myself starting again.

From that time the agitation of my mind became so great that I could not feel myself safe. Every day seemed to increase my fear, till I was unfit for work, study or rest. My friend endeavoured, but in vain, to get me to stay a week longer.

The events of the spring proved that I had not left too soon. As soon as the season for travelling fairly opened, active search was made, and my master was seen in a town, twenty miles in advance of where I had spent my six months.

The following curious fact also came out. That same brother-in-law who frightened me, was putting up one evening at a hotel some miles off, and while sitting quietly by himself in one part of the room, he overheard a conversation between a travelling pedler and several gossippers of the neighbourhood, who were lounging away the evening at the hotel.

PEDLER.—"Do you know one W. W. somewhere about here?"

GOSSIPPER.—"Yes, he lives———miles off."

PED.—"I understand he had a black boy with him last winter, I wonder if he is there yet?"

GOS.—"I don't know, he most always has a runaway nigger with him."

PED.—"I should like to find out whether that fellow is there yet."

BROTHER-IN-LAW, (turning about.)—"What does thee know about that boy?"

PED.—"Well he is a runaway."

BROTHER-IN-LAW.—"Who did he run away from?"

PED.—From Col———in———."

BROTHER-IN-LAW.—"How did thee find out that fact?"

PED.—"Well, I have been over there peddling."

BROTHER-IN-LAW.—"Where art thou from?"

PED.—"I belong in Conn."

BROTHER-IN-LAW.—"Did thee see the boy's master?"

PED.—"Yes?"

BROTHER-IN-LAW.—"What did he offer thee to find the boy?"

PED.—"I agreed to find out where he was, and let him know, and if he got him, I was to receive———."

BROTHER-IN-LAW.—"How didst thou hear the boy had been with W. W."

PED.—"Oh, he is known to be a notorious rascal for enticing away, and concealing slaves; he'll get himself into trouble yet, the slaveholders are on the look out for him."

BROTHER-IN-LAW.—"W. W. is my brother-in-law; the boy of whom thou speakest is not with him, and to save thee the trouble of abusing him, I can moreover say, he is no rascal."

PED.—"He may not be there now, but it is because he has sent him off. His master heard of him, and from the description, he is sure it must have been his boy. He could tell me pretty nigh where he was; he said he was a fine healthy boy, twenty-one, a first-rate blacksmith; he would not have taken a thousand dollars for him."

BROTHER-IN-LAW.—"I know not where the boy is, but I have no doubt he is worth more to himself than he ever was to his master, high as he fixed the price on him; and I have no doubt thee will do better to pursue thy peddling honestly, than to neglect it for the sake of serving negro-hunters at a venture."

All this happened within a month or two after I left my friend. One fact which makes this part of the story deeply interesting to my own mind is, that some years elapsed before it came to my knowledge.

CHAPTER V

Seven Months' Residence in the Family of J. K., a Member of the Society of Friends, in Chester County, Pennsylvania—Removal to New York—Becomes a Convert to Religion—Becomes a Teacher

On leaving W. W., I wended my way in deep sorrow and melancholy, onward towards Philadelphia, and after travelling two days and a night, I found shelter and employ in the family of J. K., another member of the Society of Friends,[27] a farmer.

The religious atmosphere in this family was excellent. Mrs. K. gave me the first copy of the Holy Scriptures I ever possessed, she also gave me much excellent counsel. She was a preacher in the Society of Friends; this occasioned her with her husband to be much of their time from home. This left the charge of the farm upon me, and besides put it out of their power to render me that aid in my studies which my former friend had. I, however, kept myself closely concealed, by confining myself to the limits of the farm, and using all my leisure time in study. This place was more secluded, and I felt less of dread and fear of discovery than I had before, and although seriously embarrassed for want of an instructor, I realized some pleasure and profit in my studies. I often employed myself in drawing rude maps of the solar system, and diagrams illustrating the theory of solar eclipses. I felt also a fondness for reading the Bible, and committing chapters, and verses of hymns to memory. Often on the Sabbath when alone in the barn, I would break the monotony of the hours by endeavouring to speak, as if I was addressing an audience. My mind was constantly struggling for thoughts, and I was still more grieved and alarmed at its barrenness; I found it gradually freed from the darkness entailed by slavery, but I was deeply and anxiously concerned how I should fill it with useful knowledge. I had a few books, and no tutor.

In this way I spent seven months with J. K., and should have continued longer, agreeably to his urgent solicitation, but I felt that life was fast wearing, and that as I was now free, I must adventure in search of knowledge. On leaving J. K., he kindly gave me the following certificate,—

"East Nautmeal, Chester County, Pennsylvania, *Tenth Month* 5*th*, 1828.

"I hereby certify, that the bearer, J.W.C. Pennington, has been in my employ seven months, during most of which time I have been from home, leaving my entire business in his trust, and that he has proved a highly trustworthy and industrious young man. He leaves with the sincere regret of myself and family; but as he feels it to be his duty to go where he can obtain education, so as to fit him to be more useful, I cordially commend him to the warm sympathy of the friends of humanity wherever a wise providence may appoint him a home.

Signed,   "J. K."

Passing through Philadelphia, I went to New York, and in a short time found employ on Long Island, near the city. At this time, the state of things was extremely critical in New York. It was just two years after the general emancipation in that state.[28] In the city it was a daily occurrence for slaveholders from the southern states to catch their slaves, and by certificate from Recorder Riker take them back. I often felt serious apprehensions of danger, and yet I felt also that I must begin the world somewhere.

I was earning respectable wages, and by means of evening schools and private tuition, was making encouraging progress in my studies.

Up to this time, it had never occurred to me that I was a slave in another and a more serious sense. All my serious impressions of mind had been with reference to the slavery from which I had escaped. Slavery had been my theme of thought day and night.

In the spring of 1829, I found my mind unusually perplexed about the state of the slave. I was enjoying rare privileges in attending a Sabbath school; the great value of Christian knowledge began to be impressed upon my mind to an extent I had not been conscious of before. I began to contrast my condition with that of ten brothers and sisters I had left in slavery, and the condition of children I saw sitting around me on the Sabbath, with their pious teachers, with that of 700,000, now 800,440 slave children, who had no means of Christian instruction.

The theme was more powerful than any my mind had ever encountered before. It entered into the deep chambers of my soul, and stirred the most agitating emotions I had ever felt. The question was, what can I do for that vast body of suffering brotherhood I have left behind. To add to the weight and magnitude of the theme, I learnt for the first time, how many slaves there were. The question completely staggered my mind; and finding myself more and more borne down with it, until I was in an agony; I thought I would make it a subject of prayer to God, although prayer had not been my habit, having never attempted it but once.

I not only prayed, but also fasted. It was while engaged thus, that my attention was seriously drawn to the fact that I was a lost sinner, and a slave to Satan; and soon I saw that I must make another escape from another tyrant. I did not by any means forget my fellow-bondmen, of whom I had been sorrowing so deeply, and travailing in spirit so earnestly; but I now saw that while man had been injuring me, I had been offending God; and that unless I ceased to offend him, I could not expect to have his sympathy in my wrongs; and moreover, that I could not be instrumental in eliciting his powerful aid in behalf of those for whom I mourned so deeply.

This may provoke a smile from some who profess to be the friends of the slave, but who have a lower estimate of experimental Christianity than I believe is due to it; but I am not the less confident that sincere prayer to God, proceeding from a few hearts deeply imbued with experimental Christianity about *that time*, has had much to do with subsequent happy results. At that time the 800,000 bondmen in the British Isles[29] had not seen the beginning of the end of their sufferings—at that time, 20,000 who are now free in Canada, were in bonds—at that time, there was no Vigilance Committee to aid the flying slave—at that time, the two powerful Anti-Slavery Societies[30] of America had no being.

I distinctly remember that I felt the need of enlisting the sympathy of God, in behalf of my enslaved brethren; but when I attempted it day after day, and night after night, I was made to feel, that whatever else I might do, I was not qualified to do that, as I was myself alienated from him by wicked works. In short, I felt that I needed the powerful aid of some in my behalf with God, just as much as I did that of my dear friend in Pennsylvania, when flying from man. "If one man sin against another, the judge shall judge him, but if a man sin against God, who shall entreat for him?"

Day after day, for about two weeks, I found myself more deeply convicted of personal guilt before God. My heart, soul, and body were in the greatest distress; I thought of neither food, drink or rest, for days and nights together. Burning with a recollection of the wrongs man had done me—mourning for the injuries my brethren were still enduring, and deeply convicted of the guilt of my own sins against God. One evening, in the third week of the struggle, while alone in my chamber, and after solemn reflection for several hours, I concluded that I could never be happy or useful in that state of mind, and resolved that I would try to become reconciled to God. I was then living in the family of an Elder of the Presbyterian Church. I had not made known my feelings to any one, either in the family or out of it; and I did not suppose that any one had discovered my feelings. To my surprise, however, I found that the family had not only been aware of my state for several days, but were deeply anxious on my behalf. The following Sabbath Dr. Cox was on a visit in Brooklyn to preach, and was a guest in the family; hearing of my case, he expressed a wish to converse with me, and without knowing the plan, I was invited into a room and left alone with him. He entered skilfully and kindly into my feelings, and after considerable conversation he invited me to attend his service that afternoon. I did so, and was deeply interested.

Without detaining the reader with too many particulars, I will only state that I heard the doctor once or twice after this, at his own place of worship in New York City, and had several personal interviews with him, as the result of which, I hope, I was brought to a saving acquaintance with Him, of whom Moses in the Law and the Prophets did write; and soon connected myself with the church under his pastoral care.

I now returned with all my renewed powers to the great theme—slavery. It seemed now as I looked at it, to be more hideous than ever. I saw it now as an evil under the moral government of God—as a sin not only against man, but also against God. The great and engrossing thought with me was, how shall I now employ my time and my talents so as to tell most effectually upon this system of wrong! As I have stated, there was no Anti-Slavery Society then—there was no Vigilance Committee. I had, therefore, to select a course of action, without counsel or advice from any one who professed to sympathize with the slave. Many, many lonely hours of deep meditation have I passed during the years 1828 and 1829, before the great anti-slavery movement, on the questions, What shall I do for the slave? How shall I act so that he will reap the benefit of my time and talents? At one time I had resolved to go to Africa, and to react from there; but without bias or advice from any mortal, I soon gave up that, as looking too much like feeding a hungry man with a long spoon.

At length, finding that the misery, ignorance, and wretchedness of the free coloured people was by the whites tortured into an argument for slavery; finding myself now among the free people of colour in New York, where slavery was so recently abolished; and finding much to do for their elevation, I resolved to give my strength in that direction. And well do I remember the great movement which commenced among us about this time, for the holding of General Conventions,[31] to devise ways and means for their elevation, which continued with happy influence up to 1834, when we gave way to anti-slavery friends, who had then taken up the labouring oar. And well do I remember that the first time I ever saw those tried friends, Garrison, Jocelyn, and Tappan, was in one of those Conventions, where they came to make our acquaintance, and to secure our confidence in some of their preliminary labours.

My particular mode of labour was still a subject of deep reflection; and from time to time I carried it to the Throne of Grace. Eventually my mind fixed upon the ministry as the desire of my whole heart. I had mastered the preliminary branches of English education, and was engaged in studying logic, rhetoric, and the Greek Testament, without a master. While thus struggling in my laudable work, an opening presented itself which was not less surprising than gratifying. Walking on the street one day, I met a friend, who said to me, "I have just had an application to supply a teacher for a school, and I have recommended you." I said, "My dear friend, I am obliged to you for the kindness; but I fear I cannot sustain an examination for that station." "Oh," said he, "try." I said, "I will," and we separated. Two weeks afterwards, I met the trustees of the school, was examined, accepted, and agreed with them for a salary of two hundred dollars per annum; commenced my school, and succeeded. This was five years, three months, and thirteen days after I came from the South.

As the events of my life since that have been of a public professional nature, I will say no more about it. My object in writing this tract is now completed. It has been to shew the reader the hand of God with a slave; and to elicit your sympathy in behalf of the fugitive slave, by shewing some of the untold dangers and hardships through which he has to pass to gain liberty, and how much he needs friends on free soil; and that men who have felt the yoke of slavery, even in its mildest form, cannot be expected to speak of the system otherwise than in terms of the most unqualified condemnation.

There is one sin that slavery committed against me, which I never can forgive. It robbed me of my education; the injury is irreparable; I feel the embarrassment more seriously now than I ever did before. It cost me two years' hard labour, after I fled, to unshackle my mind; it was three years before I had purged my language of slavery's idioms; it was four years before I had thrown off the crouching aspect of slavery; and now the evil that besets me is a great lack of that general information, the foundation of which is most effectually laid in that part of life which I served as a slave. When I consider how much now, more than ever, depends upon sound and thorough education among coloured men, I am grievously overwhelmed with a sense of my deficiency, and more especially as I can never hope now to make it up. If I know my own heart, I have no ambition but to serve the cause of suffering humanity; all that I have desired or sought, has been to make me more efficient for good. So far I have some consciousness that I have done my utmost; and should my future days be few or many, I am reconciled to meet the last account, hoping to be acquitted of any wilful neglect of duty; but I shall have to go to my last account with this charge against the system of slavery, *"Vile monster! thou hast hindered my usefulness, by robbing me of my early education."*

Oh! what might I have been now, but for this robbery perpetrated upon me as soon as I saw the light. When the monster heard that a man child was born, he laughed, and said, "It is mine." When I was laid in the cradle, he came and looked on my face, and wrote down my name upon his barbarous list of chattels personal, on the same list where he registered his horses, hogs, cows, sheep, and even his *dogs!* Gracious Heaven, is there no repentance for the misguided men who do these things!

The only harm I wish to slaveholders is, that they may be speedily delivered from the guilt of a sin, which, if not repented of, must bring down the judgment of Almighty God upon their devoted heads. The least I desire for the slave is, that he may be speedily released from the pain of drinking a cup whose bitterness I have sufficiently tasted, to know that it is insufferable.

CHAPTER VI

Some Account of the Family I Left in Slavery—Proposal to Purchase Myself and Parents—How Met by my Old Master

It is but natural that the reader should wish to hear a word about the family I left behind.

There are frequently large slave families with whom God seems to deal in a remarkable manner. I believe my family is an instance.

I have already stated that when I fled, I left a father, mother, and eleven brothers and sisters. These were all, except my oldest brother, owned by the man from whom I fled. It will be seen at once then how the fear of implicating them embarrassed me in the outset. They suffered nothing, however, but a strong suspicion, until about six months after I had left; when the following circumstance took place:—

When I left my friend W. W. in Pennsylvania to go on north, I ventured to write a letter back to one of my brothers, informing him how I was; and this letter was directed to the care of a white man who was hired on the plantation, who worked in the garden with my father, and who professed a warm friendship to our family; but instead of acting in good faith, he handed the letter to my master. I am sorry that truth compels me to say that that man was an Englishman.

From that day the family were handled most strangely. The history begins thus: they were all sold into Virginia, the adjoining state. This was done lest I should have some plan to get them off; but God so ordered that they fell into kinder hands. After a few years, however, their master became much embarrassed, so that he was obliged to pass them into other hands, at least for a term of years. By this change the family was divided, and my parents, with the greater part of their children, were taken to New Orleans. After remaining there several years at hard labour,—my father being in a situation of considerable trust, they were again taken back to Virginia; and by this means became entitled by the laws of that state to their freedom. Before justice, however, could take its course, their old master in Maryland, as if intent to doom them for ever to bondage, repurchased them; and in order to defeat a similar law in Maryland, by which they would have been entitled to liberty, he obtained from the General Assembly of that state the following special act. This will show not only something of his character as a slaveholder, but also his political influence in the state. It is often urged in the behalf of slaveholders, that the law interposes an obstacle in the way of emancipating their slaves when they wish to do so, but here is an instance which lays open the real philosophy of the whole case. They make the law themselves, and when they find the laws operate more in favour of the slaves than themselves, they can easily evade or change it. Maryland being a slave-exporting state, you will see why they need a law to prohibit the importation of slaves; it is a protection to that sort of trade. This law he wished to evade.

"*An act for the Relief of*————*of*————*County. Passed January* 17*th,* 1842.

"Whereas it is represented to this General Assembly that————of————county, brought into this state from the state of Virginia, sometime in the month of March last, two negro slaves, to wit,————and————his wife, who are slaves for life, and who were acquired by the said————by purchase, and whereas, the said————is desirous of retaining said slaves in this state. THEREFORE, BE IT ENACTED, *by the General Assembly* of Maryland, that the said————be, and he is thereby authorized to retain said negroes as slaves for life within this state, provided that the said————shall within thirty days after the passage of this act, file with the clerk of the————county court, a list of said slaves so brought into this state, stating their ages, with an affidavit thereto attached, that the same is a true and faithful list of the slaves so removed, and that they were not brought into this state for the purpose of sale, and that they are slaves for life. And *provided also*, that the sum of fifteen dollars for each slave, between the ages of twelve and forty-five years, and the sum of five dollars for each slave above the age of forty-five years and under twelve years of age, so brought into this state, shall be paid to the said clerk of————county court: to be paid over by him to the treasurer of the western shore, for the use and benefit of the Colonization Society of this state.

State of Connecticut, Office of Secretary of State.

"I hereby certify, that the foregoing is a true copy of an act passed by the General Assembly of Maryland, January 17th, 1842, as it appears in the printed acts of the said Maryland, in the Library of the state.

In testimony whereof, I have hereunto set my hand and seal of said state, at Hartford, this 17th day of August, 1846.

CHARLES W. BEADLEY,
(SEAL.)   Secretary of State.

Thus, the whole family after being twice fairly entitled to their liberty, even by the laws of two slave states, had the mortification of finding themselves again, not only recorded as slaves for life, but also a premium paid upon them, professedly to aid in establishing others of their fellow-beings in a free republic on the coast of Africa; but the hand of God seems to have been heavy upon the man who could plan such a stratagem to wrong his fellows.

The immense fortune he possessed when I left him, (bating one thousand dollars I brought with me in my own body,) and which he seems to have retained till that time, began to fly, and in a few years he was insolvent, so that he was unable to hold the family, and was compelled to think of selling them again. About this time I heard of their state by an underground railroad passenger,[32] who came from that neighbourhood, and resolved to make an effort to obtain the freedom of my parents, and to relieve myself from liability. For this purpose, after arranging for the means to purchase, I employed counsel to make a definite offer for my parents and myself. To his proposal, the following evasive and offensive answer was returned.

January 12*th,* 1846.

J. H———, Esq.

"Sir,—Your letter is before me. The ungrateful servant in whose behalf you write, merits no clemency from me. He was guilty of theft when he departed, for which I hope he has made due amends. I have heard he was a respectable man, and calculated to do some good to his fellow-beings. Servants are selling from five hundred and fifty to seven hundred dollars, I will take five hundred and fifty dollars, and liberate him. If my proposition is acceded to, and the money lodged in Baltimore, I will execute the necessary instrument, and deliver it in Baltimore, to be given up on payment being made.

"Yours, &c.,
"———."

"Jim was a first-rate mechanic, (blacksmith) and was worth to me one thousand dollars."

Here he not only refuses to account for my parents, by including them in his return and proposition, but he at the same time attempts to intimidate me by mooting the charge of theft.

I confess I was not only surprised, but mortified, at this result. The hope of being once more united to parents whom I had not seen for sixteen years, and whom I still loved dearly, had so excited my mind that I disarranged my business relations, disposed of a valuable library of four hundred volumes, and by additional aid obtained among the liberal people of Jamaica, I was prepared to give the extravagant sum of five hundred dollars each for myself, and my father and mother. This I was willing to do, not because I approve of the principle involved as a general rule. But supposing that, as my former master was now an old man not far from his grave, (about which I was not mistaken) and as he knew, by his own shewing, that I was able to do some good, he would be inclined, whatever might have been our former relations and misunderstandings, to meet my reasonable desire to see my parents, and to part this world in reconciliation with each other, as well as with God. I should have rejoiced had his temper permitted him to accede to my offer. But I thought it too bad, a free man of Jesus Christ, living on "free soil," to give a man five hundred dollars for the privilege of being let alone, and to be branded as a thief into the bargain, and that too after I had served him twenty prime years, without the benefit of being taught so much as the alphabet.

I wrote him with my own hand, sometime after this, stating that no proposition would be acceded to by me, which did not include my parents; and likewise fix the sum for myself more reasonable, and also retract the offensive charge; to this he maintained a dignified silence. The means I had acquired by the contributions of kind friends to redeem myself, I laid by, in case the worst should come; and that designed for the purchase of my parents, I used in another kind of operation, as the result of which, my father and two brothers are now in Canada. My mother was sold a second time, south, but she was eventually found. Several of my sisters married free men, who purchased their liberty; and three brothers are owned, by what may be called conscience slaveholders, who hold slaves only for a term of years. My old master has since died; my mother and he are now in the other world together, she is at rest from him. Sometime after his death, I received information from a gentleman, intimate with his heirs, (who are principally females) that the reduced state of the family, afforded not only a good opportunity to obtain a release upon reasonable terms, but also to render the children of my oppressor some pecuniary aid; and much as I had suffered, I must confess this latter was the stronger motive with me, for acceding to their offer made by him.

I have many other deeply interesting particulars touching our family history, but I have detailed as many as prudence will permit, on account of those members who are yet south of Mason and Dixon's line.[33]

I have faith in the hand that has dealt with us so strangely, that all our remaining members will in time be brought together; and then the case may merit a reviewed and enlarged edition of this tract, when other important matter will be inserted.

CHAPTER VII

The Feeding and Clothing of the Slaves in the Part of Maryland where I Lived, &c

The slaves are generally fed upon salt pork, herrings and Indian corn.

The manner of dealing it out to them is as follows:—Each workingman, on Monday morning, goes to the cellar of the master where the provisions are kept, and where the overseer takes his stand with some one to assist him, when he, with a pair of steel-yards, weighs out to every man the amount of three-and-a-half pounds, to last him till the ensuing Monday—allowing him just half-a-pound per day. Once in a few weeks there is a change made, by which, instead of the three-and-a-half pounds of pork, each man receives twelve herrings, allowing two a-day. The only bread kind the slaves have is that made of Indian meal. In some of the lower counties, the masters usually give their slaves the corn in the ear; and they have to grind it for themselves by night at hand-mills. But my master had a quantity sent to the grist-mill at a time, to be ground into coarse meal, and kept it in a large chest in his cellar, where the woman who cooked for the boys could get it daily. This was baked in large loaves, called "steel poun bread." Sometimes as a change it was made into "Johnny Cake,"[34] and then at others into mush.

The slaves had no butter, coffee, tea, or sugar; occasionally they were allowed milk, but not statedly; the only exception to this statement was the "harvest provisions." In harvest, when cutting the grain, which lasted from two to three weeks in the heat of summer, they were allowed some fresh meat, rice, sugar, and coffee; and also their allowance of whiskey.

At the beginning of winter, each slave had one pair of coarse shoes and stockings, one pair of pantaloons, and a jacket.

At the beginning of summer, he had two pair of coarse linen pantaloons and two shirts.

Once in a number of years, each slave, or each man and his wife, had one coarse blanket and enough coarse linen for a "bed-tick."[35] He never had any bedstead or other furniture kind. The men had no hats, waistcoats or handkerchiefs given them, or the women any bonnets. These they had to contrive for themselves. Each labouring man had a small "patch" of ground allowed him; from this he was expected to furnish himself and his boys hats, &c. These patches they had to work by night; from these, also, they had to raise their own provisions, as no potatoes, cabbage, &c., were allowed them from the plantation. Years ago the slaves were in the habit of raising broom-corn, and making brooms to supply the market in the towns; but now of later years great quantities of those and other articles, such as scrubbing-brushes, wooden trays, mats, baskets, and straw hats, which the slaves made, are furnished by the shakers and other small manufacturers, from the free states of the north.

Neither my master or any other master, within my acquaintance, made any provisions for the religious instruction of his slaves. They were not worked on the Sabbath. One of the "boys" was required to stay at home and "feed," that is, take care of the stock, every Sabbath; the rest went to see their friends. Those men whose families were on other plantations usually spent the Sabbath with them; some would lie about at home and rest themselves.

When it was pleasant weather my master would ride "into town" to church, but I never knew him to say a word to one of us about going to church, or about our obligations to God, or a future state. But there were a number of pious slaves in our neighbourhood, and several of these my master owned; one of these was an exhorter. He was not connected with a religious body, but used to speak every Sabbath in some part of the neighbourhood. When slaves died, their remains were usually consigned to the grave without any ceremony; but this old gentleman, wherever he heard of a slave having been buried in that way, would send notice from plantation to plantation, calling the slaves together at the grave on the Sabbath, where he'd sing, pray, and exhort. I have known him to go ten or fifteen miles voluntarily to attend these services. He could not read, and I never heard him refer to any Scripture, and state and discourse upon any fundamental doctrine of the gospel; but he knew a number of "spiritual songs by heart," of these he would give two lines at a time very exact, set and lead the tune himself; he would pray with great fervour, and his exhortations were amongst the most impressive I have heard.

The Methodists at one time attempted to evangelize the slaves in our neighbourhood, but the effort was sternly resisted by the masters. They held a Camp Meeting in the neighbourhood, where many of the slaves attended. But one of their preachers, for addressing words of comfort to the slaves, was arrested and tried for his life.

My master was very active in this disgraceful affair, but the excellent man, Rev. Mr. G., was acquitted and escaped out of their hands. Still, it was deemed by his brethren to be imprudent for him to preach any more in the place, as some of the more reckless masters swore violence against him. This good man's name is remembered dearly, till this day, by slaves in that county. I met with a fugitive about a year ago, who remembered distinctly the words spoken by Mr. G., and by which his own mind was awakened to a sense of the value of his soul. He said, in the course of his preaching, addressing himself to the slaves, "You have precious immortal souls, that are worth far more to you than your bodies are to your masters;" or words to that effect. But while these words interested many slaves, they also made many masters exceedingly angry, and they tortured his words into an attempt to excite the slaves to rebellion.

Some of my master's slaves who had families, were regularly married, and others were not; the law makes no provision for such marriages, and the only provision made by the master was, that they should obtain his leave. In some cases, after obtaining leave to take his wife, the slave would ask further leave to go to a minister and be married. I never knew him to deny such a request, and yet, in those cases where the slave did not ask it, he never required him to be married by a minister. Of course, no Bibles, Tracts, or religious books of any kind, were ever given to the slaves; and no ministers or religious instructors were ever known to visit our plantation at any time, either in sickness or in health. When a slave was sick, my master being himself a physician, sometimes attended, and sometimes he called other physicians. Slaves frequently sickened and died, but I never knew any provision made to administer to them the comforts, or to offer to them the hopes of the gospel, or to their friends after their death.

There is no one feature of slavery to which the mind recurs with more gloomy impressions, than to its disastrous influence upon the families of the masters, physically, pecuniarily, and mentally.

It seems to destroy families as by a powerful blight, large and opulent slaveholding families often vanish like a group of shadows at the third or fourth generation. This fact arrested my attention some years before I escaped from slavery, and of course before I had any enlightened views of the moral character of the system. As far back as I can recollect, indeed, it was a remark among slaves, that every generation of slaveholders are more and more inferior. There were several large and powerful families in our county, including that of my master, which affords to my mind a melancholy illustration of this remark. One of the wealthiest slaveholders in the county, was General R., a brother-in-law to my master. This man owned a large and highly valuable tract of land, called R.'s Manor. I do not know how many slaves he owned, but the number was large. He lived in a splendid mansion, and drove his coach and four.[36] He was for some years a member of Congress. He had a numerous family of children.

The family showed no particular signs of decay until he had married a second time, and had considerably increased his number of children. It then became evident that his older children were not educated for active business, and were only destined to be a charge. Of sons, (seven or eight), not one of them reached the eminence once occupied by the father. The only one that approached to it, was the eldest, who became an officer in the navy, and obtained the doubtful glory of being killed in the Mexican war.[37]

General R. himself ran through his vast estate, died intemperate, and left a widow and large number of daughters, some minors, destitute, and none of his sons fitted for any employment but in the army and navy.

Slaves have a superstitious dread of passing the dilapidated dwelling of a man who has been guilty of great cruelties to his slaves, and who is dead, or moved away. I never felt this dread deeply but once, and that was one Sabbath about sunset, as I crossed the yard of General R.'s residence, which was about two miles from us, after he had been compelled to leave it.

To see the once fine smooth gravel walks, overgrown with grass—the redundances of the shrubbery neglected—the once finely painted pricket fences rusted and fallen down—a fine garden in splendid ruins—the lofty ceiling of the mansion thickly curtained with cobwebs—the spacious apartments abandoned, while the only music heard within as a substitute for the voices of family glee that once filled it, was the crying cricket and cockroaches! Ignorant slave as I was at that time, I could but pause for a moment, and recur in silent horror to the fact, that a strange reverse of fortune had lately driven from that proud mansion a large and once opulent family. What advantage was it now to the members of that family, that the father and head had for near half a century stood high in the counsels of the state, and had the benefit of the unrequited toil of hundreds of his fellow-men, when they were already grappling with the annoyances of that poverty, which he had entailed upon others.

My master's family, in wealth and influence, was not inferior to General R.'s originally. His father was a member of the convention that framed the present constitution of the state; he was, also, for some years chief justice of the state.

My master was never equal to his father, although he stood high at one time. He once lacked but a few votes of being elected Governor of the state: he once sat in the Assembly, and was generally a leading man in his own county. His influence was found to be greatest when exerted in favour of any measure in regard to the control of slaves. He was the first mover in several cruel and rigid municipal regulations in the county, which prohibited slaves from going over a certain number of miles from their master's places on the Sabbath, and from being seen about the town. He once instigated the authorities of the town where he attended service, to break up a Sabbath-school some humane members of the Methodist and Lutheran denominations had set up to teach the free negroes, lest the slaves should get some benefit of it.

But there was still a wider contrast between my master and his own children, eight in number, when I left him. His eldest daughter, the flower of the family, married a miserable and reckless gambler. His eldest son was kind-hearted, and rather a favourite with the slaves on that account; but he had no strength of mind or weight of character. His education was limited, and he had no disposition or tact for business of any kind. He died at thirty-six, intestate; leaving his second wife (a sister to his father's second wife) with several orphan children, a widow with a small estate deeply embarrassed. The second son was once sent to West Point to fit for an officer. After being there a short time, however, he became unsteady, and commenced the study of medicine, but he soon gave that up and preferred to live at home and flog the slaves; and by them was cordially dreaded and disliked, and among themselves he was vulgarly nicknamed on account of his cruel and filthy habits.

These two families will afford a fair illustration of the gloomy history of many others that I could name. This decline of slaveholding families is a subject of observation and daily remark among slaves; they are led to observe every change in the pecuniary, moral, and social state of the families they belong to, from the fact, that as the old master declines, or as his children are married off, they are expecting to fall into their hands, or in case of insolvency on the part of the old master, they expect to be sold; in either case, it involves a change of master—a subject to which they cannot be indifferent. And it is very rarely the case that a slave's condition is benefited by passing from the old master into the hands of one of his children. Owing to the causes I have mentioned, the decline is so rapid and marked, in almost every point of view, that the children of slaveholders are universally inferior to themselves, mentally morally, physically, as well as pecuniarily, especially so in the latter point of view; and this is a matter of most vital concern to the slaves. The young master not being able to own as many slaves as his father, usually works what he has more severely, and being more liable to embarrassment, the slaves' liability to be sold at an early day is much greater. For the same reason, slaves have a deep interest, generally, in the marriage of a young mistress. Very generally the daughters of slaveholders marry inferior men; men who seek to better their own condition by a wealthy connection. The slaves who pass into the hands of the young master has had some chance to become acquainted with his character, bad as it may be; but the young mistress brings her slaves a new, and sometimes an unknown master. Sometimes these are the sons of already broken down slaveholders. In other cases they are adventurers from the north who remove to the south, and who readily become the most cruel masters.

APPENDIX

These two letters are simply introduced to show what the state of my feeling was with reference to slavery at the time they were written. I had just heard several facts with regard to my parents, which had awakened my mind to great excitement.

To My Father, Mother, Brothers, and Sisters.
The following was written in 1844:

DEARLY BELOVED IN BONDS,

About seventeen long years have now rolled away, since in the Providence of Almighty God, I left your embraces, and set out upon a daring adventure in search of freedom. Since that time, I have felt most severely the loss of the sun and moon and eleven stars from my social sky. Many, many a thick cloud of anguish has pressed my brow and sent deep down into my soul the bitter waters of sorrow in consequence. And you have doubtless had your troubles and anxious seasons also about your fugitive star.

I have learned that some of you have been sold, and again taken back by Colonel———. How many of you are living and together, I cannot tell. My great grief is, lest you should have suffered this or some additional punishment on account of my *Exodus*.[38]

I indulge the hope that it will afford you some consolation to know that your son and brother is yet alive. That God has dealt wonderfully and kindly with me in all my way. He has made me a Christian, and a Christian Minister, and thus I have drawn my support and comfort from that blessed Saviour, who came *to preach good tidings unto the meek, to bind up the broken hearted, to proclaim liberty to the captives, and the opening of the prison to them that are bound. To proclaim the acceptable year of the Lord and the day of vengeance of our God; to comfort all that mourn. To appoint unto them that mourn in Zion,*[39]*to give unto them beauty for ashes, the oil of joy for mourning, the garment of praise for the spirit of heaviness, that they might be called trees of righteousness, the planting of the Lord that he might be glorified.*[40]

If the course I took in leaving a condition which had become intolerable to me, has been made the occasion of making that condition worse to you in any way, I do most heartily regret such a change for the worse on your part. As I have no means, however, of knowing if such be the fact, so I have no means of making atonement, but by sincere prayer to Almighty God in your behalf, and also by taking this method of offering to you these consolations of the gospel to which I have just referred, and which I have found to be preeminently my own stay and support. My dear father and mother; I have very often wished, while administering the Holy Ordinance of Baptism to some scores of children brought forward by doting parents, that I could see you with yours among the number. And you, my brothers and sisters, while teaching hundreds of children and youths in schools over which I have been placed, what unspeakable delight I should have had in having you among the number; you may all judge of my feeling for these past years, when while preaching from Sabbath to Sabbath to congregations, I have not been so fortunate as even to see father, mother, brother, sister, uncle, aunt, nephew, niece, or cousin in my congregations. While visiting the sick, going to the house of mourning, and burying the dead, I have been a constant mourner for you. My sorrow has been that I know you are not in possession of those hallowed means of grace. I am thankful to you for those mild and gentle traits of character which you took such care to enforce upon me in my youthful days. As an evidence that I prize both you and them, I may say that at the age of thirty-seven, I find them as valuable as any lessons I have learned, nor am I ashamed to let it be known to the world, that I am the son of a bond man and a bond woman.

Let me urge upon you the fundamental truths of the Gospel of the Son of God. Let repentance towards God and faith in our Lord Jesus Christ have their perfect work in you, I beseech you. Do not be prejudiced against the gospel because it may be seemingly twisted into a support of slavery. The gospel rightly understood, taught, received, felt and practised, is anti-slavery as it is anti-sin. Just so far and so fast as the true spirit of the gospel obtains in the land, and especially in the lives of the oppressed, will the spirit of slavery sicken and become powerless like the serpent with his head pressed beneath the fresh leaves of the prickly ash of the forest.

There is not a solitary decree of the immaculate God that has been concerned in the ordination of slavery, nor does any possible development of his holy will sanctify it.

He has permitted us to be enslaved according to the invention of wicked men, instigated by the devil, with intention to bring good out of the evil, but He does not, He cannot approve of it. He has no need to approve of it, even on account of the good which He will bring out of it, for He could have brought about that very good in some other way.

God is never straitened; He is never at a loss for means to work. Could He not have made this a great and wealthy nation without making its riches to consist in our blood, bones, and souls? And could He not also have given the gospel to us without making us slaves?

My friends, let us then, in our afflictions, embrace and hold fast the gospel. The gospel is the fulness of God. We have the glorious and total weight of God's moral character in our side of the scale.

The wonderful purple stream which flowed for the healing of the nations, has a branch for us. Nay, is Christ divided? "The grace of God that bringeth salvation hath appeared to (for) all men, teaching us that denying ungodliness and worldly lust, we should live soberly, righteously, and godly in this present world, looking for that blessed hope and glorious appearing of the great God and our Saviour Jesus Christ, who gave himself for us that he might redeem us from all iniquity, and purify unto himself a peculiar people, zealous of good works."—Titus ii. 11–14.

But you say you have not the privilege of hearing of this gospel of which I speak. I know it; and this is my great grief. But you shall have it; I will send it to you by my humble prayer; I can do it; I will beg our heavenly Father, and he will preach this gospel to you in his holy providence.

You, dear father and mother cannot have much longer to live in this troublesome and oppressive world; you cannot bear the yoke much longer. And as you approach another world, how desirable it is that you should have the prospect of a different destiny from what you have been called to endure in this world during a long life.

But it is the gospel that sets before you the hope of such a blessed rest as is spoken of in the word of God, Job iii. 17, 19. "There the wicked cease from troubling, and there the weary be at rest; there the prisoners rest together; they hear not the voice of the oppressors. The small and great are there; and the servant is free from his master."

Father, I know that thy eyes are dim with age and weary with weeping, but look, dear father, yet a little while toward that haven. Look unto Jesus, "the author and finisher of thy faith,"[41] for the moment of thy happy deliverance is at hand.

Mother, dear mother, I know, I feel, mother, the pangs of thy bleeding heart, that thou hast endured, during so many years of vexation. Thy agonies are by a genuine son-like sympathy mine; I will, I must, I do share daily in those agonies of thine. But I sincerely hope that with me you bear your agonies to Christ who carries our sorrows.

O come then with me, my beloved family, of weary heart-broken and care-worn ones, to Jesus Christ, "casting all your care upon him, for he careth for you."—2 Peter v. 7.

With these words of earnest exhortation, joined with fervent prayer to God that He may smooth your rugged way, lighten your burden, and give a happy issue out of all your troubles, I must bid you adieu.

Your son and brother,
JAS.P.
Alias J.W.C. PENNINGTON.

To Colonel F———T———, Of H———, Washington County, Md. 1844.

DEAR SIR,

It is now, as you are aware, about seventeen years since I left your house and service, at the age of twenty. Up to that time, I was, according to your rule and claim, your slave. Till the age of seven years, I was, of course, of little or no service to you. At that age, however, you hired me out, and for three years I earned my support; at the age of ten years, you took me to your place again, and in a short time after you put me to work at the blacksmith's trade, at which, together with the carpentering trade, &c., I served you peaceably until the day I left you with exception of the short time you had sold me to S———H———, Esq., for seven hundred dollars. It is important for me to say to you, that I have no consciousness of having done you any wrong. I called you master when I was with you from the mere force of circumstances; but I never regarded you as my master. The nature which God gave me did not allow me to believe that you had any more right to me than I had to you, and that was just none at all. And from an early age, I had intentions to free myself from your claim. I never consulted any one about it; I had no advisers or instigators; I kept my own counsel entirely concealed in my own bosom. I never meditated any evil to your person or property, but I regarded you as my oppressor, and I deemed it my duty to get out of your hands by peaceable means.

I was always obedient to your commands. I laboured for you diligently at all times. I acted with fidelity in any matter which you entrusted me. As you sometimes saw fit to entrust me with considerable money, to buy tools or materials, not a cent was ever coveted or kept.

During the time I served you in the capacity of blacksmith, your materials were used economically, your work was done expeditiously, and in the very best style, a style second to no smith in your neighbourhood. In short, sir, you know well that my habits from early life were advantageous to you. Drinking, gambling, fighting, &c., were not my habits. On Sabbaths, holidays, &c., I was frequently at your service, when not even your body-servant was at home.

Times and times again, I have gone on Sunday afternoon to H———, six miles, after your letters and papers, when it was as much my privilege to be *"out of the way,"* as it was C———.

But what treatment did you see fit to return me for all this? You, in the most unfeeling manner, abused my father for no cause but speaking a word to you, as a man would speak to his fellow-man, for the sake simply of a better understanding.

You vexed my mother, and because she, as a tender mother would do, showed solicitude for the virtue of her daughters, you threatened her in an insulting brutal manner.

You abused my brother and sister without cause, and in like manner you did to myself; you surmised evil against me. You struck me with your walking-cane, called me insulting names, threatened me, swore at me, and became more and more wrathy in your conduct, and at the time I quitted your place, I had good reason to believe that you were meditating serious evil against me.

Since I have been out of your hands, I have been signally favoured of God, whence I infer that in leaving you, I acted strictly in accordance with his holy will. I have a conscience void of offence towards God and towards all men, yourself not excepted. And I verily believe that I have performed a sacred duty to God and myself, and a kindness to you, in taking the blood of my soul peaceably off your soul. And now, dear sir, having spoken somewhat pointedly, I would, to convince you of my perfect good will towards you, in the most kind and respectful terms, remind you of your coming destiny. You are now over seventy years of age, pressing on to eternity with the weight of these seventy years upon you. Is not this enough without the blood of some half-score of souls?

You are aware that your right to property in man is now disputed by the civilized world. You are fully aware, also, that the question, whether the Bible sanctions slavery, has distinctly divided this nation in sentiment. On the side of Biblical Anti-slavery, we have many of the most learned, wise and holy men in the land. If the Bible affords no sanction to slavery, (and I claim that it cannot,) then it must be a sin of the deepest dye; and can you, sir, think to go to God in hope with a sin of such magnitude upon your soul?

But admitting that the question is yet doubtful, (which I do only for the sake of argument,) still, sir, you will have the critical hazard of this doubt pressing, in no very doubtful way, upon your declining years, as you descend the long and tedious hill of life.

Would it not seem to be exceedingly undesirable to close an eventful probation of seventy or eighty year and leave your reputation among posterity suspended upon so doubtful an issue? But what, my dear sir, is a reputation among posterity, who are but worms, compared with a destiny in the world of spirits? And it is in light of that destiny that I would now have you look at this subject. You and I, and all that you claim as your slaves, are in a state of probation; our great business is to serve God under His righteous moral government. Master and slave are the subjects of that government, bound by its immutable requirements, and liable to its sanctions in the next world, though enjoying its forbearance in this. You will pardon me then for pressing this point in earnest good faith. You should, at this stage, review your life without political bias, or adherence to long cherished prejudices, and remember that you are soon to meet those whom you have held, and do hold in slavery, at the awful bar of the impartial Judge of all who doeth right. Then what will become of your own doubtful claims? What will be done with those doubts that agitated your mind years ago; will you answer for threatening, swearing, and using the cowhide among your slaves?

What will become of those long groans and unsatisfied complaints of your slaves, for vexing them with insulting words, placing them in the power of dogish and abusive overseers, or under your stripling, misguided, hot-headed son, to drive and whip at pleasure, and for selling parts or whole families to Georgia? They will all meet you at that bar. Uncle James True, Charles Cooper, Aunt Jenny, and the native Africans; Jeremiah, London, and Donmore, have already gone a-head, and only wait your arrival—Sir, I shall meet you there. The account between us for the first twenty years of my life, will have a definite character upon which one or the other will be able to make out a case.

Upon such a review as this, sir, you will, I am quite sure, see the need of seriousness. I assure you that the thought of meeting you in eternity and before the dread tribunal of God, with a complaint in my mouth against you, is to me of most weighty and solemn character. And you will see that the circumstances from which this thought arises are of equal moment to yourself. Can the pride of leaving your children possessed of long slave states, or the policy of sustaining in the state the institution of slavery, justify you in overlooking a point of moment to your future happiness?

What excuse could you offer at the bar of God, favoured as you have been with the benefits of a refined education, and through a long life with the gospel of love, should you, when arraigned there, find that you have, all your life long, laboured under a great mistake in regard to slavery, and that in this mistake you had died, and only lifted up your eyes in the light of eternity to be corrected, when it was too late to be corrected in any other way.

I could wish to address you (being bred, born, and raised in your family) *as a father in Israel, or as an elder brother in Christ, but I cannot; mockery is a sin*. I can only say then, dear sir, farewell, till I meet you at the bar of God, where Jesus, who died for us, will judge between us. Now his blood can wash out our stain, break down the middle wall of partition, and reconcile us not only to God but to each other, then the word of his mouth, the sentence will set us at one. As for myself, I am quite ready to meet you face to face at the bar of God. I have done you no wrong; I have nothing to fear when we both fall into the hands of the just God.

I beseech you, dear sir, to look well and consider this matter soundly. In yonder world you can have no slaves—you can be no man's master—you can neither sell, buy, or whip, or drive. Are you then, by sustaining the relation of a slaveholder, forming a character to dwell with God in peace?

With kind regards,

I am, sir, yours respectfully,

J.W.C. PENNINGTON.

NOTES

1. William L. Andrews, *To Tell a Free Story: The First Century of Afro-American Autobiography, 1760–1865* (Urbana: University of Illinois Press, 1986), 160–65.

2. R. J. M. Blackett, *Beating Against the Barriers: Biographical Essays in Nineteenth-Century Afro-American History* (Baton Rouge: Louisiana State University Press, 1986), 7–9.

3. Herman E. James Thomas, *W. C. Pennington: African American Churchman and Abolitionist* (New York: Garland Publishing, 1995), 8–9; Howard Holman Bell, *A Survey of the Negro Convention Movement, 1830–1861* (New York: Arno Press, 1969), 10–37.

4. Benjamin Quarles, *Black Abolitionists* (New York: Oxford University Press, 1969), 54–55, 133–42.

5. Blackett, *Beating Against the Barriers*, 73.

6. Blackett, *Beating Against the Barriers*, 42–80.

7. Rayford W. Logan and Michael R. Winston, eds., *Dictionary of American Negro Biography* (New York: Norton, 1982), 488–90; Blackett, *Beating Against the Barriers*, 80–84.

8. Pennington successfully escaped slavery in 1827. His narrative was published over twenty years later.

9. Jesus. An allusion to Isaiah 9:6, "For unto us a child is born, unto us a son is given: and the government shall be upon his shoulder: and his name shall be called Wonderful, Counsellor, The mighty God, The everlasting Father, The Prince of Peace."

10. Gerrit Smith (1797–1874) was an American abolitionist, reformer, philanthropist, and founder of the Liberty Party. Smith was initially interested in colonizing blacks, but, by 1835, had become a strong supporter of abolition. He was a member of the American Anti-Slavery Society, involved himself with the Underground Railroad, and contributed funds to John Brown. He served in the House of Representatives in 1853 and 1854.

11. Theodore Wright (?–1847) was a minister at the First Colored Presbyterian Church in New York City. After his death, Pennington was called to the position.

12. The Fugitive Slave Act was part of the Compromise of 1850. It imposed substantial penalties on those who failed to participate in the recovery of, or aided, runaway slaves.

13. Welts caused by whipping.

14. One who believed in maintaining the chattel slave system forever and who therefore opposed either immediate abolition or gradual emancipation.

15. Ground corn.

16. The star in the Northern Hemisphere to which the axis of the earth nearly points. Because of that, it appears stationary. The star was used by escaping slaves as a point of reference.

17. Commonly speaking, a ship. More specifically, though, packets were government ships used to transport mail. Because of that, packets had fixed sailing days.

18. A stone marker indicating the distance in miles to a given point.

19. A highly contagious disease characterized by small running sores that usually leave a pit or scar.

20. A stableman (a variation of holster).

21. A measure of length containing 5 1/2 yards or 16 1/2 feet.

22. Job 26:9.

23. The place after death where God judges and decides who will enter heaven.

24. Abraham (circa 1800 BC–circa 1500 BC) was, along with Isaac and Jacob, one of the founding fathers of the Jews. According to Genesis, Abraham was born in Ur (a city in Mesopotamia, which is now mostly Iraq). Abraham was led by God to settle in Canaan, which God promised would belong to Abraham and his descendants. Lot was Abraham's nephew and assisted Abraham in leading his followers to Canaan. Once in Canaan, Lot settled in Sodom, which along with the city of Gomorrah, was known for its wickedness. When God decided to destroy the cities, Lot and his family were told to depart without

looking back. Lot's wife disobeyed the order and, as punishment, was turned into a pillar of salt (Genesis 19:26).

25. One of the founding fathers of the Jews (Abraham, Isaac, and Jacob).

26. Benjamin Banneker (1731–1806) is probably best known as the black man who assisted the surveyor who created the boundaries of the District of Columbia in 1791. Banneker served in that position in part due to the recommendation Thomas Jefferson (who was then secretary of state) made to President George Washington. Phillis Wheatley (1753?–1784) was the first significant black American poet. She is best known for *Poems on Various Subjects, Religious and Moral* (1773). She was originally brought from Africa to America to be the servant of Boston merchant John Wheatley. Francis Williams (?–?) was a Jamaican who, because of his intelligence, was selected early in the eighteenth century by the Duke of Montagu to be educated at Cambridge University. Montagu hoped to use Williams to learn something about the intellectual capabilities of blacks.

27. The group was commonly referred to as Quakers and was originally founded in England in 1647 by George Fox (1624–1691). Their beliefs encourage humanitarianism, racial equality, prison reform, and quality education.

28. New York universally emancipated its slaves on July 4, 1827.

29. Britain abolished slavery in the West Indies on August 1, 1834.

30. Though there are a number of organizations to which Pennington might allude, this reference may be toward the New England Anti-Slavery Society, organized by William Lloyd Garrison in 1831, and the American Anti-Slavery Society, founded in 1833.

31. The first annual meeting of the Negro Convention movement was held in Philadelphia in 1831. The convention was founded a year earlier by the Reverend Richard Allen, who had earlier organized the African Methodist Episcopal church and was, at the time, serving as its bishop. The convention was initially established to organize a response to Ohio's decision to enforce its black code. In 1830, a group of blacks from Ohio subsequently resettled in the Wilberforce settlement in Ontario, Canada. The convention eventually expanded its focus to include education, economic self-determination, and other issues relevant to the well-being of the black race. See Blackett, *Beating Against the Barriers*, 7–9.

32. A runaway slave who was assisted by a system of cooperation among antislavery supporters by which fugitive slaves were secretly helped to reach the North or Canada. See Blockson, *The Underground Railroad*.

33. Though commonly seen as the line dividing the North and the South (and free states from slave states), it is more accurately the boundary line between Pennsylvania and Maryland. The surveyors Charles Mason and Jeremiah Dixon completed their survey of the land in 1767 in an effort to resolve the dispute the two colonies had about the boundary.

34. A kind of cake made of corn meal, flour, eggs, milk, etc.

35. Mattress.

36. Most likely a coach drawn by four horses.

37. The Mexican War (1846–1848) was fought to resolve the dispute concerning the boundary between Mexico and the United States. According to the Treaty of Guadalupe Hidalgo, the United States acquired a region that included what is now California, Nevada, Utah, and parts of Arizona, New Mexico, Colorado, and Wyoming. Many saw the war as an unnecessary attack by the United States on a weaker country.

38. Jacob's son Joseph was sold into slavery in Egypt. As a reward for correctly interpreting pharaoh's dreams, Joseph was appointed prime minister to the pharaoh. When famine arrived in Canaan, Joseph invited the Israelites to come to Egypt. They lived peacefully until a new pharaoh enslaved them. Moses led the Israelites in their exodus. The Israelites were eventually able to return to their homeland in Canaan.

39. The place on a hill in Jerusalem where King David built his royal palace. It was originally named the City of David. It is also the site where King Solomon later built the Temple. It came to refer to the homeland of the Israelites. Among Christians, Zion often refers to a heavenly city or heavenly home.

40. Isaiah 61:1–3.

41. Hebrews 12:2, "Looking unto Jesus the author and the finisher of our faith; who for the joy that was set before him endured the cross, despising the shame, and is set down at the right hand of the throne of God."

■ CHAPTER 6
William (1826?–1900) and Ellen Craft (1826–1891)

RUNNING A THOUSAND MILES FOR FREEDOM

Though William and Ellen Craft contributed one of the most thrilling and compelling narratives of escape from slavery, theirs is the story of a lifetime of political activity and social involvement. Both were born slaves in Georgia before being brought to Macon, Georgia, where they met in the 1840s and married sometime near 1846.[1] By 1848, they had formulated their plan to escape to the north. Ellen, who had a very fair complexion, would pose as a male slave owner accompanied by her servant William. The 1,000-mile trip north from Macon to Philadelphia was relatively brief and ultimately successful. They basically used public conveyances, financed by William's apprentice work as a carpenter and employment as a waiter in a local hotel, traveling by train, boat, and carriage from Macon through Savannah, Charleston, Wilmington, Richmond, Washington, and Baltimore before arriving four days later at the farm of Quaker supporters just outside of Philadelphia.

The ingenuity of their escape was widely publicized in both the proslavery and antislavery press. *The Liberator* notes that "We would look in vain through the most trying times of our revolutionary history . . . for an incident of courage and noble daring to equal that of the escape of William and Ellen Craft; and future historians and poets would tell this story as one of the most thrilling in the nation's annals."[2]

They became involved with the antislavery lecture circuit and often shared the platform with William Wells Brown. Though the Crafts relocated to Boston in 1849, they still, under the provisions of the Fugitive Slave Act of 1850, risked capture and return to the South. This possibility was especially evident when the Craft's former owners petitioned President Millard Fillmore to release federal aid to help the owners reclaim their property. President Fillmore declined direct aid in his letter of response, but indicated a willingness, at the appropriate moment, to mobilize federal troops. In response, the Crafts departed for Liverpool, England, in November 1850. British abolitionists immediately recognized the importance of William and Ellen Craft to the British antislavery movement. In a letter to the editor of the *Anti-Slavery Standard*, Richard D. Webb, a prominent Irish abolitionist, argued that "If they do come they will excite a hearty interest for American slaves and an increasing contempt and repugnance for their republican masters. There is no truer saying than 'by their fruits ye shall know them'—and a troupe of fugitive slaves—true heroes—lecturing through England must diffuse strange ideas of the peculiar institution."[3]

British audiences were certainly familiar with the experiences of such well-known fugitive slaves as Frederick Douglass, Moses Roper, and Josiah Henson, among others, who had preceded the arrival of the Crafts. The Crafts were joined in the United Kingdom at this time by William Wells Brown, Henry Highland Garnet, James W. C. Pennington, Henry "Box" Brown, and Alexander Crummell, all of whom were speaking throughout England, Scotland, and Ireland in an effort to mobilize the British antislavery movement against the actions of American slaveholders and the American government. In 1851, the Crafts attended the Ockham school in Ockham, Surrey, where they remained as students (and where William eventually taught carpentry and Ellen taught sewing) until 1854, when they returned to their antislavery activities.

William accepted an invitation from the African Aid Society (formed in Britain in July 1860) to travel to Dahomey in hopes of convincing Dahomey's citizens to expand commerce along the Niger River, grow cotton, eliminate human sacrifice, accept Christianity, and allow the British to bring "culture" to the region. William raised the necessary funds and departed for Dahomey in November 1862. Though he made some progress toward achieving his goal, it became increasingly clear to William that he was being used to advance British colonization plans in the region. Though Ellen seems to have remained active in the British antislavery movement, little is known of her activities during the time William was away. What is known, however, is that William's activities in Dahomey were a financial failure. The Company of African Merchants, which had helped send William, held him responsible for the losses. The Crafts sold their home in 1867 and planned to return with their family, which now included four children, to Georgia.

The South in general (and Georgia in particular) had been devastated by the war. The Crafts decided to lease at $300 per year a rundown plantation, hire tenant farmers, and open a school. Their students numbered approximately twenty or thirty by the conclusion of 1873.[4] Ultimately the crops raised did not bring in enough money to support their tenants. Revenues were low, and the costs of rebuilding the plantation and attracting tenants by undercutting the demands of neighboring plantations was high. The family fell deeper into debt by 1875. Their economic problems were compounded by an economic downturn in 1873, numerous crop failures, local political opposition, a precipitous increase in Ku Klux Klan activity, and the failure of the Freedman's Bank in 1874. Neighboring planters—possibly annoyed at being undercut by the terms offered tenant farmers by the Crafts—seem to have conspired to attack the Crafts, who were accused of misappropriating funds from the plantation for their personal use. They lost a lengthy and expensive libel case and were forced to close the school. The Crafts returned to the plantation and attempted to pay their debts by raising rice and cotton (and most likely borrowing additional funds against their crop).

Ellen died in 1891, and losses associated with the plantation continued to increase. William eventually lost the plantation to debt foreclosure and died in 1900.

The narrative reprinted here is from the original text, published in London in 1860.

Further Reading

Barrett, Lindon. "Hand-Writing: Legibility and the White Body in *Running a Thousand Miles for Freedom*." *American Literature* 69 (June 1997): 315–36; R. J. M. Blackett, *Beating against the Barriers: Biographical Essays in Nineteenth-Century Afro-American History*. Baton Rouge: Louisiana State University Press, 1986; Bland, Sterling Lecater, Jr. *Voices of the Fugitives: Runaway Slave Stories and Their Fictions of Self-Creation*. Westport, CT: Greenwood Press, 2000; Doyle, Mary Ellen. "The Slave Narratives as Rhetorical Art." In *The Art of Slave Narrative: Original Essays in Criticism and Theory*, edited by John Sekora and Darwin T. Turner, 83–95. Macomb: Western Illinois University, 1982; Keetley, Dawn. "Racial Conviction, Racial Confusion: Indeterminate Identities in Women's Slave Narratives and Southern Courts." *A–B: Auto-Biography Studies* 10 (Fall 1995): 1–20; McCaskill, Barbara. "'Yours Very Truly': Ellen Craft—The Fugitive as Text and Artifact." *African American Review* 28 (Winter 1994): 509–29; Weinauer, Ellen M. "'A Most Respectable Looking Gentleman': Passing, Possession, and Transgression in *Running a Thousand Miles for Freedom*." In *Passing and the Fictions of Identity*, edited by Elaine K. Ginsberg, 37–56. Durham, NC: Duke University Press, 1996.

Ellen Craft. (Illustrated London News/Getty Images)

RUNNING A THOUSAND MILES FOR FREEDOM; OR, THE ESCAPE OF WILLIAM AND ELLEN CRAFT FROM SLAVERY.

"Slaves cannot breathe in England: if their lungs
Receive our air, that moment they are free;
They touch our country, and their shackles fall."

COWPER.

London:
William Tweedie, 337, Strand.
1860.

London:
Richard Barrett, Printer,
Mark Lane.

PREFACE.

HAVING heard while in Slavery that "God made of one blood all nations of men,"[5] and also that the American Declaration of Independence says, that "We hold these truths to be self-evident, that all men are created equal; that they are endowed by their Creator with certain inalienable rights; that among these, are life, liberty, and the pursuit of happiness;" we could not understand by what right we were held as "chattels." Therefore, we felt perfectly justified in undertaking the dangerous and exciting task of "running a thousand miles"[6] in order to obtain those rights which are so vividly set forth in the Declaration.

I beg those who would know the particulars of our journey, to peruse these pages.

This book is not intended as a full history of the life of my wife, nor of myself; but merely as an account of our escape; together with other matter which I hope may be the means of creating in some minds a deeper abhorrence of the sinful and abominable practice of enslaving and brutifying our fellow-creatures.

Without stopping to write a long apology for offering this little volume to the public, I shall commence at once to pursue my simple story.

W. CRAFT.

12, CAMBRIDGE ROAD, HAMMERSMITH, LONDON.

PART I

> "God gave us only over beast, fish, fowl,
> Dominion absolute; that right we hold
> By his donation. But man over man
> He made not lord; such title to himself
> Reserving, human left from human free."
> MILTON.[7]

My wife and myself were born in different towns in the State of Georgia, which is one of the principal slave States. It is true, our condition as slaves was not by any means the worst; but the mere idea that we were held as chattels, and deprived of all legal rights—the thought that we had to give up our hard earnings to a tyrant, to enable him to live in idleness and luxury—the thought that we could not call the bones and sinews that God gave us our own: but above all, the fact that another man had the power to tear from our cradle the new-born babe and sell it in the shambles like a brute, and then scourge us if we dared to lift a finger to save it from such a fate, haunted us for years.

But in December, 1848, a plan suggested itself that proved quite successful, and in eight days after it was first thought of we were free from the horrible trammels of slavery, rejoicing and praising God in the glorious sunshine of liberty.

My wife's first master was her father, and her mother his slave, and the latter is still the slave of his widow.

Notwithstanding my wife being of African extraction on her mother's side, she is almost white—in fact, she is so nearly so that the tyrannical old lady to whom she first belonged became so annoyed, at finding her frequently mistaken for a child of the family, that she gave her when eleven years of age to a daughter, as a wedding present. This separated my wife from her mother, and also from several other dear friends. But the incessant cruelty of her old mistress made the change of owners or treatment so desirable, that she did not grumble much at this cruel separation.

It may be remembered that slavery in America is not at all confined to persons of any particular complexion; there are a very large number of slaves as white as any one; but as the evidence of a slave is not admitted in court against a free white person, it is almost impossible for a white child, after having been kidnapped and sold into or reduced to slavery, in a part of the country where it is not known (as often is the case), ever to recover its freedom.

I have myself conversed with several slaves who told me that their parents were white and free; but that they were stolen away from them and sold when quite young. As they could not tell their address, and also as the parents did not know what had become of their lost and dear little ones, of course all traces of each other were gone.

The following facts are sufficient to prove, that he who has the power, and is inhuman enough to trample upon the sacred rights of the weak, cares nothing for race or colour:—

In March, 1818, three ships arrived at New Orleans, bringing several hundred German emigrants from the province of Alsace, on the lower Rhine. Among them were Daniel Muller and his two daughters, Dorothea and Salomé, whose mother had died on the passage. Soon after his arrival, Muller, taking with him his two daughters, both young children, went up the river to Attakapas parish, to work on the plantation of John F. Miller. A few weeks later, his relatives, who had remained at New Orleans, learned that he had died of the fever of the country. They immediately sent for the two girls; but they had disappeared, and the relatives, notwithstanding repeated and persevering inquiries and researches, could find no traces of them. They were at length given up for dead. Dorothea was never again heard of; nor was any thing known of Salomé from 1818 till 1843.

In the summer of that year, Madame Karl, a German woman who had come over in the same ship with the Mullers, was passing through a street in New Orleans, and accidentally saw Salomé in a wine-shop, belonging to Louis Belmonte, by whom she was held as a slave. Madame Karl recognised her at once, and carried her to the house of another German woman, Mrs. Schubert, who was Salomé's cousin and godmother, and who no sooner set eyes on her than, without having any intimation that the discovery had been previously made, she unhesitatingly exclaimed, "My God! here is the long-lost Salomé Muller."

The *Law Reporter*, in its account of this case, says:—

"As many of the German emigrants of 1818 as could be gathered together were brought to the house of Mrs. Schubert, and every one of the number who had any recollection of the little girl upon the passage, or any acquaintance with her father and mother, immediately identified the woman before them as the long-lost Salomé Muller. By all these witnesses, who appeared at the trial, the identity was fully established. The family resemblance in every feature was declared to be so remarkable, that some of the witnesses did not hesitate to say that they should know her among ten thousand; that they were as certain the plaintiff was Salomé Muller, the daughter of Daniel and Dorothea Muller, as of their own existence."

Among the witnesses who appeared in Court was the midwife who had assisted at the birth of Salomé. She testified to the existence of certain peculiar marks upon the body of the child, which were found, exactly as described, by the surgeons who were appointed by the Court to make an examination for the purpose.

There was no trace of African descent in any feature of Salomé Muller. She had long, straight, black hair, hazel eyes, thin lips, and a Roman nose. The complexion of her face and neck was as dark as that of the darkest brunette. It appears, however, that, during the twenty-five years of her servitude, she had been exposed to the sun's rays in the hot climate of Louisiana, with head and neck unsheltered, as is customary with the female slaves, while labouring in the cotton or the sugar field. Those parts of her person which had been shielded from the sun were comparatively white.

Belmonte, the pretended owner of the girl, had obtained possession of her by an act of sale from John F. Miller, the planter in whose service Salomé's father died. This Miller was a man of consideration and substance, owning large sugar estates, and bearing a high reputation for honour and honesty, and for indulgent treatment of his slaves. It was testified on the trial that he had said to Belmonte, a few weeks after the sale of Salomé, "that she was white, and had as much right to her freedom as any one, and was only to be retained in slavery by care and kind treatment." The broker who negotiated the sale from Miller to Belmonte, in 1838, testified in Court that he then thought, and still thought, that the girl was white!

The case was elaborately argued on both sides, but was at length decided in favour of the girl, by the Supreme Court declaring that "she was free and white, and therefore unlawfully held in bondage."

The Rev. George Bourne, of Virginia, in his *Picture of Slavery*,[8] published in 1834, relates the case of a white boy who, at the age of seven, was stolen from his home in Ohio, tanned and stained in such a way that he could not be distinguished from a person of colour, and then sold as a slave in Virginia. At the age of twenty, he made his escape, by running away, and happily succeeded in rejoining his parents.

I have known worthless white people to sell their own free children into slavery; and, as there are good-for-nothing white as well as coloured persons everywhere, no one, perhaps, will wonder at such inhuman transactions: particularly in the Southern States of America, where I believe there is a greater want of humanity and high principle amongst the whites, than among any other civilized people in the world.

I know that those who are not familiar with the working of "the peculiar institution," can scarcely imagine any one so totally devoid of all natural affection as to sell his own offspring into returnless bondage. But Shakspeare, that great observer of human nature, says:—

"With caution judge of probabilities.
Things deemed unlikely, e'en impossible,
Experience often shows us to be true."

My wife's new mistress was decidedly more humane than the majority of her class. My wife has always given her credit for not exposing her to many of the worst features of slavery. For instance, it is a common practice in the slave States for ladies, when angry with their maids, to send them to the calybuce[9] sugar-house, or to some other place established for the purpose of punishing slaves, and have them severely flogged; and I am sorry it is a fact, that the villains to whom those defenceless creatures are sent, not only flog them as they are ordered, but frequently compel them to submit to the greatest indignity. Oh! if there is any one thing under the wide canopy of heaven, horrible enough to stir a man's soul, and to make his very blood boil, it is the thought of his dear wife, his unprotected sister, or his young and virtuous daughters, struggling to save themselves from falling a prey to such demons!

It always appears strange to me that any one who was not born a slaveholder, and steeped to the very core in the demoralizing atmosphere of the Southern States, can in any way palliate slavery. It is still more surprising to see virtuous ladies looking with patience upon, and remaining in different to, the existence of a system that exposes nearly two millions of their own sex in the manner I have mentioned, and that too in a professedly free and Christian country. There is, however, great consolation in knowing that God is just, and will not let the oppressor of the weak, and the spoiler of the virtuous, escape unpunished here and hereafter.

I believe a similar retribution to that which destroyed Sodom is hanging over the slaveholders. My sincere prayer is that they may not provoke God, by persisting in a reckless course of wickedness, to pour out his consuming wrath upon them.

I must now return to our history.

My old master had the reputation of being a very humane and Christian man, but he thought nothing of selling my poor old father, and dear aged mother, at separate times, to different persons, to be dragged off never to behold each other again, till summoned to appear before the great tribunal of heaven. But, oh! what a happy meeting it will be on that great day for those faithful souls. I say a happy meeting, because I never saw persons more devoted to the service of God than they. But how will the case stand with those reckless traffickers in human flesh and blood, who plunged the poisonous dagger of separation into those loving hearts which God had for so many years closely joined together—nay, sealed as it were with his own hands for the eternal courts of heaven? It is not for me to say what will become of those heartless tyrants. I must leave them in the hands of an all-wise and just God, who will, in his own good time, and in his own way, avenge the wrongs of his oppressed people.

My old master also sold a dear brother and a sister, in the same manner as he did my father and mother. The reason he assigned for disposing of my parents, as well as of several other aged slaves, was, that "they were getting old, and would soon become valueless in the market, and therefore he intended to sell off all the old stock, and buy in a young lot." A most disgraceful conclusion for a man to come to, who made such great professions of religion!

This shameful conduct gave me a thorough hatred, not for true Christianity, but for slaveholding piety.

My old master, then, wishing to make the most of the rest of his slaves, apprenticed a brother and myself out to learn trades: he to a blacksmith, and myself to a cabinet-maker. If a slave has a good trade, he will let or sell for more than a person without one, and many slaveholders have their slaves taught trades on this account. But before our time expired, my old master wanted money; so he sold my brother, and then mortgaged my sister, a dear girl about fourteen years of age, and myself, then about sixteen, to one of the banks, to get money to speculate in cotton. This we knew nothing of at the moment; but time rolled on, the money became due, my master was unable to meet his payments; so the bank had us placed upon the auction stand and sold to the highest bidder.

My poor sister was sold first: she was knocked down to a planter who resided at some distance in the country. Then I was called upon the stand. While the auctioneer was crying the bids, I saw the man that had purchased my sister getting her into a cart, to take her to his home. I at once asked a slave friend who was standing near the platform, to run and ask the gentleman if he would please to wait till I was sold, in order that I might have an opportunity of bidding her good-bye. He sent me word back that he had some distance to go, and could not wait.

I then turned to the auctioneer, fell upon my knees, and humbly prayed him to let me just step down and bid my last sister farewell. But, instead of granting me this request, he grasped me by the neck, and in a commanding tone of voice, and with a violent oath, exclaimed, "Get up! You can do the wench no good; therefore there is no use in your seeing her."

On rising, I saw the cart in which she sat moving slowly off; and, as she clasped her hands with a grasp that indicated despair, and looked pitifully round towards me, I also saw the large silent tears trickling down her cheeks. She made a farewell bow, and buried her face in her lap. This seemed more than I could bear. It appeared to swell my aching heart to its utmost. But before I could fairly recover, the poor girl was gone;—gone, and I have never had the good fortune to see her from that day to this! Perhaps I should have never heard of her again, had it not been for the untiring efforts of my good old mother, who became free a few years ago by purchase, and, after a great deal of difficulty, found my sister residing with a family in Mississippi. My mother at once wrote to me, informing me of the fact, and requesting me to do something to get her free; and I am happy to say that, partly by lecturing occasionally, and through the sale of an engraving of my wife in the disguise in which she escaped, together with the extreme kindness and generosity of Miss Burdett Coutts, Mr. George Richardson of Plymouth, and a few other friends, I have nearly accomplished this. It would be to me a great and ever-glorious achievement to restore my sister to our dear mother, from whom she was forcibly driven in early life.

I was knocked down to the cashier of the bank to which we were mortgaged, and ordered to return to the cabinet shop where I previously worked.

But the thought of the harsh auctioneer not allowing me to bid my dear sister farewell, sent red-hot indignation darting like lightning through every vein. It quenched my tears, and appeared to set my brain on fire, and made me crave for power to avenge our wrongs! But, alas! we were only slaves, and had no legal rights; consequently we were compelled to smother our wounded feelings, and crouch beneath the iron heel of despotism.

I must now give the account of our escape; but, before doing so, it may be well to quote a few passages from the fundamental laws of slavery; in order to give some idea of the legal as well as the social tyranny from which we fled.

According to the law of Louisiana, "A slave is one who is in the power of a master to whom he belongs. The master may sell him, dispose of his person, his industry, and his labour; he can do nothing, possess nothing, nor acquire anything but what must belong to his master."—*Civil Code, art.* 35.

In South Carolina it is expressed in the following language:—"Slaves shall be deemed, sold, taken, reputed and judged in law to be *chattels personal* in the hands of their owners and possessors, and their executors, administrators, and assigns, *to all intents, constructions, and purposes whatsoever.*—2 *Brevard's Digest*, 229.

The Constitution of Georgia has the following (Art. 4, sec. 12):—"Any person who shall maliciously dismember or deprive a slave of life, shall suffer such punishment as would be inflicted in case the like offense had been committed on a free white person, and on the like proof, except in case of insurrection of such slave, and unless SUCH DEATH SHOULD HAPPEN BY ACCIDENT IN GIVING SUCH SLAVE MODERATE CORRECTION."—*Prince's Digest*, 559.

I have known slaves to be beaten to death, but as they died under "moderate correction," it was quite lawful; and of course the murderers were not interfered with.

"If any slave, who shall be out of the house or plantation where such slave shall live, or shall be usually employed, or without some white person in company with such slave, shall *refuse to submit* to undergo the examination of *any* white person, (let him be ever so drunk or crazy), it shall be lawful for such white person to pursue, apprehend, and moderately correct such slave; and if such slave shall assault and strike such white person, such slave may be *lawfully killed.*"—2 *Brevard's Digest*, 231.

"Provided always," says the law, "that such striking be not done by the command and in the defence of the person or property of the owner, or other person having the government of such slave; in which case the slave shall be wholly excused."

According to this law, if a slave, by the direction of his overseer, strike a white person who is beating said overseer's pig, "the slave shall be wholly excused." But, should the bondman, of his own accord, fight to defend his wife, or should his terrified daughter instinctively raise her hand and strike the wretch who attempts to violate her chastity, he or she shall, saith the model republican law, suffer death.

From having been myself a slave for nearly twenty-three years, I am quite prepared to say, that the practical working of slavery is worse than the odious laws by which it is governed.

At an early age we were taken by the persons who held us as property to Maçon, the largest town in the interior of the State of Georgia, at which place we became acquainted with each other for several years before our marriage; in fact, our marriage was postponed for some time simply because one of the unjust and worse than Pagan laws under which we lived compelled all children of slave mothers to follow their condition. That is to say, the father of the slave may be the President of the Republic; but if the mother should be a slave at the infant's birth, the poor child is ever legally doomed to the same cruel fate.

It is a common practice for gentlemen (if I may call them such), moving in the highest circles of society, to be the fathers of children by their slaves, whom they can and do sell with the greatest impunity; and the more pious, beautiful, and virtuous the girls are, the greater the price they bring, and that too for the most infamous purposes.

Any man with money (let him be ever such a rough brute), can buy a beautiful and virtuous girl, and force her to live with him in a criminal connexion; and as the law says a slave shall have no higher appeal than the mere will of the master, she cannot escape, unless it be by flight or death.

In endeavouring to reconcile a girl to her fate, the master sometimes says that he would marry her if it was not unlawful.* However, he will always consider her to be his wife, and will treat her as such; and she, on the other hand, may regard him as her lawful husband; and if they have any children, they will be free and well educated.

I am in duty bound to add, that while a great majority of such men care nothing for the happiness of the women with whom they live, nor for the children of whom they are the fathers, there are those to be found, even in that heterogeneous mass of licentious monsters, who are true to their pledges. But as the woman and her children are legally the property of the man, who stands in the anomalous relation to them of husband and father, as well as master, they are liable to be seized and sold for his debts, should he become involved.

There are several cases on record where such persons have been sold and separated for life. I know of some myself, but I have only space to glance at one.

I knew a very humane and wealthy gentleman, that bought a woman, with whom he lived as his wife. They brought up a family of children, among whom were three nearly white, well educated, and beautiful girls.

On the father being suddenly killed it was found that he had not left a will; but, as the family had always heard him say that he had no surviving relatives, they felt that their liberty and property were quite secured to them, and, knowing the insults to which they were exposed, now their protector was no more, they were making preparations to leave for a free State.

But, poor creatures, they were soon sadly undeceived. A villain residing at a distance, hearing of the circumstance, came forward and swore that he was a relative of the deceased; and as this man bore, or assumed, Mr. Slator's name, the case was brought before one of those horrible tribunals, presided over by a second Judge Jeffreys, and calling itself a court of justice, but before whom no coloured person, nor an abolitionist, was ever known to get his full rights.

A verdict was given in favour of the plaintiff, whom the better portion of the community thought had wilfully conspired to cheat the family.

The heartless wretch not only took the ordinary property, but actually had the aged and friendless widow, and all her fatherless children, except Frank, a fine young man about twenty-two years of age, and Mary, a very nice girl, a little younger than her brother, brought to the auction stand and sold to the highest bidder. Mrs. Slator had cash enough, that her husband and master left, to purchase the liberty of herself and children; but on her attempting to do so, the pusillanimous

---

* It is unlawful in the slave States for any one of purely European descent to intermarry with a person of African extraction; though a white man may live with as many coloured women as he pleases without materially damaging his reputation in Southern society.

scoundrel, who had robbed them of their freedom, claimed the money as his property; and, poor creature, she had to give it up. According to law, as will be seen hereafter, a slave cannot own anything. The old lady never recovered from her sad affliction.

At the sale she was brought up first, and after being vulgarly criticised, in the presence of all her distressed family, was sold to a cotton planter, who said he wanted the "proud old critter to go to his plantation, to look after the little woolly heads, while their mammies were working in the field."

When the sale was over, then came the separation, and

"O, deep was the anguish of that slave mother's heart,
When called from her darlings for ever to part;
The poor mourning mother of reason bereft,
Soon ended her sorrows, and sank cold in death."

Antoinette, the flower of the family, a girl who was much beloved by all who knew her, for her Christ-like piety, dignity of manner, as well as her great talents and extreme beauty, was bought by an uneducated and drunken slave-dealer.

I cannot give a more correct description of the scene, when she was called from her brother to the stand, than will be found in the following lines—

"Why stands she near the auction stand!
That girl so young and fair;
What brings her to this dismal place?
Why stands she weeping there!

Why does she raise that bitter cry!
Why hangs her head with shame,
As now the auctioneer's rough voice
So rudely calls her name!

But see! she grasps a manly hand,
And in a voice so low,
As scarcely to be heard, she says,
"My brother, must I go?"

A moment's pause: then, midst a wail
Of agonizing woe,
His answer falls upon the ear,—
"Yes, sister, you must go!

No longer can my arm defend,
No longer can I save
My sister from the horrid fate
That waits her as a SLAVE!"

> Blush, Christian, blush! for e'en the dark
> Untutored heathen see
> Thy inconsistency, and lo!
> They scorn thy God, and thee!"

The low trader said to a kind lady who wished to purchase Antoinette out of his hands, "I reckon I'll not sell the smart critter for ten thousand dollars; I always wanted her for my own use." The lady, wishing to remonstrate with him, commenced by saying, "You should remember, Sir, that there is a just God." Hoskens not understanding Mrs. Huston, interrupted her by saying, "I does, and guess its monstrous kind an' him to send such likely niggers for our convenience." Mrs. Huston finding that a long course of reckless wickedness, drunkenness, and vice, had destroyed in Hoskens every noble impulse, left him.

Antoinette, poor girl, also seeing that there was no help for her, became frantic. I can never forget her cries of despair, when Hoskens gave the order for her to be taken to his house, and locked in an upper room. On Hoskens entering the apartment, in a state of intoxication, a fearful struggle ensued. The brave Antoinette broke loose from him, pitched herself head foremost through the window, and fell upon the pavement below.

Her bruised but unpolluted body was soon picked up—restoratives brought—doctor called in; but, alas! it was too late: her pure and noble spirit had fled away to be at rest in those realms of endless bliss, "where the wicked cease from troubling, and the weary are at rest."[10]

Antoinette like many other noble women who are deprived of liberty, still

> "Holds something sacred, something undefiled;
> Some pledge and keepsake of their higher nature.
> And, like the diamond in the dark, retains
> Some quenchless gleam of the celestial light."

On Hoskens fully realizing the fact that his victim was no more, he exclaimed "By thunder I am a used-up man!" The sudden disappointment, and the loss of two thousand dollars, was more than he could endure: so he drank more than ever, and in a short time died, raving mad with *delirium tremens*.[11]

The villain Slator said to Mrs. Huston, the kind lady who endeavoured to purchase Antoinette from Hoskens, "Nobody needn't talk to me 'bout buying them ar likely niggers, for I'm not going to sell em." "But Mary is rather delicate," said Mrs. Huston, "and, being unaccustomed to hard work, cannot do you much service on a plantation." I don't want her for the field," replied Slator, "but for another purpose." Mrs. Huston understood what this meant, and instantly exclaimed, "Oh, but she is your cousin!" "The devil she is!" said Slator; and added, "Do you mean to insult me Madam, by saying that I am related to niggers?" "No," replied Mrs. Huston, "I do not wish to offend you, Sir. But wasn't Mr. Slator, Mary's father, your uncle?" "Yes, I calculate he was," said Slator; "but I want you and everybody to understand that I'm no kin to his niggers." "Oh, very well," said Mrs. Huston; adding, "Now what will you take for the poor girl?" "Nothin'," he replied; "for, as I said before, I'm not goin' to sell, so you needn't trouble yourself no more. If the critter behaves herself, I'll do as well by her as any man."

Slator spoke up boldly, but his manner and sheepish look clearly indicated that

"His heart within him was at strife
With such accursed gains;
For he knew whose passions gave her life,
Whose blood ran in her veins."

"The monster led her from the door,
He led her by the hand,
To be his slave and paramour
In a strange and distant land!"

Poor Frank and his sister were handcuffed together, and confined in prison. Their dear little twin brother and sister were sold, and taken where they knew not. But it often happens that misfortune causes those whom we counted dearest to shrink away; while it makes friends of those whom we least expected to take any interest in our affairs. Among the latter class Frank found two comparatively new but faithful friends to watch the gloomy paths of the unhappy little twins.

In a day or two after the sale, Slator had two fast horses put to a large light van, and placed in it a good many small but valuable things belonging to the distressed family. He also took with him Frank and Mary, as well as all the money for the spoil; and after treating all his low friends and bystanders, and drinking deeply himself, he started in high glee for his home in South Carolina. But they had not proceeded many miles, before Frank and his sister discovered that Slator was too drunk to drive. But he, like most tipsy men, thought he was all right; and as he had with him some of the ruined family's best brandy and wine, such as he had not been accustomed to, and being a thirsty soul, he drank till the reins fell from his fingers, and in attempting to catch them he tumbled out of the vehicle, and was unable to get up. Frank and Mary there and then contrived a plan by which to escape. As they were still handcuffed by one wrist each, they alighted, took from the drunken assassin's pocket the key, undid the iron bracelets, and placed them upon Slator, who was better fitted to wear such ornaments. As the demon lay unconscious of what was taking place, Frank and Mary took from him the large sum of money that was realized at the sale, as well as that which Slator had so very meanly obtained from their poor mother. They then dragged him into the woods, tied him to a tree, and left the inebriated robber to shift for himself, while they made good their escape to Savannah. The fugitives being white, of course no one suspected that they were slaves.

Slator was not able to call any one to his rescue till late the next day; and as there were no railroads in that part of the country at that time, it was not until late the following day that Slator was able to get a party to join him for the chase. A person informed Slator that he had met a man and woman, in a trap,[12] answering to the description of those whom he had lost, driving furiously towards Savannah. So Slator and several slave hunters on horseback started off in full tilt, with their blood-hounds, in pursuit of Frank and Mary.

On arriving at Savannah, the hunters found that the fugitives had sold the horses and trap, and embarked as free white persons, for New York. Slator's disappointment and rascality so preyed upon his base mind, that he, like Judas,[13] went and hanged himself.

As soon as Frank and Mary were safe, they endeavoured to redeem their good mother. But, alas! she was gone; she had passed on to the realm of spirit life.

In due time Frank learned from his friends in Georgia where his little brother and sister dwelt. So he wrote at once to purchase them, but the persons with whom they lived would not sell them. After failing in several attempts to buy them, Frank cultivated large whiskers and moustachios, cut off his hair, put on a wig and glasses, and went down as a white man, and stopped in the neighbourhood where his sister was; and after seeing her and also his little brother, arrangements were made for them to meet at a particular place on a Sunday, which they did, and got safely off.

I saw Frank myself, when he came for the little twins. Though I was then quite a lad, I well remember being highly delighted by hearing him tell how nicely he and Mary had served Slator.

Frank had so completely disguised or changed his appearance that his little sister did not know him, and would not speak till he showed their mother's likeness; the sight of which melted her to tears,—for she knew the face. Frank might have said to her

> "'O, Emma! O, my sister, speak to me!
> Dost thou not know me, that I am thy brother!
> Come to me, little Emma, thou shalt dwell
> With me henceforth, and know no care or want.'
> Emma was silent for a space, as if
> 'Twere hard to summon up a human voice."

Frank and Mary's mother was my wife's own dear aunt.

After this great diversion from our narrative, which I hope, dear reader, you will excuse, I shall return at once to it.

My wife was torn from her mother's embrace in childhood, and taken to a distant part of the country. She had seen so many other children separated from their parents in this cruel manner, that the mere thought of her ever becoming the mother of a child, to linger out a miserable existence under the wretched system of American slavery, appeared to fill her very soul with horror; and as she had taken what I felt to be an important view of her condition, I did not, at first, press the marriage, but agreed to assist her in trying to devise some plan by which we might escape from our unhappy condition, and then be married.

We thought of plan after plan, but they all seemed crowded with insurmountable difficulties. We knew it was unlawful for any public conveyance to take us as passengers, without our master's consent. We were also perfectly aware of the startling fact, that had we left without this consent the professional slave-hunters would have soon had their ferocious bloodhounds baying on our track, and in a short time we should have been dragged back to slavery, not to fill the more favourable situations which we had just left, but to be separated for life, and put to the very meanest and most laborious drudgery; or else have been tortured to death as examples, in order to strike terror into the hearts of others, and thereby prevent them from even attempting to escape from their cruel taskmasters. It is a fact worthy of remark, that nothing seems to give the slaveholders so much pleasure as the catching and torturing of fugitives. They had much rather take the keen and poisonous lash, and with it cut their poor trembling victims to atoms, than allow one of them to escape to a free country, and expose the infamous system from which he fled.

The greatest excitement prevails at a slave-hunt. The slaveholders and their hired ruffians appear to take more pleasure in this inhuman pursuit than English sportsmen do in chasing a fox or a stag. Therefore, knowing what we should have been compelled to suffer, if caught and taken back, we were more than anxious to hit upon a plan that would lead us safely to a land of liberty.

But, after puzzling our brains for years, we were reluctantly driven to the sad conclusion, that it was almost impossible to escape from slavery in Georgia, and travel 1,000 miles across the slave States. We therefore resolved to get the consent of our owners, be married, settle down in slavery, and endeavour to make ourselves as comfortable as possible under that system; but at the same time ever to keep our dim eyes steadily fixed upon the glimmering hope of liberty, and earnestly pray God mercifully to assist us to escape from our unjust thraldom.

We were married, and prayed and toiled on till December, 1848, at which time (as I have stated) a plan suggested itself that proved quite successful, and in eight days after it was first thought of we were free from the horrible trammels of slavery, and glorifying God who had brought us safely out of a land of bondage.

Knowing that slaveholders have the privilege of taking their slaves to any part of the country they think proper, it occurred to me that, as my wife was nearly white, I might get her to disguise herself as an invalid gentleman, and assume to be my master, while I could attend as his slave, and that in this manner we might effect our escape. After I thought of the plan, I suggested it to my wife, but at first she shrank from the idea. She thought it was almost impossible for her to assume that disguise, and travel a distance of 1,000 miles across the slave States. However, on the other hand, she also thought of her condition. She saw that the laws under which we lived did not recognize her to be a woman, but a mere chattel, to be bought and sold, or otherwise dealt with as her owner might see fit. Therefore the more she contemplated her helpless condition, the more anxious she was to escape from it. So she said, "I think it is almost too much for us to undertake; however, I feel that God is on our side, and with his assistance, notwithstanding all the difficulties, we shall be able to succeed. Therefore, if you will purchase the disguise, I will try to carry out the plan."

But after I concluded to purchase the disguise, I was afraid to go to any one to ask him to sell me the articles. It is unlawful in Georgia for a white man to trade with slaves without the master's consent. But, notwithstanding this, many persons will sell a slave any article that he can get the money to buy. Not that they sympathize with the slave, but merely because his testimony is not admitted in court against a free white person.

Therefore, with little difficulty I went to different parts of the town, at odd times, and purchased things piece by piece, (except the trowsers which she found necessary to make,) and took them home to the house where my wife resided. She being a ladies' maid, and a favourite slave in the family, was allowed a little room to herself; and amongst other pieces of furniture which I had made in my overtime, was a chest of drawers; so when I took the articles home, she locked them up carefully in these drawers. No one about the premises knew that she had anything of the kind. So when we fancied we had everything ready the time was fixed for the flight. But we knew it would not do to start off without first getting our master's consent to be away for a few days. Had we left without this, they would soon have had us back into slavery, and probably we should never have got another fair opportunity of even attempting to escape.

Some of the best slaveholders will sometimes give their favourite slaves a few days' holiday at Christmas time; so, after no little amount of perseverance on my wife's part, she obtained a pass[14] from her mistress, allowing her to be away for a few days. The cabinet-maker with whom I worked gave me a similar paper, but said that he needed my services very much, and wished me to return as soon as the time granted was up. I thanked him kindly; but somehow I have not been able to make it convenient to return yet; and, as the free air of good old England agrees so well with my wife and our dear little ones, as well as with myself, it is not at all likely we shall return at present to the "peculiar institution"[15] of chains and stripes.[16]

On reaching my wife's cottage she handed me her pass, and I showed mine, but at that time neither of us were able to read them. It is not only unlawful for slaves to be taught to read, but in some of the States there are heavy penalties attached, such as fines and imprisonment, which will be vigorously enforced upon any one who is humane enough to violate the so-called law.

The following case will serve to show how persons are treated in the most enlightened slaveholding community.

"INDICTMENT.

COMMONWEALTH OF VIRGINIA, NORFOLK COUNTY, *ss*.
In the Circuit Court.

The Grand Jurors empannelled and sworn to inquire of offences committed in the body of the said County on their oath present, that Margaret Douglass, being an evil disposed person, not having the fear of God before her eyes, but moved and instigated by the devil, wickedly, maliciously, and feloniously, on the fourth day of July, in the year of our Lord one thousand eight hundred and fifty-four, at Norfolk, in said County, did teach a certain black girl named Kate to read in the Bible, to the great displeasure of Almighty God, to the pernicious example of others in like case offending, contrary to the form of the statute in such case made and provided, and against the peace and dignity of the Commonwealth of Virginia.

"VICTOR VAGABOND, *Prosecuting Attorney.*"

"On this indictment Mrs. Douglass was arraigned as a necessary matter of form, tried, found guilty of course; and Judge Scalawag, before whom she was tried, having consulted with Dr. Adams, ordered the sheriff to place Mrs. Douglass in the prisoner's box, when he addressed her as follows: 'Margaret Douglass, stand up. You are guilty of one of the vilest crimes that ever disgraced society; and the jury have found you so. You have taught a slave girl to read in the Bible. No enlightened society can exist where such offences go unpunished. The Court, in your case, do not feel for you one solitary ray of sympathy, and they will inflict on you the utmost penalty of the law. In any other civilized country you would have paid the forfeit of your crime with your life, and the Court have only to regret that such is not the law in this country. The sentence for your offence is, that you be imprisoned one month in the country jail, and that you pay the costs of this prosecution. Sheriff, remove the prisoner to jail.' On the publication of these proceedings, the Doctors of Divinity preached each a sermon on the necessity of obeying the laws; the *New York Observer* noticed with much pious gladness a revival of religion on Dr. Smith's plantation in Georgia, among his slaves; while the *Journal of Commerce* commended this political preaching of the Doctors of Divinity because it favoured slavery. Let us do nothing to offend our Southern brethren."

However, at first, we were highly delighted at the idea of having gained permission to be absent for a few days; but when the thought flashed across my wife's mind, that it was customary for travellers to register their names in the visitors' book at hotels, as well as in the clearance or Custom-house book at Charleston, South Carolina—it made our spirits droop within us.

So, while sitting in our little room upon the verge of despair, all at once my wife raised her head, and with a smile upon her face, which was a moment before bathed in tears, said, "I think I have it!" I asked what it was. She said, "I think I can make a poultice[17] and bind up my right hand in a sling, and with propriety ask the officers to register my name for me." I thought that would do.

It then occurred to her that the smoothness of her face might betray her; so she decided to make another poultice, and put it in a white handkerchief to be worn under the chin, up the cheeks, and to tie over the head. This nearly hid the expression of the countenance, as well as the beardless chin.

The poultice is left off in the engraving, because the likeness could not have been taken well with it on.

My wife, knowing that she would be thrown a good deal into the company of gentlemen, fancied that she could get on better if she had something to go over the eyes; so I went to a shop and bought a pair of green spectacles. This was in the evening.

We sat up all night discussing the plan, and making preparations. Just before the time arrived, in the morning, for us to leave, I cut off my wife's hair square at the back of the head, and got her to dress in the disguise and stand out on the floor. I found that she made a most respectable looking gentleman.

My wife had no ambition whatever to assume this disguise, and would not have done so had it been possible to have obtained our liberty by more simple means; but we knew it was not customary in the South for ladies to travel with male servants; and therefore, notwithstanding my wife's fair complexion, it would have been a very difficult task for her to have come off as a free white lady, with me as her slave; in fact, her not being able to write would have made this quite impossible. We knew that no public conveyance would take us, or any other slave, as a passenger, without our master's consent. This consent could never be obtained to pass into a free State. My wife's being muffled in the poultices, &c., furnished a plausible excuse for avoiding general conversation, of which most Yankee[18] travellers are passionately fond.

There are a large number of free negroes residing in the southern States; but in Georgia (and I believe in all the slave States,) every coloured person's complexion is *primâ facie*[19] evidence of his being a slave; and the lowest villain in the country, should he be a white man, has the legal power to arrest, and question, in the most inquisitorial and insulting manner, any coloured person, male or female, that he may find at large, particularly at night and on Sundays, without a written pass, signed by the master or some one in authority; or stamped free papers, certifying that the person is the rightful owner of himself.

If the coloured person refuses to answer questions put to him, he may be beaten, and his defending himself against this attack makes him an outlaw, and if he be killed on the spot, the murderer will be exempted from all blame; but after the coloured person has answered the questions put to him, in a most humble and pointed manner, he may then be taken to prison; and should it turn out, after further examination, that he was caught where he had no permission or legal right to be, and that he has not given what they term a satisfactory account of himself, the master will have to pay a fine. On his refusing to do this, the poor slave may be legally and severely flogged by public officers. Should the prisoner prove to be a free man, he is most likely to be both whipped and fined.

The great majority of slaveholders hate this class of persons with a hatred that can only be equalled by the condemned spirits of the infernal regions.[20] They have no mercy upon, nor sympathy for, any negro whom they cannot enslave. They say that God made the black man to be a slave for the white, and act as though they really believed that all free persons of colour are in open rebellion to a direct command from heaven, and that they (the whites) are God's chosen agents to pour out upon them unlimited vengeance. For instance, a Bill has been introduced in the Tennessee Legislature to prevent free negroes from travelling on the railroads in that State. It has passed the first reading. The bill provides that the President who shall permit a free negro to travel on any road within the jurisdiction of the State under his supervision shall pay a fine of 500 dollars; any conductor permitting a violation of the Act shall pay 250 dollars; provided such free negro is not under the control of a free white citizen of Tennessee, who will vouch for the character of said free negro in a penal bond of one thousand dollars. The State of Arkansas has passed a law to banish all free negroes from its bounds, and it came into effect on the 1st day of January, 1860. Every free negro found there after that date will be liable to be sold into slavery, the crime of freedom being unpardonable. The Missouri Senate has before it a bill providing that all free negroes above the age of eighteen years who shall be found in the State after September, 1860, shall be sold into slavery; and that all such negroes as shall enter the State after September, 1861, and remain there twenty-four hours, shall also be sold into slavery for ever. Mississippi, Kentucky, and Georgia, and in fact, I believe, all the slave States, are legislating in the same manner. Thus the slaveholders make it almost impossible for free persons of colour to get out of the slave States, in order that they may sell them into slavery if they don't go. If no white persons travelled upon railroads except those who could get some one to vouch for their character in a penal bond of one thousand dollars, the railroad companies would soon go to the "wall." Such mean legislation is too low for comment; therefore I leave the villanous acts to speak for themselves.

But the Dred Scott decision[21] is the crowning act of infamous Yankee legislation. The Supreme Court, the highest tribunal of the Republic, composed of nine Judge Jeffries's, chosen both from the free and slave States, has decided that no coloured person, or persons of African extraction, can ever become a citizen of the

United States, or have any rights which white men are bound to respect. That is to say, in the opinion of this Court, robbery, rape, and murder are not crimes when committed by a white upon a coloured person.

Judges who will sneak from their high and honourable position down into the lowest depths of human depravity, and scrape up a decision like this, are wholly unworthy the confidence of any people. I believe such men would, if they had the power, and were it to their temporal interest, sell their country's independence, and barter away every man's birthright for a mess of pottage.[22] Well may Thomas Campbell say—

> United States, your banner wears,
> Two emblems,—one of fame;
> Alas, the other that it bears
> Reminds us of your shame!
> The white man's liberty in types
> Stands blazoned by your stars;
> But what's the meaning of your stripes?
> They mean your Negro-scars.

When the time had arrived for us to start, we blew out the lights, knelt down, and prayed to our Heavenly Father mercifully to assist us, as he did his people of old, to escape from cruel bondage; and we shall ever feel that God heard and answered our prayer. Had we not been sustained by a kind, and I sometimes think special, providence,[23] we could never have overcome the mountainous difficulties which I am now about to describe.

After this we rose and stood for a few moments in breathless silence,—we were afraid that some one might have been about the cottage listening and watching our movements. So I took my wife by the hand, stepped softly to the door, raised the latch, drew it open, and peeped out. Though there were trees all around the house, yet the foliage scarcely moved; in fact, everything appeared to be as still as death. I then whispered to my wife, "Come my dear, let us make a desperate leap for liberty!" But poor thing, she shrank back, in a state of trepidation. I turned and asked what was the matter; she made no reply, but burst into violent sobs, and threw her head upon my breast. This appeared to touch my very heart, it caused me to enter into her feelings more fully than ever. We both saw the many mountainous difficulties that rose one after the other before our view, and knew far too well what our sad fate would have been, were we caught and forced back into our slavish den. Therefore on my wife's fully realizing the solemn fact that we had to take our lives, as it were, in our hands, and contest every inch of the thousand miles of slave territory over which we had to pass, it made her heart almost sink within her, and, had I known them at that time, I would have repeated the following encouraging lines, which may not be out of place here—

"The hill, though high, I covet to ascend,
The *difficulty will not me offend*;
For I perceive the way to life lies here:
Come, pluck up heart, let's neither faint nor fear;
Better, though difficult, the right way to go,—
Than wrong, though easy, where the end is woe."

However, the sobbing was soon over, and after a few moments of silent prayer she recovered her self-possession, and said, "Come, William, it is getting late, so now let us venture upon our perilous journey."

We then opened the door, and stepped as softly out as "moonlight upon the water." I locked the door with my own key, which I now have before me, and tiptoed across the yard into the street. I say tiptoed, because we were like persons near a tottering avalanche, afraid to move, or even breathe freely, for fear the sleeping tyrants should be aroused, and come down upon us with double vengeance, for daring to attempt to escape in the manner which we contemplated.

We shook hands, said farewell, and started in different directions for the railway station. I took the nearest possible way to the train, for fear I should be recognized by some one, and got into the negro car in which I knew I should have to ride; but my *master* (as I will now call my wife) took a longer way round, and only arrived there with the bulk of the passengers. He obtained a ticket for himself and one for his slave to Savannah, the first port, which was about two hundred miles off. My master then had the luggage stowed away, and stepped into one of the best carriages.

But just before the train moved off I peeped through the window, and, to my great astonishment, I saw the cabinet-maker with whom I had worked so long, on the platform. He stepped up to the ticket-seller, and asked some question, and then commenced looking rapidly through the passengers, and into the carriages. Fully believing that we were caught, I shrank into a corner, turned my face from the door, and expected in a moment to be dragged out. The cabinet-maker looked into my master's carriage, but did not know him in his new attire, and, as God would have it, before he reached mine the bell rang, and the train moved off.

I have heard since that the cabinet-maker had a presentiment that we were about to "make tracks for parts unknown;" but, not seeing me, his suspicions vanished, until he received the startling intelligence that we had arrived safely in a free State.

As soon as the train had left the platform, my master looked round in the carriage, and was terror-stricken to find a Mr. Cray—an old friend of my wife's master, who dined with the family the day before, and knew my wife from childhood—sitting on the same seat.

The doors of the American railway carriages are at the ends. The passengers walk up the aisle, and take seats on either side; and as my master was engaged in looking out of the window, he did not see who came in.

My master's first impression, after seeing Mr. Cray, was, that he was there for the purpose of securing him. However, my master thought it was not wise to give any information respecting himself, and for fear that Mr. Cray might draw him into conversation and recognise his voice, my master resolved to feign deafness as the only means of self-defence.

After a little while, Mr. Cray said to my master, "It is a very fine morning, sir." The latter took no notice, but kept looking out of the window. Mr. Cray soon repeated this remark, in a little louder tone, but my master remained as before. This indifference attracted the attention of the passengers near, one of whom laughed out. This, I suppose, annoyed the old gentleman; so he said, "I will make him hear;" and in a loud tone of voice repeated, "It is a very fine morning, sir."

My master turned his head, and with a polite bow said, "Yes," and commenced looking out of the window again.

One of the gentlemen remarked that it was a very great deprivation to be deaf. "Yes," replied Mr. Cray, "and I shall not trouble that fellow any more." This enabled my master to breathe a little easier, and to feel that Mr. Cray was not his pursuer after all.

The gentlemen then turned the conversation upon the three great topics of discussion in first-class circles in Georgia, namely, Niggers, Cotton, and the Abolitionists.

My master had often heard of abolitionists, but in such a connection as to cause him to think that they were a fearful kind of wild animal. But he was highly delighted to learn, from the gentlemen's conversation, that the abolitionists were persons who were opposed to oppression; and therefore, in his opinion, not the lowest, but the very highest, of God's creatures.

Without the slightest objection on my master's part, the gentlemen left the carriage at Gordon, for Milledgeville (the capital of the State).

We arrived at Savannah early in the evening, and got into an omnibus, which stopped at the hotel for the passengers to take tea. I stepped into the house and brought my master something on a tray to the omnibus, which took us in due time to the steamer, which was bound for Charleston, South Carolina.

Soon after going on board, my master turned in; and as the captain and some of the passengers seemed to think this strange, and also questioned me respecting him, my master thought I had better get out the flannels and opodeldoc[24] which we had prepared for the rheumatism, warm them quickly by the stove in the gentleman's saloon, and bring them to his berth. We did this as an excuse for my master's retiring to bed so early.

While at the stove one of the passengers said to me, "Buck,[25] what have you got there?" "Opedeldoc, sir," I replied. "I should think it's opo-*devil*," said a lanky swell, who was leaning back in a chair with his heels upon the back of another, and chewing tobacco as if for a wager; "it stinks enough to kill or cure twenty men. Away with it, or I reckon I will throw it overboard!"

It was by this time warm enough, so I took it to my master's berth, remained there a little while, and then went on deck and asked the steward where I was to sleep. He said there was no place provided for coloured passengers, whether slave or free. So I paced the deck till a late hour, then mounted some cotton bags, in a warm place near the funnel, sat there till morning, and then went and assisted my master to get ready for breakfast.

He was seated at the right hand of the captain, who, together with all the passengers, inquired very kindly after his health. As my master had one hand in a sling, it was my duty to carve his food. But when I went out the captain said, "You have a very attentive boy, sir; but you had better watch him like a hawk when you get on to the North. He seems all very well here, but he may act quite differently there. I know several gentlemen who have lost their valuable niggers among them d———d cut-throat abolitionists."

Before my master could speak, a rough slave-dealer, who was sitting opposite, with both elbows on the table, and with a large piece of broiled fowl in his fingers, shook his head with emphasis, and in a deep Yankee tone, forced through his crowded mouth the words, "Sound doctrine, captain, very sound." He then dropped the chicken into the plate, leant back, placed his thumbs in the armholes of his fancy waistcoat, and continued, "I would not take a nigger to the North under no consideration. I have had a deal to do with niggers in my time, but I never saw one who ever had his heel upon free soil that was worth a d———n." "Now stranger," addressing my master, "if you have made up your mind to sell that ere nigger, I am your man; just mention your price, and if it isn't out of the way, I will pay for him on this board with hard silver dollars." This hard-featured, bristly-bearded, wire-headed, red-eyed monster, staring at my master as the serpent did at Eve,[26] said, "What do you say, stranger?" He replied, "I don't wish to sell, sir; I cannot get on well without him."

"You will have to get on without him if you take him to the North," continued this man; "for I can tell ye, stranger, as a friend, I am an older cove than you, I have seen lots of this ere world, and I reckon I have had more dealings with niggers than any man living or dead. I was once employed by General Wade Hampton, for ten years, in doing nothing but breaking 'em in; and everybody knows that the General would not have a man that didn't understand his business. So I tell ye, stranger, again, you had better sell, and let me take him down to Orleans. He will do you no good, if you take him across Mason's and Dixon's line;[27] he is a keen nigger, and I can see from the cut of his eye that he is certain to run away." My master said, "I think not, sir; I have great confidence in his fidelity." "Fi*devil*," indignantly said the dealer, as his fist came down upon the edge of the saucer and upset a cup of hot coffee in a gentleman's lap. (As the scalded man jumped up the trader quietly said, "Don't disturb yourself, neighbour; accidents will happen in the best of families.") "It always makes me mad to hear a man talking about fidelity in niggers. There isn't a d———d one on 'em who wouldn't cut sticks,[28] if he had half a chance."

By this time we were near Charleston; my master thanked the captain for his advice, and they all withdrew and went on deck, where the trader fancied he became quite eloquent. He drew a crowd around him, and with emphasis said, "Cap'en, if I was the President of this mighty United States of America, the greatest and freest country under the whole univarse, I would never let no man, I don't care who he is, take a nigger into the North and bring him back here, filled to the brim, as he is sure to be, with d——d abolition vices, to taint all quiet niggers with the hellish spirit of running away. These air, cap'en, my flat-footed, every day, right up and down sentiments, and as this is a free country, cap'en, I don't care who hears 'em; for I am a Southern man, every inch on me to the backbone." "Good!" said an insignificant-looking individual of the slave-dealer stamp. "Three cheers for John C. Calhoun[29] and the whole fair sunny South!" added the trader. So off went their hats, and out burst a terrific roar of irregular but continued cheering. My master took no more notice of the dealer. He merely said to the captain that the air on deck was too keen for him, and he would therefore return to the cabin.

While the trader was in the zenith of his eloquence, he might as well have said, as one of his kit did, at a great Filibustering[30] meeting, that "When the great American Eagle gets one of his mighty claws upon Canada and the other into South America, and his glorious and starry wings of liberty extending from the Atlantic to the Pacific, oh! then, where will England be, ye gentlemen? I tell ye, she will only serve as a pocket-handkerchief for Jonathan to wipe his nose with."

On my master entering the cabin he found at the breakfast-table a young southern military officer, with whom he had travelled some distance the previous day.

After passing the usual compliments the conversation turned upon the old subject,—niggers.

The officer, who was also travelling with a man-servant, said to my master, "You will excuse me, Sir, for saying I think you are very likely to spoil your boy by saying 'thank you' to him. I assure you, sir, nothing spoils a slave so soon as saying, 'thank you' and 'if you please' to him. The only way to make a nigger toe the mark, and to keep him in his place, is to storm at him like thunder, and keep him trembling like a leaf. Don't you see, when I speak to my Ned, he darts like lightning; and if he didn't I'd skin him."

Just then the poor dejected slave came in, and the officer swore at him fearfully, merely to teach my master what he called the proper way to treat me.

After he had gone out to get his master's luggage ready, the officer said, "That is the way to speak to them. If every nigger was drilled in this manner, they would be as humble as dogs, and never dare to run away.

The gentleman urged my master not to go to the North for the restoration of his health, but to visit the Warm Springs in Arkansas.

My master said, he thought the air of Philadelphia would suit his complaint best; and, not only so, he thought he could get better advice there.

The boat had now reached the wharf. The officer wished my master a safe and pleasant journey, and left the saloon.

There were a large number of persons on the quay waiting the arrival of the steamer: but we were afraid to venture out for fear that some one might recognize me; or that they had heard that we were gone, and had telegraphed to have us stopped. However, after remaining in the cabin till all the other passengers were gone, we had our luggage placed on a fly,[31] and I took my master by the arm, and with a little difficulty he hobbled on shore, got in and drove off to the best hotel, which John C. Calhoun, and all the other great southern fire-eating states men, made their head-quarters while in Charleston.

On arriving at the house the landlord ran out and opened the door: but judging, from the poultices and green glasses, that my master was an invalid, he took him very tenderly by one arm and ordered his man to take the other.

My master then eased himself out, and with their assistance found no trouble in getting up the steps into the hotel. The proprietor made me stand on one side, while he paid my master the attention and homage he thought a gentleman of his high position merited.

My master asked for a bed-room. The servant was ordered to show a good one, into which we helped him. The servant returned. My master then handed me the bandages, I took them downstairs in great haste, and told the landlord my master wanted two hot poultices as quickly as possible. He rang the bell, the servant came in, to whom he said, "Run to the kitchen and tell the cook to make two hot poultices right off, for there is a gentleman upstairs very badly off indeed!"

In a few minutes the smoking poultices were brought in. I placed them in white handkerchiefs, and hurried upstairs, went into my master's apartment, shut the door, and laid them on the mantel-piece. As he was alone for a little while, he thought he could rest a great deal better with the poultices off. However, it was necessary to have them to complete the remainder of the journey. I then ordered dinner, and took my master's boots out to polish them. While doing so I entered into conversation with one of the slaves. I may state here, that on the sea-coast of South Carolina and Georgia the slaves speak worse English than in any other part of the country. This is owing to the frequent importation, or smuggling in, of Africans, who mingle with the natives. Consequently the language cannot properly be called English or African, but a corruption of the two.[32]

The shrewd son of African parents to whom I referred said to me, "Say, brudder, way you come from, and which side you goin day wid dat ar little don up buckra" (white man)?[33]

I replied, "To Philadelphia."

"What!" he exclaimed, with astonishment, "to Philumadelphy?"

"Yes," I said.

"By squash! I wish I was going wid you! I hears um say dat dare's no slaves way over in dem parts; is um so?"

I quietly said, "I have heard the same thing."

"Well," continued he, as he threw down the boot and brush, and, placing his hands in his pockets, strutted across the floor with an air of independence—"Gorra Mighty, dem is de parts for Pompey; and I hope when you get dare you will stay, and nebber follow dat buckra back to dis hot quarter no more, let him be eber so good."

I thanked him; and just as I took the boots up and started off, he caught my hand between his two, and gave it a hearty shake, and, with tears streaming down his cheeks, said:—

"God bless you, broder, and may de Lord be wid you. When you gets de freedom, and sitin under your own wine and fig-tree, don't forget to pray for poor Pompey."

I was afraid to say much to him, but I shall never forget his earnest request, nor fail to do what little I can to release the millions of unhappy bondmen, of whom he was one.

At the proper time my master had the poultices placed on, came down, and seated himself at a table in a very brilliant dining-room, to have his dinner. I had to have something at the same time, in order to be ready for the boat; so they gave me my dinner in an old broken plate, with a rusty knife and fork, and said, "Here, boy, you go in the kitchen." I took it and went out, but did not stay more than a few minutes, because I was in a great hurry to get back to see how the invalid was getting on. On arriving I found two or three servants waiting on him; but as he did not feel able to make a very hearty dinner, he soon finished, paid the bill, and gave the servants each a trifle, which caused one of them to say to me, "Your massa is a big bug"—meaning a gentleman of distinction—"he is the greatest gentleman dat has been dis way for dis six months." I said, "Yes, he is some pumpkins," meaning the same as "big bug."

When we left Maçon, it was our intention to take a steamer at Charleston through to Philadelphia; but on arriving there we found that the vessels did not run during the winter, and I have no doubt it was well for us they did not; for on the very last voyage the steamer made that we intended to go by, a fugitive was discovered secreted on board, and sent back to slavery. However, as we had also heard of the Overland Mail Route, we were all right. So I ordered a fly to the door, had the luggage placed on; we got in, and drove down to the Custom-house Office, which was near the wharf where we had to obtain tickets, to take a steamer for Wilmington, North Carolina. When we reached the building, I helped my master into the office, which was crowded with passengers. He asked for a ticket for himself and one for his slave to Philadelphia. This caused the principal officer—a very mean-looking, cheese-coloured fellow, who was sitting there—to look up at us very suspiciously, and in a fierce tone of voice he said to me, "Boy, do you belong to that gentleman?" I quickly replied, "Yes, sir" (which was quite correct). The tickets were handed out, and as my master was paying for them the chief man said to him, "I wish you to register your name here, sir, and also the name of your nigger, and pay a dollar duty on him."

My master paid the dollar, and pointing to the hand that was in the poultice, requested the officer to register his name for him. This seemed to offend the "highbred" South Carolinian. He jumped up, shaking his head; and, cramming his hands almost through the bottom of his trousers pockets, with a slave-bullying air, said, "I shan't do it."

This attracted the attention of all the passengers. Just then the young military officer with whom my master travelled and conversed on the steamer from Savannah stepped in, somewhat the worse for brandy; he shook hands with my master, and pretended to know all about him. He said, "I know his kin (friends) like a book;" and as the officer was known in Charleston, and was going to stop there with friends, the recognition was very much in my master's favour.

The captain of the steamer, a good-looking jovial fellow, seeing that the gentleman appeared to know my master, and perhaps not wishing to lose us as passengers, said in an off-hand sailor-like manner, "I will register the gentleman's name, and take the responsibility upon myself." He asked my master's name. He said, "William Johnson." The names were put down, I think, "Mr. Johnson and slave." The captain said, "It's all right now, Mr. Johnson." He thanked him kindly, and the young officer begged my master to go with him, and have something to drink and a cigar; but as he had not acquired these accomplishments, he excused himself, and we went on board and came off to Wilmington, North Carolina. When the gentleman finds out his mistake, he will, I have no doubt, be careful in future not to pretend to have an intimate acquaintance with an entire stranger. During the voyage the captain said, "It was rather sharp shooting this morning, Mr. Johnson. It was not out of any disrespect to you, sir; but they make it a rule to be very strict at Charleston. I have known families to be detained there with their slaves till reliable information could be received respecting them. If they were not very careful, any d——d abolitionist might take off a lot of valuable niggers."

My master said, "I suppose so," and thanked him again for helping him over the difficulty.

We reached Wilmington the next morning, and took the train for Richmond, Virginia. I have stated that the American railway carriages (or cars, as they are called), are constructed differently to those in England. At one end of some of them, in the South, there is a little apartment with a couch on both sides for the convenience of families and invalids; and as they thought my master was very poorly, he was allowed to enter one of these apartments at Petersburg, Virginia, where an old gentleman and two handsome young ladies, his daughters, also got in, and took seats in the same carriage. But before the train started, the gentleman stepped into my car, and questioned me respecting my master. He wished to know what was the matter with him, where he was from, and where he was going. I told him where he came from, and said that he was suffering from a complication of complaints, and was going to Philadelphia, where he thought he could get more suitable advice than in Georgia.

The gentleman said my master could obtain the very best advice in Philadelphia. Which turned out to be quite correct, though he did not receive it from physicians, but from kind abolitionists who understood his case much better. The gentleman also said, "I reckon your master's father hasn't any more such faithful and smart boys as you." "O, yes, sir, he has," I replied, "lots on 'em." Which was literally true. This seemed all he wished to know. He thanked me, gave me a ten-cent piece, and requested me to be attentive to my good master. I promised that I would do so, and have ever since endeavoured to keep my pledge. During the gentleman's absence, the ladies and my master had a little cosy chat. But on his return, he said, "You seem to be very much afflicted, sir." "Yes, sir," replied the gentleman in the poultices. "What seems to be the matter with you, sir; may I be allowed to ask?" "Inflammatory rheumatism, sir." "Oh! that is very bad, sir," said the kind gentleman: "I can sympathise with you; for I know from bitter experience what the rheumatism is." If he did, he knew a good deal more than Mr. Johnson.

The gentleman thought my master would feel better if he would lie down and rest himself; and as he was anxious to avoid conversation, he at once acted upon this suggestion. The ladies politely rose, took their extra shawls, and made a nice pillow for the invalid's head. My master wore a fashionable cloth cloak, which they took and covered him comfortably on the couch. After he had been lying a little while the ladies, I suppose, thought he was asleep; so one of them gave a long sigh, and said, in a quiet fascinating tone, "Papa, he seems to be a very nice young gentleman." But before papa could speak, the other lady quickly said, "Oh! dear me, I never felt so much for a gentleman in my life!" To use an American expression, "they fell in love with the wrong chap."

After my master had been lying a little while he got up, the gentleman assisted him in getting on his cloak, the ladies took their shawls, and soon all were seated. They then insisted upon Mr. Johnson taking some of their refreshments, which of course he did, out of courtesy to the ladies. All went on enjoying themselves until they reached Richmond, where the ladies and their father left the train. But, before doing so, the good old Virginian gentleman, who appeared to be much pleased with my master, presented him with a recipe, which he said was a perfect cure for the inflammatory rheumatism. But the invalid not being able to read it, and fearing he should hold it upside down in pretending to do so, thanked the donor kindly, and placed it in his waist-coat[34] pocket. My master's new friend also gave him his card, and requested him the next time he travelled that way to do him the kindness to call; adding, "I shall be pleased to see you, and so will my daughters." Mr. Johnson expressed his gratitude for the proffered hospitality, and said he should feel glad to call on his return. I have not the slightest doubt that he will fulfil the promise whenever that return takes place. After changing trains we went on a little beyond Fredericksburg, and took a steamer to Washington.

At Richmond, a stout elderly lady, whose whole demeanour indicated that she belonged (as Mrs. Stowe's Aunt Chloe expresses it) to one of the "firstest families," stepped into the carriage, and took a seat near my master. Seeing me passing quickly along the platform, she sprang up as if taken by a fit, and exclaimed, "Bless my soul! there goes my nigger, Ned!"

My master said, "No; that is my boy."

The lady paid no attention to this; she poked her head out of the window, and bawled to me, "You Ned, come to me, sir, you runaway rascal!"

On my looking round she drew her head in, and said to my master, "I beg your pardon, sir, I was sure it was my nigger; I never in my life saw two black pigs more alike than your boy and my Ned."

After the disappointed lady had resumed her seat, and the train had moved off, she closed her eyes, slightly raising her hands, and in a sanctified tone said to my master, "Oh! I hope, sir, your boy will not turn out to be so worthless as my Ned has. Oh! I was as kind to him as if he had been my own son. Oh! sir, it grieves me very much to think that after all I did for him he should go off without having any cause whatever."

"When did he leave you?" asked Mr. Johnson.

"About eighteen months ago, and I have never seen hair or hide of him since."

"Did he have a wife?" enquired a very respectable-looking young gentleman, who was sitting near my master and opposite to the lady.

"No, sir; not when he left, though he did have one a little before that. She was very unlike him; she was as good and as faithful a nigger as any one need wish to have. But, poor thing! she became so ill, that she was unable to do much work; so I thought it would be best to sell her, to go to New Orleans, where the climate is nice and warm."

"I suppose she was very glad to go South for the restoration of her health?" said the gentleman.

"No; she was not," replied the lady, "for niggers never know what is best for them. She took on a great deal about leaving Ned and the little nigger; but, as she was so weakly, I let her go."

"Was she good-looking?" asked the young passenger, who was evidently not of the same opinion as the talkative lady, and therefore wished her to tell all she knew.

"Yes; she was very handsome, and much whiter than I am; and therefore will have no trouble in getting another husband. I am sure I wish her well. I asked the speculator who bought her to sell her to a good master. Poor thing! she has my prayers, and I know she prays for me. She was a good Christian, and always used to pray for my soul. It was through her earliest prayers," continued the lady, "that

I was first led to seek forgiveness of my sins, before I was converted at the great camp-meeting."

This caused the lady to snuffle and to draw from her pocket a richly embroidered handkerchief, and apply it to the corner of her eyes. But my master could not see that it was at all soiled.

The silence which prevailed for a few moments was broken by the gentleman's saying, "As your 'July' was such a very good girl, and had served you so faithfully before she lost her health, don't you think it would have been better to have emancipated her?"

"No, indeed I do not!" scornfully exclaimed the lady, as she impatiently crammed the fine handkerchief into a little work-bag. "I have no patience with people who set niggers at liberty. It is the very worst thing you can do for them. My dear husband just before he died willed all his niggers free. But I and all our friends knew very well that he was too good a man to have ever thought of doing such an unkind and foolish thing, had he been in his right mind, and, therefore we had the will altered as it should have been in the first place."

"Did you mean, madam," asked my master, "that willing the slaves free was unjust to yourself, or unkind to them?"

"I mean that it was decidedly unkind to the servants themselves. It always seems to me such a cruel thing to turn niggers loose to shift for themselves, when there are so many good masters to take care of them. As for myself," continued the considerate lady, "I thank the Lord my dear husband left me and my son well provided for. Therefore I care nothing for the niggers, on my own account, for they are a great deal more trouble than they are worth, I sometimes wish that there was not one of them in the world; for the ungrateful wretches are always running away. I have lost no less than ten since my poor husband died. It's ruinous, sir!"

"But as you are well provided for, I suppose you do not feel the loss very much," said the passenger.

"I don't feel it at all," haughtily continued the good soul; "but that is no reason why property should be squandered. If my son and myself had the money for those valuable niggers, just see what a great deal of good we could do for the poor, and in sending missionaries abroad to the poor heathen, who have never heard the name of our blessed Redeemer. My dear son who is a good Christian minister has advised me not to worry and send my soul to hell for the sake of niggers; but to sell every blessed one of them for what they will fetch, and go and live in peace with him in New York. This I have concluded to do. I have just been to Richmond and made arrangements with my agent to make clean work of the forty that are left."

"Your son being a good Christian minister," said the gentleman, "It's strange he did not advise you to let the poor negroes have their liberty and go North."

"It's not at all strange, sir; it's not at all strange. My son knows what's best for the niggers; he has always told me that they were much better off than the free niggers in the North. In fact, I don't believe there are any white labouring people in the world who are as well off as the slaves."

"You are quite mistaken, madam," said the young man. "For instance, my own widowed mother, before she died, emancipated all her slaves, and sent them to Ohio, where they are getting a long well. I saw several of them last summer myself."

"Well," replied the lady, "freedom may do for your ma's niggers, but it will never do for mine; and, plague them, they shall never have it; that is the word, with the bark on it."

"If freedom will not do for your slaves," replied the passenger, "I have no doubt your Ned and the other nine negroes will find out their mistake, and return to their old home.

"Blast them!" exclaimed the old lady, with great emphasis, "if I ever get them, I will cook their infernal hash, and tan their accursed black hides well for them! God forgive me," added the old soul, "the niggers will make me lose all my religion!"

By this time the lady had reached her destination. The gentleman got out at the next station beyond. As soon as she was gone, the young Southerner said to my master, "What a d——d shame it is for that old whining hypocritical humbug to cheat the poor negroes out of their liberty! If she has religion, may the devil prevent me from ever being converted!"

For the purpose of somewhat disguising myself, I bought and wore a very good second-hand white beaver, an article which I had never indulged in before. So just before we arrived at Washington, an uncouth planter, who had been watching me very closely, said to my master, "I reckon, stranger, you are *'spiling'* that ere nigger of yourn, by letting him wear such a devilish fine hat. Just look at the quality on it; the President couldn't wear a better. I should just like to go and kick it overboard." His friend touched him, and said, "Don't speak so to a gentleman." "Why not?" exclaimed the fellow. He grated his short teeth, which appeared to be nearly worn away by the incessant chewing of tobacco, and said, "It always makes me itch all over, from head to toe, to get hold of every d——d nigger I see dressed like a white man. Washington is run away with *spiled* and free niggers. If I had my way I would sell every d——d rascal of 'em way down South, where the devil would be whipped out on 'em."

This man's fierce manner made my master feel rather nervous, and therefore he thought the less he said the better; so he walked off without making any reply. In a few minutes we were landed at Washington, where we took a conveyance and hurried off to the train for Baltimore.

We left our cottage on Wednesday morning, the 21st of December, 1848, and arrived at Baltimore, Saturday evening, the 24th (Christmas Eve). Baltimore was the last slave port of any note at which we stopped.

On arriving there we felt more anxious than ever, because we knew not what that last dark night would bring forth. It is true we were near the goal, but our poor hearts were still as if tossed at sea; and, as there was another great and dangerous bar to pass, we were afraid our liberties would be wrecked, and, like the ill-fated *Royal Charter*, go down for ever just off the place we longed to reach.

They are particularly watchful at Baltimore to prevent slaves from escaping into Pennsylvania, which is a free State. After I had seen my master into one of the best carriages, and was just about to step into mine, an officer, a full-blooded Yankee of the lower order, saw me. He came quickly up, and, tapping me on the shoulder, said in his unmistakable native twang, together with no little display of his authority, "Where are you going, boy?" "To Philadelphia, sir," I humbly replied. "Well, what are you going there for?" "I am travelling with my master, who is in the next carriage, sir." "Well, I calculate you had better get him out; and be mighty quick about it, because the train will soon be starting. It is against my rules to let any man take a slave past here, unless he can satisfy them in the office that he has a right to take him along."

The officer then passed on and left me standing upon the platform, with my anxious heart apparently palpitating in the throat. At first I scarcely knew which way to turn. But it soon occurred to me that the good God, who had been with us thus far, would not forsake us at the eleventh hour. So with renewed hope I stepped into my master's carriage, to inform him of the difficulty. I found him sitting at the farther end, quite alone. As soon as he looked up and saw me, he smiled. I also tried to wear a cheerful countenance, in order to break the shock of the sad news. I knew what made him smile. He was aware that if we were fortunate we should reach our destination at five o'clock the next morning, and this made it the more painful to communicate what the officer had said; but, as there was no time to lose, I went up to him and asked him how he felt. He said "Much better," and that he thanked God we were getting on so nicely. I then said we were not getting on quite so well as we had anticipated. He anxiously and quickly asked what was the matter. I told him. He started as if struck by lightning, and exclaimed, "Good Heavens! William, is it possible that we are, after all, doomed to hopeless bondage?" I could say nothing, my heart was too full to speak, for at first I did not know what to do. However we knew it would never do to turn back to the "City of Destruction," like Bunyan's[35] *Mistrust* and *Timorous*, because they saw lions in the narrow way after ascending the hill Difficulty; but press on, like noble *Christian* and *Hopeful*, to the great city in which dwelt a few "shining ones." So, after a few moments, I did all I could to encourage my companion, and we stepped out and made for the office: but how or where my master obtained sufficient courage to face the tyrants who had power to blast all we held dear, heaven only knows! Queen Elizabeth[36] could not have been more terror-stricken, on being forced to land at the traitors' gate leading to the Tower, than we were on entering that office. We felt that our very existence was at stake, and that we must either sink or swim. But, as God was our present and mighty helper in this as well as in all former trials, we were able to keep our heads up and press forwards.

On entering the room we found the principal man, to whom my master said, "Do you wish to see me, sir?" "Yes," said this eagle-eyed officer; and he added, "It is against our rules, sir, to allow any person to take a slave out of Baltimore into Philadelphia, unless he can satisfy us that he has a right to take him along." "Why is that?" asked my master, with more firmness than could be expected. "Because, sir," continued he, in a voice and manner that almost chilled our blood, "if we should suffer any gentleman to take a slave past here into Philadelphia; and should the gentleman with whom the slave might be travelling turn out not to be his rightful owner; and should the proper master come and prove that his slave escaped on our road, we shall have him to pay for; and, therefore, we cannot let any slave pass here without receiving security to show, and to satisfy us, that it is all right."

This conversation attracted the attention of the large number of bustling passengers. After the officer had finished, a few of them said, "Chit, chit, chit;" not because they thought we were slaves endeavouring to escape, but merely because they thought my master was a slaveholder and invalid gentleman, and therefore it was wrong to detain him. The officer, observing that the passengers sympathised with my master, asked him if he was not acquainted with some gentleman in Baltimore that he could get to endorse for him, to show that I was his property, and that he had a right to take me off. He said, "No;" and added, "I bought tickets in Charleston to pass us through to Philadelphia, and therefore you have no right to detain us here." "Well, sir," said the man, indignantly, "right or no right, we shan't let you go." These sharp words fell upon our anxious hearts like the crack of doom, and made us feel that hope only smiles to deceive.

For a few moments perfect silence prevailed. My master looked at me, and I at him, but neither of us dared to speak a word, for fear of making some blunder that would tend to our detection. We knew that the officers had power to throw us into prison, and if they had done so we must have been detected and driven back, like the vilest felons, to a life of slavery, which we dreaded far more than sudden death.

We felt as though we had come into deep waters and were about being overwhelmed, and that the slightest mistake would clip asunder the last brittle thread of hope by which we were suspended, and let us down for ever into the dark and horrible pit of misery and degradation from which we were straining every nerve to escape. While our hearts were crying lustily unto Him who is ever ready and able to save, the conductor of the train that we had just left stepped in. The officer asked if we came by the train with him from Washington; he said we did, and left the room. Just then the bell rang for the train to leave; and had it been the sudden shock of an earthquake it could not have given us a greater thrill. The sound of the bell caused every eye to flash with apparent interest, and to be more steadily fixed upon us than before. But, as God would have it, the officer all at once thrust his fingers through his hair, and in a state of great agitation said, "I really don't know what to do; I calculate it is all right." He then told the clerk to run and tell the conductor to "let this gentleman and slave pass;" adding, "As he is not well, it is a pity to stop him here. We will let him go." My master thanked him, and stepped out and hobbled across the platform as quickly as possible. I tumbled him unceremoniously into one of the best carriages, and leaped into mine just as the train was gliding off towards our happy destination.

We thought of this plan about four days before we left Maçon and as we had our daily employment to attend to, we only saw each other at night. So we sat up the four long nights talking over the plan and making preparations.

We had also been four days on the journey; and as we travelled night and day, we got but very limited opportunities for sleeping. I believe nothing in the world could have kept us awake so long but the intense excitement, produced by the fear of being retaken on the one hand, and the bright anticipation of liberty on the other.

We left Baltimore about eight o'clock in the evening; and not being aware of a stopping-place of any consequence between there and Philadelphia, and also knowing that if we were fortunate we should be in the latter place early the next morning, I thought I might indulge in a few minutes' sleep in the car; but I, like Bunyan's Christian in the arbour, went to sleep at the wrong time, and took too long a nap. So, when the train reached Havre de Grace, all the first-class passengers had to get out of the carriages and into a ferry-boat, to be ferried across the Susquehanna river, and take the train on the opposite side.

The road was constructed so as to be raised or lowered to suit the tide. So they rolled the luggage-vans on to the boat, and off on the other side; and as I was in one of the apartments adjoining a baggage-car, they considered it unnecessary to awaken me, and tumbled me over with the luggage. But when my master was asked to leave his seat, he found it very dark, and cold, and raining. He missed me for the first time on the journey. On all previous occasions, as soon as the train stopped, I was at hand to assist him. This caused many slaveholders to praise me very much: they said they had never before seen a slave so attentive to his master: and therefore my absence filled him with terror and confusion; the children of Israel could not have felt more troubled on arriving at the Red Sea.[37] So he asked the conductor if he had seen anything of his slave. The man being somewhat of an abolitionist, and believing that my master was really a slaveholder, thought he would tease him a little respecting me. So he said, "No, sir; I haven't seen anything of him for some time: I have no doubt he has run away, and is in Philadelphia, free, long before now." My master knew that there was nothing in this; so he asked the conductor if he would please to see if he could find me. The man indignantly replied, "I am no slave-hunter; and as far as I am concerned everybody must look after their own niggers." He went off and left the confused invalid to fancy whatever he felt inclined. My master at first thought I must have been kidnapped into slavery by some one, or left, or perhaps killed on the train. He also thought of stopping to see if he could hear anything of me, but he soon remembered that he had no money. That night all the money we had was consigned to my own pocket, because we thought, in case there were any pickpockets about, a slave's pocket would be the last one they would look for. However, hoping to meet me some day in a land of liberty, and as he had the tickets, he thought it best upon the whole to enter the boat and come off to Philadelphia, and endeavour to make his way alone in this cold and hollow world as best he could. The time was now up, so he went on board and came across with feelings that can be better imagined than described.

After the train had got fairly on the way to Philadelphia, the guard came into my car and gave me a violent shake, and bawled out at the same time, "Boy, wake up!" I started, almost frightened out of my wits. He said, "Your master is scared half to death about you." That frightened me still more—I thought they had found him out; so I anxiously inquired what was the matter. The guard said, "He thinks you have run away from him." This made me feel quite at ease. I said, "No, sir; I am satisfied my good master doesn't think that." So off I started to see him. He had been fearfully nervous, but on seeing me he at once felt much better. He merely wished to know what had become of me.

On returning to my seat, I found the conductor and two or three other persons amusing themselves very much respecting my running away. So the guard said, "Boy, what did your master want?* I replied, "He merely wished to know what had become of me." "No," said the man, "that was not it; he thought you had taken French leave,[38] for parts unknown. I never saw a fellow so badly scared about losing his slave in my life. Now," continued the guard, "let me give you a little friendly advice. When you get to Philadelphia, run away and leave that cripple, and have your liberty." "No, sir," I indifferently replied, "I can't promise to do that." "Why not?" said the conductor, evidently much surprised; "don't you want your liberty?" "Yes, sir," I replied; "but I shall never run away from such a good master as I have at present."

One of the men said to the guard, "Let him alone; I guess he will open his eyes when he gets to Philadelphia, and see things in another light." After giving me a good deal of information, which I afterwards found to be very useful, they left me alone.

I also met with a coloured gentleman on this train, who recommended me to a boarding-house that was kept by an abolitionist, where he thought I would be quite safe, if I wished to run away from my master. I thanked him kindly, but of course did not let him know who we were. Late at night, or rather early in the morning, I heard a fearful whistling of the steam-engine; so I opened the window and looked out, and saw a large number of flickering lights in the distance, and heard a

---

*I may state here that every man slave is called boy till he is very old, then the more respectable slaveholders call him uncle. The women are all girls till they are aged, then they are called aunts. This is the reason why Mrs. Stowe calls her characters Uncle Tom, Aunt Chloe, Uncle Tiff, &c.

passenger in the next carriage—who also had his head out of the window—say to his companion, "Wake up, old horse, we are at Philadelphia!"

The sight of those lights and that announcement made me feel almost as happy as Bunyan's Christian must have felt when he first caught sight of the cross. I, like him, felt that the straps that bound the heavy burden to my back began to pop, and the load to roll off. I also looked, and looked again, for it appeared very wonderful to me how the mere sight of our first city of refuge should have all at once made my hitherto sad and heavy heart become so light and happy. As the train speeded on, I rejoiced and thanked God with all my heart and soul for his great kindness and tender mercy, in watching over us, and bringing us safely through.

As soon as the train had reached the platform, before it had fairly stopped, I hurried out of my carriage to my master, whom I got at once into a cab, placed the luggage on, jumped in myself, and we drove off to the boardinghouse which was so kindly recommended to me. On leaving the station, my master—or rather my wife, as I may now say—who had from the commencement of the journey borne up in a manner that much surprised us both, grasped me by the hand, and said, "Thank God, William, we are safe!" then burst into tears, leant upon me, and wept like a child. The reaction was fearful. So when we reached the house, she was in reality so weak and faint that she could scarcely stand alone. However, I got her into the apartments that were pointed out, and there we knelt down, on this Sabbath, and Christmas-day,—a day that will ever be memorable to us,—and poured out our heartfelt gratitude to God, for his goodness in enabling us to overcome so many perilous difficulties, in escaping out of the jaws of the wicked.

PART II

AFTER my wife had a little recovered herself, she threw off the disguise and assumed her own apparel. We then stepped into the sitting-room, and asked to see the landlord. The man came in, but he seemed thunderstruck on finding a fugitive slave and his wife, instead of a "young cotton planter and his nigger." As his eyes travelled round the room, he said to me. "Where is your master?" I pointed him out. The man gravely replied, "I am not joking, I really wish to see your master." I pointed him out again, but at first he could not believe his eyes; he said "he knew that was not the gentleman that came with me."

But, after some conversation, we satisfied him that we were fugitive slaves, and had just escaped in the manner I have described. We asked him if he thought it would be safe for us to stop in Philadelphia. He said he thought not, but he would call in some persons who knew more about the laws than himself. He then went out, and kindly brought in several of the leading abolitionists of the city, who gave us a most hearty and friendly welcome amongst them. As it was in December, and also as we had just left a very warm climate, they advised us not to go to Canada as we had intended, but to settle at Boston in the United States. It is true that the constitution of the Republic has always guaranteed the slaveholders the right to come into any of the so-called free States, and take their fugitives back to southern Egypt. But through the untiring, uncompromising, and manly efforts of Mr. Garrison, Wendell Phillips, Theodore Parker,[39] and a host of other noble abolitionists of Boston and the neighbourhood, public opinion in Massachusetts had become so much opposed to slavery and to kidnapping, that it was almost impossible for any one to take a fugitive slave out of that State.

So we took the advice of our good Philadelphia friends, and settled at Boston. I shall have something to say about our sojourn there presently.

Among other friends we met with at Philadelphia, was Robert Purves, Esq., a well educated and wealthy coloured gentleman, who introduced us to Mr. Barkley Ivens, a member of the Society of Friends, and a noble and generous-hearted farmer, who lived at some distance in the country.

This good Samaritan[40] at once invited us to go and stop quietly with his family, till my wife could somewhat recover from the fearful reaction of the past journey. We most gratefully accepted the invitation, and at the time appointed we took a steamer to a place up the Delaware river, where our new and dear friend met us with his snug little cart, and took us to his happy home. This was the first act of great and disinterested kindness we had ever received from a white person.

The gentleman was not of the fairest complexion, and therefore, as my wife was not in the room when I received the information respecting him and his anti-slavery character, she thought of course he was a quadroon like herself. But on arriving at the house, and finding out her mistake, she became more nervous and timid than ever.

As the cart came into the yard, the dear good old lady, and her three charming and affectionate daughters, all came to the door to meet us. We got out, and the gentleman said, "Go in, and make yourselves at home; I will see after the baggage." But my wife was afraid to approach them. She stopped in the yard, and said to me, "William, I thought we were coming among coloured people?" I replied, "It is all right; these are the same." "No," she said, "it is not all right, and I am not going to stop here; I have no confidence whatever in white people, they are only trying to get us back to slavery." She turned round and said, "I am going right off." The old lady then came out, with her sweet, soft, and winning smile, shook her heartily by the hand, and kindly said, "How art thou, my dear? We are all very glad to see thee and thy husband. Come in, to the fire; I dare say thou art cold and hungry after thy journey."

We went in, and the young ladies asked if she would like to go upstairs and "fix" herself before tea. My wife said, "No, I thank you; I shall only stop a little while." "But where art thou going this cold night?" said Mr. Ivens, who had just stepped in.

"I don't know," was the reply. "Well, then," he continued, "I think thou hadst better take off thy things and sit near the fire; tea will soon be ready. "Yes, come Ellen," said Mrs. Ivens, "let me assist thee;" (as she commenced undoing my wife's bonnet-strings;) "don't be frightened, Ellen, I shall not hurt a single hair of thy head. We have heard with much pleasure of the marvellous escape of thee and thy husband, and deeply sympathise with thee in all that thou hast undergone. I don't wonder at thee, poor thing, being timid; but thou needs not fear us; we would as soon send one of our own daughters into slavery as thee; so thou mayest make thyself quite at ease!" These soft and soothing words fell like balm upon my wife's unstrung nerves, and melted her to tears; her fears and prejudices vanished, and from that day she has firmly believed that there are good and bad persons of every shade of complexion.

After seeing Sally Ann and Jacob, two coloured domestics, my wife felt quite at home. After partaking of what Mrs. Stowe's Mose and Pete called a "busting supper," the ladies wished to know whether we could read. On learning we could not, they said if we liked they would teach us. To this kind offer, of course, there was no objection. But we looked rather knowingly at each other, as much as to say that they would have rather a hard task to cram anything into our thick and matured sculls.

However, all hands set to and quickly cleared away the tea-things, and the ladies and their good brother brought out the spelling and copy books and slates, &c., and commenced with their new and green pupils. We had, by stratagem, learned the alphabet while in slavery, but not the writing characters; and, as we had been such a time learning so little, we at first felt that it was a waste of time for any one at our ages to undertake to learn to read and write. But, as the ladies were so anxious that we should learn, and so willing to teach us, we concluded to give our whole minds to the work, and see what could be done. By so doing, at the end of the three weeks we remained with the good family we could spell and write our names quite legibly. They all begged us to stop longer; but, as we were not safe in the State of Pennsylvania, and also as we wished to commence doing something for a livelihood, we did not remain.

When the time arrived for us to leave for Boston, it was like parting with our relatives. We have since met with many very kind and hospitable friends, both in America and England; but we have never been under a roof where we were made to feel more at home, or where the inmates took a deeper interest in our well-being, than Mr. Barkley Ivens and his dear family. May God ever bless them, and preserve each one from every reverse of fortune!

We finally, as I have stated, settled at Boston, where we remained nearly two years, I employed as cabinet-maker and furniture broker, and my wife at her needle; and, as our little earnings in slavery were not all spent on the journey, we were getting on very well, and would have made money, if we had not been compelled by the General Government, at the bidding of the slaveholders, to break up business, and fly from under the Stars and Stripes to save our liberties and our lives.

In 1850, Congress passed the Fugitive Slave Bill, an enactment too infamous to have been thought of or tolerated by any people in the world, except the unprincipled and tyrannical Yankees. The following are a few of the leading features of the above law; which requires, under heavy penalties, that the inhabitants of the *free* States should not only refuse food and shelter to a starving, hunted human being, but also should assist, if called upon by the authorities, to seize the unhappy fugitive and send him back to slavery.

In no case is a person's evidence admitted in Court, in defence of his liberty, when arrested under this law.

If the judge decides that the prisoner is a slave, he gets ten dollars; but if he sets him at liberty, he only receives five.

After the prisoner has been sentenced to slavery, he is handed over to the United States Marshal, who has the power, at the expense of the General Government, to summon a sufficient force to take the poor creature back to slavery, and to the lash, from which he fled.

Our old masters sent agents to Boston after us. They took out warrants, and placed them in the hands of the United States Marshal to execute. But the following letter from our highly esteemed and faithful friend, the Rev. Samuel May, of Boston, to our equally dear and much lamented friend, Dr. Estlin of Bristol, will show why we were not taken into custody.

"21, *Cornhill, Boston,*
"*November* 6*th*, 1850.

"My dear Mr Estlin,

"I trust that in God's good providence this letter will be handed to you in safety by our good friends, William and Ellen Craft. They have lived amongst us about two years, and have proved themselves worthy, in all respects, of our confidence and regard. The laws of this republican and Christian land (tell it not in Moscow, nor in Constantinople) regard them only as slaves—chattels—personal property. But they nobly vindicated their title and right to freedom, two years since, by winning their way to it; at least, so they thought. But now, the slave power, with the aid of Daniel Webster[41] and a band of lesser traitors, has enacted a law, which puts their dearly-bought liberties in the most imminent peril; holds out a strong temptation to every mercenary and unprincipled ruffian to become their kidnapper; and has stimulated the slaveholders generally to such desperate acts for the recovery of their fugitive property, as have never before been enacted in the history of this government.

"Within a fortnight, two fellows from Maçon, Georgia, have been in Boston for the purpose of arresting our friends William and Ellen. A writ was served against them from the United States District Court; but it was not served by the United States Marshal; why not, is not certainly known: perhaps through fear, for a general feeling of indignation, and a cool determination not to allow this young couple to be taken from Boston into slavery, was aroused, and pervaded the city. It is understood that one of the judges told the Marshal that he would not be authorised in breaking the door of Craft's house. Craft kept himself close within the house, armed himself, and awaited with remarkable composure the event. Ellen, in the meantime, had been taken to a retired place out of the city. The Vigilance Committee (appointed at a late meeting in Fanueil Hall) enlarged their numbers, held an almost permanent session, and appointed various subcommittees to act in different ways. One of these committees called repeatedly on Messrs. Hughes and Knight, the slave-catchers, and requested and advised them to leave the city. At first they peremptorily refused to do so, "till they got hold of the niggers.' On complaint of different persons, these two fellows were several times arrested, carried before one of our county courts, and held to BAIL on charges of 'conspiracy to kidnap,' and of 'defamation,' in calling William and Ellen '*slaves*.' At length, they became so alarmed, that they left the city by an indirect route, evading the vigilance of many persons who were on the look-out for them. Hughes, at one time, was near losing his life at the hands of an infuriated coloured man. While these men remained in the city, a prominent whig gentleman sent word to William Craft, that if he would submit peaceably to an arrest, he and his wife should be bought from their owners, cost what it might. Craft replied, in effect, that he was in a measure the representative of all the other fugitives in Boston, some 200 or 300 in number; that, if he gave up, they would all be at the mercy of the slave-catchers, and must fly from the city at any sacrifice; and that, if his freedom could be bought for two cents, he would not consent to compromise the matter in such a way. This event has stirred up the slave spirit of the country, south and north; the United States government is determined to try its hand in enforcing the Fugitive Slave law; and William and Ellen Craft would be prominent objects of the slaveholders' vengeance. Under these circumstances, it is the almost unanimous opinion of their best friends, that they should quit America as speedily as possible, and seek an asylum in England! Oh! shame, shame upon us, that Americans, whose fathers fought against Great Britain, in order to be free, should have to acknowledge this disgraceful fact! God gave us a fair and goodly heritage in this land, but man has cursed it with his devices and crimes against human souls and human rights. Is America the 'land of the free, and the home of the brave?'[42] God knows it is not; and we know it too. A brave young man and a virtuous young woman must fly the American shores, and seek, under the shadow of the British throne, the enjoyment of 'life, liberty, and the pursuit of happiness.'[43]

"But I must pursue my plain, sad story. All day long, I have been busy planning a safe way for William and Ellen to leave Boston. We dare not allow them to go on board a vessel, even in the port of Boston; for the writ is yet in the Marshal's hands, and he *may* be waiting an opportunity to serve it; so I am expecting to accompany them to-morrow to Portland, Maine, which is beyond the reach of the Marshal's authority; and there I hope to see them on board a British steamer.

"This letter is written to introduce them to you. I know your infirm health; but I am sure, if you were stretched on your bed in your last illness, and could lift your hand at all, you would extend it to welcome these poor hunted fellow-creatures. Henceforth, England is their nation and their home. It is with real regret for our personal loss in their departure, as well as burning shame for the land that is not worthy of them, that we send them away, or rather allow them to go. But, with all the resolute courage they have shown in a most trying hour, they themselves see it is the part of a foolhardy rashness to attempt to stay here longer.

"I must close; and with many renewed thanks for all your kind words and deeds towards us,

"I am, very respectfully yours,
"SAMUEL MAY, JUN."

Our old masters, having heard how their agents were treated at Boston, wrote to Mr. Filmore,[44] who was then President of the States, to know what he could do to have us sent back to slavery. Mr. Filmore said that we should be returned. He gave instructions for military force to be sent to Boston to assist the officers in making the arrest. Therefore we, as well as our friends (among whom was George Thompson, Esq., late M.P. for the Tower Hamlets—the slave's long-tried, self-sacrificing friend, and eloquent advocate) thought it best, at any sacrifice, to leave the mock-free Republic, and come to a country where we and our dear little ones can be truly free.—"No one daring to molest or make us afraid."[45] But, as the officers were watching every vessel that left the port to prevent us from escaping, we had to take the expensive and tedious overland route to Halifax.

We shall always cherish the deepest feelings of gratitude to the Vigilance Committee of Boston (upon which were many of the leading abolitionists), and also to our numerous friends, for the very kind and noble manner in which they assisted us to preserve our liberties and to escape from Boston, as it were like Lot from Sodom, to a place of refuge, and finally to this truly free and glorious country; where no tyrant, let his power be ever so absolute over his poor trembling victims at home, dare come and lay violent hands upon us or upon our dear little boys (who had the good fortune to be born upon British soil), and reduce us to the legal level of the beast that perisheth. Oh! may God bless the thousands of unflinching, disinterested abolitionists of America, who are labouring through evil as well as through good report, to cleanse their country's escutcheon from the foul and destructive blot of slavery, and to restore to every bondman his God-given rights; and may God ever smile upon England and upon England's good, much-beloved, and deservedly-honoured Queen, for the generous protection that is given to unfortunate refugees of every rank, and of every colour and clime.

On the passing of the Fugitive Slave Bill, the following learned doctors, as well as a host of lesser traitors, came out strongly in its defence.

The Rev. Dr. Gardiner Spring, an eminent Presbyterian Clergyman of New York, well known in this country by his religious publications, declared from the pulpit that, "if by one prayer he could liberate every slave in the world he would not dare to offer it."

The Rev. Dr. Joel Parker, of Philadelphia, in the course of a discussion on the nature of Slavery, says, "What, then, are the evils inseparable from slavery? There is not one that is not equally inseparable from depraved human nature in other lawful relations."

The Rev. Moses Stuart, D.D., (late Professor in the Theological College of Andover), in his vindication of this Bill, reminds his readers that "many Southern slaveholders are true *Christians*." That "sending back a fugitive to them is not like restoring one to an idolatrous people." That "though we may *pity* the fugitive, yet the Mosaic Law[46] does not authorize the rejection of the claims of the slaveholders to their stolen or strayed *property*."

The Rev. Dr. Spencer, of Brooklyn, New York, has come forward in support of the "Fugitive Slave Bill," by publishing a sermon entitled the "Religious Duty of Obedience to the Laws," which has elicited the highest encomiums from Dr. Samuel H. Cox, the Presbyterian minister of Brooklyn (notorious both in this country and America for his sympathy with the slaveholder).

The Rev. W. M. Rogers, an orthodox minister of Boston, delivered a sermon in which he says, "When the slave asks me to stand between him and his master, what does he ask? He asks me to murder a nation's life; and I will not do it, because I have a conscience,—because there is a God." He proceeds to affirm that if resistance to the carrying out of the "Fugitive Slave Law" should lead the magistracy to call the citizens to arms, their duty was to obey and "if ordered to take human life, in the name of God to take it;" and he concludes by admonishing the fugitives to "hearken to the Word of God, and to count their own masters worthy of all honour."

The Rev. William Crowell, of Waterfield, State of Maine, printed a Thanksgiving Sermon of the same kind, in which he calls upon his hearers not to allow "excessive sympathies for a few hundred fugitives to blind them so as that they may risk increased suffering to the millions already in chains."

The Rev. Dr. Taylor, an Episcopal Clergyman of New Haven, Connecticut, made a speech at a Union Meeting, in which he deprecates the agitation on the law, and urges obedience to it; asking,—"Is that article in the Constitution contrary to the law of Nature, of nations, or to the will of God? Is it so? Is there a shadow of reason for saying it? I have not been able to discover it. Have I not shown you it is lawful to deliver up, in compliance with the laws, fugitive slaves, for the high, the great, the momentous interests of those [Southern] States?"

The Right Rev. Bishop Hopkins, of Vermont, in a Lecture at Lockport, says, "It was warranted by the Old Testament;" and inquires, "What effect had the Gospel in doing away with slavery? None whatever." Therefore he argues, as it is expressly permitted by the Bible, it does not in itself involve any sin; but that every Christian is authorised by the Divine Law to own slaves, provided they were not treated with unnecessary cruelty.

The Rev. Orville Dewey, D.D., of the Unitarian connexion, maintained in his lectures that the safety of the Union is not to be hazarded for the sake of the African race. He declares that, for his part, he would send his own brother or child into slavery, if needed to preserve the Union between the free and the slaveholding States; and, counselling the slave to similar magnanimity, thus exhorts him:—
"*Your right to be free is not absolute, unqualified, irrespective of all consequences. If my espousal of your claim is likely to involve your race and mine together in disasters infinitely greater than your personal servitude, then you ought not to be free. In such a case personal rights ought to be sacrificed to the general good. You yourself ought to see this, and be willing to suffer for a while—one for many.*"

If the Doctor is prepared, he is quite at liberty to sacrifice his "personal rights to the general good." But, as I have suffered a long time in slavery, it is hardly fair for the Doctor to advise me to go back. According to his showing, he ought rather to take my place. That would be practically carrying out his logic, as respects "suffering awhile—one for many."

In fact, so eager were they to prostrate themselves before the great idol of slavery, and, like Baalam,[47] to curse instead of blessing the people whom God had brought out of bondage, that they in bringing up obsolete passages from the Old Testament to justify their downward course, overlooked, or would not see, the following verses, which show very clearly, according to the Doctor's own textbook, that the slaves have a right to run away, and that it is unscriptural for any one to send them back.

In the 23rd chapter of Deuteronomy, 15th and 16th verses, it is thus written:—
"Thou shalt not deliver unto his master the servant which is escaped from his master unto thee. He shall dwell with thee, even among you, in that place which he shall choose in one of thy gates, where it liketh him best: thou shalt not oppress him."

"Hide the outcast. Bewray not him that wandereth. Let mine outcasts dwell with thee. Be thou a covert to them from the face of the spoiler."—(Isa. xvi. 3, 4.)

The great majority of the American ministers are not content with uttering sentences similar to the above, or remaining wholly indifferent to the cries of the poor bondman; but they do all they can to blast the reputation, and to muzzle the mouths, of the few good men who dare to beseech the God of mercy "to loose the bonds of wickedness, to undo the heavy burdens, and let the oppressed go free."[48] These reverend gentlemen pour a terrible cannonade upon "Jonah," for refusing to carry God's message against Nineveh, and tell us about the whale in which he was entombed; while they utterly overlook the existence of the whales which trouble their republican waters, and know not that they themselves are the "Jonahs" who threaten to sink their ship of state, by steering in an unrighteous direction.[49] We are told that the whale vomited up the runaway prophet. This would not have seemed so strange, had it been one of the above lukewarm Doctors of Divinity whom he had swallowed; for even a whale might find such a morsel difficult of digestion.

"I venerate the man whose heart is warm,
Whose hands are pure; whose doctrines and whose life
Coincident, exhibit lucid proof
That he is honest in the sacred cause."

"But grace abused brings forth the foulest deeds,
As richest soil the most luxuriant weeds."

I must now leave the reverend gentlemen in the hands of Him who knows best how to deal with a recreant ministry.

I do not wish it to be understood that all the ministers of the States are of the Baalam stamp. There are those who are as uncompromising with slaveholders as Moses was with Pharaoh,[50] and, like Daniel,[51] will never bow down before the great false God that has been set up.

On arriving at Portland, we found that the steamer we intended to take had run into a schooner the previous night, and was lying up for repairs; so we had to wait there, in fearful suspense, for two or three days. During this time, we had the honour of being the guest of the late and much lamented Daniel Oliver, Esq., one of the best and most hospitable men in the State. By simply fulfilling the Scripture injunction, to take in the stranger, &c., he ran the risk of incurring a penalty of 2,000 dollars, and twelve months' imprisonment.

But neither the Fugitive Slave Law, nor any other Satanic enactment, can ever drive the spirit of liberty and humanity out of such noble and generous-hearted men.

May God ever bless his dear widow, and eventually unite them in His courts above!

We finally got off to St. John's, New Brunswick, where we had to wait two days for the steamer that conveyed us to Windsor, Nova Scotia.

On going into a hotel at St. John's, we met the butler in the hall, to whom I said, "We wish to stop here to-night." He turned round, scratching his head, evidently much put about. But thinking that my wife was white, he replied, "We have plenty of room for the lady, but I don't know about yourself; we never take in coloured folks." "Oh, don't trouble about me," I said; "if you have room for the lady, that will do; so please have the luggage taken to a bed-room." Which was immediately done, and my wife went upstairs into the apartment.

After taking a little walk in the town, I returned, and asked to see the "lady." On being conducted to the little sitting-room, where she then was, I entered without knocking, much to the surprise of the whole house. The "lady" then rang the bell, and ordered dinner for two. "Dinner for two, mum!" exclaimed the waiter, as he backed out of the door. "Yes, for two," said my wife. In a little while the stout, red-nosed butler, whom we first met, knocked at the door. I called out, "Come in." On entering, he rolled his whisky eyes at me, and then at my wife, and said, in a very solemn tone, "Did you order dinner for two, mum?" "Yes, for two," my wife again replied. This confused the chubby butler more than ever; and, as the landlord was not in the house, he seemed at a loss what to do.

When dinner was ready, the maid came in and said, "Please mum, the Missis wishes to know whether you will have dinner up now, or wait till your friend arrives?" "I will have it up at once, if you please." "Thank you, mum," continued the maid, and out she glided.

After a good deal of giggling in the passage, some one said, "You are in for it, butler, after all; so you had better make the best of a bad job." But before dinner was sent up, the landlord returned, and having heard from the steward of the steamer by which we came that we were bound for England, the proprietor's native country, he treated us in the most respectful manner.

At the above house, the boots[52] (whose name I forget) was a fugitive slave, a very intelligent and active man, about forty-five years of age. Soon after his marriage, while in slavery, his bride was sold away from him, and he could never learn where the poor creature dwelt. So after remaining single for many years, both before and after his escape, and never expecting to see again, nor even to hear from, his long-lost partner, he finally married a woman at St. John's. But, poor fellow, as he was passing down the street one day, he met a woman; at the first glance they nearly recognized each other; they both turned round and stared, and unconsciously advanced, till she screamed and flew into his arms. Her first words were, "Dear, are you married?" On his answering in the affirmative, she shrank from his embrace, hung her head, and wept. A person who witnessed this meeting told me it was most affecting.

This couple knew nothing of each other's escape or whereabouts. The woman had escaped a few years before to the free States, by secreting herself in the hold of a vessel; but as they tried to get her back to bondage, she fled to New Brunswick for that protection which her native country was too mean to afford.

The man at once took his old wife to see his new one, who was also a fugitive slave, and as they all knew the workings of the infamous system of slavery, they could (as no one else can,) sympathise with each other's misfortune.

According to the rules of slavery, the man and his first wife were already divorced, but not morally; and therefore it was arranged between the three that he should live only with the lastly married wife, and allow the other one so much a week, as long she requested his assistance.

After staying at St. John's two days, the steamer arrived, which took us to Windsor, where we found a coach bound for Halifax. Prejudice against colour forced me on the top in the rain.[53] On arriving within about seven miles of the town, the coach broke down and was upset. I fell upon the big crotchety driver, whose head stuck in the mud; and as he "always objected to niggers riding inside with white folks," I was not particularly sorry to see him deeper in the mire than myself. All of us were scratched and bruised more or less. After the passengers had crawled out as best they could, we all set off, and paddled through the deep mud and cold and rain, to Halifax.

On leaving Boston, it was our intention to reach Halifax at least two or three days before the steamer from Boston touched there, *en route* for Liverpool; but, having been detained so long at Portland and St. John's, we had the misfortune to arrive at Halifax at dark, just two hours after the steamer had gone; consequently we had to wait there a fortnight, for the *Cambria*.

The coach was patched up, and reached Halifax with the luggage, soon after the passengers arrived. The only respectable hotel that was then in the town had suspended business, and was closed; so we went to the inn, opposite the market, where the coach stopped: a most miserable, dirty hole it was.

Knowing that we were still under the influence of the low Yankee prejudice, I sent my wife in with the other passengers, to engage a bed for herself and husband. I stopped outside in the rain till the coach came up. If I had gone in and asked for a bed they would have been quite full. But as they thought my wife was white, she had no difficulty in securing apartments, into which the luggage was afterwards carried. The landlady, observing that I took an interest in the baggage, became somewhat uneasy, and went into my wife's room, and said to her, "Do you know the dark man downstairs?" "Yes, he is my husband." "Oh! I mean the black man—the *nigger?*" "I quite understand you; he is my husband." "My God!" exclaimed the woman as she flounced out and banged to the door. On going upstairs, I heard what had taken place: but, as we were there, and did not mean to leave that night, we did not disturb ourselves. On our ordering tea, the landlady sent word back to say that we must take it in the kitchen, or in our bed-room, as she had no other room for "niggers." We replied that we were not particular, and that they could send it up to our room,—which they did.

After the pro-slavery persons who were staying there heard that we were in, the whole house became agitated, and all sorts of oaths and fearful threats were heaped upon the "d——d niggers, for coming among white folks." Some of them said they would not stop there a minute if there was another house to go to.

The mistress came up the next morning to know how long we wished to stop. We said a fortnight. "Oh! dear me, it is impossible for us to accommodate you, and I think you had better go: you must understand, I have no prejudice myself; I think a good deal of the coloured people, and have always been their friend; but if you stop here we shall lose all our customers, which we can't do no-how." We said we were glad to hear that she had "no prejudice," and was such a staunch friend to the coloured people. We also informed her that we would be sorry for her "customers" to leave on our account; and as it was not our intention to interfere with anyone, it was foolish for them to be frightened away. However, if she would get us a comfortable place, we would be glad to leave. The landlady said she would go out and try. After spending the whole morning in canvassing the town, she came to our room and said, "I have been from one end of the place to the other, but everybody is full." Having a little foretaste of the vulgar prejudice of the town, we did not wonder at this result. However, the landlady gave me the address of some respectable coloured families, whom she thought, "under the circumstances," might be induced to take us. And, as we were not at all comfortable—being compelled to sit, eat and sleep, in the same small room—we were quite willing to change our quarters.

I called upon the Rev. Mr. Cannady, a truly good-hearted Christian man, who received us at a word; and both he and his kind lady treated us handsomely, and for a nominal charge.

My wife and myself were both unwell when we left Boston, and, having taken fresh cold on the journey to Halifax, we were laid up there under the doctor's care, nearly the whole fortnight. I had much worry about getting tickets, for they baffled us shamefully at the Cunard office. They at first said that they did not book till the steamer came; which was not the fact. When I called again, they said they knew the steamer would come full from Boston; and therefore we had "better try to get to Liverpool by other means." Other mean Yankee excuses were made; and it was not till an influential gentleman, to whom Mr. Francis Jackson, of Boston, kindly gave us a letter, went and rebuked them, that we were able to secure our tickets. So when we went on board my wife was very poorly, and was also so ill on the voyage that I did not believe she could live to see Liverpool.

However, I am thankful to say she arrived; and, after laying up at Liverpool very ill for two or three weeks, gradually recovered.

It was not until we stepped upon the shore at Liverpool that we were free from every slavish fear.

We raised our thankful hearts to Heaven, and could have knelt down, like the Neapolitan exiles,[54] and kissed the soil; for we felt that from slavery

"Heaven sure had kept this spot of earth uncurs'd,
To show how all things were created first."

In a few days after we landed, the Rev. Francis Bishop and his lady came and invited us to be their guests; to whose unlimited kindness and watchful care my wife owes, in a great degree, her restoration to health.

We enclosed our letter from the Rev. Mr. May to Mr. Estlin, who at once wrote to invite us to his house at Bristol. On arriving there, both Mr. and Miss Estlin received us as cordially as did our first good Quaker friends in Pennsylvania. It grieves me much to have to mention that he is no more. Everyone who knew him can truthfully say—

> "Peace to the memory of a man of worth,
> A man of letters, and of manners too!
> Of manners sweet as Virtue always wears
> When gay Good-nature dresses her in smiles."

It was principally through the extreme kindness of Mr. Estlin, the Right Hon. Lady Noel Byron, Miss Harriet Martineau, Mrs. Reid, Miss Sturch, and a few other good friends, that my wife and myself were able to spend a short time at a school in this country, to acquire a little of that education which we were so shamefully deprived of while in the house of bondage. The school is under the supervision of the Misses Lushington, daughters of the Right Hon. Stephen Lushington, D.C.L. During our stay at the school we received the greatest attention from every one; and I am particularly indebted to Thomas Wilson, Esq., of Bradmore House, Chiswick, (who was then the master,) for the deep interest he took in trying to get me on in my studies. We shall ever fondly and gratefully cherish the memory of our endeared and departed friend, Mr. Estlin. We, as well as the Anti-Slavery cause, lost a good friend in him. However, if departed spirits in Heaven are conscious of the wickedness of this world, and are allowed to speak, he will never fail to plead in the presence of the angelic host, and before the great and just Judge, for downtrodden and outraged humanity.

> "Therefore I cannot think thee wholly gone;
> The better part of thee is with us still;
> Thy soul its hampering clay aside hath thrown,
> And only freer wrestles with the ill.
>
> "Thou livest in the life of all good things;
> What words thou spak'st for Freedom shall not die;
> Thou sleepest not, for now thy Love hath wings
> To soar where hence thy hope could hardly fly.
>
> "And often, from that other world, on this
> Some gleams from great souls gone before may shine,
> To shed on struggling hearts a clearer bliss,
> And clothe the Right with lustre more divine.
>
> "Farewell! good man, good angel now! this hand
> Soon, like thine own, shall lose its cunning, too;
> Soon shall this soul, like thine, bewildered stand,
> Then leap to thread the free unfathomed blue."
>
> JAMES RUSSELL LOWELL.

In the preceding pages I have not dwelt upon the great barbarities which are practised upon the slaves; because I wish to present the system in its mildest form, and to show that the "tender mercies of the wicked are cruel."[55] But I do now, however, most solemnly declare, that a very large majority of the American slaves are over-worked, under-fed, and frequently unmercifully flogged.

I have often seen slaves tortured in every conceivable manner. I have seen them hunted down and torn by bloodhounds. I have seen them shamefully beaten, and branded with hot irons. I have seen them hunted, and even burned alive at the stake, frequently for offences that would be applauded if committed by white persons for similar purposes.

In short, it is well known in England, if not all over the world, that the Americans, as a people, are notoriously mean and cruel towards all coloured persons, whether they are bond or free.

"Oh, tyrant, thou who sleepest
On a volcano, from whose pent-up wrath,
Already some red flashes bursting up,
Beware!"

NOTES

1. The biographical details of William and Ellen Craft's lives are drawn from Blackett, *Beating against the Barriers*, 87–137.

2. *The Liberator*, January 12, February 2, 1849. Quoted in Blackett, *Beating against the Barriers*, 90.

3. *Anti-Slavery Standard*, December 26, 1850. Quoted in Blackett, *Beating against the Barriers*, 96. The biblical quotation is taken from Matthew 7:16, "Ye shall know them by their fruits. Do men gather grapes of thorns, or figs of thistles?" and Matthew 7:20, "Wherefore by their fruits ye shall know them."

4. Blackett, *Beating against the Barriers*, 127.

5. Acts 17:26, "And hath made of one blood all nations of men for to dwell on all the face of the earth, and hath determined the times before appointed, and the bounds of their habitation."

6. The distance William and Ellen traveled is roughly 1,000 miles.

7. John Milton (1608–1674) wrote *Paradise Lost* (1667) in an attempt to "justify the ways of God to man." The poem narrates the creation, Satan's fall from grace, and his attempts to get revenge on God by corrupting God's creation, Adam and Eve.

8. The Reverend George Bourne (1780–1845) was an antislavery minister who published *Picture of Slavery in the United States of America* (1834). Reverend Bourne was also known for numerous other works, including a history of Napoleon Bonaparte.

9. A calaboose is a jail.

10. Job 3:17.

11. Delirium tremens is a combination of symptoms caused by excessive use of alcohol. These symptoms include mental confusion, disorientation, and slurred speech, and is often accompanied by hallucinations.

12. A two-wheeled, one-horse carriage with springs.

13. The disciple, called Iscariot, who betrayed Christ.

14. A pass is a note or letter of permission from their owner that all slaves were required to carry during travel.

15. Black slavery, more fully called "peculiar domestic institution of the South."

16. Welts caused by whipping.

17. A soft composition of bread, bran, herbs, etc., that is heated and spread on a cloth. The concoction is then applied to sores or inflamed areas of the body to provide warmth, moisture, and, sometimes, antiseptic qualities.

18. A nickname referring to someone from the Northern states.

19. At first view.

20. Souls relegated to hell.

21. Dred Scott was enslaved to John Emerson, an army surgeon who lived in Missouri. According to the Compromise of 1820, Missouri was a slave state. In 1834, Scott accompanied Emerson to live in Illinois and the Wisconsin Territory, both free areas, before they returned to Missouri. After Emerson's death, Scott petitioned the courts for his freedom on the basis of the time he had lived in free territory. The case reached the Supreme Court, which, in 1857, ruled against Scott. The decision declared that neither slaves nor free blacks could claim United States citizenship. The court further decided that Congress could not prohibit slavery in territories of the United States. Since slaves were property, the Court ruled that violating slavery limited a slaveholder's constitutional right to property.

22. In Genesis 25:29–34, Esau sold his birthright to his younger brother Jacob for a bowl of stew. Later, his mother, Rebecca, urged Jacob to pretend to be Esau to his blind father, Isaac. Isaac blessed Jacob, thinking him Esau. When Esau discovered what had happened, his anger caused Jacob to flee for his life.

23. A benign power seen as guiding individuals through danger with care or, when necessary, intervention.

24. A soap liniment containing camphor.

25. A derogatory term for a black male.

26. Genesis 3:1–24.

27. Though commonly seen as the line dividing the North and the South (and free states from slave states), it is more accurately the boundary line between Pennsylvania and Maryland. The surveyors Charles Mason and Jeremiah Dixon completed their survey of the land in 1767 in an effort to resolve the dispute the two colonies had about the boundary.

28. To run away or escape.

29. John Caldwell Calhoun (1782–1850) was a South Carolina politician who served as vice president (1825–1832), member of the House of Representatives and Senate, secretary of war, and secretary of state. Calhoun argued for states' right as a way of helping Southern states keep slavery and other interests without seceding from the Union.

30. Plundering. The term originally referred to pirates along the Latin American coasts but came to refer to hostile expeditions by groups of Americans into foreign countries in search of plunder.

31. A covered pleasure carriage drawn by a fast horse.

32. Possibly an allusion to the Gullah dialect, which combines English and African linguistic elements. The dialect was used by slaves and their descendants. These people were originally from western Africa and inhabit the sea coast areas of South Carolina, Georgia, and northeastern Florida.

33. A white man (a master).

34. A vest.

35. John Bunyan (1628–1688) was a British preacher whose most well-known literary work is a religious allegory entitled *Pilgrim's Progress* (1678, 1684). The book, written while Bunyan was imprisoned for preaching without a license, is the story of Christian, who is attempting to travel from the City of Destruction to the Celestial City. His adventures include those who, like Apollyon and Giant Despair, try to hurt him or otherwise impede his journey and those who, like Faithful, help him. Christian is ultimately successful in reaching the Celestial City.

36. Elizabeth I (1533–1603) was queen of England (1558–1603). Elizabeth, who was the daughter of Henry VIII and his second wife, Anne Boleyn, became the focus of her half sister Mary's fears of conspiracy. Mary, against bitter Protestant opposition, sought to return England to Roman Catholicism. Elizabeth was Protestant, though she outwardly professed to be Catholic. She would have benefited if Mary had been over-thrown and Protestantism had been restored to England. In 1554, Mary had Elizabeth sent to the Tower of London after Sir Thomas Wyatt's rebellion. Elizabeth was released after two months but remained confined at Wood stock for the next year.

37. Moses, according to Exodus 14, parted the Red Sea and led the Israelites out of Egyptian captivity. In the moments preceding Moses's act, the Israelites were frightened and confused about how they would proceed.

38. An informal, hasty, or secret departure, often without paying one's debts.

39. William Lloyd Garrison (1805–1879) was a journalist and reformer. Garrison edited the *National Philanthropist* and, in 1828, began working with Benjamin Lundy. In 1831, Garrison began editing his own antislavery newspaper, *The Liberator*, which continued to be published until 1865. Wendell Phillips (1811–1884) was an American orator, reformer, and abolitionist. He joined William Lloyd Garrison's group in 1837 and advocated ending slavery, even at the expense of splitting the Union. He is well-known for his speech denouncing those who participated in the mob that lynched abolitionist editor Elijah P. Lovejoy in Alton, Illinois, in 1837. Theodore Parker (1810–1860) was an American Unitarian minister and committed abolitionist.

40. In the parable contained in Luke 10:30–37, a Samaritan helped a stranger on the road from Jerusalem to Jericho who had been beaten and robbed by thieves. The Samaritan expected no reward for his effort. Jesus encouraged his disciples to do likewise.

41. Daniel Webster (1782–1852) was an American lawyer and statesman. He served in the United States House of Representatives from 1813 to 1817 and in the Senate beginning in 1827. Webster also served as secretary of state for Presidents William Henry Harrison, John Tyler, and Millard Fillmore. Though he was personally opposed to slavery, Webster believed strongly in preserving the Union. Webster further believed that the federal government should avoid interfering with policies established within individual states. Webster drew the criticism of antislavery supporters when he sponsored the Compromise of 1850,

which contained the Fugitive Slave Act requiring the North to return escaped slaves to the South.

42. The final line of "The Star-Spangled Banner," written by Francis Scott Key during the War of 1812: "And the Star-Spangled Banner in Triumph shall wave / O'er the land of the free and the home of the brave."

43. A reference to the Declaration of Independence, "We hold these truths to be self-evident, that all men are created equal, that they are endowed by their Creator with certain unalienable Rights, that among these are Life, Liberty, and the Pursuit of Happiness."

44. Millard Fillmore (1800–1874) was the thirteenth president of the United States. He was Zachary Taylor's vice president and became president when Taylor died in office. He remained in office for thirty-two months (1850–1853). As president, he approved the Compromise of 1850. Fillmore also served in the House of Representatives (1833–1835 and 1837–1843).

45. Craft most likely alludes to Ezekiel 34:28, "And they shall no more be a prey to the heathen, neither shall the beast of the land devour them; but they shall dwell safely, and none shall make them afraid." Similar formulations appear in Leviticus 26:6, Job 11:19, Isaiah 17:2, Micah 4:4, Nahum 2:11, and Zephaniah 3:13.

46. The law given to Moses by God in Exodus 20–23. This law became ancient Judaic law.

47. Baal (or the plural, Baalim) was one of a multitude of local deities worshipped in Syria and Palestine. Each town or natural quality had its own Baal. In general, Baalim were gods of fertility. Though the Israelites believed Yahweh had led them out of Egyptian captivity, many were tempted to worship Baal in hopes of receiving an abundant harvest. Baal was also thought to have a sexual influence.

48. Isaiah 58:6.

49. According to the book of Jonah in the Old Testament, Jonah was a Hebrew prophet who was commanded by God to go to Nineveh. Jonah refused and tried to flee aboard a ship sailing for Tarshish. God sent a storm as punishment. Jonah, realizing the danger his presence posed to the others aboard the ship, told the sailors to throw him overboard to stop the storm, which they did. Jonah was swallowed by a great fish (called a whale in Matthew 12:40), in whose stomach he remained for three days before being cast out.

50. Moses was born in Egypt in the late 1300s BC. His mother hid him near the Nile River when pharaoh ordered all male Hebrew children killed. Moses was discovered by pharaoh's daughter and raised as an Egyptian. Moses was later told by God to lead the Israelites from Egypt. Once they crossed the Red Sea and reached the desert, God made a covenant with Moses, in which God promised to protect Israel if they observed the laws God gave to Moses. After leaving Egypt, the Israelites wandered in the desert for forty years before reaching Canaan. Because Moses had broken one of God's laws, Moses was allowed by God to see Canaan, but not to cross the Jordan River into Canaan.

51. According to the book of Daniel in the Old Testament, Daniel (late 600s BC?–late 500s BC?) was a Hebrew prophet who was held captive by the Babylonians. Daniel interpreted dreams for Nebuchadnezzar and the writing on the wall for Belshazzar. He was saved by God when he was cast into a den of lions for refusing to worship Darius the Mede as a god.

52. A bootblack, or one who shines boots and shoes.

53. See Litwack, *North of Slavery*, esp. pp. 30–112.

54. Napoleon I (also known as Napoleon Bonaparte) (1769–1821) crowned himself emperor of France and established an empire that included much of western and central Europe. His ambition contributed to his eventual downfall. Napoleon was exiled to Elba in 1814. He returned from the island in February 1815 and reclaimed his power. In June 1815, he was exiled again, this time to St. Helena, a tiny island in the South Atlantic Ocean.

55. Proverbs 12:10.

Bibliography

Abramson, Doris M. "William Wells Brown: America's First Negro Playwright." *Educational Theatre Journal* 20 (1968): 370–75.

Andrews, William L., ed. *From Fugitive Slave to Free Man: The Autobiographies of William Wells Brown*. New York: Mentor Books, 1993.

Andrews, William L. "Inter(racial)textuality in Nineteenth-Century Southern Narrative." In *Influence and Intertextuality in Literary History*, edited by Jay Clayton and Eric Rothstein, 298–317. Madison: University of Wisconsin Press, 1991.

Andrews, William L. "Mark Twain and James W. C. Pennington: Huckleberry Finn's Smallpox Lie." *Studies in American Fiction* 9 (Spring 1981): 103–12.

Andrews, William L. "Mark Twain, William Wells Brown, and the Problem of Authority in New South Writing." In *Southern Literature and Literary Practice*, edited by Jefferson Humphries, 1–21. Athens: University of Georgia Press, 1990.

Andrews, William L. *To Tell a Free Story: The First Century of Afro-American Autobiography, 1760–1865*. Urbana: University of Illinois Press, 1986.

Andrews, William L., ed. *Two Biographies by African-American Women*. New York: Oxford University Press, 1991.

Aptheker, Herbert. *American Negro Slave Revolts*. New York: International Publishers, 1983.

Aptheker, Herbert. *Essays in the History of the American Negro*. New York: International Publishers, 1945.

Aptheker, Herbert. *Nat Turner's Slave Rebellion. Together with the Full Text of the So-Called "Confessions" of Nat Turner Made in Prison in 1831*. New York: Humanities Press, 1966.

Barbour, James. "Nineteenth Century Black Novelists: A Checklist." *Minority Voices* 3 (1980): 27–43.

Barrett, Lindon. "African-American Slave Narratives: Literacy, the Body, Authority." *American Literary History* 7.3 (1995): 415–42.

Barrett, Lindon. "Hand-Writing: Legibility and the White Body in *Running a Thousand Miles for Freedom*." *American Literature* 69 (June 1997): 315–36.

Bayliss, John F., ed. *Black Slave Narratives*. New York: Macmillan, 1970.

Bell, Howard Holman. *A Survey of the Negro Convention Movement, 1830–1861*. New York: Arno Press, 1969.

Blackett, R. J. M. *Beating against the Barriers: Biographical Essays in Nineteenth-Century Afro-American History*. Baton Rouge: Louisiana State University Press, 1986.

Blackett, R. J. M. *Building an Antislavery Wall*. Baton Rouge: Louisiana State University Press, 1983.

Bland, Sterling Lecater, Jr. *Voices of the Fugitives: Runaway Slave Stories and Their Fictions of Self-Creation*. Westport, CT: Greenwood Press, 2000.

Blockson, Charles L. *The Underground Railroad*. New York: Prentice-Hall, 1987.

Braxton, Joanne M. *Black Women Writing Autobiography: A Tradition within a Tradition*. Philadelphia: Temple University Press, 1989.

Breen, Patrick H. "Contested Communion: The Limits of White Solidarity in Nat Turner's Virginia." *Journal of the Early Republic* 27 (Winter 2007): 685–703.

Brooks, Daphne A. *Bodies in Dissent: Spectacular Performances of Race and Freedom, 1850–1910*. Durham, NC: Duke University Press, 2006.

Browder, Laura. *Slippery Characters: Ethnic Impersonators and American Identities*. Chapel Hill: University of North Carolina Press, 2000.

Brown, William Wells. *The American Fugitive in Europe: Sketches of Places and People Abroad*. New York: Negro Universities Press, 1969.

Brown, William Wells. *Clotel; or, The President's Daughter*. Edited by Joan E. Cashin. Armonk, NY: M. E. Sharpe, 1996.

Brown, William Wells. *The Rising Son; or, The Antecedents and Advancement of the Colored Race*. New York: Johnson Reprint Corp., 1970.

Browne, Stephen Howard. "'This Unparalleled and Inhuman Massacre': The Gothic, the Sacred, and the Meaning of Nat Turner." *Rhetoric and Public Affairs* 3 (Fall 2000): 309–32.

Brusky, Sarah. "The Travels of William and Ellen Craft: Race and Travel Literature in the Nineteenth Century." *Prospects: An Annual of American Cultural Studies* 25 (2000): 177–92.

Bruss, Elizabeth W. *Autobiographical Acts: The Changing Situation of a Literary Genre*. Baltimore: Johns Hopkins University Press, 1976.

Butterfield, Stephen. *Black Autobiography in America*. Amherst: University of Massachusetts Press, 1974.

Carroll, Joseph Cephas. *Slave Insurrections in the United States 1800–1865*. New York: Negro Universities Press, 1968.

Castronovo, Russ. "Radical Configurations of History in the Era of American Slavery." *American Literature* 65 (September 1993): 523–47.

Clarke, John Henrik, ed. *William Styron's Nat Turner: Ten Black Writers Respond*. Boston: Beacon Press, 1968.

Costanzo, Angelo. *Surprising Narrative: Olaudah Equiano and the Beginnings of Black Autobiography*. Westport, CT: Greenwood Press, 1987.

David, Jay, ed. *Black Defiance: Black Profiles in Courage*. New York: Morrow, 1972.

Donaldson, Susan V. "Telling Forgotten Stories of Slavery in the Postmodern South." *Southern Literary Journal* 40, Special Issue: History, Memory, and Mourning (Spring 2008): 267–83.

Dorsey, Peter A. "De-Authorizing Slavery: Realism in Stowe's *Uncle Tom's Cabin* and Brown's *Clotel*." *ESQ* 41 (1995): 256–88.

Dorsey, Peter A. "The Slave Narratives as Rhetorical Art." In *The Art of Slave Narrative: Original Essays in Criticism and Theory*, edited by John Sekora and Darwin T. Turner, 83–95. Macomb: Western Illinois University, 1982.

duCille, Ann. "Where in the World Is William Wells Brown? Thomas Jefferson, Sally Hemings, and the DNA of African-American Literary History." *American Literary History* 12.3 (2000): 443–62.

Egerton, Douglas R. *Gabriel's Rebellion: The Virginia Slave Conspiracies of 1800 and 1802*. Chapel Hill: University of North Carolina Press, 1993.

Egerton, Douglas R. "The Scenes Which Are Acted in St. Domingo: The Legacy of Revolutionary Violence in Early National Virginia." In *Antislavery Violence: Sectional, Racial, and Cultural Conflict in Antebellum America*, edited by John R. McKivigan and Stanley Harrold, 41–64. Knoxville: University of Tennessee Press, 1999.

Ellison, Curtis W., and E. W. Metcalf Jr. *William Wells Brown and Martin R. Delany: A Reference Guide*. Boston: G. K. Hall, 1978.

Emmeluth, Nancy Elizabeth. "William Wells Brown's *My Southern Home* and the African-American Literary Tradition." PhD dissertation, State University of New York at Albany, 1995.

Ernest, John. "The Reconstruction of Whiteness: William Wells Brown's *The Escape; or, A Leap for Freedom*." *PMLA* 113 (October 1998): 1108–21.

Ernest, John. "Representing Chaos: William Craft's *Running a Thousand Miles for Freedom*." *PMLA* 121 (March 2006): 469–83.

Ernest, John. "Traumatic Theology in the *Narrative of the Life of Henry Box Brown, Written by Himself*." *African American Review* 41 (Spring 2007): 19–31.

Fabi, M. Giulia. "Representing Slavery in Nineteenth-Century Britain: The Anxiety of Non/Fictional Authorship in Charles Dickens' *American Notes* (1842) and William Wells Brown's *Clotel* (1853)." In *Images of America: Through the European Looking-Glass*, edited by William L. Chew III, 125–40. Brussels, Belgium: VUB University Press, 1997.

Fabi, M. Giulia. "The 'Unguarded Expressions of the Feelings of the Negroes': Gender, Slave Resistance, and William Wells Brown's Revisions of *Clotel*." *African American Review* 27 (Winter 1993): 639–54.

Fabricant, Daniel S. "Thomas R. Gray and William Styron: Finally, a Critical Look at the 1831 *Confessions of Nat Turner*." *American Journal of Legal History* 37 (July 1993): 332–61.

Farrison, William Edward. "Clotel, Thomas Jefferson, and Sally Hemings." *College Language Association Journal* 17 (December 1973): 147–74.

Farrison, William Edward. "The Kidnapped Clergyman and Brown's Experience." *College Language Association Journal* 18 (1975): 507–15.

Farrison, William Edward. *William Wells Brown: Author and Reformer*. Chicago: University of Chicago Press, 1969.

Faust, Drew Gilpin, ed. *The Ideology of Slavery: Proslavery Thought in the Antebellum South, 1830–1860*. Baton Rouge: Louisiana State University Press, 1981.

Filler, Louis. *The Crusade against Slavery, 1830–1860*. New York: Harper, 1960.

Fleischner, Jennifer. *Mastering Slavery: Memory, Family, and Identity in Women's Slave Narratives*. New York: New York University Press, 1996.

Foner, Eric, ed. *Nat Turner*. Englewood Cliffs, NJ: Prentice-Hall, 1971.

Foster, Frances Smith. *Witnessing Slavery: The Development of Ante-Bellum Slave Narratives.* Westport, CT: Greenwood Press, 1979.

Franklin, John Hope, and Loren Schweninger. *Runaway Slaves: Rebels on the Plantation.* New York: Oxford University Press, 1999.

Freehling, Alison Goodyear. *Drift toward Dissolution: The Virginia Slavery Debate of 1831–1832.* Baton Rouge: Louisiana State University Press, 1982.

Garraty, John A. *A Short History of the American Nation.* 2 vols. New York: Harper Collins, 1993.

Gates, Henry Louis, Jr. *Figures in Black: Words, Signs, and the "Racial" Self.* New York: Oxford University Press, 1987.

Genovese, Eugene D. *From Rebellion to Revolution: Afro-American Slave Revolts in the Making of the Modern World.* Baton Rouge: Louisiana State University Press, 1979.

Genovese, Eugene D. *Roll, Jordan, Roll: The World the Slaves Made.* New York: Pantheon Books, 1974.

Gilmore, Paul. "'De Genewine Artekil': William Wells Brown, Blackface Minstrelsy, and Abolitionism." *American Literature* 69 (December 1997): 743–80.

Greenberg, Kenneth S., ed. *The Confessions of Nat Turner and Related Documents.* Boston: Bedford Books of St. Martin's Press, 1996.

Greenspan, Ezra. *William Wells Brown: An African American Life.* New York: W. W. Norton and Co., 2014.

Harding, Vincent. *There Is a River: The Black Struggle for Freedom in America.* New York: Harcourt Brace Jovanovich, 1981.

Harding, Vincent. "You've Taken My Nat and Gone." In *The Critical Response to William Styron,* edited by Daniel W. Ross, 133–39. Westport, CT: Greenwood Press, 1995.

Harrold, Stanley. *The Abolitionists and the South, 1831–1861.* Lexington: University of Kentucky Press, 1995.

Haskett, Norman D. "Afro-American Images of Africa: Four Antebellum Authors." *Ufahamu* 3 (1972): 29–40.

Hedin, Robert. "The American Slave Narrative: The Justification of the Picaro," *American Literature* 53 (January 1982): 630–45.

Heermance, J. Noel. *William Wells Brown and* Clotelle*: A Portrait of the Artist in the First Negro Novel.* Hamden, CT: Archon, 1969.

Heller, Murray. "The Names of Slaves and Masters: Real and Fictional." *Literary Onomastics Studies* 6 (1979): 130–48.

Hooper, M. Clay. "'It Is Good to Be Shifty': William Wells Brown's Trickster Critique of Black Autobiography." *Modern Language Studies* 38, Collaborations: NeMLA at 40 (Winter 2009): 28–45.

Huggins, Nathan Irvin. *Black Odyssey: The Afro-American Ordeal in Slavery.* New York: Pantheon Books, 1977.

Jefferson, Paul, ed. *The Travels of William Wells Brown, including the Narrative of William Wells Brown, a Fugitive Slave, and the American Fugitive in Europe, Sketches of Places and People Abroad.* New York: Markus Weiner Publishers, 1991.

Joyner, Charles. "A Single Southern Culture: Cultural Interaction in the Old South." In *Black and White Cultural Interaction in the Antebellum South,* edited by Ted Ownby, 3–22. Jackson: University Press of Mississippi, 1993.

Jugurtha, Lillie Butler. "Point of View in the Afro-American Slave Narratives: A Study of Narratives by Douglass and Pennington." In *The Art of Slave Narrative: Original Essays in Criticism and Theory*, edited by John Sekora and Darwin T. Turner, 110–19. Macomb: Western Illinois University, 1982.

Katz, William L. *Eyewitness: The Negro in American History*. New York: Pitman Publishing Corporation, 1967.

Kaye, Anthony E. "Neighborhoods and Nat Turner: The Making of a Slave Rebel and the Unmaking of a Slave Rebellion." *Journal of the Early Republic* 27 (Winter 2007): 705–20.

Keetley, Dawn. "Racial Conviction, Racial Confusion: Indeterminate Identities in Women's Slave Narratives and Southern Courts." *A–B: Auto-Biography Studies* 10 (Fall 1995): 1–20.

Kolchin, Peter. *Unfree Labor: American Slavery and Russian Serfdom*. Cambridge, MA: Belknap Press of Harvard University Press, 1987.

Levine, Lawrence W. *Black Culture and Black Consciousness: Afro-American Folk Thought from Slavery to Freedom*. New York: Oxford University Press, 1977.

Levine, Robert S. "'Whiskey, Blacking, and All': Temperance and Race in William Wells Brown's *Clotel*." In *The Serpent in the Cup: Temperance in American Literature*, edited by David S. Reynolds and Debra J. Rosenthal, 93–114. Amherst: University of Massachusetts Press, 1997.

Lewis, Richard O. "Irony in the Fiction of William Wells Brown and Charles Waddell Chesnutt." PhD dissertation, State University of New York at Buffalo, 1978.

Lewis, Richard O. "Literary Conventions in the Novels of William Wells Brown." *College Language Association Journal* 29 (December 1985): 129–56.

Loewenberg, Bert James, and Ruth Bogin, eds. *Black Women in Nineteenth-Century American Life: Their Words, Their Thoughts, Their Feelings*. University Park: Pennsylvania State University Press, 1976.

Lowance, Mason, ed. *Against Slavery: An Abolitionist Reader*. New York: Penguin Books, 2000.

Lucasi, Stephen. "William Wells Brown's 'Narrative' and Traveling Subjectivity." *African American Review* 41 (Fall 2007): 521–39.

MacKethan, Lucinda H. "Huck Finn and the Slave Narratives: Lighting Out as Design." *Southern Review* 20 (Spring 1984): 247–64.

MacKethan, Lucinda H. "Metaphors of Mastery in the Slave Narratives." In *The Art of Slave Narrative: Original Essays in Criticism and Theory*, edited by John Sekora and Darwin T. Turner, 55–69. Macomb: Western Illinois University, 1982.

Magdol, Edward. *The Antislavery Rank and File: A Social Profile of the Abolitionists' Constituency*. Westport, CT: Greenwood Press, 1986.

Mayer, Henry. *All on Fire: William Lloyd Garrison and the Abolition of Slavery*. New York: St. Martin's Press, 1998.

McBride, Dwight. *Impossible Witnesses: Truth, Abolition, and Slave Testimony*. New York: New York University Press, 2001.

McCaskill, Barbara. "'Yours Very Truly': Ellen Craft—The Fugitive as Text and Artifact." *African American Review* 28 (Winter 1994): 509–29.

McCoy, Beth A. "Race and the (Para)Textual Condition." *PMLA* 121.1 (2006): 156–69.

McMichael, George, ed. *Anthology of American Literature: Volume I: Colonial through Romantic*. New York: Macmillan, 1974.

McMillan, Uri. "Ellen Craft's Radical Techniques of Subversion." *e-misférica* 5.2 (2008): n.p. http://hemisphericinstitute.org/hemi/en/e-misferica-52/mcmillan.

Miller, Ruth, and Peter J. Katopes. "Modern Beginnings: William Wells Brown, Charles Waddell Chesnutt, Martin R. Delany, Paul Laurence Dunbar, Sutton E. Griggs, Frances Ellen Watkins Harper, and Frank J. Webb." In *Black American Writers: Bibliographical Essays*, vol. 1, *The Beginnings through the Harlem Renaissance and Langston Hughes*, edited by M. Thomas Inge, Maurice Duke, and Jackson R. Bryer, 133–60. New York: St. Martin's, 1978.

Millette, HollyGale. "Exchanging Fugitive Identity: William and Ellen Craft's Transatlantic Reinvention (1850–69)." *Imagining Transatlantic Slavery*, edited by Cora Kaplan and John Oldfield, 61–76. New York: Palgrave 2010.

Mitchell, Angelyn. "Her Side of His Story: A Feminist Analysis of Two Nineteenth-Century Antebellum Novels—William Wells Brown's *Clotel* and Harriet E. Wilson's *Our Nig*." *American Literary Realism* 24 (Spring 1992): 7–21.

Mitchell, Verner D. "To Steal Away Home: Tracing Race, Slavery, and Difference in Selected Writings of Thomas Jefferson, David Walker, William Wells Brown, Ralph Waldo Emerson, and Pauline Elizabeth Hopkins." PhD dissertation, Rutgers University, 1995.

Morton, Patricia, ed. *Discovering the Women in Slavery: Emancipating Perspectives on the American Past*. Athens: University of Georgia Press, 1996.

Mulvey, Christopher. "The Fugitive Self and the New World of the North: William Wells Brown's Discovery of America." In *The Black Columbiad: Defining Moments in African American Literature and Culture*, edited by Werner Sollors and Maria Diedrich, 99–111. Cambridge, MA: Harvard University Press, 1994.

Nichols, Charles H. *Many Thousand Gone: The Ex-Slaves' Account of Their Bondage and Freedom*. Leiden, Netherlands: E. J. Brill, 1963.

Oates, Stephen B. *The Fires of Jubilee: Nat Turner's Fierce Rebellion*. New York: Harper and Row, 1975.

Olney, James. "'I Was Born': Slave Narratives, Their Status as Autobiography and as Literature." In *The Slave's Narrative*, edited by Charles T. Davis and Henry Louis Gates Jr., 148–75. New York: Oxford University Press, 1985.

Osofsky, Gilbert. *Puttin' on Ole Massa: The Slave Narratives of Henry Bibb, William Wells Brown, and Solomon Northrup*. New York: Harper and Row, 1969.

Parramore, Thomas C. *Southampton County, Virginia*. Charlottesville: University Press of Virginia, 1978.

Paulin, Diana R. "Acting Out Miscegenation." In *African American Performance and Theater History: A Critical Reader*, edited by Harry J. Elam and David Krasner. New York: Oxford University Press, 2001.

Pease, Jane H., and William H. Pease. *They Who Would Be Free: Blacks' Search for Freedom, 1830–1861*. New York: Atheneum, 1974.

Perry, Lewis. *Radical Abolitionism: Anarchy and the Government of God in Antislavery Thought*. Ithaca, NY: Cornell University Press, 1973.

Quarles, Benjamin. *Black Abolitionists*. New York: Oxford University Press, 1969.

Quarles, Benjamin. *Frederick Douglass*. Washington DC: Associated Publishers, 1948.

Raboteau, Albert J. *Slave Religion: The "Invisible Institution" in the Antebellum South*. New York: Oxford University Press, 1978.

Rice, C. Duncan. *The Rise and Fall of Black Slavery*. London: Macmillan, 1975.

Richardson, Marilyn, ed. *Maria Stewart: America's First Black Woman Political Writer*. Bloomington: Indiana University Press, 1987.

Robbins, Hollis. "The Deliverance of Henry 'Box' Brown and Antebellum Postal Politics." *American Studies* 50 (Spring/Summer 2009): 5–25.

Rosselot, Gerald S. "*Clotel*, a Black Romance." *College Language Association Journal* 23 (1980): 296–302.

Ruff, Loren K. "William Wells Brown: Dramatic Apostle Abolition." *New England Theatre Journal* 2 (1991): 73–83.

Ruggles, Jeffrey. *The Unboxing of Henry Brown*. Richmond: Library of Virginia, 2003.

Samuels, Ellen. "'A Complication of Complaints': Untangling Disability, Race, and Gender in William and Ellen Craft's *Running a Thousand Miles for Freedom*." *MELUS* 31, Race, Ethnicity, Disability, and Literature (Fall 2006): 15–47.

Scales, Laura Thiemann. "Narrative Revolutions in Nat Turner and Joseph Smith." *American Literary History* 24 (Summer 2013): 205–33.

Scully, Randolph Ferguson. "'I Come Here Before You Did and I Shall Not Go Away': Race, Gender, and Evangelical Community on the Eve of the Nat Turner Rebellion." *Journal of the Early Republic* 27 (Winter 2007): 661–84.

Sengupta, Ashis. "William Wells Brown's *Clotel*: A Critique of Slave Life in America." In *Indian Views on American Literature*, edited by Desai A. A. Mutalik, 117–25. New Delhi, India: Prestige, 1998.

Simpson, Mark. *Trafficking Subjects: The Politics of Mobility in Nineteenth Century America*. Minneapolis: University of Minnesota Press, 2005.

Simson, Rennie. "Christianity: Hypocrisy and Honesty in the Afro-American Novel of the Mid-Nineteenth Century." *University of Dayton Review* 15 (Spring 1982): 11–16.

Sloss, Phyllis Ann. "Hierarchy, Irony, and the Thesis of Death in William Wells Brown's *Clotel; or, The President's Daughter*." PhD dissertation, State University of New York at Buffalo, 1976.

Sobel, Mechal. *Trabelin' On: The Slave Journey to an Afro-Baptist Faith*. Princeton, NJ: Princeton University Press, 1988.

Sollors, Werner. "A British Mercenary and American Abolitionists: Literary Retellings from 'Inkle and Yarico' and John Gabriel Stedman to Lydia Maria Child and William Wells Brown." In *(Trans)Formations of Cultural Identity in the English-Speaking World*, edited by Jochen Achilles and Carmen Birkle, 95–123. Heidelberg, Germany: Carl Winter Universitatsverlag, 1998.

Starling, Marion Wilson. *The Slave Narrative: Its Place in American History*, 2nd ed. Washington, D.C.: Howard University Press, 1988.

Stepto, Robert B. *From behind the Veil: A Study of Afro-American Narrative*. Urbana: University of Illinois Press, 1979.

Stetson, Erlene. "Studying Slavery: Some Literary and Pedagogical Considerations on the Black Female Slave." In *All the Women Are White, All the Blacks Are Men, but Some of Us Are Brave: Black Women's Studies*, edited by Gloria T. Hull, Patricia Bell Scott, and Barbara Smith, 61–84. Old Westbury, NY: Feminist Press, 1982.

Stone, Albert E. *The Return of Nat Turner: History, Literature, and Cultural Politics in Sixties America*. Athens: University of Georgia Press, 1992.

Styron, William. *The Confessions of Nat Turner*. New York: Modern Library, 1994. Originally published New York: Random House, 1967.

Sundquist, Eric J. *To Wake the Nations: Race in the Making of American Literature*. Cambridge, MA: Belknap Press of Harvard University Press, 1993.

Swift, David E. *Black Prophets of Justice: Activist Clergy before the Civil War*. Baton Rouge: Louisiana State University Press, 1989.

Swindells, Julia. *The Uses of Autobiography*. London: Taylor and Francis, 1995.

Taylor, Yuval. *I Was Born a Slave: An Anthology of Classic Slave Narratives*. 2 vols. Chicago: Lawrence Hill Books, 1999.

Thomas, Herman E. *James W. C. Pennington: African American Churchman and Abolitionist*. New York: Garland Publishing, 1995.

Tragle, Henry Irving. *The Southampton Slave Revolt of 1831: A Compilation of Source Material*. Amherst: University of Massachusetts Press, 1971.

Wardrop, Daneen. "Ellen Craft and the Case of Salomé Muller in *Running a Thousand Miles for Freedom*." *Women's Studies* 33 (2004): 961–84.

Warner, Lucille Schulberg. *From Slave to Abolitionist: The Life of William Wells Brown*. New York: Dial Press, 1976.

Washington, James Melvin. *Frustrated Fellowship: The Black Baptist Quest for Social Power*. Macon, GA: Mercer, 1986.

Weinauer, Ellen M. "'A Most Respectable Looking Gentleman': Passing, Possession, and Transgression in *Running a Thousand Miles for Freedom*." In *Passing and the Fictions of Identity*, edited by Elaine K. Ginsberg, 37–56. Durham, NC: Duke University Press, 1996.

West, James L. W., III, ed. *Conversations with William Styron*. Jackson: University Press of Mississippi, 1985.

White, Deborah Gray. *Ar'n't I a Woman? Female Slaves in the Plantation South*. New York: Norton, 1985.

Wilentz, Gay. "Authenticating Experience: North Carolina Slave Narratives and the Politics of Race." *North Carolina Literary Review* 1 (Summer 1992): 115–37.

Wolff, Cynthia Griffin. "Passing Beyond the Middle Passage: Henry 'Box' Brown's Translations of Slavery." *Massachusetts Review* 37 (Spring 1996): 23–44.

Wood, Marcus. "'All Right!': The Narrative of Henry Box Brown as a Test Case for the Racial Prescription of Rhetoric and Semiotics." *Proceedings of the American Antiquarian Society* 107 (April 1997): 65–104.

Wood, Marcus. *Blind Memory: Visual Representations of Slavery in England and America 1780–1865*. New York: Routledge, 2000.

Wood, Peter H. "Nat Turner: The Unknown Slave as Visionary Leader." In *Black Leaders of the Nineteenth Century*, edited by Leon Litwack and August Meier, 21–40. Urbana: University of Illinois Press, 1988.

Yellin, Jean Fagan. *The Intricate Knot: Black Figures in American Literature, 1776–1863*. New York: New York University Press, 1972.

Yellin, Jean Fagan, and John C. Van Horne, eds. *The Abolitionist Sisterhood: Women's Political Culture in Antebellum America*. Ithaca, NY: Cornell University Press, 1994.

Index

abolitionist movement: beginnings, 4–6; black involvement, 6–7; conflict within, 9–10; expansion, 6–7; New England, 3; religion and, 7–8, 9; slave narratives and, 3; women and, 8–10. *See also* abolitionist organizations; abolitionists; lecture circuit, abolitionist

abolitionist organizations: American Antislavery Society, 75; Connecticut State Anti-Slavery Society, 180; Massachusetts Abolition Society, 9; Massachusetts Anti-Slavery Society, 9; New England Anti-Slavery Society, 9; Western New York Anti-Slavery Society, 74, 117. *See also* abolitionist movement; abolitionists

abolitionists: British, 238; William Wells Brown, 73–74, 116–117; in Craft narrative, 260, 266, 272, 273, 274–275, 279; Frederick Douglass, 73–74, 238; William Lloyd Garrison, 5, 9, 116, 275; Benjamin Lundy, 5, 116; need for slave narratives, 3; James W. C. Pennington, 179, 218; as sponsors of slave narratives, 1, 3, 8, 11; traditional religious practice and, 8; Richard D. Webb, 238. *See also* abolitionist movement; abolitionist organizations; lecture circuit, abolitionist; May, Samuel J.

Adams, John Quincy: thoughts on slavery, 4

Adventures of Huckleberry Finn (Twain), 2

Africa, African American emigration to: James W. C. Pennington opposition to, 180, 218, 221

Africa, Dahomey: William Craft trip to, 238

African Aid Society, 238

African American literature: *Autobiography of Malcolm X* (Malcolm X), 2; *Behind the Scenes: Thirty Years a Slave and Four Years in the White House* (Keckley), 14; *Beloved* (Morrison), 2; black autobiography versus white autobiography, 12; *Black Boy* (Wright), 2; *The Black Man, His Antecedents, His Genius, and His Achievements* (W. W. Brown), 74; *Book of American Negro Poetry* (Johnson), 14; *Clotel; or, The President's Daughter* (W. W. Brown), 74; *Dessa Rose* (Williams), 20; eighteenth-century slave narratives, 2–4; *The Escape; or, A Leap for Freedom: A Drama in Five Acts* (W. W. Brown), 74; first-person narrative voice in, 14; *The Known World* (Jones), 2; legacy of slave narratives, 13–15; *My Southern Home, or The South and Its People* (W. W. Brown), 74; *Narrative of the Life of Frederick Douglass* (Douglass), xi; nineteenth-century slave narratives, xi–xii, 1–4, 6–8, 10–15; *Ol' Prophet Nat* (Panger), 20; *The Rising Son; or, The Antecedents and Advancement of the Colored Race* (W. W. Brown), 74; *The Souls of Black Folk* (Du Bois), xii; *A Text Book of the Origin and History, &c. & c. of Colored People* (Pennington) 180; *Up from Slavery* (Washington), 14. See also *Confessions of Nat Turner, The* (original edition, 1831); *Fugitive Blacksmith; or, Events in the History of James W. C. Pennington, The* (third edition, 1850); *Narrative of Henry Box Brown* (first edition, 1849); *Narrative of Lunsford Lane, The* (third edition, 1845); *Narrative of William W. Brown, A Fugitive Slave* (second edition, 1848); *Running*

301

a Thousand Miles for Freedom; or, The Escape of William and Ellen Craft from Slavery (original text, 1860)
African Methodist Episcopal Church, 180, 185
alcohol, problems with: in W. Brown narrative, 85, 100, 106; in Craft narrative, 247, 249, 250, 251; James W. C. Pennington, 180
Allen, John F., 145–148; on religion of the South, 148; on slaves and religion, 147; swearing habit, 147; treatment of sick tobacco worker, 146; on white people and religion, 148
Allen, Richard, 180
American Antislavery Society, 75
Anti Slavery Bugle, 1
anti-slavery movement. *See* abolitionist movement; abolitionist organizations; abolitionists; lecture circuit, abolitionist
Anti-Slavery Standard, William and Ellen Craft article in, 238
Arkansas: ban on free blacks, 257
auctions, slave, 10, 74; in H. Brown narrative, 141, 154; in W. Brown narrative, 92–93, 96, 107; in Craft narrative, 245, 246, 248–249; preparing old slaves for, 92. *See also* slaves, selling
Autobiography of Malcolm X, 2

Baker, Kyle: *Nat Turner*, 20
Baltimore, Maryland, 122, 237; in H. Brown narrative, 169; in Craft narrative, 269, 270, 271; in Pennington narrative, 198, 199, 222
baptism: in H. Brown narrative, 132, 135–136; of Lunsford Lane, 54; in Pennington narrative, 229; slave, 30, 135–136; of Nat Turner, 30; in Turner narrative, 30
Baptist Church: in H. Brown narrative, 144; in W. Brown narrative, 91; in Lane narrative, 54
Behind the Scenes: Thirty Years a Slave and Four Years in the White House (Keckley), 14
Belmonte, Louis, 242, 243
Beloved (Morrison), 2
bill of sale, slave: in Lane narrative, 54, 55, 60, 69–71; in Pennington narrative, 183
Bishop, Francis, 285
Black Abolitionists (Quarles), 180
Black Boy (Wright), 2
Black Man, His Antecedents, His Genius, and His Achievements. The (W. W. Brown), 74
Book of American Negro Poetry (Johnson), 14

Boston, Massachusetts, 8, 74, 122, 237; in H. Brown narrative, 157, 163, 167, 169; in Craft narrative, 275, 276, 277, 278, 279, 284, 285; in Lane narrative, 61, 62, 63, 64, 69
Bourne, George: *Picture of Slavery*, 243
Bouve, Pauline Carrington Rust: *Their Shadows Before: A Story of the Southampton Insurrection*, 20
Brave Music of a Distant Drum (Herbstein), 2
British antislavery movement, 238
Brown, Henry "Box," 43, 121–122, 238; abolitionist lecture circuit, 122, 157–158; becoming Baptist, 144; escape from slavery, 121, 122, 154–156; marriage and family, 121, 148–149; relocation to England, 122; tobacco factory work, 121, 142, 144–145. See also *Narrative of Henry Box Brown* (first edition, 1849)
Brown, Wells, 114, 115
Brown, William Wells, 2, 13, 43, 73–74, 237, 238; abolitionist speaker, 74, 117; birth, 73, 82; *The Black Man, His Antecedents, His Genius, and His Achievements*, 74; Civil War and, 74; *Clotel; or, The President's Daughter*, 74; death, 74; *The Escape; or, A Leap for Freedom: A Drama in Five Acts*, 74; escape from slavery, 73, 111–114; father, 73, 74, 82; freedom, 73, 116; helping slaves escape to Canada, 73, 116–117; hiring out to slave trader, 73, 91–96; mother, 82, 106; *My Southern Home, or The South and Its People*, 74; as physician, 74; relocation from Kentucky to Missouri, 73, 85; *The Rising Son; or, The Antecedents and Advancement of the Colored Race*, 74. See also *Narrative of William W. Brown, A Fugitive Slave* (second edition, 1848)
Byron, Noel, 286

California, 169
Canada: William Wells Brown helping slaves escape to, 73, 116–117; William Wells Brown thoughts of escaping to, 88, 101, 108; in Craft narrative, 279, 282–285
chattel principle, 183, 184, 186, 246
children, slave: biracial offspring of slaveholder and slave, 250–252; in H. Brown narrative, 131–133; in Craft narrative, 242–244, 250–253; in Lane narrative,

47–48; master's children treatment of, 191; in Pennington narrative, 190–191; separated from mother, 252–253; in Turner narrative, 27–28; white, 242–244

Christianity, 20, 121, 238; in W. Brown narrative, 81; in Craft narrative, 245; Fugitive Slave Act defenders and, 280–281; in James Pennington narrative, 217; in slave narratives, 10, 13; slaveholding religion versus true, 121, 133; in Turner narrative, 29–30. *See also* God; Jesus; religion

civil rights, 6; Maria W. Stewart and, 9

Civil War, 10; African Americans fighting in, 74; William Wells Brown and, 74; James W. C. Pennington and, 180

Cleveland, Ohio, 73, 115, 116

Clotel; or, The President's Daughter (W. W. Brown), 74

Colburn, John, 86

Company of African Merchants, 238

Compromise of 1850, 122. *See also* Fugitive Slave Act of 1850

Confessions of Nat Turner, The (original edition, 1831), 19–20; "Commonwealth, vs. Nat Turner," 37–38; "Confession," 27–37; fictional accounts, 20; God and religion, 20, 29–30; introductory material, 24–27; "A list of murdered in the Insurrection," 38; "A List of Negroes Brought before the Court of Southampton," 39–40; Savior, 29, 30; title page, 23

Confessions of Nat Turner (Styron), 2, 20

Connecticut, 180; abolitionist organization, 180; in Pennington narrative, 221. *See also* Hartford, Connecticut

Connecticut State Anti-Slavery Society, 180

Coutts, Burdett, 246

Cox, Samuel H.: Fugitive Slave Act defender, 280

Craft, Ellen, 43, 126, 237–239; anti-slavery lecture circuit, 237; death, 239; father, 242; mother, 242, 252; Ockham school student, 238, 286; relocation to England, 237. *See also* Craft, William; Craft family; *Running a Thousand Miles for Freedom; or, The Escape of William and Ellen Craft from Slavery* (original text, 1860)

Craft, William, 43, 126, 237–239; anti-slavery lecture circuit, 237; death, 239; Ockham school student, 238, 286; relocation to England, 237; travel to Dahomey, Africa, 238. *See also* Craft, Ellen; Craft family; *Running a Thousand Miles for Freedom; or, The Escape of William and Ellen Craft from Slavery* (original text, 1860)

Craft family: closing school, 239; debt, 238–239; lease of plantation, 238; opening school, 238; return to Georgia from England, 238. *See also* Craft, Ellen; Craft, William; *Running a Thousand Miles for Freedom; or, The Escape of William and Ellen Craft from Slavery* (original text, 1860)

Crowell, William: Fugitive Slave Act defender, 280

Crummell, Alexander, 238

Culver, William B., 85

death sentence, 26, 247. *See also* hanging

Delaware River, 275

Dessa Rose (Williams), 20

Dewey, Orville: Fugitive Slave Act defender, 281

double consciousness, xii

Douglass, Frederick, 73–74, 79, 238; marriage to Anna Murray, 180; *Narrative of the Life of Frederick Douglass,* xi

Douglass, Margaret: jailing of, 255

Dred: A Tale of the Great Dismal Swamp (Stowe), 20

Dred Scott decision, 257–258

Du Bois, W. E. B.: *The Souls of Black Folk,* xii

education, 73, 74, 179, 238, 239; in Craft narrative, 254–255, 286; in Lane narrative, 47, 48; laws prohibiting for slaves, 2, 254–255; literacy barriers for slaves, 11, 74; in Pennington narrative, 212, 218, 219, 227; reading restrictions for slaves, 11; in Turner narrative, 28; 36

England: abolitionists in, 238; Henry "Box" Brown relocation to, 122; William and Ellen Craft relocation to, 237, 238, 285–286; Ockham school, 238, 286; relocation of former slaves to, 122, 237, 285–286. *See also* lecture circuit entrepreneurship: Lunsford Lane childhood ventures, 48–49; Lunsford Lane lumber business, 54; Lunsford Lane tobacco manufacturing, 51–52, 54–55

Episcopal Church, 54, 146, 151, 195

escape: Henry "Box" Brown, 121, 122, 154–156, 172; William Wells Brown, 73, 111–114; William and Ellen Craft, 258–274; motif in nineteenth-century slave narratives, 4, 6, 7; James W. C. Pennington, 179, 197–211

Escape; or, A Leap for Freedom: A Drama in Five Acts, The (W. W. Brown), 74

Estlin, John Bishop, 277, 285, 286

family. *See* children, slave; fathers, slave; marriage and family, slave; mothers, slave

fathers, slave: William Wells Brown, 73, 74, 82; James W. C. Pennington, 193; Ellen Craft, 242. *See also* marriage and family

field work: in W. Brown narrative, 82–83, 84, 89, 105; in Craft narrative, 243, 249; in Lane narrative, 47, 48; in Pennington narrative, 199

Fillmore, Millard: owners of William and Ellen Craft petition and, 237, 279

Florida, 180

food, slave, 50–51, 223–224

free states, 4; in H. Brown narrative, 138, 157, 159; in W. Brown narrative, 86, 88, 110, 111; in Craft narrative, 248, 256, 259, 270, 275, 277, 283; in Pennington narrative, 189, 196, 224. *See also* California; Connecticut; Illinois; Maine; Massachusetts; New York State; Ohio; Pennsylvania

Freeland, Robert, 85

friends, importance of to slaves, 141–142

Fugitive Blacksmith; or, Events in the History of James W. C. Pennington, The (third edition, 1850), 179–181; author's note, 182; beating by master, 194; birth and childhood, 179, 190; carpentry work, 192; Christianity, 217; decline of slaveholding families, 226–227; escape, 179, 197–211; escape decision, 193, 196; escape preparation, 196–197; family left behind, 220–223; father's beating by master, 193; God, 189, 196, 206, 211, 216, 217, 218, 219, 220, 222, 224, 228, 229, 230, 231, 232, 233; "great moral dilemma" of fabricating story during escape, 179, 201–204, 206; hiring out to blacksmith, 179, 192; hiring out to stone mason, 179, 191; Jesus, 212, 222, 229, 230, 233; letters, 228–233; master's children treatment of slave children, 191; narrative first edition, 181; narrative prefaces, 182–190; narrative title page, 182; opposition to African American emigration to Africa, 180, 218, 221; overseer cruelty, 191, 194–195; as pastor, 180; Quaker help during escape, 211–215; religion, 224–225; slave children, 190–191; slave clothing in Maryland, 224; slave food in Maryland, 223–224; slave marriage, 225; slave religion and religious instruction, 224–225; slave spying for master, 195; slavery and education, 219; taken captive for no papers, 200–201; teaching job, 218–219; travels to Long Island, 216

Fugitive Slave Act of 1850, 74, 122, 180, 237, 277, 278; clergy as defenders of, 280–282

Garnet, Henry Highland, 238

Garrison, William Lloyd, 5, 9, 116, 275

Genius of Universal Emancipation, The (Lundy), 5, 116

Georgia, 179, 237, 238; in H. Brown narrative, 153; in W. Brown narrative, 96; in Craft narrative, 241, 246–247, 252, 253, 255, 256, 260, 263, 266, 277; in Pennington narrative, 202, 232; slave code and laws, 246–247, 254, 257

God: in H. Brown narrative, 128, 130, 131, 132, 133, 135, 138, 144, 145, 150, 152, 153, 154, 155, 156, 157, 159, 164, 165, 166, 171; in W. Brown narrative, 81, 104, 107, 112, 113; in Craft narrative, 241, 242, 244, 245, 253, 254, 257, 258, 259, 260, 270, 271, 274, 276, 277, 278, 279, 282; Fugitive Slave Act defenders and, 280–281; in Lane narrative, 50, 53, 54, 69; in Pennington narrative, 189, 196, 206, 211, 216, 217, 218, 219, 220, 222, 224, 228, 229, 230, 231, 232, 233; slavemaster seen as, 132; Maria W. Stewart and, 9; in Turner narrative, 29, 30. *See also* Christianity; Jesus; religion

Gray, Thomas R.: *The Confessions of Nat Turner and*, 19–20, 24–26

half-hanging, 143
hanging: of Gabriel Prosser, 19; of Nat Turner, 1, 20. *See also* Lynch law
Harned, William, 185, 186
Hartford, Connecticut: Talcott Street Church, 180
Haskell, Friend, 85, 89
Hathaway, J. C.: preface to *Narrative of William W. Brown, A Fugitive Slave*, 74, 80–82
Henson, Josiah, 238
Herbstein, Manu: *Brave Music of a Distant Drum*, 2
Hill, J. B., 105
hiring out slaves, 44, 121, 179; to blacksmiths, 179, 192; in H. Brown narrative, 142, 144–145; in W. Brown narrative, 85–86, 88–96, 105, 106–111; carpentry work, 192; in Pennington narrative, 191, 192; public house and hotel work, 85–86; to slave traders, 73, 91–96; to steamboat captains, 88–89, 105, 106–109; steamboat work, 88–89, 105, 106–111; to stone masons, 179, 191; tobacco factory work, 121, 142, 144–145
Homoselle (Tiernan), 20
Hopkins, John Henry: Fugitive Slave Act defender, 281
house servants, 73; in W. Brown narrative, 83, 90, 93, 94; in Lane narrative, 47, 50, 53

Illinois, 102
Ivens, Barkley, 275

Jackson, Francis, 285
jail: for accusations of being abolitionist, 63–65; in H. Brown narrative, 151, 169; in W. Brown narrative, 85, 92, 93, 97, 98, 100, 101, 104, 105; in Craft narrative, 255; Margaret Douglass in, 255; in Lane narrative, 56, 63–65; for teaching slave to read, 255; in Turner narrative, 24, 25, 27, 38
James, G.P.R.: *The Old Dominion; or the Southampton Massacre*, 20
Jesus: in H. Brown narrative, 127, 132, 144; in Pennington narrative, 212, 222, 229, 230, 233; slavemaster's son seen as, 132. *See also* Christianity; God; religion

Johnson, James Weldon: *Book of American Negro Poetry*, 14
Jones, Edward P.: *The Known World*, 2

Keckley, Elizabeth: *Behind the Scenes: Thirty Years a Slave and Four Years in the White House*, 14
Kentucky, 73; in W. Brown narrative, 82, 90; in Craft narrative, 257; in Pennington narrative, 183, 190
Known World, The (Jones), 2

Lane, Lunsford, 12, 43–44; buying freedom/ manumission, 44, 52, 54; marriage, 44, 49–50; tobacco manufacturer, 44, 51–52, 54–55. *See also Narrative of Lunsford Lane, The* (third edition, 1845)
lecture circuit: abolitionist, 122, 237, 238; Henry "Box" Brown, 122, 157–158; William Wells Brown, 74, 117; William and Ellen Craft, 237; James W. C. Pennington, 180
Liberator, The, 9, 116; William and Ellen Craft escape story in, 237
Locke, Alain: *New Negro, The*, 14
Louisiana, 153, 190, 194, 201, 243; slave code/ laws, 246; slave revolt, 5. *See also* New Orleans
L'Ouverture, Toussaint: Saint-Domingue slave uprising, 2
Lovejoy, Elijah P., 86, 87, 88, 169
Lundy, Benjamin: *The Genius of Universal Emancipation*, 5, 116
Lutheran Church, 227
Lynch law, 166

Maine, 279
Malcolm X: *Autobiography of Malcolm X*, 2
manumission, 52, 54. *See also* Lane, Lunsford; *Narrative of Lunsford Lane, The* (third edition, 1845)
marriage and family, slave, 44, 121, 238–239; in H. Brown narrative, 135, 140–141, 148–152; in W. Brown narrative, 86, 109–110; in Craft narrative, 253; in Lane narrative, 49–50, 53, 55; in Pennington narrative, 220–223, 225. *See also* children, slave; fathers, slave; mothers, slave
Martineau, Harriet, 286

Maryland, 179; in Pennington narrative, 183, 184, 185, 188, 190, 191, 192, 196, 199, 220, 221, 223; slave clothing in, 224; slave food in, 223–224. *See also* Baltimore, Maryland

Massachusetts: abolitionist organizations, 9; in H. Brown narrative, 157; in W. Brown narrative, 115; in Craft narrative, 275; in Lane narrative, 63, 64, 69. *See also* Boston, Massachusetts

Massachusetts Abolition Society, 9

Massachusetts Anti-Slavery Society, 9

May, Samuel J., 122, 172; anti-slavery speech in H. Brown narrative, 158–171; letter regarding William and Ellen Craft, 277–279, 285

McIntosh, Francis, 87

McKinney, Samuel, 88

Methodist Church, 50, 152, 184, 192, 195, 225, 227

Miller, John F., 242, 243

Missions of Freedmen, Presbyterian Committee of, 180

Mississippi: in H. Brown narrative, 153, in Craft narrative, 246, 257; in Pennington narrative, 183; slave codes/laws in, 257

Mississippi River, 5, 73, 85, 88. See also *Narrative of William W. Brown, a Fugitive Slave* (second edition, 1848)

Missouri, 73; in W. Brown narrative, 82, 83, 87, 104, 105, 107; slave code, 257. *See also* St. Louis, Missouri

Missouri River, 82, 94

Missouri Territory, 73

Morrison, Toni: *Beloved,* 2

mothers, slave: in H. Brown narrative, 131; in W. Brown narrative, 82, 83, 105–106; children separated from, 252–253; Ellen Craft, 242, 252; in Craft narrative, 252–253. *See also* marriage and family, slave

Muller, Daniel, 242, 243

Muller, Dorothea, 242, 243

Muller, Salomé, 242–243

murder, 5; in H. Brown narrative, 143, 169; in W. Brown narrative, 87, 99; in Craft narrative, 247, 253, 257, 258; in Lane narrative, 50; in Turner narrative, 24, 25, 31–33, 37. *See also* Turner's Rebellion, Nat

My Southern Home, or The South and Its People (W. W. Brown), 74

"Narrative of Fugitive Slaves" (Peabody), vii

Narrative of Henry Box Brown (first edition, 1849), 121–122; abolitionist lecture circuit, 122, 157–158; anti-slavery speech by Samuel J. May, 158–171; author's introduction, 129–130; birth and infancy, 130–131; boyhood waiting on master and mistress, 133; breaking up families, 140–141; broken promises of freedom upon payment, 121, 140; Christianity, 121, 133; escape box engraving, 172; escape box journey to freedom, 122, 154–156, 172; escape decision, 153; family connections, 121; God, 128, 130, 131, 132, 133, 135, 138, 144, 145, 150, 152, 153, 154, 155, 156, 157, 159, 164, 165, 166, 171; half-hanging of slaves, 143; hope of freedom, 140; "Hymn of Thanksgiving," 128; importance of friends to slaves, 141–142; and Jesus, 127, 132, 144; joining Baptist Church, 144; marriage and wife's sale, 148–149; Massachusetts stay, 157; master as God, 132; master's death, 142; master's son as Jesus Christ, 132; master's son as new master, 142; masters and female slaves, 135; mother's influence, 131; narrative preface, 125–128; narrative publisher's note, 125; narrative title page, 124; Northern hypocrisy, 135, 144; old master, 138–139; overseer treatment of slaves, 139; parents, 131; payment of family's room and board, 149; and religion, 121, 132, 133, 135–136, 144; religion in narrative preface, 125–128; relocation to England, 122; resolve to escape, 121–122; sale of author's family, 150–152; slave codes, 143; slave marriage, 135; slave religion and baptism, 135–136; slave treatment post–Nat Turner's Rebellion, 143; slaveholders encouraging stealing, 121, 137–138; slaveholders versus non-slaveholders, 136–137; tobacco manufactory overseer, 145–148; tobacco manufactory work, 142, 144–145; true Christianity versus slaveholding religion, 121, 133; vow to speak for slaves, 153; whippings and slavery, 136, 137, 143, 167; wife and children, 121; witnessing other slaves, 134; worry about becoming field slave, 133–134

Narrative of the Life of Frederick Douglass (Douglass), xi

Narrative of Lunsford Lane, The (third edition, 1845), 43–44; author's note, 46; birth and infancy, 47; buying family's freedom, 55; buying freedom/manumission, 52, 54; church and baptism, 54; court and jail regarding abolitionist accusations, 63–65; early boyhood, 47–48; early entrepreneur days, 48–49; family, 53; feeling free, 52–53; first child, 50; first plan to become free, 48; food, 50–51; God, 50, 53, 54, 69; hiring out, 51; as house servant, 53; journey to Raleigh from Boston, 62–63; leaving New York for Boston, 61; leaving North Carolina for New York, 61; legal order to leave North Carolina, 55–58; lumber business, 54; marriage, 49–50; masters, 47, 48, 53; master's death, 51; narrative first edition, 44; narrative preface, 46–47; narrative title page, 45; petitioning legislature to remain in North Carolina, 58–60; questioning regarding abolitionist activities, 66; religion, 54; return to family and their journey north, 67–69; seeking permission to return to North Carolina to retrieve family, 62; slave bills of sale, 54, 55, 60, 69–71; tarring and feathering, 66–67; tobacco manufacturer, 51–52, 54–55; whipping slaves, 50

Narrative of William W. Brown, a Fugitive Slave (second edition, 1848), 73–75; abolitionist activities, 74, 116–117; beating by Samuel McKinney, 88; birth, 82; Christianity, 81; cruelty toward slaves, 74, 83–84, 86, 87, 91, 93–98; everyday life of field hands, 82–83; family members sold to different people, 86; father, 82; field work, 89; God, 81, 104, 107, 112, 113; helping slaves get to Canada, 116–117; hiring out to J. Colburn, 86; hiring out to M. Freeland, 85; hiring out to J. B. Hill on steamer *Otto,* 105, 106–108; hiring out to E. P. Lovejoy, 86–88; hiring out to E. Price, 108–111; hiring out to O. Reynolds on steamboat *Enterprise,* 88–89; hiring out to J. Walker as soul driver, 91–96; as house slave, 90; introductory letter from Edmund Quincy, Esq., 79; literacy barriers, 74; master, 82; mother, 82, 83, 105–106; move to St. Louis, 85; narrative note, 79; narrative preface by J. C. Hathaway, 74, 80–82; narrative style and structure, 74; narrative title page, 78; new name, 74, 115; overseer Friend Haskell, 85, 89; preparing old slaves for market, 92; printer's helper, 86–87; religion, 74, 90; sent back to Samuel Willi, 108; sent to find new master and decision to escape to Canada, 101; slave auctions, 74, 107; slave drivers, 107; slave marriage, 109–110; slave pens, 92–93, 96; slaveholding religion, 74, 90; smoking of, 85; sold to tailor Samuel Willi, 105; stay in Cleveland on way to Canada, 116; steamboat *Missouri* work, 85; successful escape attempt, 74, 111–114; taken in by Wells Brown, 114–115; temperance work, 117; thoughts of escaping to Canada, 88, 101, 108; trip to fortune teller, 110–111; unsuccessful escape attempts, 74, 85, 102–104; whippings, 83, 85, 86, 87, 88, 91, 93, 97, 98, 105, 107, 110, 112, 121; white people sold into slavery, 99–100; witness to killing of slave, 99

Negro Convention, first annual meeting of, 180

New England Anti-Slavery Society, 9

New Negro Renaissance, 14

New Orleans, 73; in W. Brown narrative, 89, 91, 92, 93, 94, 96, 99, 100, 104, 105, 110, 220; in Craft narrative, 242, 267

New York City, 179, 180; Brooklyn, 179; in Craft narrative, 268; First Colored Presbyterian Church, 180; in Lane narrative, 52, 61, 68, 69; in Pennington narrative, 184, 216, 218

New York Herald, 4

New York State: abolitionist organization, 74, 117; Buffalo, 73; in Craft narrative, 252; Long Island, 216; in Pennington narrative, 196, 218; Western, 81

New York Sun, 4

North Carolina, 43; in H. Brown narrative, 152; in Craft narrative, 264, 265; in Lane narrative, 47, 55–56, 58, 61, 70, 71; slave code, 56. *See also* Raleigh, North Carolina

Nottoway River, 34

Ohio, 73; in W. Brown narrative, 110, 111, 115, 116; in Craft narrative, 243, 269. *See also* Cleveland, Ohio

Ohio River, 111
Ol' Prophet Nat (Panger), 20
Old Dominion; or the Southampton Massacre, The (James), 20
Oliver, Daniel, 282
overseers, 4, 121; abuse of children, 191; abusive, 232; John F. Allen, 145–148, 154; Blackstone, 191; in H. Brown narrative, 131, 136, 139, 142, 143, 144–148, 154; in W. Brown narrative, 82, 83, 84, 85, 89, 90, 105; G. Cook, 82, 83, 84; in Craft narrative, 247; cruel, 50, 191, 194–195; Friend Haskell, 85, 89, 90, 105; in Lane narrative, 50, 54; murdered in Turner's Rebellion, 38; in Pennington narrative, 184, 191, 194–195, 212, 223, 232; in Turner narrative, 29, 38

Panger, Daniel: *Ol' Prophet Nat,* 20
Parker, Joel: Fugitive Slave Act defender, 280
Parker, Nate: *The Birth of a Nation*, 20
Parker, Theodore, 275
passing. See Craft, Ellen; *Running a Thousand Miles for Freedom; or, The Escape of William and Ellen Craft from Slavery* (original text, 1860)
Peabody, Ephraim: "Narrative of Fugitive Slaves," vii
Pennington, James W. C., 2, 13, 179–180, 238; alcoholism, 180; anti-slavery speaking engagements, 180; birth and childhood, 179, 190; death, 180; destitution, 180; escape, 179, 197–211; honorary doctorate, 180; officiant at Frederick Douglass and Anna Murray wedding, 180; opposition to African American emigration to Africa, 180, 218, 221; as pastor, 180; *Text Book of the Origin and History, &c. & c. of Colored People, A.,* 180; Underground Railroad, 180, 221. See also *Fugitive Blacksmith; or, Events in the History of James W. C. Pennington, The* (third edition, 1850)
Pennsylvania: in Craft narrative, 270, 276, 285; in Pennington narrative, 196, 211, 216, 217, 220. See also Philadelphia, Pennsylvania
Philadelphia, Pennsylvania, 179, 237; in H. Box narrative, 122, 155, 156, 157, 172; in Craft narrative, 262, 263, 264, 266, 270, 271, 272, 273, 274, 275; in Lane narrative, 60, 65, 68, 69; in Pennington narrative, 215, 216

Phillips, Wendell, 275
Picture of Slavery (Bourne), 243
preachers and pastors: in H. Brown narrative, 143, 144; in W. Brown narrative, 90, 107, 132; Methodist, 225; James, W. C. Pennington, 180; in Pennington narrative, 185, 206, 215, 225; Quaker, 215; silencing of black, 143; Nat Turner, 20
Price, Enoch, 108, 110, 114
Prosser, Gabriel: hanging of, 19; Richmond, Virginia, slave uprising, 2, 19
punishment, slave: beating, 88, 193, 194; in H. Brown narrative, 136, 137, 143, 167; in W. Brown narrative, 83, 85, 86, 87, 88, 91, 93, 97, 98, 105, 107, 110, 112, 121; burning, 87; in Craft narrative, 257; half-hanging, 143; in Lane narrative, 50, 66–67; in Pennington narrative, 194; smoking, 85; tarring and feathering, 66–67; whipping, 50, 83, 85, 86, 87, 88, 91, 93, 97, 98, 105, 107, 112, 121, 136, 137, 143, 167, 257. *See also* death sentence; hanging; jail
Purves, Robert, 275

Quakers: William Wells Brown and, 73, 114–115; William and Ellen Craft and, 237, 285; James W. C. Pennington and, 179, 211–215. *See also* Society of Friends
Quarles, Benjamin: *Black Abolitionists,* 180
Quincy, Edmund, 79
Raleigh, North Carolina, 43; in Lane narrative, 47, 49, 52, 54, 57, 59, 60, 61, 62, 63, 65, 66, 67, 68, 69, 70, 71
reading. *See* education, slave
religion, 74, 121; abolitionist movement and, 7–8, 9; abolitionist practice of, 8; African Methodist Episcopal, 180, 185; John F. Allen comments on, 147–148; Baptist, 54, 91, 136, 144; in H. Brown narrative, 132, 133, 135–136, 144; in H. Brown narrative preface, 125–128; in W. Brown narrative, 90; Episcopal, 54, 146, 151, 195; former slave as pastor, 180; in Lane narrative, 54; Lutheran, 227; Methodist, 50, 152, 184, 192, 195, 225, 227; in Pennington narrative, 224–225; Quaker, 211–215, 237, 275; questioning traditional practices of, 8; slave, 135–136, 224–225; slave and baptism, 135–136; slave and religious instruction,

224–225; in slave narratives, 7, 10, 13; slaveholding, 74, 90; Maria W. Stewart language and, 9; true Christianity versus slaveholding, 121, 133; Turner's Rebellion and slaveholder religious rhetoric, 20. *See also* Christianity; God; Jesus; preachers and pastors

Reynolds, Otis, 88, 89, 90

Richardson, George, 246

Rising Son; or, The Antecedents and Advancement of the Colored Race, The (W. W. Brown), 74

robbery and theft, 6, 13, 121; in H. Brown narrative, 137–138, 165; in Craft narrative, 258; in Lane narrative, 53; slaveholders encouraging, 121, 137–138; in Turner narrative, 28, 33, 36

Rogers, W. M.: Fugitive Slave Act defender, 280

Roper, Moses, 238

Running a Thousand Miles for Freedom; or, The Escape of William and Ellen Craft from Slavery (original text, 1860), 237–239; Christianity, 238, 245; Ellen's mistress, 244; Ellen's parents and early life, 242, 252; England arrival, 285; escape, 258–274; escape preparation, 254, 256; free in Philadelphia, 274–276; God, 241, 242, 244, 245, 253, 254, 257, 258, 259, 260, 270, 271, 274, 276, 277, 278, 279, 282; living in Boston, 276; marriage, 253; narrative preface by William Craft, 241; narrative title page, 240; old masters' letters to Millard Fillmore, 237, 279; slave laws, 246–247, 254; slave owners and female slaves, 247–248; slaveholder's biracial children, 250–252; travel to Halifax, Nova Scotia, 279, 282–285; whipping slaves, 257; white children sold as slaves, 242–244; William in slave auction, 245; William's old master, 244–245; William's plan to disguise Ellen as white master, 253–254

Scott, Alexander, 96

slave codes and laws, 2, 143, 246–247, 254; Arkansas, 257; Georgia, 246–247, 254, 257; Kentucky, 257; Louisiana, 246; Mississippi, 257; Missouri, 257; North Carolina, 56; South Carolina, 246; striking slaves and, 247; teaching reading and, 254–255; Tennessee, 257. *See also* Dred Scott decision; Fugitive Slave Act of 1850

slave driver: in W. Brown narrative, 86, 107, 111, 153

slave narratives, eighteenth-century, 2–3; African origins and, 3; birth-of-narrator beginning, 4; idealized African experiences in, 4; inhumane European culture in, 4; nautical adventures in, 4

slave narratives, nineteenth-century: abolition of slavery as primary focus, 3; abolitionist movement and, 3; abolitionist sponsorship, 1; birth-of-narrator beginning, 4; bondage-to-freedom narrative, 13; Christianity in, 10, 13; conclusion, 11; didactive purpose, 13; disparity between blackness and assimilation in, 6; education and reading restrictions for slaves, 11; episodic structure, 7; escape attempts, 11; escape desire, 7, 12; escape motif, 4, 6, 7; escape plotting, 7, 12; farms and plantations in, 3, 4; historical importance, 1; introductory material, 10, 12; literary importance, 2; literary legacy of, 13–15; new life in free territory, 7; oral, 6, 7; popularity, 1, 4; reflections on slavery, 7; sensationalism in, 3; slave auctions in, 10; slave owners in, 4, 10; slavery description, 4; structural and thematic sameness among, 10–11; supplementary material, 11; sympathetic characters in, 4, 6, 8; taking new last name, 12; as triangular, 13; white audience and, 12–13. See also *Confessions of Nat Turner, The* (original edition, 1831); *Fugitive Blacksmith; or, Events in the History of James W. C. Pennington, The* (third edition, 1850); *Narrative of Henry Box Brown* (first edition, 1849); *Narrative of Lunsford Lane, The* (third edition, 1845); *Narrative of William W. Brown, A Fugitive Slave* (second edition, 1848); *Running a Thousand Miles for Freedom; or, The Escape of William and Ellen Craft from Slavery* (original text, 1860)

slave narrators, 3; audience approach strategies, 12–13; female, 10; reconstructive voice, 11–13. *See also* Brown, Henry "Box"; Brown, William Wells; Craft, Ellen; Craft,

William; Lane, Lunsford; Pennington, James W. C.; Turner, Nat
slave religion: baptism and, 135–136; religious instruction and, 224–225. *See also* Christianity; God; Jesus; religion
slave states: in Craft narrative, 241, 244, 246, 251, 253, 254, 256, 257, 260, 263; in Pennington narrative, 190, 191, 221, 233. *See also* Arkansas; Florida; Georgia; Kentucky; Louisiana; Maryland; Mississippi; Missouri; North Carolina; South Carolina; Tennessee; Texas; Virginia
slave trader, William Wells Brown and, 73, 91–96. *See also* slave driver
slave uprisings, 2, 5–6, 7; Charleston, South Carolina, 2, 5; effects of on blacks, 2; Richmond, Virginia, 2, 19; Saint-Domingue (Santo Domingo), 2, 19; Southampton, Virginia, 1, 2, 5, 19–20, 143. *See also Confessions of Nat Turner, The* (original edition, 1831)
slaveholding religion, 74, 90; true Christianity versus 121, 133
slavery: John Quincy Adams thoughts on, 4; chattel principle and, 183, 184, 186, 246; descriptions of in slave narratives, 4; Northern hypocrisy about, 135, 144; reflections on in slave narratives, 7; white people sold into, 99–100, 242–244
Slavery as It Is (Weld), 99
slaves, selling: in H. Brown narrative, 148–149; in W. Brown narrative, 80, 86, 93; in Craft narrative, 243; in Lane narrative, 53; in Pennington narrative, 184, 192, 221. *See also* auction, slave; bill of sale, slave
Smith, Gerrit, 187–188
smoking punishment, 85
Society of Friends, 275. *See also* Quakers
"soul driver," 80, 91
Souls of Black Folk, The (Du Bois), xii
South Carolina: in Craft narrative, 246, 251, 256, 260, 263; slave codes/laws, 246; slave uprisings, 2, 5
Spring, Gardiner: Fugitive Slave Act defender, 280
spying: slave on slaves for master, 195
St. Louis, Missouri, 73; in W. Brown narrative, 85, 86, 87, 88, 89, 92, 93, 94, 99, 100, 101, 103, 104, 105, 107, 108, 109, 110, 114

steamboats, 85; in H. Brown narrative, 155; William Wells Brown work on, 73, 85–86, 88–89, 91–96, 105, 106–107, 110–111, 116; *Carlton,* 92; *Chester,* 110; *Enterprise,* 88, 91; *Flora,* 87; *North America,* 96; *Otto,* 105; *Trenton,* 99
Stewart, Maria W., 8–9; black civil rights and, 9; religious language used by, 9; women's rights and, 9
Stowe, Harriet Beecher: *Dred: A Tale of the Great Dismal Swamp,* 20; *Uncle Tom's Cabin,* 2
Stuart, Moses: Fugitive Slave Act defender, 280
Styron, William: *Confessions of Nat Turner,* 2, 20
Susquehanna River, 272

tarring and feathering, 66–67
temperance movement, 6, 62; William Wells Brown and, 74, 117; James W. C. Pennington and, 188
Tennessee: in W. Brown narrative, 107; in Craft narrative, 257; ban on free blacks, 257
Texas, 153
Text Book of the Origin and History, &c. & c. of Colored People, A. (Pennington), 180
Their Shadows Before: A Story of the Southampton Insurrection (Bouve), 20
Thompson, George, 279
Tiernan, Mary Spear: *Homoselle,* 20
tobacco: Henry "Box" Brown work with, 121, 142, 144–145; Lunsford Lane manufacturing enterprise, 44, 51–52, 54–55
Turner, Nat, 19–20; birth and youth, 27–28; religion and, 20, 29–30; slave uprising in Southampton, Virginia, 1, 2, 5, 19–20; trial and hanging, 1, 20, 37–38. *See also Confessions of Nat Turner, The* (original edition, 1831)
Turner's Rebellion, Nat, 1, 2, 5, 19–20, 143; murder victims, 38; religious rhetoric of slaveholders and, 20; slave treatment after, 143; suspects brought before the court, 39–40; U.S. troops and, 144. *See also Confessions of Nat Turner, The* (original edition, 1831); Turner, Nat
Twain, Mark: *Adventures of Huckleberry Finn,* 2

Uncle Tom's Cabin (Stowe), 2
Underground Railroad, James W. C. Pennington and, 180, 221

Union Missionary Society, 180
Up from Slavery (Washington), 14

Vesey, Denmark: slave uprising in Charleston, South Carolina, 2, 5
Vigilance Committee of Boston, 279
Virginia, 121, 179; in H. Brown narrative, 144, 153; in Craft narrative, 244, 255, 265; in Pennington narrative, 183, 185, 190, 202, 220, 221; Prosser's slave revolt in, 2, 19; Turner's Rebellion in, 1, 2, 5, 19, 24, 26. See also *Confessions of Nat Turner, The* (original edition, 1831)

Walker, James, 73, 91–96
Washington, Booker T.: *Up from Slavery,* 14
Webb, Richard D., 238
Webster, Daniel, 277
Weld, Theodore D.: *Slavery as It Is,* 99
Western New York Anti-Slavery Society, 74
whipping slaves: in H. Brown narrative, 136, 137, 143, 167; in W. Brown narrative, 83, 85, 86, 87, 88, 91, 93, 97, 98, 105, 107, 110, 112, 121; in Craft narrative, 257; in Lane narrative, 50
white people: as slave narrative audience, 12–13; as slaves, 99–100, 242–244
Willi, Samuel, 105, 108
Williams, Sherley Anne: *Dessa Rose,* 20
Wilson, Thomas, 286
women: abolitionist movement and, 8–10; in H. Brown narrative, 135; in Craft narrative, 247–248; slave narrators, 10; slave owners and, 135, 247–248. *See also* Craft, Ellen; mothers, slave; *Running a Thousand Miles for Freedom; or, The Escape of William and Ellen Craft from Slavery* (original text, 1860); Stewart, Maria W.; women's rights movement
women's rights movement, 6; Maria W. Stewart and, 9
work. *See* field work; hiring out slaves; house servants; tobacco
World Anti-Slavery Convention, second, 180
Wright, Richard: *Black Boy,* 2

About the Editor

STERLING LECATER BLAND JR., is an associate professor of English, African American Studies, and American Studies at Rutgers University in Newark, New Jersey, where he has previously served as associate dean of the Graduate School–Newark and chair of the Department of African American and African Studies. He has published or edited *Voices of the Fugitives: Runaway Slave Stories and Their Fictions of Self-Creation* (Praeger, 2000); *African American Slave Narratives: An Anthology* (Greenwood, 2001, 3 volumes); and *The* Pedro Gorino*: The Adventures of a Negro Sea-Captain* (2011). "Fire and Romance: African American Literature Since World War II" appeared in *A Concise Companion to Postwar American Literature and Culture*, edited by Josephine Hendin (2004).

In addition to his extensive work on slave narrative writing, he has published numerous articles and book chapters in the area of African American literature and culture. His research and teaching interests include nineteenth-century American literature, African American literature and culture, autobiography, narrative theory, theory of the novel, and jazz studies.

www.ingramcontent.com/pod-product-compliance
Lightning Source LLC
Chambersburg PA
CBHW060508300426
44112CB00017B/2582